PENGUIN CLASSICS

ENDLESS SONG

ARCHANA VENKATESAN is associate professor of religious studies and comparative literature at the University of California, Davis. She has received numerous grants, including fellowships from the Guggenheim Foundation, the National Endowment for the Arts, National Endowment for the Humanities, American Institute of Indian Studies and Fulbright. She is the author of *The Secret Garland: Āṇṭāḷ's Tiruppāvai and Nācciyār Tirumoḻi* and translator of Nammālvār's *Tiruviruttam*, as *A Hundred Measures of Time*. You can find her at archana.faculty.ucdavis.edu

ADVANCE PRAISE FOR THE BOOK

'Nammāḻvār was immersed in god. *Endless Song* in turn demonstrates Archana Venkatesan's complete immersion in Nammāḻvār: the poetry, the theology and the living millennium-old tradition of the text. This translation—as A.K. Ramanujan might have said—is a superb example of poetry winning without scholarship losing. Reading this mellifluous translation, English readers, much like Tamil devotees, are likely to declare, "Nammāḻvār is *our* Āḻvār!"'—A.R. Venkatachalapathy, editor of *Love Stands Alone: Selections from Tamil Sangam Poetry*

'Archana Venkatesan's translation of Nammāḻvār's *Tiruvāymoḻi* is shored up by her profound knowledge of the text in context as well as in performance. Her renditions are elegant, disciplined, and made with a profound attunement. Celebrating beauty and the love for god in all of its expressions, Venkatesan captures the rush of emotion in the text, and while there is light in each poem, there is also a probing quality as Nammāḻvār yearns for his dark, glittering god'—Martha Ann Selby, professor of South Asian studies, The University of Texas at Austin

ENDLESS SONG

Tiruvāymoḻi

Nammāḻvār

Translated from the Tamiḻ by
Archana Venkatesan

Foreword by
DAVID SHULMAN

PENGUIN BOOKS
An imprint of Penguin Random House

PENGUIN BOOKS

USA | Canada | UK | Ireland | Australia
New Zealand | India | South Africa | China | Singapore

Penguin Books is part of the Penguin Random House group of companies whose addresses can be found at global.penguinrandomhouse.com

Published by Penguin Random House India Pvt. Ltd
4th Floor, Capital Tower 1, MG Road,
Gurugram 122 002, Haryana, India

First published in Penguin Books by Penguin Random House India 2020

10 9 8 7 6 5 4 3 2

ISBN 9780143067986

Typeset in Adobe Devanagari by Manipal Technologies Limited, Manipal
Printed at Repro India Limited

www.penguin.co.in

Contents

Acknowledgements

Over a decade ago, at the Annual Conference of the American Academy of Religion, Professor Frank Clooney sat me down and asked me if I would consider working with him on a translation of the *Tiruvāymoḻi*. Frank has spent a lifetime on the *Tiruvāymoḻi*: he already had a draft translation of the entire text inflected by his deep reading of the Śrīvaiṣṇavas' commentarial traditions. To collaborate with someone like him was an extraordinary opportunity, and despite my trepidation, I agreed. We secured a contract from Penguin, and began working together. We met a couple of times, once at Harvard and once in Davis, and communicated as much as possible over email. The plan had been that both he and I would prepare independent translations and we would then work on reconciling them. We collaborated effectively on the first sixty verses, but life, distance, our other commitments, and my own slowness as a translator, proved difficult hurdles to overcome. In the end, when it became apparent that it would take another ten years for us to finish the planned collaboration, we mutually agreed that I would publish my translation independently. Frank's voice is everywhere in this translation, influenced as much by his own translations as by his many articles and books that have engaged the *Tiruvāymoḻi*. I would never have thought to dive into the *Tiruvāymoḻi*, had it not been for him and for that long-ago proposition. It has been life altering to do this work, and for that, I am indebted to Frank. Although we were not able to bring this work out together, I am honoured that Frank agreed to contribute a reflection on his own engagement with the *Tiruvāymoḻi* to it.

This book has been made possible through the generous support of a number of granting agencies. A translation grant from the National Endowment of the Arts (2012) marked the beginning of my first serious and sustained thinking with the *Tiruvāymoḻi* and its translation. A faculty grant from Harvard University (2010) allowed me to travel to Boston to collaborate with Frank Clooney on the first thirty verses of the *Tiruvāymoḻi*. Fellowships from the National Endowment for the Humanities (2007–2008) and a Fulbright FLEX (2017–2019) have funded fieldwork on the Adhyayanotsavam (Festival of Recitation), which has immeasurably added to my understanding and appreciation of the *Tiruvāymoḻi*. The Indian Culture and Heritage Trust has provided invaluable logistical support for research on the Nava Tirupati temples. A miraculous Guggenheim Fellowship in 2018–2019, conjured a one-year sabbatical that gifted me time and silence, without which I would never have finished this book.

My work on the *Tiruvāymoḻi* overlapped with my long-term research project, begun in 2007, on the Adhyayanotsavam celebrated in the temples of the Tirunelveli region of southern Tamil Nadu. The festival commemorates the *Tiruvāymoḻi* and its poet through recitation and ritual. My observation, documentation and study of this festival, particularly at the sites of Alvar Tirunagari (the birthplace of Nammāḻvār), Tirukkurungudi and Nanguneri have deepened my understanding of the text. The warm generosity of the pontiffs, priests, reciters, women, children and various community members opened my eyes to the affective dimensions of the poem, and the ways in which poetry makes and unmakes worlds, both sacred and not.

The Adhyayanotsavam project itself has intersected with another long-term collaborative project on the Nava Tirupati temples. My fellow travellers, Crispin Branfoot, Leslie Orr and Anna Seastrand, have challenged me to place the *Tiruvāymoḻi* in the broader context of temple ritual, art and architecture. Their scholarship and companionship have helped me see anew the ways of transmission, and what the inscriptional record can tell us about the history of the *Tiruvāymoḻi*'s reception.

My first encounter of the Adhyayanotsavam was Vasudha Narayanan's eye-opening *Vernacular Veda* (1994), and it changed the trajectory of my academic life. I devoured everything she had written, and then wrote to her, asking her how I could enter this amazing world. She replied, almost instantly, with a message of such kindness and generosity, offering me advice that still echoes in my head. Her scholarship has remained a lodestar—elegant, accessible and erudite—and I hope that my own work, so indelibly guided by hers, can live up to her example.

I owe a great debt to fellow translators, Steven Hopkins and Martha Ann Selby, who have modelled new and always thoughtful approaches to translation. George Hart, my teacher at UC Berkeley, first introduced me to the idea of translation as scholarship in its own right. It has taken me a long time to imbibe that lesson, and I have at last come to see the value of his insight. Indira Peterson continues to mentor me with typical kindness and ferocious large-heartedness, while her wide-ranging, careful scholarship challenges me to stretch myself. David Shulman is a sensitive interlocutor and an indefatigable cheerleader, and our ongoing conversations about poetry and translation have enriched both mind and heart. I am deeply grateful to him for the time he took to read and comment on the *Tiruvāymoḻi* translation, and for his generous foreword to this book.

As I worked on the translation of the *Tiruvāymoḻi*, I began a project that engaged with the performative aspects of *āḻvār* poetry. I was exploring ways to incorporate the fluidity of text—the ability to rearrange, split and interpenetrate verses—into my translation praxis. While these experiments did not directly affect the *Tiruvāymoḻi* translations, they helped me develop a clearer more melodic voice. For this, I thank my musical collaborator, Sikkil Gurucharan. His lovely musical interpretations, our discussions and interplay in performance, enlivened my own engagements with the text, and constantly reminded me to feel the poems in my body. It reframed the project of translation as bodily and sensory experience. I am grateful to the Sacramento Poetry Center, to Prakriti Foundation, Chennai, and Poet's House, New York, for giving us a space to share these experiments.

I owe thanks to all the librarians who have procured obscure books for me, particularly Narenthiran Rajagopal, of the French Institute of Pondicherry, and the dogged and dedicated staff of UC Davis's Interlibrary Loan services. Kannan, also of the French Institute of Pondicherry, has been a cherished friend and much-admired colleague from my first years of graduate school. I have always valued his insight and his encyclopaedic knowledge of Tamiḻ literature. A timely publication assistance grant from UC Davis's Office of Research and the Letters and Science Dean's Office allowed me to hire Manasvin Rajagopalan to help me with the final editing, indexing and proofreading of the manuscript. Manas brought his usual enthusiasm, care and diligence to this project, and I am very grateful to him for undertaking this additional work even while preparing for his Qualifying Exams.

The editorial team at Penguin has been exemplary and a pleasure to work with. Kamini Mahadevan, now enjoying a well-earned retirement, brought me to Penguin. Richa Burman, who tended my earlier book, *A Hundred Measures of Time*, with such care through its long labour, brought equal parts of tenderness and firmness to this book and its even longer gestation and labour. I am fortunate that she has stuck with me through all the delays and my eccentricities as a translator. The eagle eyes of Paloma Dutta and Clare Stewart caught every typo, every misplaced comma, and have saved me from excruciating grammar embarrassment. Manju Khanna helped prepare the Index, and made this book that much more reader-friendly. Parag Chitale designed a stunning cover that not only captures the feel and spirit of the poem, but also complements the jacket of *A Hundred Measures of Time*. This would have been impossible without Olivia Fraser granting us permission to use her painting *Breathe II* (2017). I am delighted that yet again, her gorgeous, haunting, jewel-toned painting invites the reader into one of my books.

Translation is both a solitary journey and one undertaken in community. One never reads the *Tiruvāymoḻi* alone. The voices of learned commentators of old are constant companions. I have sat at their feet, and tried to absorb a smidgen of their vast learning and their even vaster feeling for this monumental work. My debt to them is unpayable. I have shamelessly mined the minds of fellow scholars of the Śrīvaiṣṇava *sampradāya*s: Ajay Rao, Bharati Jagannathan, Elisa Freschi, Frank Clooney, Lynn Ate, Manasicha Akepiyapornchai, Patricia Mumme, Ranjeeta Dutta, Srilata Raman, Sucharita Adluri, Suganya Anandakichenin, Steven Hopkins, Ute Huesken and Vasudha Narayanan. Their work has made mine possible. I have learnt so much from the cohort of scholars of bhakti, particularly, Anand Venkatkrishnan, Christian Novetzke, Cynthia Packert, Elaine Craddock, Gil Ben-Herut,

Jack Hawley, John Cort, Jon Keune, Karen Pechilis, Linda Hess, Richard Davis, Tracy Coleman and Patton Burchett. They have opened new paths of inquiry and have added immeasurably to my own understanding of bhakti. Anne Monius, a tireless cheerleader, brilliant scholar, and the editor of my first book, passed away unexpectedly in August 2019. Neither she nor I ever thought I would finish the *Tiruvāymoḻi*, but here it is at last, but Anne is gone. Her loss is incalculable. Davesh Soneji is a shining example of what it means to practise exceptional, ethical scholarship, and our steadfast friendship over many long years has always been a source of strength and comfort.

Writing is also a solitary endeavour, but impossible to accomplish without an army of people who protect you in ways both small and great. My family has been that army. My parents, Jayashree and Venkatesan, my sister, Aarathi, her husband, Venkatesh, my two precious nieces, my uncle Ragu, have enveloped me in love, kindness and unshakeable faith, that even the impossible became possible because of them. The strategically timed love-ambushes of my feline companions, Tiny Artemis and Bajarangi-Merlin, infuse my life with joy, and remind me every day that all is well with a warm, purring cat (or two) to cuddle.

On a particularly difficult day, at a time when this book seemed insurmountable, my husband, Layne, pressed a small, exquisite, gently smiling Nammāḻvār into the palm of my hand. It was exactly the right thing at exactly the right moment. That image now sits on my desk, beaming out love, and nothing seems insurmountable. To this amazing man, who has the hugest heart of anyone I know, I dedicate this book. *Aṭiyēṉ.*

Sacramento, CA
May 2019

A Note on Transliteration

I have employed a transliteration system that will make Indic words easy to pronounce, both for native and non-native speakers. I have transliterated Tamiḻ and Maṇipravāḷa, but have let Sanskrit remain in its anglicized form (over Saṁskṛta). Within the translation, I have largely transliterated Tamiḻ words according to the conventions of the *Tamiḻ Lexicon*. Sanskrit words used in a Tamiḻ context retain their Sanskritic forms, but I have indigenized them to Tamiḻ by including the final nasal. Thus, mokṣam instead of mōkkam, Mādhavaṉ instead of Mādhava, Indran instead of Intiraṉ, and so forth. When a name is used as a vocative, I have included the final long vowel—so Mādhavā, rather than Mādhava. This is to distinguish from those moments where the name does not appear as a vocative or with the final nasal. I have transliterated the poet's name as Śaṭhakōpaṉ instead of Caṭakōpaṉ. Within the translation and notes, place names and the names of historical figures are all transliterated in a manner that hews closely to the ways in which they are pronounced; thus Śrīraṅgam instead of Śrīraṅkam, Varamaṅgai instead of Varamaṅkai, and Nañjīyar instead of Nañcīyar. In the materials that accompany the translation, such as the Introduction, Annotations, Indices, etc., I have rendered Tamiḻ and Sanskrit words according to the most common conventions. In the Introduction and Annotations, I have used the most well-known contemporary spelling for place names (without diacritical marks), so Tirukkurungudi, Nanguneri and Srirangam.

Tamiḻ has twelve vowels, which are classified into five short vowels (*a, i, u, e, o*), five long vowels (*ā, ī, ū, ē, ō*) and two diphthongs (*ai* and *au*). There are eighteen consonants.

Below is a pronunciation guide.

Vowels

a pronounced like the *u* in *cut*
Tamiḻ e.g. *akam* (interior)

ā pronounced like the *a* in *father*
Tamiḻ e.g. *ākam* (body)

i pronounced like the *i* in *it*
Tamiḻ e.g. *itu* (this)

ī pronounced like the *ee* in *feet*
Tamiḻ e.g. *īcaṉ* (lord)

u pronounced like the *u* in *put*
Tamiḻ e.g. *uvaṉ* (the middle he)

ū pronounced like the *oo* in *root*
Tamiḻ e.g. *ūr* (town)

e pronounced like the *e* in *set*
Tamiḻ e.g. *etu* (which)

ē pronounced like the *a* in *rate*
Tamiḻ e.g. *ētu* (how)

o pronounced like the *o* in *hotel*
Tamiḻ e.g. *oru* (one)

ō pronounced like the *o* in *go*
Tamiḻ e.g. *ōcai* (sound)

ai	pronounced like the *ie* in *pie* Tamiḻ e.g. *aivar* (the five)
au	pronounced like the *ow* in *cow* Tamiḻ e.g. *auvai* (matron)

Consonants

k (guttural)	pronounced like the *k* in *kite* Tamiḻ e.g. *kal* (stone)
c (palatal)	pronounced like the *ch* in *chalk*. It can also be pronounced as a sibilant, like *s* in *sieve* Tamiḻ e.g. *col* (word)
ṭ (retroflex)	pronounced like the *t* in *toe* Tamiḻ e.g. *vaṇṭu* (insect)
t (dental)	pronounced like the *th* in *thing* Tamiḻ e.g. *vantu* (having come)
p	pronounced like *p-s* in prop Tamiḻ e.g. *pal* (teeth)
ṅ (nasal, paired with k)	pronounced like the nk in *ink* Tamiḻ e.g. *maṅkai* (girl)
ñ (nasal, paired with c)	pronounced like the *gn* in *gnosis* Tamiḻ e.g. *neñcu* (heart)
ṇ (nasal paired with ṭ)	pronounced like the *n* in *friend* Tamiḻ e.g. *vaṇṭu* (insect)
n (nasal paired with t)	pronounced like the *n* in *now* Tamiḻ e.g. *vantu* (having come)
ṉ (alveolar nasal, occurs at the end of words)	pronounced like the *n* in *now*, but with the tongue pressed closer to the teeth Tamiḻ e.g. *avaṉ* (he)

m (nasal paired with p)	pronounced like the *m* in *marriage* Tamiḻ e.g. *mayil* (peacock)
y	pronounced like the *y* in *your* Tamiḻ e.g. *yār* (who)
r	pronounced like the *r* in *your* Tamiḻ e.g. *yār* (who)
ṟ	pronounced like the *dr* in *drill* Tamiḻ e.g. *aṉṟu* (then)
l	pronounced like the *l* in *light* Tamiḻ e.g. *ilai* (leaf)
ḷ (retroflex)	pronounced like the *l* in *blah*, but with more emphasis. It is pronounced with the tongue curled back, to touch the roof of the mouth. Tamiḻ e.g. *avaḷ* (she)
v	pronounced like the *v* in *victory* Tamiḻ e.g. *vīṭu* (house)
ḻ	No English equivalent. Pronounced as a gentle rolled sound similar to the North American use of the *r* sound, as in *American*. Tamiḻ e.g. *moḻi* (language)

Foreword

Archana's Nammāḻvār

DAVID SHULMAN

Not every translator, even a pretty good one, knows what it means to translate a single verse, a line, a clause, a sentence. Archana knows. A verse may live in her, or she in it, for weeks or months or even years before she lets it go, usually unwillingly. A thousand-some-verse work like Nammāḻvār's *Tiruvāymoḻi* thus demands huge blocks of time, maybe an infinity of time. At some point the translation pauses long enough to go to press. The echo chamber in the true translator's head goes on with its business, night and day.

The *Tiruvāymoḻi* is commensurate with Archana's passion and her talent. She's the best translator from Tamiḻ in this generation, because she knows what it means. It's not about satisfaction, an unreachable goal. You have this perfect verse, a miracle of sound and flow and texture and, after all the above, meaning; and you know for sure that only 3 per cent of that will go into English. So you wake up in the middle of the night hoping to extend the number to, say, 3.5 per cent. That would be a huge achievement. After that, the verse keeps coming back at you, at odd times, when you're least expecting it, and then you want to cut out one more syllable, thus reaching towards 3.6. Only someone with Archana's stamina has a chance to make this happen.

She has, I think, an aversion to punctuation. The line breaks are meant to suffice in suggesting a pause in the syntactic flow. This method, a reasonable one, demands a certain kind of listening on the part of the reader. I recommend reading the English out loud. Nammāḻvār, in particular, deserves the aural dimension, in Tamiḻ, of course, but also in Archana's English.

This was a poet who changed the nature of a poetic line in Tamiḻ. He invented a form of syntax that is at once light, intelligible at first or second hearing, and dense with suggestion, much of it derived from the combinations of syllables that he was able to imagine into being. Later Tamiḻ poets, such as Kampaṉ, the author of the Tamiḻ *Rāmāyaṇa*, probably two centuries or more after Nammāḻvār, learnt the poetic art from listening to the *Tiruvāymoḻi*. Kampaṉ, too, was capable of producing that specific density of lightness. It comes with a very rich emotional texture, so much so that many of the verses in this volume, like verses of Kampaṉ or Tirumaṅkaiyāḻvār, can easily generate tears in a good reader. Just after the tears comes a cognitive moment, when the reader finds herself amazed at what the poet has just said.

The art of reading this translation has a lot to do with the intrinsic texture of the decad form, and not only on the printed page. Decads of this text are still recited in what is called *viruttam* performance. The singer—today often a professional Carnatic musician, like Sikkil Gurucharan or Aruna Sairam or T.M. Krishna—takes up a phrase, sings it, then begins to play with it, sometimes turning the syntax upside down, or paring it down to two or three syllables, or shifting scale or register. She or he has the liberty to repeat a phrase as many times as is necessary in order to let the listener fully understand its unique beauty and its placement within the sentence or the verse as a whole. Viruttam recitation of an entire decad takes time, because it allows the listener to hear, perhaps unconsciously, the patterns of aural and semantic coherence that are the true life of all ten verses. The singer helps bind them together, thereby also highlighting particular themes or twinges of feeling. The listener has a part to play in this creative process—even in English. Archana makes it relatively easy: she is sensitive to the integrity of the decad. Try reading all ten verses aloud, as slowly as possible. Try singing them in viruttam style.

I had the privilege of seeing early drafts of some of these poems. Often at dawn, still sleepy, after peering closely at the Tamiḻ, I would respond with queries or hints or even suggestions. Then there would be some days of watching those early-morning question marks bounce back and forth across the oceans that separate California from Jerusalem. Often I was surprised at the next versions. Sometimes I thought it was the delicious Madras street Tamiḻ that Archana knew from childhood that infused her translations with a natural south Indian musicality and at the same time made her keep honing and rehearing them, in the viruttam mode. Street Tamiḻ, strange to say, is continuous with Nammāḻvār's style. Not everyone can hear it.

Here's one example of how she works. The first verse of the second decad of the *Tiruvāymoḻi* reads in Tamiḻ: *vīṭumiṉ muṟṟavum vīṭu ceyt' umm uyir/vīṭ'uṭaiyāṉ iṭai vīṭu ceymmiṉe.* The metre is a very short, compressed one, and even from the transliteration above anyone can see or hear that what has been compressed is subject to conspicuous syllabic repetition. The two syllables *vīṭu* occur four times (out of a total of twenty-three syllables, although what counts in Tamiḻ poetry is the number of morae or short-syllable beats). The verb *viṭu* means to leave or put aside, abandon, let go; the noun *vīṭu* is the Tamiḻ word for release, *mokṣa* or *mukti* in Sanskrit—the great goal of much of Indian religion. Here is how Archana translates this bewitching line:

When you've let go everything let your life
go to him who owns all letting go.

You can see what sort of problem the Tamiḻ poses for a translator. It sounds at first hearing like 'let go something something letting go something something letting go something something let go'. And along with finding a way to capture the beautiful assonance of the original, there is a semantic, or even theological, problem—because in Tamiḻ 'release' means finding one's way to the god and not to some disembodied, abstract quality of freedom from the world, as in other Indian systems.

Here is where the punctuation aversion serves a real purpose. One might expect a comma after 'everything' in the first line, neatly separating the initial action from what follows. Instead, the line tumbles straight on into the imperative that echoes the opening verb and then into the line break with its surprising enjambment (let your life/go). There's a lot of this letting go; if only we could figure out who is doing what when . . . But in a way, that run-on jumble is the point. We are swept along in a flood of viṭu instants, something much stronger than we are and not easily understood; our very life, *uyir*, is at stake. And indeed that 'everything' in the first line is almost floating, spilling over into what is to come even as it looks backward over its shoulder, as if to tell us that this verse is literally about everything, about life itself and how to live it.

Now look at how Archana puts the verb 'go' in the middle of the first line and then at the start and end of the second. She's made an inspired choice. Going to the god is what it means to let go, to become free, and Lord Viṣṇu himself is defined here as *vīṭ'uṭaiyān*, 'him who owns all letting go'. It's his very nature, also the promise held out to someone who loves him. In a brief flash, as brief as the burst of sound in the original, the English beautifully coincides with the Tamil̲, both in sound and meaning. It's also worth noticing that the Tamil̲ consonant *ṭ*, which fills the original verse like a continuous drumbeat, is there in the highlighted and repeated English 'leT/ leTTing go'. Occasionally the gods themselves intervene and send the translator a little sign.

The *Tiruvāymoḻi* is recited in its entirety once every year by the Araiyar singers in the temples of Srivilliputtur and Alvar Tirunagari, in the far south of the Tamil̲ country, and in the great temple of Srirangam at the centre. The setting is the Adhyayanotsavam festival, which Archana has seen and documented several times; she is the world's expert on this exceedingly complex ritual form. She herself would say that even to begin to understand Nammāl̲vār's massive poem one has to hear it performed out loud, with accompanying hand gestures, over the days and nights of the festival, with the poet himself present in his image, placed in close proximity to the god. I am sure she is right. Hidden within the text is a vast drama of distance and closeness, agonizing separateness, longing, loving and eventual (temporary) merging. These opposing vectors are at play in the god himself and in every Nammāl̲var verse. They create a trajectory made visible in the course of the ritual processions and enactments of critical moments in the biographies of both poet and deity. As you read the translation, try to imagine that you are sitting in one of those temples, in the crowd and heat, fighting off the deadly mosquitoes, hearing the priests chant the poems as the incantations they are meant to be.

Nammāḻvār was born an accomplished yogi. They say that immediately at birth he crawled around the temple in his village, Alvar Tirunagari, and then came to rest under a tamarind tree, where he remained in silent meditation for many years. That silence still haunts the Tamiḻ poems we have; you should listen for it. It takes a lot of good karma from earlier births, and along with it the personal benefice of the god, to live that kind of life and to sing that kind of poetry. I think the good karma lasted some 1200 years and eventually produced Archana as the translator of this book. I'm sure she's still not satisfied, and that is how things should be. But, like her translation of Nammāḻvār's *Tiruviruttam*, this new, complete translation of the core work by this great poet is a priceless gift. There is a lot to say for having it as a whole since, incredibly, those thousand verses were conceived as a circular chain, each decad linked to the next by its final syllables, and the final decad linked in the same way to the first. One needs the four lines of any verse to understand even one phrase, as one needs the decad to understand one poem, and as one needs the entire book to understand a decad. And what does one need to understand the whole book? That is a question that a new generation of readers might want to address.

Preface

FRANCIS X. CLOONEY, SJ

Archana Venkatesan has produced a very fine, subtle and sensitive translation of Śaṭhakōpaṉ's *Tiruvāymoḻi.* It will surely be for years to come the go-to translation of *Tiruvāymoḻi* for those who want to read the songs in English, get a feel for the text as a whole and for its underlying cultural, spiritual and theological depths. It stands very nicely alongside her translation of Śaṭhakōpaṉ's *Tiruviruttam*, and her earlier rendering of Āṇṭāḷ's *Tiruppāvai* and *Nācciyār Tirumoḻi*, and confirms her status as today's best translator of the Tamiḻ Vaiṣṇava religious classics. As was the case with those earlier works, this is a simple translation that is nonetheless wonderfully informed by the great commentarial tradition: the annotations are remarkable, helpful without being wordy, simply inviting readers who want more to go deeper; the appendices give new readers much of what they need to get started. With great sensitivity she has also included Madurakavi's *Kaṇṇinuṇ ciṟu tāmpu*, verses in praise of Śaṭhakōpaṉ by his first disciple; these are verses that any reader might be advised to read at the beginning and end of study. Archana also has written an informative and comprehensive introduction, and there is little that I can or need to add to it. So the reader will permit me to use this space, at her kind invitation, to add to the joyful moment of the appearance of this translation just a few recollections of my life with *Tiruvāymoḻi*.

I first encountered these one hundred songs when A.K. Ramanujan was finishing his lovely *Hymns for the Drowning* and I was a new graduate student in the Department of South Asian Languages and Civilizations at the University of Chicago. Only a year into my study of Tamiḻ, I was honoured to proofread the galleys for him. Over the next months, he then read with me some of the verses, and we dipped ever so slightly into the commentaries, which greatly interested me, him much less. Raman loved the verses, each on its own, as if *Tiruvāymoḻi* was a *caṅkam* anthology of mysterious solitary gems. He found a common ground with such gems, selecting a few to carry over, alive, into his incomparable English. I was fascinated by the poetry as a garland adorning the lord and the community, but also, from the start, by *Tiruvāymoḻi*'s significance as a canon of scripture, extended in commentary and the words of many teachers. I most warmly remember reading with Raman verse VIII.8.3:

He is unique among those rich in understanding, but by his grace
I placed him in my understanding to hold him there,
But even that is by his sweet grace, and so he made me realize
that all understanding and life and body and the infinite too are
mere nothing,
And for understanding beyond all that, he ended up as me, himself
myself.

I found that this verse marked a path for an advaita distinguished by love, in the tradition of Rāmānuja: non-dualism as an event culminating a love relationship. Surprisingly, the commentators read this verse along with the famed 'That Thou Art' (*tat tvam asi*) of the *Chāndogya Upaniṣad* 6. It was on this fascinating meeting between Tamil̲ devotion and Vedānta that I wrote my first article related to *Tiruvāymol̲i*, which appeared in 1983 in *Śrīrāmānujavāṇi*, a small journal in Madras.

After being introduced to *Tiruvāymol̲i* by Raman, in the middle and late 1980s, I kept reading and translating the songs, first of all as a way of improving my Tamil̲! Norman Cutler and I joked that insofar as I was a Tamil̲ scholar at all, I'd be more at home at ninth-century Tiruveṅkaṭam than on the streets of today's Chennai. But while improving my beginner's Tamil̲ little by little, I was also caught by songs, drawn into the world of *Tiruvāymol̲i*, which replicates in small form an entire religious universe.

During 1992–1993, I had the opportunity to devote myself to the study of *Tiruvāymol̲i* full time. I was in Mylapore that year, working on a project that became *Seeing through Texts* (1996). I studied rather intensively with several teachers. A few times a week, sometimes daily, I cycled (as one could still dare to do in those days) to the home of Sri Sampath Kumaran, a philosophy professor at Vivekananda College, whose first love was *Tiruvāymol̲i*. He was a descendant of Maṇavāḷamāmuni, and long ago retired to Śrīraṅgam. Professor M.A. Venkatakrishnan at the University of Madras also generously found time to read some verses and commentary with me. I was also on and off part of a small group that met regularly at the home of Sri Kumaravati Ramanujacharya ('Tirumāl'). Most members of this small group were learned devotees, proud to be lifelong students. They aimed simply to study the whole of the 1102 verses and Vaṭakkutiruvītipiḷḷai's great commentary, the *Īṭu*, a full three times with their teacher. I unfortunately was the one who was in a hurry. Sabbaticals are short, so it was not possible for me to immerse myself completely in a regime of study that would never end, since one never quite masters the *Bhagavat Viṣayam* tradition. But I did try to go deeper. I visited the Mylapore temples very frequently, and when I travelled, a number of the temples mentioned by Śaṭhakōpaṉ; I remember with particular pleasure a week I spent at his birthplace, Alvar Tirunagari, during the winter festival. To listen to the songs as well as read them, I frequented temple recitations when I could, and by means of cassettes I bought in the bazaar near Luz Corner, I listened to several complete songs each day; I would cover the 1102 verses in about three months, and then start over again. I continued this practice even back in Boston, until the book was finished.

Early on in my stay in Myaplore, I was interviewed about my studies: Why would an American professor be interested in *Tiruvāymoḻi* and the *Bhagavat Viṣayam*? Then I was asked which was my favourite verse. I chose II.3.3,

In that time when I did not know you, you made me love
your service,
There, in my great unknowing confusion, you made me
your servant,
Unknown, a dwarf, you begged, 'Three steps of earth, great Bali,'
You tricked him who didn't know—and now you've mingled
inside my self.

The interview made the cover of the popular magazine *Kuṃutam*, and for a few days I—never one to blend in with the crowds in the back streets of Mylapore—stood out even more, as something of a celebrity. They didn't ask, but in fact I chose that verse in part because when I read it I was also thinking of St Augustine's famous plaint:

> Late have I loved Thee, O Beauty so ancient and so new; late have I loved Thee! For behold Thou were within me, and I outside; and I sought Thee outside and in my unloveliness fell upon those lovely things that Thou hast made. Thou were with me and I was not with Thee. I was kept from Thee by those things, yet had they not been in Thee, they would not have been at all. Thou didst call and cry to me and break open my deafness: and Thou didst send forth Thy beams and shine upon me and chase away my blindness: Thou didst breathe fragrance upon me, and I drew in my breath and do not pant for Thee: I tasted Thee, and now hunger and thirst for Thee: Thou didst touch me, and I have burned for Thy peace. (*Confessions* X; F.J. Sheed translation)

Śaṭhakōpaṉ and Augustine, at least in this instance (though not in many others!), seem soulmates, their hearts and words resonating wonderfully together. But *Tiruvāymoḻi* has always resonated with my Catholic tradition, evoking memories of texts I know well, and of other texts that reading Śaṭhakōpaṉ prompted me to look up and study in more depth.

My *Kumutam* moment happened in 1992, as I was learning the songs, but in fact, I had a very rough but complete translation of *Tiruvāymoḻi* already in hand by the time I reached Madras in 1992. I have now and then puttered with the translations, as needed for one or another lecture or class or piece of writing; other parts of it I probably haven't corrected in thirty years. The most recent time I drew on *Tiruvāymoḻi* was in writing *His Hiding Place Is Darkness* (2013), in which I read together *Tiruvāymoḻi* and the Biblical *Song of Songs*. My goal was to trace the acutely felt absence of the previously intensely present beloved in both of these very beautiful texts. In *Tiruvāymoḻi*, I focused particularly on five songs: I.4 (the first of the woman's messenger songs), V.4 (her anguished love, alone in the dark of night), V.9 (her sense of the just out of reach proximity of the lord, near but across the river), VII.3 (her desperation to reach Tiruppēreyil, where her beloved now dwells, holding her heart hostage), IX.6 (a moment of intense union, between two songs of all the more painful absence), and X.3 (her fear that once Kṛṣṇa has returned, he will only go away again). As always, I read all these songs as explicated by generations of Śrīvaiṣṇavas in the great tradition of the *Bhagavat Viṣayam*, alongside the Song as read and preached by Bernard of Clairvaux and his great monastic successors. The intense resonance I found will not be surprising for a reader who understands how mystical traditions, though never the same, often end up resonating: 'Deep calls to deep at the thunder of your cataracts; all your waves and your billows have gone over me.' (Psalm 42) Many of the problems that inevitably face interreligious learning have seemed, relatively speaking, incidental, whenever *Tiruvāymoḻi* was near at hand. For me as a comparative theologian, there have been innumerable possibilities for learnings from Hindu traditions in Sanskrit and Tamiḻ. But there has been no better venue for my interreligious learning than *Tiruvāymoḻi*. These lovely linked songs, so well rendered for us by Archana, draw the reader into a world of ideas and images, sentiments and insights, times and places.

As Archana kindly notes, I was part of a translation project some thirty years ago, with A.K. Ramanujan himself, John Carman (Harvard, and a premier Rāmānuja scholar) and Vasudha Narayanan (University of Florida, scholar of Śrīvaiṣṇava traditions, and also a sensitive reader in whom Nammāḻvār seems naturally, deeply, richly alive). What a team! Gathering at Vasu's home, we made good progress for a while (while enjoying her hospitality and her excellent idli and dosa), painstakingly reading and discussing each verse, quickly looking into the commentaries, even if in the end, wearied and ready to move on, we often deferred to Raman's elegant, very personal translation style. Some of these translations made it into Vasu's book *The Vernacular Veda*, while our work together aided me in correcting my own translations over the years. But the project quietly came to an end after Raman's untimely death in 1993.

Years later, it was therefore a joy for me to link up with Archana, as she recounts, with the idea once again of doing the translation together. We indeed had a wonderful time in translating some verses together, the sixty-plus verses of songs I.1 to I.6. As she also explains, time together was precious and rare, three thousand miles lay between Davis, California and Cambridge, Massachusetts, and our sabbaticals never coincided. Our styles were compatible but different enough that the work of agreeing on every verse would have been exhilarating and very time-consuming. So, in the end, this collaboration too turned out not to be possible. But I am relieved that this fine book has now come to light, a work to be proud of. Who better than Archana, who has so well translated the *Tiruviruttam* and the *Tiruppāvai*?

In fact, I've never been inclined to publish my own translation, and am glad that Archana has done the needful so brilliantly. My reticence is in part because I am not a native Tamiḻ speaker, nor am I a poet: though I love reading poetry, I lack the ear for the writing of it, in any language, and I find myself ever 'workmanlike' in translations that fall short poetically, even if I erase little and add little to the poet's words. But it is never enough, and no surprise: even Śaṭhakōpaṉ himself had trouble finishing off his words:

Could I ever be done with praising him,
The lord whose lovely hand holds the discus,

Even if earth and sky and water all melt into one and I drink them up?
But he has made unlovely me himself, and
To his own glory sung by me these sweet songs. (VII.9.8)

Not only are the words beautiful, but they open up into world upon world of insight and love; and to write them sweetly in an alien tongue (English) is even harder, though Archana has brought us very close indeed.

As a theologian, though, I realize that I have suffered a deeper qualm about getting my translation into print: my impossible desire has been really to translate the commentaries that comprise the *Bhagavat Viṣayam* along with *Tiruvāymoḻi*, so that the verses don't stand alone, apart from the community of learning around them. This is nearly impossible, even for a single set of eleven verses, since in English the commentaries might take up 50–100 pages. As Archana explains, the *Bhagavat Viṣayam* is a deep and vast ocean of wisdom of five related commentaries with a few sub-commentaries too, that has lived on in the twentieth century through new printings, and with the commentaries of P.B. Annangaracharíar and Uttamur Viraraghavachariar, and Purusottama Naidu's rendering of the *Īṭu* in modern Tamiḻ. I can only hope that more Śrīvaiṣṇavas in the West will now take up the work that Archana is doing, and render many more of the āḻvār works, and commentaries too, in good, modern English.

If *Tiruvāymoḻi* is to have its deserved place in the modern world and as a core text in modern Śrīvaiṣṇava theology and piety, and at the centre of Hindu–Christian interreligious theology, we need also to read *with* the tradition. Otherwise, it would appear alone and bereft, apart from the tradition it generated and with which it has been read for a thousand years. Fortunately, another reason to be grateful to Archana is that she is so conscientious in consulting the commentaries in the course of her work of translation, reading expertly and concisely, but also with a willingness to hear the voices of tradition. And then there is the much larger oral tradition of teachers and students who have gathered perhaps for a millennium to read the text, recite it, and in various ways ancient and modern, enact it, even nowadays by innumerable discourses one can find on YouTube.

Yet people also want to make it all short, intense, brief. As Archana notes, the tradition that made *Tiruvāymoḻi* larger and larger also preserved *Tiruvāymoḻi* in small form, as if to make it easier for the faithful to carry it with them everywhere. They sought to catch the essence of *Tiruvāymoḻi* in Sanskrit words, as in Vedānta Deśika's *Dramiḍopaniṣad Tātparyaratnāvali*—one word in Sanskrit for each of the 1102 verses in Tamiḻ—and in the often overlooked *Dramiḍopaniṣad Saṃgati* of Vātikēsari Aḻakiya Maṇavāḷa Jīyar, which catches each song's meaning in just two Sanskrit lines. Maṇavāḷamāmuni's *Tiruvāymoḻi Nuṟṟantāti* is a Tamiḻ condensation into one hundred short verses that directly imitate the original in style and meaning, and thus in a directly living manner extend beautifully *Tiruvāymoḻi* as a living, lived reality. In my recent *Reading the Hindu and Christian Classics* (University of Virginia, 2019), I drew on the *Nuṟṟantāti* as my primary Hindu text in a chapter on 'participation': some of the texts we study draw us inside them first as puzzles, then as poems, then as spiritual and theological missives, and finally, unless we stop along the way, as powerful living voices that possess us and become our own voice.

Or still more simply, the commentators often enough correlate the songs of *Tiruvāymoḻi* with the three holy mantras—the Tirumantra, a simple word of praise; the Carama Śloka, Kṛṣṇa's invitation to take refuge; and, above all, the Dvaya Mantra, the very words of that refuge, act of surrender. Thus correlations at first make little sense to the newcomer to these matters, but in the long run, the wisdom becomes apparent, simple prayers that contain in a moment's time the entirety of *Tiruvāymoḻi*'s psychological complexity, human desire and bewilderment, and depth and passion. Taking refuge is most beautifully and famously linked to VI.10.10, here in Archana's translation:

'I won't part from you for an instant'
says Śrī who rests on your chest,
lord of matchless fame,
holder of the three worlds
my king, master of Vēṅkaṭam
dear to peerless immortals and sages
with nowhere else to go, I've settled at your feet.

And yet, of course, four hundred more verses of *Tiruvāymoḻi* are still to come, as both Śaṭhakōpaṉ and his lord come to terms with the act of faith and surrender that has here taken place. There is always more to come, no verse is really the last.

We end up reading the verses again and again, the deep meanings never exhausted, and yet tempted to make them simple and succinct, just a few right words that in turn are always too few. If it is true that *Tiruvāymoḻi* is to be received not only as Tamiḻ poetry from over a millennium ago, but also as the scripture—surrounded by all the other āḻvār works—generative of a still living tradition, then the opportunity is there for the reader to use this lovely translation as a pathway into that tradition, and then, as Raman might say, to be immersed entirely in the ocean of Śaṭhakōpaṉ's holy words of mouth.

Advice to the reader: read these pages slowly, regularly, over time. You will find that as with any classic holy word, its deepest meanings are never exhausted, and never cease to have their effect. This conscious reader, at first innocently just reading a lovely translation, may well end up finding herself being translated into Śaṭhakōpaṉ's world, engaged in a personal and then communal process that never ends, but rather only intensifies over time.

I must stop here, but I cannot but help quote one more verse, the tenth of the last song, this time twice over, my old translation and Archana's fresh rendering of the same:

Surrounding, spreading, deep, uplifting the great expanse unlimited,
Surrounding that and greater still, unfolding flowers of light,
Surrounding that and greater still, the radiant bliss of knowledge,
Surrounding that and greater still, my desire for you
And that too you finish off, surrounding me.

Swirling spreading deep high endless vastness
Swirling growing beyond that
a great blossoming light
Swirling growing beyond even that
the luminous bliss of wisdom
Swirling growing beyond even that
my love for you. You cut that too
and engulfed me.

Introduction

The Poem: The Tiruvāymoḻi

The five senses torment even
the celestials who serve you. What will they do
to me here on earth if you abandon me?
Supreme lord, hidden in song, the secret in poems,
heart of devotion, you
dwell in my eyes, live in my heart
are in my words, come
say something to me.

Tiruvāymoḻi VII.1.6

Sometime in the ninth century, a man about whom we know little, composed an extraordinary Tamiḻ poem, which came to be known as the *Tiruvāymoḻi* (Sacred Utterance/Sacred Truth). It appeared during a tumultuous period in the Tamiḻ-speaking regions of peninsular southern India, where emergent ecstatic devotionalism (bhakti) challenged the well-established religious traditions of Buddhism and Jainism. This is not a key preoccupation of the text though it refutes as well as accepts into its world view alternative religious traditions, be they Buddhist, Jain or Śaiva.[1] Even with this occasionally capacious vision, the text's own commitments are decidedly and irrefutably Vaiṣṇava. The poet, who calls himself Māraṉ-Śaṭhakōpaṉ, is Viṣṇu's devotee, and if we take his claims in the *Tiruvāymoḻi* seriously, descended from a long line of Vaiṣṇavas. Viṣṇu, transcendent and omnipotent, is the poet's sole refuge, and his only goal is to exist in eternal service to him, in a state of unbreakable, uninterrupted union. The poem's subject is the relationship between god (Viṣṇu) and the devotee (the poet), which is characterized by brief moments of blissful union and protracted periods of desolate separation.

The *Tiruvāymoḻi*'s 1102 verses are divided into ten books of a hundred verses called Pattu (Ten); each Pattu consists of ten decads, referred to as a Tiruvāymoḻi or Tirumoḻi. Each (except one) Tiruvāymoḻi is composed of ten individual verses termed a *pāsuram*, with a concluding eleventh benedictory meta-verse, which is a *phala-śruti*.[2] Thus, the above pāsuram, VII.1.6, refers to the sixth verse in the first decad of the Seventh Hundred of the text, or more simply, verse 668.[3] The *Tiruvāymoḻi* is held together by the *antāti*, a form of interlinked verses that the poet, Śaṭhakōpaṉ, favoured. The antāti (end to beginning) uses strategies such as syllabic play, homonyms and repetition to ensure that every pāsuram, every Tiruvāymoḻi, every Pattu in the poem, is woven together to produce an endless, infinite garland of words, where every beginning is also an ending, and vice versa. Traditionally though, the poem does start somewhere—with a contemplation of the ineffability of god—and it ends somewhere—with the poet achieving the highest state. The poem signals these thematic orientations with the word *uyar* (high) that opens and concludes it.[4]

The poem's circular structure suits the iterative nature of the poet's quest, allowing for the possibility of an infinite number of entry points that trace the oscillation between union and separation, between bliss and melancholy, between wisdom and ignorance. The text's striking and distinctive structural flexibility is not without discipline, bound as it is by the interlinked antāti and the thematic unity of individual decads. If one is reading the text from any beginning to any end—say from V.4.1—we are obliged to read the decads in sequence, until we reach V.3.11.[5] If one seeks to read just a single decad within the *Tiruvāymoḻi*, one must start with the Ten's first verse and read until its eleventh verse—V.4.1 through V.4.11—to maintain its thematic integrity. Despite the stringent boundaries that antāti and theme impose on the text, there is a way to disassemble it to create new meanings; tracing the use of particular words, epithets or myths across the text is an obvious approach.

Frank Clooney offers one such reading by focusing on the enigmatic vocative, Neṭiyāy (Tall One).[6] Is it simply a way to describe god's towering nature, his transcendence, his beauty? Is it a reference to his actions as Trivikrama, when he grew to take over worlds? These few possibilities do not foreclose other readings: 'Tall one does not mean anything we want it to mean; it evokes some words and some memories, and echoes throughout *Tiruvāymoḻi* in a particular way that invites the more attentive and learned reader to a heightened appreciation.'[7] Similarly, one can, as the traditional commentators do, see the entire text encapsulated in a single verse.[8] The most obvious example of this is *Tiruvāymoḻi* I.1.1,

Who possesses the highest good?
Him.
Who cuts delusion grants a good clear mind?
Him.

Who's the master of unforgetting untiring immortals?
Him.
Sunder grief, worship his luminous feet, bow down, rise up
my mind.

which is said to distil the *arthapañcaka*, the five categories of inquiry. These are god (*īśvara*), the self (*jīva*), the path to mokṣa (*upāya*), the obstacles (*virodhi*) and the final goal (*puruṣārtha*). God, the master of the immortals, is beyond pain and is supreme; he cuts the obstacles represented by delusion; worshipping his feet is the path, and service to him is the final goal, one that assures a clear, exalted mind.[9] One can also take each Hundred as its own unit, representing a fully realized narrative—one that may begin in separation, say II.1 (a messenger poem) and end with the poet extolling the virtue of a specific site, II.10 (on Tirumaliruncolai). We could assemble verses on specific sites, and consider how the poet understands Viṣṇu's immanence; we could just read the *Tiruvāymoḻi*'s female-voiced poems to learn something of the theology of divine absence, and to understand its opposite, divine presence; we could weave together all the decads and verses where god is a poet, and so on.

The *Tiruvāymoḻi*'s division—single verses set into tens, embedded into ten sets of hundreds—offers limitless possibilities for the reader/listener, even within the antāti framework. We can approach the text as a series of involutions, of contractions, where we find the perfect pearl of an idea in a single verse. Alternatively, we can see it as ever expansive and outward moving, where the one becomes ten becomes hundred becomes a thousand. The poem's accordion-like quality is in keeping with all the ways the poet conceptualizes god: as one, two, three, many, and that entire multitude inevitably collapsing into singularity. This preoccupation is clear in the very first myth Śaṭhakōpaṉ invokes, of Viṣṇu (as yet unnamed) eating the world (I.1.7). Come the end time, the entire multifarious universe is absorbed back into his body, only to be spewed forth when the time of creation is at hand. A deliberate choice, the myth tells us something about this yet unnamed deity, about his enigmatic nature, as the maker and destroyer of worlds. Like this narrative allusion, every myth and motif, every name and place in the poem is deliberate and is orientated towards a larger, overarching point. Thus, the poem's protean quality, exemplified by this first story, embodies Viṣṇu's paradoxical nature—as limitless, multitudinous, singular and fixed. Equally, the poem's garland-like form articulates the causality of action, and the endless circularity of *saṁsāra*, in which the poet finds himself and from which he seeks release. Just as god and devotee are inextricably bound, so too are these two ways of understanding the repetitive structure of the *Tiruvāymoḻi*.

The Poet: Māṟaṉ Śaṭhakōpaṉ

Māṟaṉ Śaṭhakōpaṉ from Kurukūr
who wears a garland of fragrant makiḻ flowers
sang with love these ten verses from a thousand
on the one who rules, him who holds the disc.
Those who learn them reach Vaikuṇṭha, never to return.

Tiruvāymoḻi IV.10.11

The *Tiruvāymoḻi* provides us with two internal sources for information about its author. The first and most obvious are the hundred phala-śrutis,[10] meṭa-verses rendered in the third person, which conclude each Tiruvāymoḻi. In addition to revealing the merits of hearing, reciting, singing or mastering the preceding

Ten, these benedictory verses also provide us with a hazy outline of the poet, one that hagiography will colour in. We learn that his name is Śaṭhakōpaṉ, and that he is associated with the town of Kurukur (present-day Alvar Tirunagari), a town on the banks of the Tamiraparani. Not unlike other Tamiḻ poets, he extols his city as a wealthy, fertile home to the devout.[11] He sometimes employs the epithet, Māṟaṉ or Kārimāṟaṉ, and identifies himself as belonging to the fertile Vaḻuti lands (Pāṇṭiya country). It is this last piece of information that has allowed scholars to propose a connection between Śaṭhakōpaṉ and Pāṇṭiya kings, and through this, date the poet to the late eighth or early ninth century.[12]

More nebulous but no less compelling, is Śaṭhakōpaṉ as he presents himself within each cycle of Ten. Even a cursory review of the *Tiruvāymoḻi* reveals a poet of formidable erudition, with an easy command of Vaiṣṇava myth (pan-Sanskritic and more local), ritual and theology, in addition to the Tamiḻ literary past. Like his bhakti-poet peers, he is present in his poetry, both as author and character. Over the course of the *Tiruvāymoḻi*'s eleven hundred verses, Śaṭhakōpaṉ speaks in many voices. He explicitly identifies himself as god's poet (ex. III.9.10), or as a poet through whom god speaks (ex. VII.9.6) and as belonging to a long lineage of Vaiṣṇava devotees (ex. VI.10.1). He is a wise adviser, offering counsel to fellow devotees or those who have yet to find their way to Viṣṇu. He is a young woman in love, her mother, her friend, a fortune teller. Finally, he styles himself in abject ways, as ill-fated, governed by his senses, as low and unworthy, but redeemed as god's servant, and as a servant to the servants of god.[13]

All of these disparate elements, some biographical and others poetical, form the bedrock of Śaṭhakōpaṉ's story as he slowly assumes the position as the first teacher (*ācārya*) of what will eventually become the Śrīvaiṣṇava tradition. The first stage of this process is Madurakavi's eleven-verse laudatory poem, *Kaṇṇinuṇ ciṟu tāmpu*, in which he accepts Śaṭhakōpaṉ as his teacher, his sole refuge, and characterizes the *Tiruvāymoḻi* as distilling the meaning of the Veda.[14] Although the Śrīvaiṣṇava tradition tells us that Madurakavi received the first revelation of the *Tiruvāymoḻi*, making him Śaṭhakōpaṉ's contemporary, his poem adds nothing biographical to the brief portrait we already have from the *Tiruvāymoḻi*'s phala-śrutis. A century later, Nāthamuni, the Śrīvaiṣṇavas' first preceptor, begins the process of canonizing the *Tiruvāymoḻi*, and systematizing the works of other Tamiḻ Vaiṣṇava poets, the āḻvārs, who lived between the sixth and ninth centuries. A Sanskrit *taṉiyaṉ*, a laudatory verse attributed to Nāthamuni, is appended to the *Tiruvāymoḻi*. While Madurakavi's poem focuses on the figure of Śaṭhakōpaṉ as teacher, Nāthamuni, in keeping with his canonization project, praises the text and pointedly refers to it as the Drāviḍa Veda (Southern/Tamiḻ Veda). Neither Madurakavi nor Nāthamuni gives us much information about Śaṭhakōpaṉ, the person or the poet; for that, we have to turn to the vast body of Śrīvaiṣṇava hagiographic literature.[15]

The Legend of Śaṭhakōpaṉ: Carita

He sang the deep meaning of the Veda,
known only to great brahmins,
and set it firmly in my heart.
The moment I was filled with love to serve
Śaṭhakōpaṉ, my king
in that very instant, I received
the gift of service to him.

Kaṇṇinuṇ ciṟu tāmpu 9

The legend of Śaṭhakōpaṉ is collected in a number of Śrīvaiṣṇava hagiographies composed in Tamiḻ, Sanskrit and Maṇipravāḷa, between the thirteenth and fifteenth centuries in Tamiḻ-speaking south India.[16] While hagiographies continue to be authored in various Indian languages, including in English, the tradition reveres the two *Guruparamparaprabāvams* (The Splendour of the Lineage of Teachers) and the *Divyasūricaritam* (The Stories of Divine Beings) as authoritative.[17]

The contours of the story are as follows: A pious childless Velala couple, Kāṟi and Uṭayanaṅgai, pray to Viṣṇu for a child, and is blessed with a boy, who is none other than Viṣṇu himself. However, their infant does not cry, eat, and keeps its eyes and mouth closed. He is named Śaṭhakōpaṉ. The distraught parents take the child to the temple of Ādināthaṉ in Kurukur, seeking to leave him there. The baby astonishes them by crawling to a tamarind tree, under which he sits, assuming a posture of meditation. He sits silently for sixteen long years, until Madurakavi follows a light in the sky that leads to the meditating boy. The much older brahmin Madurakavi, who has been seeking a teacher, is bewildered by the mute youth, and drops a stone next to him to determine if he is conscious or not. He opens his eyes; taking this as a sign, Madurakavi poses a riddle: 'If the small thing is born in the belly of a dead thing, what will it eat and where will it lie?' The boy answers obliquely, 'It will eat that and it will lie there.'[18] With these words, Śaṭhakōpaṉ having broken his silence, reveals four compositions to Madurakavi, of which the first is the *Tiruviruttam* and the last is the *Tiruvāymoḻi*.[19]

The story, however, does not end here, as after this first transmission, the *Tiruvāymoḻi* is lost for an indeterminate number of years. Nāthamuni, a brahmin Vaiṣṇava teacher, chances upon a group of itinerant performers singing sweet Tamiḻ verses that begin with the words *āra amutē* (the nectar that does not sate), and end with the tantalizing information that the decad is part of a thousand verses.[20] Moved by the beauty of the songs that he had never heard before, he asks them to sing the remaining verses. To his disappointment, the singers tell him that these are all they know. He finds his way to Kurukur, where Madurakavi's student instructs him to repeat his teacher's *Kaṇṇinuṇ ciṟu tāmpu* 12,000 times. At the end of this liturgical meditation, pleased by Nāthamuni's piety, Śaṭhakōpaṉ appears, and reveals his four compositions for a second time. In addition, he also shares three thousand verses composed by ten other poets. Nāthamuni compiles these four thousand verses into a book, which comes to be known as the *Nālāyira Divya Prabandham* (The Divine Collection of Four Thousand).[21] Further, he establishes a performance tradition to ensure the accurate transmission of the texts and to guard against textual loss. The twelve authors of the *Divya Prabandham* are revered as the āḻvār (those who are immersed), and the poet Śaṭhakōpaṉ is elevated above all, given the epithet, Nammāḻvār (Our Āḻvār).[22]

Although these stories tell us very little about the poet, they help us uncover the histories of an emergent Śrīvaiṣṇava sampradāya, and the singular importance of Nammāḻvār to that history.[23] At least since the period of Rāmānuja (1017–1137, traditional dates), the Śrīvaiṣṇavas have consciously constructed themselves as open to everyone, regardless of caste or gender.[24] Nammāḻvār makes this very point in the *Tiruvāymoḻi*,[25] and the list of twelve āḻvār-poets includes a woman, and men representing different caste groups. Our Āḻvār's[26] story emphasizes this pioneering approach to social relations, which reversed the customary hierarchy, making the young, non-brahmin Nammāḻvār teacher to the older brahmin Madurakavi. Asserting Vedic status for the Tamil̲ *Tiruvāymoḻi* similarly underlined that secret, esoteric knowledge was for everyone, and could be rendered in a language other than Sanskrit.[27] If the first revelation to Madurakavi describes the spontaneity and other-worldly composition of the *Tiruvāymoḻi*, its second revelation to Nāthamuni speaks to its institutionalization. Held by another brahmin, it moves from the streets, sung by wandering musicians, into a temple, to be performed by brahmin men as part of a ritual practice.[28] It evokes a different phase and a different manner of affirming the *Tiruvāymoḻi*'s Vedic status.

Later visual or textual versions of the Nammāḻvār narrative embellish it in two significant ways.[29] First, they not only assert the Vedic authority of the *Tiruvāymoḻi*, but also seek to have it accepted as a great Tamil̲ poem. In these tellings, poets of the legendary Tamil̲ Saṅgam test the text by writing a single phrase from the *Tiruvāymoḻi* (*kaṇṇan̲ kaḻalin̲ai*, X.5.1) on a palm leaf, and placing it on the Saṅgam plank (*caṅkappalakai*) to be judged. Even this brief phrase (*śeṣam*) is sufficient to throw off the works of the three hundred poets of the Tamil̲ Saṅgam,[30] definitively proving the superiority of Nammāḻvār's work, and inspiring the chief poet of the Tamil̲ academy to praise the *Tiruvāymoḻi* and its poet in a laudatory verse. This is how the Nammāḻvār–Madurakavi story concludes—with an acknowledgement of the *Tiruvāymoḻi*'s exemplary status in both the Sanskrit and Tamil̲ worlds, and the disciple's singular commitment to ensuring its propagation.[31]

The later narratives also reveal a preoccupation with the writing of the *Tiruvāymoḻi*, signalling a shift away from Nammāḻvār's oral transmission to Madurakavi and Nāthamuni.[32] In these later iterations, Madurakavi, armed with stylus and palm leaf, copies down the poet's words as he speaks them. This version becomes so embedded in the consciousness of the Śrīvaiṣṇavas that paintings and sculptures from the fifteenth century onward depict Nammāḻvār flanked by Madurakavi, stylus in hand, and Nāthamuni holding a pair of cymbals. These representations encapsulate the text's double revelation, its two modes of transmission and the two distinct lineages that ensured its preservation.[33]

God in the Tiruvāymoḻi: Tirumāl

See him
the one with lotus eyes who ate the world
who became earth sky people gods,
who became this this this this
He became luminous wisdom
created everything
He became light fiery and intense
then he became three.

Tiruvāymoḻi III.6.1

In the *Tiruvāymoḻi,* god is Viṣṇu-Nārāyaṇa, a deity of a thousand names and thousand forms, who is singular, transcendent, inscrutable, formless, distant, multiple, immanent, knowable, embodied and intimate.[34] As everything in this monumental work, Nammāḻvār's vision of Viṣṇu is complex, informed by both knowledge and experience. He knows god by his many names, in his many places, and through his legendary deeds. Simultaneously, he feels god as a corporeal presence that he sees, tastes, drinks, and one who in turn, fills and consumes him.[35] Although Śaṭhakōpaṉ does not name his god in the poem's opening decad—he is simply *avaṉ* (him)—these ten verses already allude to many of these themes: a supreme deity impossible to know as any one thing (I.1.6), yet all paths ultimately reach him alone (I.1.5). He is beyond the conception of the gods (I.1.7), but is as intimate as breath in the body (I.1.7). As the first four decads of the *Tiruvāymoḻi* (I.1 to I.4) unfold, the poet incrementally reveals something new about this elusive, impossible god. We hear his name—Nāraṇaṉ—for the first time in I.2.10, reminding his audience that this is one in whom all things abide. Next, we learn of him as avatāra, embodied and accessible (I.3.1), as the one in whom both Śiva and Brahmā exist (I.3.9), as sovereign over the worlds (I.3.10), and finally, in physical terms, as the one dark as storm clouds (I.3.10). In the fourth Ten, even the intimacy of the avatāra is superseded, for he is now a longed for but absent beloved, and it is in this context that we hear the god's first Tamiḻ names: Tirumāl (I.4.7), Neṭumāl (I.4.8), and most importantly, Kaṇṇaṉ (I.4.11), domesticating far-off transcendent Nāraṇaṉ (I.4.5, I.4.9) to the sweet intimacy of Tamiḻ. The pattern of juxtaposing Sanskrit and Tamiḻ names is evident throughout the *Tiruvāymoḻi*, but it is clear from the sheer number of times it occurs, that Kaṇṇaṉ (the Tamiḻ form for Kṛṣṇa), with all its mythic and embodied associations, holds a precious place in the Āḻvār's heart. Curiously then, this name disappears as the poem reaches its climax—used for the last time in X.5.11—midway through the final Hundred, replaced thereafter with a cascade of lofty Sanskrit names—Keśavaṉ, Nāraṇaṉ Mādhavaṉ, Vaikuṇṭhaṉ—with a sprinkling of a Tirumāl here and a Kōvalaṉ there. As the poem concludes, it folds back into the themes that open it, but with the poet Śaṭhakōpaṉ unmistakably present.

In the opening Tiruvāymoḻis, god is described objectively, as though from a great distance. In contrast, as we move through the Tenth Hundred, the vast space between god and devotee shrinks. Even as the poet-devotee describes god in familiarly transcendent ways—as the highest one (X.4.7), as inscrutable to the gods (X.5.9), as the lord of Vaikuṇṭha (X.9), he is also a friend, Āttaṉ (X.1.6), one whose feet adorn the poet's head (X.4.4, X.6.6), and who dwells inside the poet (X.8.2, X.8.6).[36] In the glorious, final decad (X.10), the poet and god drink each other, like hot iron placed in water (X.10.5), their thirst and desire for each other unquenchable, for they are to each other, ārā amutē, nectar that does not sate. In the end though, god is not the distant third person (avaṉ/*avar*) of the *Tiruvāymoḻi*'s opening decads. He has become and is known in the intimate second person, swirling around, surrounding, embracing, engulfing the poet (X.10.9, X.10.10):

Swirling spreading deep high endless vastness
Swirling growing beyond that
a great blossoming light
Swirling growing beyond even that
the luminous bliss of wisdom
Swirling growing beyond even that
my love for you. You cut that too
and engulfed me.

Tiruvāymoḻi X.10.10.

The *Tiruvāymoḻi*'s pāsurams and Pattu-s lead us to this point, not in a linear or even systematic manner. Rather, motifs, ideas, descriptions swirl, repeat, return, like breezes scented with the fragrance of a thousand flowers. They work in isolation and in concert, as the poet paints a picture of a beautiful, mercurial deity, a god of tricks and cunning, a magical poet, his mother, father and every kind of kin, an indifferent, even cruel beloved, a generous giver of grace and love.[37] He is described as the natural world,[38] and within it, dark as gathering storm clouds, his lips red as a ripe fruit, his body glowing, and tender as a freshly bloomed lotus—surrounding him, and yet apart. And when the clouds arrive and he does not, when the fruits ripen to red and the flowers bloom, it is his absence that the encircling natural world marks.[39] To the rest of us, on the outside, god is knowable through his myths—eating, spewing, measuring worlds, defeating demons, stealing butter—but to Śaṭhakōpaṉ, god is experienced physically, seen riding his eagle Garuḍa, holding aloft his conch and disc.[40] In the abstract, he glows like a mountain of emeralds, like a tower of light, like an incandescent flame. Most strikingly, god is a poet, a magical one at that, who uses Nammāḻvār as his amanuensis to sing of himself. Within the theological world of the *Tiruvāymoḻi*, an unknowable god is knowable only through the poet's words, yet these very words are nothing but god's own utterances. God sings to reveal himself, and the poet sings to know himself. Such apophatic involution is a distinctive feature of the *Tiruvāymoḻi*, which is ultimately as much about god—who is whatever we wish him to be, true to those who believe in him and untrue to others—as it is about the devotee who seeks him with a passionate single-minded devotion. Poetry makes worlds, makes gods, makes poets.

The Devotee in the Tiruvāymoḻi: Aṭiyār

In the *Tiruvāymoḻi*, Nammāḻvār oscillates between two poles—of individual longing and communal belonging. He is a lonely seeker, set apart by his singular desire, which no one can understand. He is atiyēṉ (I who am at the feet [of god]) or *toṇṭaṉ* (bonded servant/slave), assuming the stance that god solely owns him: god is his life, his breath and his only refuge. He asserts this nowhere more powerfully than in the opening verse of the final Hundred:

Silent sage four-faced one three-eyed father
my perfect dark jewel

with berry-red lips and lotus-bright eyes,
my cunning thief.
I am alone and you are my precious life
at last you're here resting on my head.
I won't let you go now
Please, no more tricks.

Tiruvāymoḻi X.10.1

In this mode of aloneness, he assumes the female persona of the Parāṅkuśa Nāyikā, who gives voice to her crippling love, utterly natural to her, but inexplicable to everyone else. She is enslaved by this desire, which subsumes and subjugates her.[41] This is a toṇṭaṉ of a different kind:

Mothers, why do you scold me?
I saw beautiful Tirukkuṟuṅkuṭi Nambi.
Now my heart can only follow
his conch his disc,
his lovely lotus eyes,
his lush red lips.

Tiruvāymoḻi V.5.1

Elsewhere, this *nāyikā* (heroine) seeks sympathy from the natural world that surrounds her, because either it reminds her of the beloved or its longing for Tirumāl is as sharp as her own. Tiruvāymoḻi II.1 exemplifies the mood and mode. In this gentle and poignant decad, the heroine asks the sleepless birds, the roaring sea, the waning moon if they suffer as she does. They too belong to him as completely as she does:

Young moon, you fade like me
No longer dispelling the darkness of the night sky
you've lost your light. Did you trust the promises
of the great lord with the disc, him
asleep on the serpent with five heads
and lose yourself?

Tiruvāymoḻi II.1.6

A counterpoint to this quiet lament is a decad like VII.7, where the heroine (the *talaivi*) is unable to distinguish between the world that surrounds her and the beauty of her beloved, and turns to her silent, befuddled mother(s) and companions for advice:

Is it death come in a pair
to devour the life of the wretched or
the beautiful eyes of Kaṇṇaṉ
dark as the sea
I can't tell. They surround me
like lotuses in full bloom
Friends, mothers, I am suffering
What should I do?

Tiruvāymoḻi VII.7.1

Diametrically opposed to such tragic, bleak despair highlighted by the Āḻvār's solitariness is the joy the poet finds in a community of devotees.[42] He not only asserts that he comes from a long line of Vaiṣṇavas (II.7.1), but that his only kin are fellow devotees (III.7.8). They rule him, and he lives to serve them, desiring such service even more than union with Viṣṇu, even more than Vaikuṇṭha:

If I win the three worlds,
even if I become him
can it equal the joy
of serving at his supplicants' feet?
Their victory is to shelter under his feet
covered in flowers
He's the one dark as storm clouds.

Tiruvāymoḻi VIII.10.2

In the company of devotees, his loneliness abates, for they alone can appreciate his great, consuming love for god:

He destroys the wickedness
in his devotees with his many weapons
the disc conch sword bow staff
Eternal youth, father of love
I am alone, but
exalted in the company
of his servants' servants' servants.

Tiruvāymoḻi VIII.10.9

Even as he exults in the friendship and company of the pious, he also remains apart from them. He subjugates himself to them, even to the vilest devotee, but also assumes a position of authority, providing advice and guidance. He urges them to visit temple sites—go to Tirumaliruncolai before youth is lost (II.10), reach him in Venkatam (III.3), circumambulate Tirumokur (X.10.5). He teaches them the right way to worship, warns them away from other paths and a worldly life. He counsels poets against praising ordinary mortal kings, cautions these same poets (III.9) that they may find themselves taken over by a miraculous poet (X.7). He exhorts his listeners to sing, leap, dance and proclaim their love for Māl, for silently uttering his names will not suffice:

My father is up north in Vēṅkaṭam
amidst pools and lovely waterfalls.
Speak his many names, and
people may call you mad.
Roam through cities, and
the world will mock you.
Dance, let your passion build, and
even the immortals will bow before you.

Tiruvāymoḻi III.5.8

Love for god ought to overwhelm the body, such that it bursts its boundaries, upends social norms and reverses traditional hierarchies. In this, he is the exemplar as is his nāyikā. The heroine's mother often despairs that her daughter's love is unseemly, that the girl (nor her friend) cares not at all for the shame it may bring her family or the gossip it attracts. Her desire is immodest and ungovernable—it refuses to be quieted and expressed in ways that are socially sanctioned. The girl is aware of these external expectations, but she also knows that to love god wholly is to care for nothing else. The most radical expression of the sentiment is found in two verses in the Fifth Hundred, in which the talaivi declares that she will ride the *maṭal*, co-opting a typically male act of public declaration. The town may gasp and stand aghast, but his cool *tuḷasi* will protect her from the scorching heat of their disapproval:

I'll ride the maṭal,
I'll be shameless in every street
Tongues will wag, women will heap abuse
the city will clamour, but
I'll be wearing the cool tuḷasi of the lord
who holds the disc in his beautiful hand.

Tiruvāymoḻi V.3.10

One way to approach the *Tiruvāymoḻi* is to read it as a guide on how to become a devotee, an *aṭiyār*, how to lead a good, worthy life grounded in piety. The Āḻvār tells us to worship in decorous ways, offering flowers and incense. He asks us to proclaim our love indecorously, unmindful of what the world might think of us. Don't sing of mortal kings, he warns fellow poets, yet styles himself in the phala-śrutis as Vaḻuti Nāḍaṉ (a cultivated man of the Pāṇṭiya land) and as Māṟaṉ, a title that affirms his own connection to Pāṇṭiya kings.[43] The push and pull of the world animates the *Tiruvāymoḻi*, and is reflected in the final benedictory verses that promise both earthly and divine rewards. In these verses, the poet twins the value of the text itself with mastering it, singing it and performing it, promising the virtuoso devotee, Vaikuṇṭha (IV.8.11), a happy family life (VIII.10.11), the love of women (VI.1.11) and eternal service (VIII.9.11).

In the final sum, there can be no doubt that the *Tiruvāymoḻi* sees service to god and to his devotees as a key Vaiṣṇava value. As if to affirm this position, the text's penultimate Ten describes an ascent to Vaikuṇṭha, not the poet's own, but that of other devotees. It is what he imagines and wishes for himself, but it is telling he does not place himself in that longed-for realm in the decad proper; he does so only in its phala-śruti (X.9.11). When the final Tiruvāymoḻi (X.10) begins, we find ourselves in a reversal, the poet is once again alone, desperate for lasting union. When that union eventually comes, it is for him alone. He alone is surrounded, engulfed; it is his desire alone that is cut, as he is immersed in the towering presence of Neṭumāl. Even the decad's phala-śruti, the poem's very last verse (X.10.11), gives no quarter, promising nothing more than an exalted birth to those who master the *Tiruvāymoḻi*. The juxtaposition of the themes in X.9 and X.10 revives the tension between particular, individual experience and one shared in a community, which animates so much of the poem's drama. In the end, as is typical of this chimerical text, the *Tiruvāymoḻi* offers us an answer on how to *be* an aṭiyār, but leaves us to work out what that might mean for each of us.

Watchers and Listeners in the Tiruvāymoḻi: Kāṭci

I am all the land you see
the sky you see, I am that too
I am the hot flame, this wind that blows
and all the ocean, I am.
Has the one dark as the ocean
the one who sees all entered her?
You stand as witness in this world
seeing everything my girl does
what shall I say?

Tiruvāymoḻi V.6.3

Nammāḻvār's first poem, the *Tiruviruttam*, opens with a clear sense of its audience and the poet's intended effect on that audience. Stand here, steadfastly, firmly, and truly *listen* to what I ask of you (*mey niṉṟu kēṭṭaruḷāy*), give me grace, begs the poet, framing his poem as a plea, *viṇappam*, to Viṣṇu.[44] The *Tiruvāymoḻi* gives us no such aid, as its audiences, listeners and watchers multiply in a deliberately destabilizing fashion, with the poem's opening verses setting the tone. In I.1.1, god is abstract, and the poet obscure. He is the speaker of the verse and its audience, a spiralling involution characteristic of this poem. 'Who is the highest one, the god of gods, who grants clarity of mind?' queries the poet in a kind of public dialogue. Someone, perhaps the poet himself, replies repeatedly, him, him, him. Then, with sudden violence, he issues what appears to be a public command—cut grief and suffering (*tuyar aṟu*), something we experience inwardly but emerges from external factors. In this vein, he exhorts the audience to bow low at god's luminous feet, and to then rise up. Only with the verse's final two words do we understand that the outward-facing voice is, in fact, turned inward. This is not a public conversation, but a private one—the poet addressing himself, insisting to himself—cut sorrow, bow at his feet, rise up *my* mind (*eṉ maṉam*). In the next verse (I.1.2), the poet first absents himself, *my* mind gives way to a generic mind, free of delusion, and of a god beyond even its conception. Poet and audience are slowly set apart, to mimic the distance between god and devotee, and to begin the journey of the *Tiruvāymoḻi*. Then, just as abruptly, the distance is erased as he (god) becomes the poet's very life. The pattern of an audience that is both outside the poem and within it is repeated in the third verse (I.1.3), but now, the *I* and *my* give way to the collective—*we* draw near him (*naṇukiṉam nāmē*), he says, drawing not just his mind, but also all beings into a circle of aspirants.

The Śrīvaiṣṇava hagiographies and commentaries read the *Tiruvāymoḻi* as an external expression of an internal contemplation, a poem that emerges fully formed in the instant that Madurakavi and Śaṭhakōpaṉ meet.[45] In this remembering, Śaṭhakōpaṉ is both the poem's author and its first audience. However, this too is complicated by the multiple instances in which the poet claims that Viṣṇu uses him to sing sweet songs in praise of himself. Let us examine two examples from VII.9, a decad of extended meditation on this dynamic between god and devotee:

What can I sing? He's merged with my sweet life
my words are his sweet songs, his own
words of praise of himself. He's mysterious
he stands before me, three forms, singular.

Tiruvāymoḻi VII.9.2

God has mingled with the poet to such a degree there can be nothing to differentiate the two—the poet's words are god's own. The poet's words of praise, which help us apprehend god, become god's own way of making himself known. The verse turns again, in the final line, where god stands, as in the *Tiruviruttam*'s opening verse, apart from the poet, granting Śaṭhakōpaṉ the audience for which he yearns. In the next verse, Nammāḻvār shifts the focus again, stretching the externality a little further:

He makes it clear 'I am singular cause'
burrows into my tongue to sing sweet songs
of himself for his devotees. He rests on my lips
always first, my father, how can I ever forget him?

Tiruvāymoḻi VII.9.3

God and poet are commingled, both of them united in their authorship, to address a third entity (us) that exists outside of them. The sweet songs are for neither of them, for they already know each other; it is for those others (us), on whose lips god does not rest, on whose tongue he has not made himself at home.

The *Tiruvāymoḻi* is as much an archive of a poet's growing self-understanding as it is a document that maps the way to god-understanding. The poem maintains a consistent dialogue between those who know (which means to see and feel), and those who cannot understand, doomed to always remain on the outside. The female-voiced songs are the most poignant and powerful expression of this dynamic. Śrīvaiṣṇava commentators read the heroine as contiguous with the poet, appearing whenever the poet finds himself apart from Māl. In such moments, when the pain of separation is unbearable, it seems only a woman's voice can capture the corporeal and sensory dimensions of desire.[46] The woman, though, is rarely alone. There are always witnesses to her suffering—some are sympathetic but befuddled, still others are cruel and apathetic, while her mother is usually distraught and helpless in the face of a love she cannot understand. Here is the young woman, speaking to the natural world:

I turn pale, fade
as the ages pass. How much longer?
Spotless white herons, be kind
One day when you see him
the king of celestials
his hair dark glossy perfect
Tell him 'She has eyes for no one but you.'

Tiruvāymoḻi VI.8.8

With the king of celestials absent from her presence, she must rely on others to listen to her, so that they can make *him* listen.

While she, a passive figure, must await his arrival, the birds, free to roam the skies, can come into his presence at any time. The urgent question that provides the delicious tension of the verse is not if her messengers will *see* him, but if they will *tell* him. To see is to hear—tell him she sees no one but you—to hear is to witness, and to witness is to know, whether it is the birds and bees that surround her or the mysterious Māl who has absented himself from her sight.

There are, however, different ways to see and to know. The girl's mother, who carefully watches her daughter, sees her suffering, hears her strange babbling, cannot quite comprehend how she came to be this way, or what it even means. Perhaps, she does see and knows more than she is willing to acknowledge, for she will take the silent, absent god to task—what do you plan to do about *her*, she'll demand later (VII.2.4):

She cups her palms and says,
'He sleeps on the ocean'
She points to the red sun and says,
'There's Śrīdharaṉ'
Her tears flow freely, she falls
crying 'Nāraṇaṉ.'
I don't understand anything
my blessed child does.

Tiruvāymoḻi IV.4.2

If the mother's seeing is tinged with wariness and a certain watchfulness, the talaivi's friend refuses to dissemble. She stands as a forceful witness to the heroine's love, and can even foresee its conclusion. Perhaps, the friend is really the heroine in another guise, at another time, at some other point in this long, endless poem. In IV.6, when she is first introduced, the friend speaks to the clueless mother(s)[47] about the girl's love, which these maternal figures have mistaken for possession. Little do they know that it *is* possession, an incurable kind, a welcome, consuming love-disease that can only be abated by words like 'conch' and 'disc' and Māl's honey-sweet tuḷasi. Does the friend speak these wise words for she too knows this special longing? In these verses of friendship, the heroine (Nammāḻvār?) is absent and silent, like the beloved, who too remains outside the frame. She rarely speaks, or if she does, it is through her friend. She is the object of sight and hearing, known only by what the friend reveals about her.[48] In IV.6, when the friend returns, we hear the friend admonish the mothers for their foolishness in allowing their girl to *see* her beloved's city:

You took her to Tolaivillimaṅgalam
and showed this pitiful girl
that blazing light, the lord with bright lotus eyes
From that moment, her eyes wept like clouds,
absorbed, her mind rests in him
she bows and looks
only in his direction.

Tiruvāymoḻi VI.5.5

From this moment, she is lost to them, completely his. At first, she is passive—taken to this city, shown the beautiful form of the storm-dark god—and then, once sight takes hold, once she has had her audience of him, she can see nothing *but* him, hear of nothing but him, can speak of nothing but him (VI.5.7–VI.5.10).

Even as her eyes flood with tears, obscuring sight, she the watcher, awaits vision, and until it appears, she creates it with words. In this, she is indeed like Nammāḻvār, who longs to see, and when he cannot, seeks to manifest the mysterious hidden god through the force of his words:

I haven't abandoned
acts that bring sorrow
I haven't worshipped your feet
without pause
ancient pervasive beautiful Kaṇṇā
my supreme light, I call out to see you.
Where should I call to see you?

Tiruvāymoḻi III.2.8

One answer to this question—where can I call to see you—is that Kaṇṇaṉ lives within the poet, returning us to the beginning, to the inward-looking gaze, to a place where the poet sees and makes the god with words, who then sees himself through the poet's words:

I know you well, I see you clearly, deep
within myself as the full perfect form of wisdom,
I've kept you there. I'm done
with the nonsense of birth and death, of being.
Lord adorned in garlands of tuḷasi I've found you.

Tiruvāymoḻi IV.7.7

What does one do, when Māl goes quiet, when he is too well hidden to be seen? How does one seek? Of what does one speak?

In the *Tiruvāymoḻi*, you build him temples out of your words, you sing him into being.

The Places of the Tiruvāymoḻi: Iṭam

In the sky, atop the mountain,
asleep on the ocean, walking the earth
you live hidden in every place
in worlds far beyond measure, you're there too
You're within me dancing
Why hide yourself from me?

Tiruvāymoḻi VI.9.5

Although for Śaṭhakopaṉ-Nammāḻvār and his fellow āḻvār poets, Viṣṇu exists in all things and is everywhere, they nonetheless locate and fix him in specific terrestrial places.[49] This is a familiar aspect of Tamiḻ bhakti poetry, which allows god—either Śiva or Viṣṇu—to replicate infinitely and indivisibly, making a home for himself in the land and within the landscapes familiar to the poet. Nammāḻvār is no different in this regard, and sings in praise of thirty-five sacred sites (thirty-three terrestrial and two non-terrestrial), both near and far. This praise is not methodical—the sites do not appear in any discernible order; they do not map pilgrimage routes, are not clustered regionally, nor are they linked thematically. Always, though, the place is imbued with god's presence, signalled by its prosperity, fertility, beauty and virtue. In addition to this beauty, the poet often signals his reverence for the Vedic tradition, using it as a shorthand to speak of the site's sacrality and the piety of its inhabitants. Two verses from the same decad demonstrate the ways in which Nammāḻvār envisions the places Viṣṇu inhabits:

I am not there, I am not here
mad to see you, I am nowhere.
Lord who destroyed Laṅkā, you are
in Śrīvaramaṅgala, city of mansions limned by the moon
You who hold conch and disc
I am alone, give me grace.

For the five you staged a war, razed
the hostile armies of the hundred, reduced them to ash
My father, lord who dug up the earth
you abide in Śrīvaramaṅgala where the wise
perform Vedic sacrifices without pause
Where shall I call out to reach you?

Tiruvāymoḻi V.7.2; V.7.4

The hagiographic tradition holds that Śaṭhakōpaṉ, the silent sage, went nowhere, that his experience of sites was visionary. The internal evidence of the *Tiruvāymoḻi* does not provide definitive evidence to argue either for or against such an assertion. He was clearly familiar with the temples in his vicinity; of the thirty-three terrestrial places he praises, twenty-four are in the Pāṇṭiya and Cēra regions, eleven of which are very close to Kurukur, his home town. In some instances, for temples a bit farther afield, Nammāḻvār provides specific topographical details that help locate them. At other times, he describes devotional activities one should undertake when visiting a special place, offering us a glimpse of a nascent Vaiṣṇava pilgrimage culture.[50] G. Damodaran argues that Nammāḻvār visited those places that he describes as having seen (*kaṇṭēṉ*), reached (*aṭaintēṉ*) or entered (*pukuntēṉ*), while he expresses a wish to see those shrines to which he has yet to travel.[51] These small clues coupled with his consistent exhortation to his fellow devotees to leap, sing, wander, visiting shrine after shrine, suggest that it is possible that Nammāḻvār physically made a pilgrimage to some, if not all, of the temples and sacred places on which he composes songs.

While some shrines are just mentioned in a single verse, several sacred places are chosen for elaborate expositions. Of these, the two most significant are the ancient shrines of Venkatam (Tirumala-Tirupati) in the northern limits of Tamiḻ *akam*, and Tirumaliruncolai, in the heart of Pāṇṭiya country. If we bracket out the customary mention of Kurukur in each concluding verse, Venkatam is the first terrestrial site evoked (II.8.3) in a brief couplet.[52] In this glancing instance, Nammāḻvār offers us no specific details about it, simply describing it as a place praised by even the gods, where Viṣṇu has made his home. What appears a throwaway reference hides the immense importance of Venkatam, which will receive two separate cycles of praise in its honour (III.3; VI.10). The latter decad is of seminal importance for Śrīvaiṣṇavas, as it represents the place and moment of Nammāḻvār's *prapatti* (total surrender). The first decad, III.3, establishes a close relationship between the devotee and the unnamed deity at this specific site. In its penultimate verse (III.3.10), it urges devotees to rush to Venkatam before they grow old, echoing the sentiment that opens the decad on Tirumaliruncolai (II.10), the only other site which receives two decads of praise. While Venkatam is the first terrestrial site praised, Maliruncolai is the first place with a Tiruvāymoḻi devoted to it. In this first decad, he praises its cloud-touched mountains filled with peacocks and elephant herds as much as he does the god enshrined within it. Cut the pull of worldly pleasures and rush to Maliruncolai, the poet counsels his listeners. The next time he invokes this mountain shrine on the northern edge of Pāṇṭiya country, it is at the poem's very end, in X.7. Again, it is a Ten in an advisory mode, but the warning is not to errant and foolish people wasting their youth away, but to poets. Nammāḻvār warns fellow poets that they stand in danger of being taken over by a magical poet, just like him, describing in loving detail this divine possession. Here, god is the cunning trickster, who just happens to reside amidst the forests and flowers of Maliruncolai:

Poets of fine words, take care. The cunning thief
the great trickster of Tirumāliruñcōlai
stole into my heart and into my life, a magical poet
he dissolved into me, remained there unknown
devoured my heart and my life
then filled me with himself.

Tiruvāymoḻi X.7.1

As the Māliruñcōlai-Tiruvāymoḻi progresses, everything within the poet is displaced to make room for this beautiful, generous god. He is emptied of himself—his ego, his action, his breath, his life—so our Āḻvār's body becomes one of god's many places, perhaps his very favourite place:

My head, the hills of Tirumāliruñcōlai
and the ocean of milk. My body, Tirumāl's Vaikuṇṭha
and his cool Tiruvēṅkaṭam. He won't leave me,
my ordinary life my mind my speech my karma,
not for an instant will he stay away. Him
the singular primordial cause of time.

Tiruvāymoḻi X.7.8

In the Venkatam and Maliruncolai Tens we hear the poet speak to others of the sanctity of a site and to offer them counsel. In several other territorial decads—nine to be precise—he describes the site in the female voice, the voice of loss and longing.[53] Two examples, one spoken by the talaivi and the other by her mother, will illustrate how the *Tiruvāymoḻi* conceives a topography of absent-presence. First, let us hear the girl, who longs to join her beloved in Tiruvallaval. She addresses her uncomprehending friends—when will I go, when will I be with him, when will I be full again—these are her insistent questions, that are all about departure. Here the verse speaks of her longing, not her longing for the god, but her longing to *go*, to be mobile, to reach the god, who is fixed and (apparently) immovable in Tiruvallaval:

Gentle doe-eyed women, look at me
waste away day by day. I am doomed.
When will I reach the feet of the king
who dwells in Tiruvallavāḻ
with its kamuku trees that touch the sky
and its air sweet with honey and jasmine?
I am his.

Tiruvāymoḻi V.9.1

In contrast, hear the mother, speaking of loss, her gentle, timid fawn-like creature gone with unexpected boldness in search of his place, forgetting kin, home, and everything else. Now it is the mother rooted in place, unable (unwilling, perhaps) to follow her daughter. She feels the loss of her daughter keenly, now gone, and in an extraordinary reversal, melts and dissolves much like her girl does in yearning for the beloved:

Saying 'Everything good is for my Kaṇṇaṉ'
my love-mad girl abandoned all this, went to Tirukkōḷūr
The village gossips, still she walks away,
not thinking of me.

Tiruvāymoḻi VI.7.9

Then, there are the messenger poems, where the abandoned heroine, unable to hold on to Māl, tries to fix him in a single place—you will find him in Tirumulikkulam she says—for she cannot hold him either within her or even keep him by her side. She recruits cranes, bees, clouds to link herself faceless and placeless to him embodied and emplaced; or the two lovers, separated by their own rootedness and fixedness, can only be united by those that have no such ties:

Bees and dragonflies
feasting in these gardens,
speak well of me to him
dark as a kāya bloom, to him
with tuḷasi in his hair, to him
who's made Tirumūḻikkaḷam his home.

Tiruvāymoḻi IX.7.8

In these messenger poems, we never learn where the poet, or his alter ego, the nāyikā is; we only know where god is—somewhere distant, unreachable, unseeable. Each is fixed in their place, the god willingly and the girl unwillingly, and the empty space between them is filled with the chatter of birds, the buzz of bees, the swish of clouds and her own thunderous longing.

The talaivi often speaks of distance, of god existing somewhere outside and apart from her. When Nammāḻvār speaks in his own voice, he dissolves this distance, to fix god on to his body, and even more radically, to map himself on to god. The *Tiruvāymoḻi* is full of verses, indeed decads, about the commingling of god and devotee, each within the other, ouroboros-like. This mutual entrenchment is a process of mutual emplacement, each making a claim on the body of the other. In a striking decad in the First Hundred, Nammāḻvār describes a systematic visualization process by which he places Viṣṇu first on to and then into his body: he's beside him, on his lap, in his heart, upon his shoulders, rooted into his tongue, in his eye, until he finally rests on his head (I.9). In the Fourth Hundred, the visualization is reversed, as the poet maps himself on to god, his heart, his words, his life become the god's adornments (IV.3). Two verses from each decad will elucidate the *Tiruvāymoḻi*'s articulations of bodies, both human and divine, as vast places of uncertain boundaries:

The mysterious lord is in my heart
it is so for everyone.
He's body and breath, wind and fire
he's both far and near
beyond thought, beyond the senses
the pure dazzling bewildering lord
rests on my shoulders.

Tiruvāymoḻi I.9.6

My life is a garland, my love is
your crown of light your countless jewels
your fine silks.

It is even the songs of praise
chanted in the three worlds
for Kaṇṇaṉ my lord my master
who wields the disc of time.

Tiruvāymoḻi IV.3.5

Commentaries and the Tiruvāymoḻi: Anubhava

At the centre of the reception of the *Tiruvāymoḻi* is experience (*anubhava*), both of the text and in the text. An ability to experience the text deeply, determined the ability to interpret it correctly. Experience is neither intuitive nor wholly spontaneous; it is cultivated through learning, usually under the tutelage of an esteemed teacher. The earliest stories about the transmission of the *Tiruvāymoḻi*, from Nammāḻvār to Madurakavi, and again from Nammāḻvār to Nāthamuni, contour its reception as the Tamiḻ Veda. Madurakavi's *Kaṇṇinuṇ ciṟu tāmpu* is our earliest extant record of a person's encounter and engagement with the *Tiruvāymoḻi*. In it, Nammāḻvār is hailed as the guru and the *Tiruvāymoḻi* is extolled as the distillation of the Sanskrit Veda. The first Sanskrit taṉiyaṉ attributed to Nāthamuni (c. tenth century) reiterates the notion of the *Tiruvāymoḻi* as the southern Veda, an idea picked up in the twelfth-century taṉiyaṉs composed by the famous Śrīvaiṣṇava teacher, Parāśara Bhaṭṭar. Indeed, both Bhaṭṭar and his father, Kūrattāḻvāṉ (eleventh century), who were Rāmānuja's prime disciples, included praise of Nammāḻvār and the *Tiruvāymoḻi* in their panegyrics (*stotra*). As Nancy Ann Nayar asserts, both father and son deployed the stotra to establish the key Śrīvaiṣṇava formulation of *Ubhaya Vedānta* (Dual Vedānta) that accepted the primacy of Sanskrit and Tamiḻ scriptural sources.

Nammāḻvār and his *Tiruvāymoḻi* were a seminal component of this effort. Nammāḻvār was a seer (*ṛṣi*) and his text, a revelation, like the Sanskrit Vedas, one that spoke of the experience of god rather than only the truth of god. In this manner, Kūrattāḻvāṉ and Bhaṭṭar elevated the *Tiruvāymoḻi*, and by extension, the *Divya Prabandham* as a whole, all while subtly delineating the difference between the Sanskrit and Tamiḻ sources of scriptural authority.[54]

The *Kaṇṇinuṇ*, the taṉiyaṉ and stotras offer the scaffolding upon which the Śrīvaiṣṇava tradition will build its edifice of Ubhaya Vedānta, primarily through the medium of authorized commentaries. While Rāmānuja composed the definitive commentaries on Sanskrit scriptural sources to explicate Viśiṣṭādvaita, his disciples took up the task of interpreting the *Tiruvāymoḻi*, to establish its equivalence with the Veda and to read it in accordance with the philosophical arguments that Rāmānuja systematized. It is the first text from the *Divya Prabandham* to receive sustained written exegetical treatment; the remaining three thousand verses will have to wait until the thirteenth century when Periyavāccāṉ Piḷḷai authors his masterful commentaries on the Śrīvaiṣṇavas' Tamiḻ canon.

The *Tiruvāymoḻi*'s first commentaries, undertaken in the formative periods of the Śrīvaiṣṇava sampradāya, took the form of oral dialogue and discourse.[55] The commentaries are filled with anecdotes about the tradition's pre-eminent teachers teaching and learning the great text, generally in a private setting, suggesting the tradition carefully regulated access to it, befitting its stature within the community, as a work of revelation.[56] This produced a textual community, a tight-knit group of authorized interpreters, who not only had the erudition to decipher a difficult, sacred text, but also prodigious feeling for it. Thus, we have multiple narratives that record points of disagreement around interpretation of specific phrases or verses, alongside an equal number of examples of the text's various interlocutors overcome by emotion, anubhava, as they contemplated the Āḻvār's words.[57] These stories suggest several things—that the tradition perceived the *Tiruvāymoḻi* as a capacious text; the process of interpretation was dialogic, with conversation unearthing ever-new ways of understanding it; that to understand the *Tiruvāymoḻi* was to experience it—anubhava.

Even as the commentarial tradition moved from oral to the written, the new form still centred on the primacy of experience, and preserved the commentarial tradition's dialogic quality. This is evident in the narrative about the *Tiruvāymoḻi*'s first written commentary. Piḷḷāṉ (b.1161), Rāmānuja's disciple, requested his teacher to compose a commentary on the text. Rāmānuja refused, knowing that his interpretation would foreclose further readings. Instead, he authorized Piḷḷāṉ to write the commentary, to preserve the many interpretations of the *Tiruvāymoḻi*, and to keep it open to further exegesis.[58] This commentary, the 6000 (*Āṟāyirappaṭi*), inaugurates nearly two centuries of productive engagement with the *Tiruvāymoḻi*, as interpretations of ever-increasing length are produced. Each of these is composed in Maṇipravāḷa, a hybrid language combining Tamiḻ and Sanskrit, a telling linguistic choice for a community intent on drawing equally from the source-wells of both languages. It is also a secret language, particular to and domesticated by Śrīvaiṣṇava teachers to help establish and preserve the sanctity of the *Tiruvāymoḻi*.[59] Piḷḷāṉ's first written commentary on the *Tiruvāymoḻi* was indeed a radical act, claiming for a non-Sanskrit text, and one authored by a non-brahmin, elevated scriptural authority.[60] The four major commentaries that follow Piḷḷāṉ's, each longer than the preceding one, follow an illustrious lineage, leading back to Rāmānuja, via his prime disciple, Parāśara Bhaṭṭar. The 9000 (*Oṉpatināyirappaṭi*) is composed by Nañjīyar, Bhaṭṭar's student. Although Nampiḷḷai (c. thirteenth century), Nañjīyar's prized pupil, did not himself write a commentary, he inspired three major ones—the *Īṭu Muppattāṟayirappaṭi* (the 36,000) by Vaṭakkutiruvītippiḷḷai, Periyavāccāṉ Piḷḷai's *Irupattunālāyirappaṭi* (the 24,000) and Vātikesari Aḻakiya Maṇavāḷa Perumāḷ Jīyar's *Paṉṉirāyiṟappaṭi* (the 12,000).[61] These five commentaries written over a period of approximately three hundred years are collectively called the *Bhagavat Viṣayam* (Literally, Pertaining to God/On the Divine).[62] Together they represent the Śrīvaiṣṇavas' continuing dialogue with the *Tiruvāymoḻi*, the vigour of that discourse and the tradition's synthetic impulses.[63]

If the *Bhagavat Viṣayam* consolidated an ever-expanding approach to the *Tiruvāymoḻi*, the next century witnessed a desire to move in the opposite direction, to compress its meaning into lucid summaries. Vedānta Deśika's (1269–1369) Sanskrit *Dramiḍopaniṣad Tātparya Ratnāvali* (Gem Garland of Meaning of the Tamiḻ Upaniṣad) and Maṇavāḷa Māmuṉikaḷ's (1370–1450) Tamiḻ *Tiruvāymoḻi Nūṟṟantāti* (The Tiruvāymoḻi in a Hundred Antāti) both adopt the same approach—composing a single verse for every Ten in the *Tiruvāymoḻi* to explicate its central theme. For instance, in verse 13 of Deśika's text, which is equivalent to *Tiruvāymoḻi* I.3, he describes god as allowing himself to be bound by his devotees (I.3.1), names him as Nārāyaṇa (I.3.3), lauds him as one in whom Śiva abides (I.3.7), and praises him as the world-strider (I.3.10). Māmuṉikaḷ's summary in Tamiḻ is even more condensed, but like Deśika, he too stresses god's accessibility as the decad's principal focus, and begins and ends his verse quoting directly from the opening lines of *Tiruvāymoḻi* I.3.1 and those of I.4.1.[64] Both poet-theologians affirm that these are the words of the Āḻvār, identified as Śaṭhakōpaṉ by Deśika and Māṟaṉ by Māmuṉikaḷ (in the aforementioned verse).[65]

Each of the *Tiruvāymoḻi*'s traditional commentators boasts a lofty lineage, which grants him access to the text, and bestows upon him the authority to explicate it. Despite the Śrīvaiṣṇava traditions' claims of openness, caste, gender and other forms of hierarchal authority have circumscribed our reception of the *Tiruvāymoḻi*. Against this stark background of exclusion, one woman stands out. Her name is Tirukkōnēri Dāsyai. She likely lived in the thirteenth century and was the author of the *Tiruvāymoḻi Vācakamālai* (A Garland of Words on the Tiruvāymoḻi). The commentary survives in a partial seventeenth-century manuscript that a scholar with Tanjavur's Saraswathi Mahal Library edited and published in 1950. Although not systematic in the manner of the *Bhagavat Viṣayam*, Dāsyai brings a fresh perspective, reading the entire *Tiruvāymoḻi* through the lens of its opening verse. Although she provides us with a theological lineage, we do not know if anyone authorized her commentary, or if she learnt her interpretation from a specific teacher. She is an enigma and the story of her commentary a mystery.[66]

Despite Dāsyai's tantalizing presence, the *Tiruvāymoḻi* is guarded ferociously for the next several centuries, available primarily to a select, elite few. Its importance is undiminished as the text cements its place at the centre of Śrīvaiṣṇavas' emotional lives. The *Tiruvāymoḻi* is finally printed in the late nineteenth century, and the *Bhagavat Viṣayam* follows soon after, appearing in ten volumes in the early twentieth century. Once the sacred text enters public print culture, it gradually gathers new interpreters of all kinds—Śrīvaiṣṇavas, women, non-Hindus, non-brahmins—writing in a variety of registers, but all with great feeling for this astonishing text.

Feeling the Tiruvāymoḻi: Utsavam

Those who master these ten verses
from the musical thousand in Tamiḻ
about the black-bodied god with large bright eyes
sung by the master of Vaḻuti,
land of gardens swarming with bees,
will rule heaven and find the great release.

Tiruvāymoḻi II.8.11

Performance weaves through the *Divya Prabandham*, sometimes a quiet deep pool from which the poet draws, and in other moments, the inevitable expression of an ungovernable river of feeling with little regard for dams or boundaries. The twelve āḻvār poets consistently exhort listeners to discipline themselves by reciting, singing and mastering their works, promising the devout student rewards both earthly and divine. In turn, they characterize their poetry as sweet and musical, emerging from within them, furious with longing, a poetry not just said, but also sung into existence. As we have seen, the earliest versions of the transmission narrative of the *Tiruvāymoḻi* affirm these themes, for the *Tiruvāymoḻi* comes into the world through a powerful oral-aural encounter between Nammāḻvār and Madurakavi. Another feat of exceptional orality—Nāthamuni's recitation of the *Kaṇṇinuṇ ciṟu tāmpu*—retrieves the *Divya Prabandham* from the abyss of loss and restores it to prominence. Subsequently, Nāthamuni ensures the survival of the text by instituting a festival of recitation, and then placing it on the bodies of two nephews, Kīḻayakattāḻvāṉ and Mēlakayattāḻvāṉ.[67] Another narrative, recorded in the Srirangam temple's *Kōyil Oḻuku*, pushes the date of the *Tiruvāymoḻi* festival even earlier, to the lifetime of Tirumaṅkai Āḻvār. Tirumaṅkai requests permission from Viṣṇu to honour the *Tiruvāymoḻi* through recitation. Viṣṇu grants the petition and authorizes the recitation, ensuring the *Tiruvāymoḻi* a place on par with the Sanskrit Veda.[68]

All of these stories emphasize the centrality of recitation, as an act of revelation, recovery and remembrance; simultaneously, they establish the authority of the *Tiruvāymoḻi*, as a text worthy of memorization and memorialization. It is therefore unsurprising that the recitation of this text is attested to very early in the formation of the nascent Śrīvaiṣṇava community. We find several eleventh-century inscriptions that record arrangements for the recitation of the *Tiruvāymoḻi* at various temples, such as Uttaramerur, Tirukkoyilur and Srirangam, particularly in the northern and central regions of Tamiḻ-speaking south India.[69] The thirteenth century brings a further wealth of inscriptions, and hints at the establishment of a Ten Day Festival of recitation for the *Tirumoḻi* (i.e. *Tiruvāymoḻi*), such as the possibly thirteenth-century inscription at the Tirukkoshtiyur temple in the reign of one Sundara Pāṇṭiya, who directed the temple manager to receive betel and *prasāda* for making the arrangements for the *Tirumoḻi* recitation.[70] Another inscription, from Kanchi, dated 1242 CE, mentions a group of fifty-eight brahmins reciting the *Tirumoḻi* (*Tiruvāymoḻi*).[71] Within two centuries, the recitation of the *Tiruvāymoḻi* along with other *Divya Prabandham* texts is a clearly established practice in several major Śrīvaiṣṇava temples, such as at Srirangam, and at the Varadarāja Perumāḷ temple in Kanchipuram,[72] as well as at the Tirumala (Tiruvenkatam) temple.[73] Beginning in the seventeenth century, under the Nāyaka kings, as temple complexes grow and festival activities are reimagined, the Adhyayanotsavam too becomes more elaborate and spectacular. Today, it is celebrated in a variety of ways in Śrīvaiṣṇava temples across the globe in a twenty-day ritual extravaganza that honours the works of all twelve āḻvār poets.[74]

The contemporary twenty-day Adhyayanotsavam is divided into two equal halves called *Pakal Pattu* (Morning Ten) and *Irā Pattu* (Night Ten).[75] Pakal Pattu is devoted to the recitation of the first two thousand verses of the *Nālāyira Divya Prabandham*, while the *Tiruvāymoḻi* is the focus of the Irā Pattu.[76] The festival's two parts are linked by Vaikuṇṭha Ekādaśī,[77] the day on which the doors to heaven open and Viṣṇu descends for the sole purpose of hearing the *Tiruvāymoḻi*, and granting Nammāḻvār the mokṣa he so desires. Over the next ten nights, Viṣṇu makes the journey from Vaikuṇṭha (the temple's *garbha gṛha*) to cross the threshold of the cosmic doorway (Vaikuṇṭha Vācal/Paramapada Vācal) to enter this, our world. In doing so, he leaves behind the eternal realm (*nitya vibhūti*) to take up temporary residence here in the realm of play (*līlā vibhūti*), where he will both stage and serve as the audience for the drama of Nammāḻvār's quest for union. Over the next ten nights, Nammāḻvār will greet Viṣṇu and usher him into our world. Then, via the resonant voices of Śrīvaiṣṇava brahmin men, he'll speak his longing through the *Tiruvāymoḻi*—one hundred verses at a time—urging god to listen to his petition, to grant him grace.[78] At night's end, Viṣṇu returns to Vaikuṇṭha (i.e. the garbha gṛha), leaving the Āḻvār behind, his desire still unfulfilled. Viṣṇu's nightly descent and return during Irā Pattu replicates the endless and fated cycle of union and separation that is the central concern of the *Tiruvāymoḻi*. The tension builds every evening, until it resolves on the last night as the recitation of the Tenth Hundred draws to a close, with the god's descent and the Āḻvār's ascent. In *Tiruvāymoḻi* X.9, Nammāḻvār imagines an ascent to heaven—the beating drums, the fragrant incense, showers of flowers, the gods lining up to greet the fortunate soul—and it is precisely how the Tiruvāymoḻi Festival ends. Amidst the throb of percussion and the resonant roar of the conch, the priests raise the image of Nammāḻvār aloft and slowly usher him towards the waiting god. He is gently placed at his feet, and in that instant the gathered men burst into a rousing, slow recitation of the final Ten (X.10). The priest begins to heap fistfuls of tuḷasi over the Āḻvār, until he is no longer visible; this is union. In the *Tiruvāymoḻi*, the poet speaks of the torment of the breeze that comes to him scented with the beloved's tuḷasi. He yearns for that same tuḷasi, wants to wear it, longs to see the god adorned in it. In the end, engulfed and surrounded by the god of his heart, he too is perfumed by that tuḷasi, inseparable at last from the one who rules him.[79]

As is clear from the historical and historiographical record, the Adhyayanotsavam asserts the Vedic status of the *Divya Prabandham* and the *Tiruvāymoḻi*, a concern for the Śrīvaiṣṇava community in its formative period. With the sacred, revealed status of these texts now assured, the festival has shifted towards nurturing a deeply felt anubhava of the *Tiruvāymoḻi*. This occurs despite the many ways in which the *Tiruvāymoḻi* is heavily mediated during the Adhyayanotsavam, particularly for women and non-brahmins. Only Śrīvaiṣṇava brahmin men are allowed into the arena to recite the text; only the priests may touch the images; lines of sight are carefully regulated, with those closest to the images privy to an unhindered viewing. Despite all the distance, both literal and figurative, that such mediations bring, the very permeability of the text allows even those on the outside to enter its world. Through the ten days, we hear the slow unfolding of Nammāḻvār's meditation, listen to his keening calls, the rapid rush of words that describe the indescribable, even if we cannot see, or only partially see. The devotees participate, marvelling at his love, at his wisdom, wishing for some part of such single-minded devotion, but grateful for his words that allow them to feel as well. The Āḻvār's love is impossible for us, even alien to us, but the

Tiruvāymoḻi makes it possible for us to wear his feeling as if it were a guise, to know that feeling in pretence. Like the characters of the *Tiruvāymoḻi*, we are relegated to the role of the voyeuristic watcher, always at a slight distance, but nonetheless, present as witnesses to a grand drama. In the final sum, the Adhyayanotsavam creates a temporary world of liquid, dynamic, multidirectional anubhava for us to live in, in which heaven and earth are contiguous, where god is porous to the Āḻvār, and the Āḻvār is porous to us.

Inhabiting the Tiruvāymoḻi: Translation

It is no small thing to commit to translate the *Tiruvāymoḻi*. Not only is the text long—1102 verses—it is often inscrutable, the simplicity and directness of the Tamiḻ masking complexity of thought and ineffability of experience. The text, its poet and its commentators are demanding taskmasters, asking of the translator a commitment of both understanding and experience. Neither permits a respectful, clinical distance, where the poem makes itself known through diagnostic probes of metres, syllables, phonemes, syntax, and the translator, surgeon-like, sews it into English, a simulacrum of itself. The method, which had worked well for me, failed me spectacularly in this instance; I hit nothing but arteries as I probed, and every version of the English I produced, felt dead or near-dead. Eventually, I had to learn a new way to translate, a gentler and kinder way to be with it, to allow my own sense of smallness before its grandeur to seep into whatever I created in this other language, so far removed from the ethos and sensibility of Tamiḻ. In more than the decade that I have worked on the *Tiruvāymoḻi*, very slowly, I have taught myself to abandon what I knew, and to embrace all that I did not know, all that I could not know. I had to learn to read the text both with the commentators and on my own, every time with fresh eyes; to mediate the many voices of the poet; to negotiate between poet and commentator; to think of myself full of words and yet empty of them too.

I am not the *Tiruvāymoḻi*'s first English translator; several people—academics, poets, Śrīvaiṣṇavas, or some combination thereof—have set themselves to this daunting task. Below, I offer a brief survey of some of the most significant translations of this text. My intention is not to provide an evaluation of each effort, to diminish or critique them as a way to distinguish my own offering. I regard each of these as contributing to the afterlife of the *Tiruvāymoḻi*, and I see myself as part of a long lineage, keeping company with those who have had the courage and commitment to tackle such a challenging and demanding work.

One of the earliest, if not the earliest reference, to the *Tiruvāymoḻi* in a European language, appears in Roberto De Nobili's (1577–1656) Latin treatise *On Indian Customs* (1610). In a subsection of the fourth chapter 4.4.5, 'Concerning the Brahmin Sects . . .' Nobili says that the Śaivas follow the Āgamas, while the laws of the Vaiṣṇavas is called the *Tiruvāymoḻi.*[80] It is clear that De Nobili did not know the *Tiruvāymoḻi* as a text, and was simply reporting what he heard from an informant. Some two hundred years later, Francis Whyte Ellis (1777–1819), a British civil servant, does much better.[81] In his masterful commentary on the *Tirukkuṟaḷ*, Ellis provides a translation of a few verses from the *Tiruvāymoḻi* to illustrate the importance of the reverence for god's feet. He uses it to explicate the following *kuṟaḷ*: *piṟavi-p peruṅkaṭa ṉiṉttuvar nīntār/iṟaiva ṉaṭicērā tār* (10),

Only those who reach the feet of god
can swim the great sea of life.

placing the *Tiruvāymoḻi* in conversation with verses from Māṇikkavācakar's *Tiruvācakam* and the Śivavākkiyam. He provides no information about Nammāḻvār or the poem, except to say that it represents the views of modern Vaiṣṇavas or the Viśiṣṭādvaita sect.[82] He offers translations of five verses culled from various parts of the text—he begins with two verses from the Sixth Hundred—VI.9.1 and VI.9.2, follows this with the opening verses of the *Tiruvāymoḻi* (I.1.1 and I.1.2) and concludes with a single verse from the Third Hundred—III.4.10.[83] Ellis's *Tirukkuṟaḷ* commentary was published posthumously around 1819, likely making this the earliest appearance of any part of the *Tiruvāymoḻi* in English.[84]

Kurattalvar Ayyangar, a Telugu pandit employed at St. Joseph's College, a Jesuit institution, in Trichy, Tamil Nadu, produced the first English translation of the *Tiruvāymoḻi*.[85] Published in ten slim volumes of just thirty-two pages, over a period of four years (1925–1929), he provides an accessible prose rendition of each verse. In his short, page-and-a-half introduction, he paints a quick picture of the text and its reception. He begins by telling us that it is sung in Vaiṣṇava temples during Mārkaḻi. This allusion to the Adhyayanotsavam is followed by the well-known description of the *Tiruvāymoḻi* as containing the essence of the Vedas and Upaniṣads and its status as the Tamiḻ Veda. He adds the additional information that the text explicates Viśiṣṭādvaita philosophy, reiterating the position of the text's commentators. Although he mentions these erudite commentators and commentaries, identifying that they were composed between the twelfth and fourteenth centuries, his own translation is free of reference annotations, commentary or notes.[86] There are occasional clarifying footnotes—for instance, in his translation of X.9, which describes the ascent to Vaikuntha, he tells us that the 'āḻvār saw and realized and enjoyed' all of this in a state of *samādhi*.[87] In the Sixth Hundred, we are offered a tantalizing window into Ayyangar's translation process, which appears to have been both disciplined and quick. Above the translated text of several of the decads, he provides us with a date and time. He seems to have begun his translation on 13 May 1897 at 2 p.m. (VI.1), continuing through the Hundred on successive days. VI.4, 15 May 1897, 9–10 a.m.; 16 May seems to have been particularly productive, for he completes three hundreds—VI.5, VI.7 and VI.8—between 6 a.m. and 7 p.m., while he devotes two one-hour blocks to a single decad—VI.9—on 17 May. Although he gives us neither date nor time for several decads (VI.2, VI.6 or VI.10), from the information we do possess, we can hypothesize that he completed his translation of the sixth decad in the latter half of May of 1897, and that he did not revise them much after his first draft. However, his translation calendar in the Sixth Hundred, suggests that he had begun working on a translation of the *Tiruvāymoḻi* almost three decades before it was actually published.[88]

Kurattalvar Ayyangar's translation emerges at a particularly productive time in the publication history of Śrīvaiṣṇava materials. In 1859, Rajagopala Pillai issued the *Tiruvāymoḻi* with commentary out of the Sabhapathi Mudaliyar Parankusa Vilasa Press in Chennai. Twenty years later, in 1879, Vatapatrasayi Araiyar of Alvar Tirunagari worked with a group of men, including Ranga Pillai and Krishnaswami Mudaliar to issue another *Tiruvāymoḻi* edition, also out of the Kalanidhi Press in Chennai. The *Bhagavat Viṣayam* is published in ten volumes, beginning in 1924, out of a press in Tiruvallikkeni (Triplicane), then a suburb of Madras (present-day Chennai). It is possible that this flurry of activity inspired Ayyangar's own work—he was after all a member of the Srirangam-based Tiruvāymoḻi Assembly, presumably a study group of some sort. Perhaps this group, which included a Cambridge-based Englishwoman, I.J. Pitt, used one of these printed editions for their discussions. Ayyangar does not provide any clues as to an edition he used. He may have used no printed edition, and simply worked from memory, for like many Śrīvaiṣṇava brahmin men, he likely knew the *Tiruvāymoḻi* by heart. What he does tell us, though, in his short preface, is that he felt inadequate to the task—not unlike *this* translator—but was so moved by the Āḻvār's words that he felt compelled to set himself to it.[89]

After nearly six decades of relative silence, the 1980s usher in a rejuvenation of interest in the *Tiruvāymoḻi*. The next complete translation of the text appears in 1981, published by the Ananthacharya Indological Research Institute in Bombay, and undertaken by Satyamurthi Ayyangar of Gwalior. The multi-volume set, titled *Tiruvāymoḻi Glossary*, comes with a short introduction, translation of the text's six taṉiyaṉs and copious notes on each verse, derived from the traditional commentaries (he does not tell us which ones). It is also a bilingual translation, with the Tamiḻ text presented in Roman script. The translation moves between prose and poetry, and uses a Victorian style, even as Sanskrit words (līlā vibhūti) or philosophical ideas (god as the inner-controller) are sprinkled throughout.

That same year, 1981, Princeton University Press brought out A.K. Ramanujan's iconic *Hymns for the Drowning*. It presents a selection of seventy-six verses, picked from various sections of the *Tiruvāymoḻi*. Arranged thematically (The Works of Viṣṇu, Love's Messengers, No More Kings, etc.) and rendered in his distinctive modernist style, these translations gently introduce the reader into the wondrous, intra-textual world of the *Tiruvāymoḻi*. By juxtaposing independent verses from different decads, it invites the reader to read across the text, paying attention to motifs and metaphors, images and ideas. This is a masterful poet's translation of another masterful poet, and predictably, the focus is firmly on bringing over the poem's incandescent literary quality, rather than its theological commitments. The commentators are largely absent from *Hymns for the Drowning*, although Ramanujan, too, develops a narrative arc for his poet and his poem: 'My arrangement also enacts the progression: from wonder at the Lord's works, his play, his contrariety, to the experience of loving him and missing him ... to moods of questioning and despair, and on to an experience of being devoured . . . until the very poems that speak of him are of his own speaking.'[90] There is little question that *Hymns for the Drowning* is a consequential and remarkable work, and is most often, the general public's first encounter with Nammāḻvār. For this and other reasons, it is justifiably anthologized repeatedly, in collections on bhakti poetry, like Arundhathi Subramaniam's *Eating God* (2014) or in Hinduism source books, such as Wendy Doniger's *Norton Anthology of World Religions* (2015),[91] ensuring a place in the firmament of literary and religious literature for a great poet and his great translator.[92]

The Śrīvaiṣṇava scholar and revivalist, Srirama Bharati and his wife, Sowbhagya Lakshmi, produced an English rendering of the entire *Tiruvāymoḻi* (1987). Their translation, undertaken while in Alvar Tirunagari, is a complement to their larger project to reconstruct and revive the musical traditions associated with *Divya Prabandham*. The translations in four-line verses of varying length are direct and clear, with almost no theological vocabulary. While there are no explanatory notes, the aim is clearly to produce a readable translation that can reach a broad, English-speaking audience. In 2000, Srirama Bharati reproduced his *Tiruvāymoḻi* in a prose format, in his complete bilingual translation of the *Nālāyira Divya Prabandham*.

In the same year as Bharati and Lakshmi published their *Tiruvāymoḻi*, Norman Cutler translated several verses as an appendix to *Songs of Experience* (1987). Placed into dialogue with several Tamiḻ Śaiva and Vaiṣṇava poets, his translations help us understand both what Nammāḻvār shared with his fellow poets, and all the ways in which he broke the mould. Cutler also brackets out the phala-śruti, giving them their own subsection with the translation, throwing the meta-quality of these verses into stark relief. John Carman and Vasudha Narayanan's *Tamiḻ Veda* (1989), is not only a comprehensive study of Piḷḷāṉ's commentary of the *Tiruvāymoḻi*, but also provides lovely, clean translations of selected decads, accompanied by translations of Piḷḷāṉ's commentary for each verse. Their choices were governed by several criteria: some verses are from the *Kōyil Tiruvāymoḻi*, the twelve (plus one, VII.4) liturgically important decads, some are theologically significant, and others reveal something unique about the commentator's art.[93] Their economical translations capture the startling, dense brevity of Nammāḻvār's Tamiḻ, which contrasts with the equally dense prose interpretation of Piḷḷāṉ, his commentator. This is the first attempt to juxtapose the *Tiruvāymoḻi* and a specific commentator's exegesis over a sustained number of verses. As such, it is an important window into Śrīvaiṣṇava reading and interpretive practices, allowing us to engage simultaneously with the text and its reception. Vasudha Narayanan's *Vernacular Veda* (1994), a study of the *Tiruvāymoḻi*'s other receptive lives—particularly in liturgy and ritual—offers a complete translation of the 143 verses of the *Kōyil Tiruvāymoḻi* in the book's appendix. Translated in a collaborative effort by Vasudha Narayanan, A.K. Ramanujan, Frank Clooney and John Carman, the verses are lyrical and compact. Unobtrusive commentarial and editorial notes run along the margins of important verses, as a helpful guide to the reader. Frank Clooney has published large sections of the *Tiruvāymoḻi*, a product of his lifelong engagement with this text. Some of these have appeared in articles, while others are in his monographs, of which *Seeing through Texts* (1996) and *His Hiding Place Is Darkness* (2014), are the most important. The latter features a number of fine, sensitive English renditions of what he terms the girl songs of the *Tiruvāymoḻi.*

My offering in this book owes itself to each of these predecessors, to their formidable learning in, and profound anubhava of, the *Tiruvāymoḻi.* Initially, this was to be a collaborative effort, and in that spirit, I worked with Frank's version open before me, as I crafted my own. Our dream to merge our two translations never came to be, and what we have here is a *Tiruvāymoḻi* in my voice, one that joins Nammāḻvār's many voices, and those of his translators, commentators and interpreters. I have stayed close to the simplicity of his diction, the economy of his phrasing, and the text's rich and playful ambiguity, and have sought to foreground the poet's unmistakable sensuality and unbridled emotion. I have kept punctuation to a minimum to bring over the density of Tamiḻ. While I could not (and did not wish to) replicate Tamiḻ prosody, I have used resources like alliteration and eye rhymes to infuse musicality into the English. Wherever possible, I have attempted to preserve the antāti or to recreate the effect through other means. I have injected a Tamiḻ flavour into the English by using Tamiḻ names and noun endings wherever possible, and when there are no readily available, lovely-sounding English equivalents for flora, I have left them untranslated. Wherever the poet uses a Tamiḻ version of a Sanskrit word (for example, mōkkam for mokṣa), I have used the more recognizable Sanskrit. Even as I have read the commentaries, and understood that they are critical to our reception of the text, my translation consciously privileges the poetic over the theological. This is a *beautiful* poem—intricately built, virtuosic in its use of language, sound and sense, and full of wonder and desire. My hope has been to capture some of these qualities, for it is the very beauty of the poem, beautifully endless and endlessly beautiful as the god it celebrates, that seduces us into an infinite loop of contemplation, rereading, and further contemplation.

TIRUVĀYMOḺI

The First Hundred

Tiruvāymoḻi I.1 (1–11)
uyarvaṟa uyar nalam

I.1.1 Who possesses the highest good?
Him.
Who cuts delusion grants a good clear mind?
Him.
Who's the master of unforgetting untiring immortals?
Him.
Sunder grief, worship his luminous feet, bow down, rise up
my mind.

I.1.2 A mind severed from filth
blooms and rises
He's beyond even its knowing beyond
what the senses feel
He's complete bliss wholly good
He's the future present past
This peerless one
is my precious life.

I.1.3 Think he's not that, he's not this
and you can't know him
The earth and sky are his,
him of form and formlessness
He's in the senses but not of the senses
He's endless, pervasive
He alone is pure goodness,
and at last we draw near him.

I.1.4 We, that him, this he, the in-between other,
that her this she the other in-between whoever.
Them there, they here, that there
this here, the in-between whichever.
All that dies, this thing, these in-between,
those things, the good the bad,
that which is, which will be,
he becomes all. There.

I.1.5 Each knows what they know,
each finds a different path
Each has their god
each reaches his feet
Each of these gods lacks nothing,
everyone is fated
to find their way to the great lord
who's always there.

I.1.6 He stands he sits he reclines
he wanders
He doesn't stand or sit
he doesn't recline he doesn't wander
You can't know him
as just one thing
He's always there,
constant firm.

I.1.7 As sky fire wind water earth
spread out
he was everything entire,
within each in all things

he is as breath in the body,
hidden and pervasive
He's in the luminous śruti,
this god who's eaten everything.

I.1.8 He's beyond the ken of the gods,
beginning with sky
he's everything, the creator's creator,
the great one who ate it all
He burned the three cities,
gifted wisdom to the gods,
as both Araṉ and Ayaṉ
he unmakes and remakes worlds.

I.1.9 If you say he is,
all these forms are his
If you say he isn't,
all these non-forms are his
If you say he is and he isn't
then he exists as both
without limit
pervading everything.

I.1.10 He's in the cool vast water,
in every drop, he's everywhere
in the wide world, in the earth in the sky,
limitless, he's hidden
in the smallest things,
luminous in every place
he pervades all,
the one who ate it all.

I.1.11 On the highest one
who abides
as sky fire wind water earth,
who is
sound vigour strength love serenity,
Kurukūr's Śaṭhakōpaṉ composed
these ten verses from his perfect thousand.
They are your release.

Tiruvāymoḻi I.2 (12–22)
vīṭumiṉ muṟṟavum

I.2.1 When you've let go everything let your life
go to him who owns all letting go.

I.2.2 The body its breath is brief as lightning
think about that for a moment.

I.2.3 Root out the you-s and yours, join him
life has no greater fullness than this.

I.2.4 His form isn't what isn't neither is it what is
sever ties that bind, love that limitless bliss.

I.2.5 If you cut desire life finds heaven, cut that too
be fixed on what lasts forever, get him.

I.2.6 Nothing binds him, he abides in everything
cut your ties too, yield into his fullness.

I.2.7 Look at all this lovely lushness, it's all him
yield into him, become his treasure.

I.2.8 Mind word deed—think well on these three
finish them, dissolve them into him.

I.2.9 When you're with him everything falls away
await the moment you'll leave your body.

I.2.10 Infinitely good, luminous, of limitless glory
is Nāraṇaṉ. Reach his feet.

I.2.11 These ten verses from a finely woven set of thousand
are the words of Śaṭhakōpaṉ of Kurukūr, city of lakes.

Tiruvāymoḻi I.3 (23–33)
pattuṭai aṭiyārkku

I.3.1 A friend to those who love him, obscure to others
the astonishing lord, beloved of Śrī is hard to gain.
He filched butter, then tied tightly to a mortar, he wept.
How simple he is.

I.3.2 He's open, his births countless and limitless
luminous, wholly good, without beginning, undying
the end, the imperishable clarity of release, he's everything
this giver of grace lives both inside and out.

I.3.3 The perfect law of all things, the highest good
the perfection of creation, destruction, the spaces in between
the immortals, everything, everyone, even himself,
all this is Nāraṇaṉ. Who can know his mystery?

I.3.4 It's hard to know his nature, even for the wise
he's easy to know especially for the simple, our lord

has a thousand names countless forms,
he has no name no form. That's the dispute.

I.3.5 He cut through the squabbles of six different systems
decreed the right path, primordial Bhagavan̲ of limitless good.
Walk the path of loving austerity, abandon other ways,
shed your bonds, know him through knowing.

I.3.6 Even if you think, think more, think deeply about this form,
even when you think and know its state you can't know him,
little lives, keep thinking, think more, speak, speak more
of Hari, Ayan̲, Aran̲. Then worship the one in your mind.

I.3.7 His form is hard to know as one or many, he's beautiful
Nāraṇan̲, Nān̲mukan̲, Aran̲ too, place the only one in your heart,
think then cut the double bind, commit yourself to the good
that is him. Do it in this very life.

I.3.8 The old deeds that torment us every day will vanish,
we'll want nothing at all, our mind devoid of desire, cleansed
we always bow to the lovely feet of Śrī's lord, then
even the day of death will be a good thing.

I.3.9 The one who razed the three cities is on his right,
in his navel the one who created every good world,
you can see him as himself in this world, you could say
it's all in his belly: wonder.

I.3.10 He bewilders even clear-thinking immortals
his mysteries vaster than the sky, one dark as storm clouds,
his feet measured worlds. I'll sing of him, I'll hold him,
I'll worship him, I'll never forget him.

I.3.11 Śaṭhakōpaṉ of wealthy Kurukūr offered as simple service
these ten from his sweet thousand verses about him,
worshipped by the gods, him who churned the sea.
Master them, rise to heaven free from the bonds of birth.

Tiruvāymoḻi I.4 (34–44)

añciṟaiya maṭa nārāy

I.4.1 Lovely little crane be kind
you and your handsome mate must help me.
Take my message to the one with the mighty eagle,
and if he locks you up, would it be so bad?

I.4.2 Does it cost you anything to take a message
to my lord with eyes bright as lotus? Cuckoos, please do it.
My past has kept me from even trying to serve him
Must this ever be my fate?

I.4.3 Lucky geese, you're forever with your mates
I've lost my mind to that thief who stole worlds.
Tell him I've become witless and confused
Will my past never end?

I.4.4 My beloved dark as storm clouds sees my plight,
but feels no pity. He doesn't say, 'This isn't right.'
What can I say? Black aṉṟil, tell him 'She won't last.'
Will you or won't you?

I.4.5 He tends the seven worlds with care
but he has no such kindness for me. Little herons
hunting fish in the garden's full streams, if you see Nāraṇaṉ
say something. My eyes overflow with tears.

I.4.6 'You've withheld your favour. Before her life wilts
give her grace, fly your eagle down her street just once'
If you see that ocean of mercy, speak to him, pretty bees
How have I erred?

I.4.7 The winter breeze pierces me, a needle in my bones
Tirumāl favours me by recalling only my faults
Sweet parrot who torments me, ask him
'How has she erred?' I raised you, didn't I?

I.4.8 Little black bird, when I asked you to tell Neṭumāl
of my sickness, you just stayed without saying a word
My beauty's gone, my lustre too.
Better find someone else to feed you now.

I.4.9 To place rare flowers each day at Nāraṇaṉ's feet
that's what we're made for. What can you do
when alone, cleaved, forsaken by luck? Go ask him,
winter breeze, then return to pierce my bones.

I.4.10 He's release from the cycle of birth, he's life
and everything else. On the deep ocean he made himself
he sleeps, a fiery disc in his hand. Guileless heart, if you see him
tell him, you'll stay until I am with him.

I.4.11 Śaṭhakōpaṉ of fertile Kurukūr with its rich fields
sang these ten from a thousand endless verses
on Kaṇṇaṉ, lord of all who live in the seven worlds,
Those who master them will gain the great wealth of heaven.

Tiruvāymoḻi I.5 (45–55)
vaḷvēḻ ulakiṉ

I.5.1 He's the seed of these seven fine worlds, and I call him
the god of gods, a thief of butter. I'm a wretch, still I say
'King of cowherds who tamed seven bulls for Piṉṉai,
with a smile lovely as jasmine buds, my father.'
I think of all this and wither.

I.5.2 Gods and sages think of you, swoon dissolve melt
they worship you with flowers water sandal incense
You are the seed, the reason of all things
known only to a steady heart, mysterious lord
Can your greatness ever diminish?

I.5.3 He said 'Birth the celestials and sages'
and birthed perfect learned Nāṉmukaṉ.
He is beyond the reach of knowledge, one
who spanned the directions with his feet
Mother to all life, he is singular.

I.5.4 His form is singular, he's the sole seed, the source
of the three, of the celestials, sages and everything else
He made within himself a great ocean, then
rested on it. God of gods, great mystery
Master of Vaikuṇṭha, my lord.

I.5.5 The doe-eyed woman rests on your chest, Mādhavā
with your bow you unbent her back, Govindā
light of the heavens, jewel-bright Madhusūdā

let me reach your flower-like feet,
I am ill-fated, grant me this gift.

I.5.6 You are the cure to end my fate, god of gods
Keśavā, cowherd-chief, great mystery, Mādhavā
Śrīdharā whose single arrow pierced seven great trees,
these are your deeds, these are your names
I say this and melt. I am bound to you.

I.5.7 He's difficult to know even for the wise
Kaṇṇaṉ who wears a garland of cool tuḷasi
Tirumāl who frees devotees from unruly bodies
I'm of little knowledge, still I weep longing to see you
Is there greater foolishness than this?

I.5.8 You ate, spat out the seven worlds, then
in base human form ate butter. Like us mere mortals
did you need a little something
to dissolve the last bits of earth?
Lord of mystery.

I.5.9 You turned the evil ghoul's poison-milk to nectar
innocent child, lord of mystery, peerless god of gods
beloved of your woman, mother of all life
master of yourself, my lord
I cling to you, death is at an end.

I.5.10 He warded off the twin deeds that cling to me
cut their deluding hold, then turned my mind to him
who grants heaven. He's the flame of perfect knowledge
him of immeasurable form, all pervasive Neṭumāl,
Life in all things.

I.5.11 Graced by Māl, love-struck Śaṭhakōpaṉ of Kurukūr
cried out 'Māl, mysterious lord, great trickster.'
Those who master these ten verses from his thousand
spread far and wide by scholars musicians devotees
will never suffer.

Tiruvāymoḻi I.6 (56–66)
parivatil īcaṉai

I.6.1 Seekers of the highest goal
sing without pause of the one
beyond suffering
offer him water flowers incense.

I.6.2 He wears the honey-sweet tuḷasi,
he's the cause of the ancient Veda
don't wonder
'How shall I serve him?' Simply do.

I.6.3 He doesn't distinguish between high and low
my heart won't leave him,
my tongue
sings his songs, I dance possessed.

I.6.4 I dance possessed, I bow, worship him
His virtues are so abundant
the gods
can only babble in delirium.

I.6.5 He has neither likes nor dislikes
neither contempt nor desire

He's nectar
to those who melt wanting nothing else.

I.6.6 Neṭumāl who wields the fiery disc
fed nectar to the immortals.
He's sweeter
than nectar, him asleep on the roaring sea.

I.6.7 He slashed the arms of Laṅkā's king
city embraced by the sea,
bow at his feet
and pass your ocean of days.

I.6.8 Stop, devotees. Worship him, he'll kill
the fates that stop your path
and give you wealth
that never wanes.

I.6.9 He's the fruit of right action
beloved of Śrī, the glorious
great lord
will end your deeds.

I.6.10 In a blink of an eye
he ends evil deeds,
Mādhavaṉ
whose banner bears the fierce eagle.

I.6.11 Śaṭhakōpaṉ spoke these ten verses
from a perfect thousand before Mādhavaṉ.
Recite them well
and never be reborn.

Tiruvāymoḻi I.7 (67–77)
piṟavittuyar aṟa

I.7.1 To cut the grief of birth they abide in wisdom
renouncing everything for the flame of self-knowledge
They never forget the righteous one who wields the disc
forever holding him in their hearts.

I.7.2 He's treasure, he's medicine, he won't let
wicked fate or the five senses plague his devotees
He's the good everywhere, the highest bliss
he's the child of our cowherd clan.

I.7.3 The child of cowherds yielded to a beating,
that lord of mystery is my fire-bright jewel.
I drank deeply of him, a pure nectar
I cut the delusion of birth.

I.7.4 To end my delusions he entered my mind
a beautiful bright flame who gives only wisdom
first among the unforgetting immortals,
what can I say? How can I leave you?

I.7.5 Will I leave my light? My master
entered the very heart of my life
he lifts me up, the lord who made eyes
at the young girls of the cowherd clans.

I.7.6 He lifted the vast earth, that lord
wearing sweet tuḷasi in his hair,
the lord of mystery pierced the trees,
even if he won't stay, I won't let him go.

I.7.7 I didn't say 'Stick close to me, stay.'
He came anyway, tricked my lonely heart
fused himself to my body, merged in my breath
That's his way. What if he leaves me now?

I.7.8 Even if he slips from me
he can't make my good heart leave.
The great one delights in Piṉṉai's embrace
primordial lord, first among the gods.

I.7.9 The very source of the immortals,
primordial lord, child of cowherds
who gave the immortals nectar, my life
has mingled with him. How could we now part?

I.7.10 If you leave, he leaves. If you draw close he does too
He's hard to enter, my lord so easy to reach
I never tire of singing of my peerless one
immersed in him night and day.

I.7.11 These ten verses from a thousand
tied tightly together by Śaṭhakōpaṉ of Kurukūr
who reached him who wears fragrant tuḷasi in his hair
will drive away every illness.

Tiruvāymoḻi I.8 (78–88)
ōṭum puḷ

I.8.1 He rides the swift eagle, wears the cool tuḷasi
the lord dances amidst things that endure.

I.8.2 The lord became so many lives, Kaṇṇaṉ
with bright eyes who split the horse's massive jaws.

I.8.3 Dear to those on earth and those in the sky
the ruler of gods resides in cool Vēṅkaṭam.

I.8.4 He lifted a mountain and felt no fatigue
I'll speak of the lord's qualities eternally.

I.8.5 He stirred butter ate it with both hands
finished with that, he merged into me.

I.8.6 He merged into me, my lord makes me good
He bewitched the senses, the youth who took the world.

I.8.7 He subdued seven bulls, he ate seven worlds
he's created a place for himself in my thoughts.

I.8.8 'He became cowherd fish pig'
these limitless births, they're all for me.

I.8.9 He holds the conch and disc in his lovely hands
our lord becomes himself everywhere.

I.8.10 The lord whose feet took the world rules me
the Veda roar his praise like the sea.

I.8.11 Śaṭhakōpaṉ composed these ten verses
part of a thousand on the one who is like water.

Tiruvāymoḻi I.9 (89–99)
ivaiyum avaiyum

I.9.1 These those and the in-between,
this he that him the in-between other,
within himself he becomes all things and all people
he makes them protects them,
primordial lord, my master, Kaṇṇaṉ,
my sweet nectar, sweetness itself
Śrī's beloved is beside me.

I.9.2 He's the master of many tricks
long ago he became a boar to lift the earth
he broke the mad elephant's tusk
he's Keśavaṉ, my lord
beyond the understanding of even the gods
rests on the deep dark sea
He's now close to me.

I.9.3 He's the faultless primordial source
of the immortals,
his body a dark-blue gem, his eyes red lotuses
he delights in riding his eagle with mighty wings
Śrī's beloved fed me a taste of the only path
now he stays with me
He won't leave.

I.9.4 Seated beside him are three women
Śrī, Bhū and the innocent cowherd girl
He rules three worlds,
the very ones he eats.
My lord rests on a banyan leaf, Kaṇṇaṉ

great master of mystery vaster than the sea
is on my lap.

I.9.5 When she placed him in her lap to nurse
he drank her milk and drained her life
The great lord made the naked god,
Ayaṉ, Indraṉ and all the rest
appear instantly.
The lord of mystery
is in my heart.

I.9.6 The mysterious lord is in my heart
it is so for everyone.
He's body and breath, wind and fire
he's both far and near
beyond thought, beyond the senses
the pure dazzling bewildering lord
rests on my shoulders.

I.9.7 He wears the cool lovely tuḷasi
across his shoulders, over his lovely chest,
in his hair, on his feet,
the peerless lord, his body radiant light
doesn't leave,
not for a moment.
He's on my tongue.

I.9.8 He's the spirit and body of all art,
wisdom that blossoms on the tongue
He protects them, destroys them too
the lord with four arms soft as flowers
who bears the great war-disc and battle conch

his dark body and lotus eyes
have entered my eye.

I.9.9 The lotus-eyed lord is in my eye.
I see with his eye, gaze open to faults
and the five senses made right
He brings forth Ayaṉ in his lotus, and
the god with the third eye.
He makes the perfect immortals and their worlds
He's now on my brow.

I.9.10 He rests on my brow, rules me,
lovely Kaṇṇaṉ
with flowers on his feet and tuḷasi in his hair.
He's worshipped by him
who wears the crescent moon,
Nāṉmukaṉ, Indraṉ and all the immortals.
He now rests on my head.

I.9.11 His feet will crown
those who beseech him
with these ten verses from a thousand
sung by Śaṭhakōpaṉ of wealthy Kurukūr
for Kaṇṇaṉ
the god of gods
who rests on his head.

Tiruvāymoḻi I.10 (100–110)
porumā nīḷpaṭai

I.10.1 He bears the great war-disc and the conch
The seven worlds praise his large great feet

He came as a chaste youth, grew tall
that dark gem dwells in my eyes.

I.10.2 If I worship him with love, he's here in an instant
dwelling in my eyes. What more do I need?
As earth water fire the cool wind sky
my lord spreads everywhere.

I.10.3 My lord is master to my father, his father, his father's father
His eyes are cool as lotuses, on his chest rests the woman
her slender waist curved like vine, or is it a snake?
Guileless heart, worship him.

I.10.4 Good good heart, with your aid what can we not do?
What would we lack? Even in times of suffering
hold on to that warrior, never leave
Śrī's beloved.

I.10.5 Heart, our karma ripen of their accord
He ate the seven worlds
took them in three steps
you too have seen him.

I.10.6 Heart, if you and I stand before him
illness won't touch us. He became mother and father
he entered this world, my lord
bright as a gem, my father.

I.10.7 'My father, my lord' wicked though I am
I said these words, placed them in my mind
The gods too call out 'My father, my lord'
holding in their mind the greatest wealth.

I.10.8 I hear the words auspicious Nāraṇa
and my eyes fill with tears. I seek it—a wonder.
Night and day he stays with me
the great one never leaves.

I.10.9 The great one blazes golden
in southern Kuṟuṅkuṭi. First among gods
beautiful light, my master
what could I say to forget him?

I.10.10 Forgetting or wisdom, I know neither.
Lest I forget, to end my forgetfulness
the lotus-eyed one dwells in me
now how can I forget my jewel-bright lord?

I.10.11 Śaṭhakōpaṉ of southern Kurukūr offered in service
this ten from a set of thousand in praise
of the celestials' jewel, an ornament to himself.
Those who master this knowledge will always flourish.

The Second Hundred

Tiruvāymoḻi II.1 (111–121)
vāyum tiraiukaḷum

II.1.1 Innocent crane of the seashore
where rolling waves leap and crash
even if mother and the immortals sleep,
you don't.
You suffer, turning pale like me
has Tirumāl stolen your heart too?

II.1.2 Sharp-voiced aṉṟil, your heart stolen
you too don't sleep through the long night
Are you like me
caught by the one on the serpent,
longing for the garlands of cool tuḷasi
adorning his feet?

II.1.3 You lost what you craved,
whether it's night or day, you don't sleep
your heart melts, you yearn.
Do you pine like me
for the feet of the one who burned Laṅkā?
Live long, lamenting sea.

II.1.4 Cool breeze, touching seas hills sky
like me you don't sleep
in bright night or burning day.
Is it to see the master
who wields the fierce war-disc
that you sicken, age after age?

II.1.5 Age upon age you bring water to the world,
then dissolve like my friends and me.
Clouds, live long
Has Madhusūdaṉ bound you too?
Do you also suffer
because you love him?

II.1.6 Young moon, you fade like me
No longer dispelling the darkness of the night sky
you've lost your light. Did you trust the promises
of the great lord with the disc, him
asleep on the serpent with five heads
and lose yourself?

II.1.7 I lost my simple heart to our great lord
to Nāraṇaṉ.
I weep my grief. Now you're here
more cruel than enemies,
will you do this through the ages?
Live long, dense darkness.

II.1.8 Salt marsh, dark as dense black night
bewildered, you don't sleep, not
even when night and day end.
Do you yearn for the great lord's kindness,
him who kicked the rolling cart?
Is that why you suffer now?

II.1.9 Fading from lovesickness that won't end,
your gentle spirit withers, undying flame
I pity you. Do you burn with desire

for the garland of cool tuḷasi
of my lord
his lips red as fruit, his eyes bright as lotuses?

II.1.10 This burning endless lovesickness
wilts my gentle spirit. You draw me to you
through relentless nights and days, then turn away.
You tore open the horse's mouth, crawled
between maruta trees, measured worlds,
primordial lord, don't leave me now.

II.1.11 Those who master
these ten verses from the thousand
uttered by Kurukūr's Śaṭhakōpaṉ
who had endless love for that radiant light
who is cause of all things,
they will never leave Vaikuṇṭha.

Tiruvāymoḻi II.2 (122–132)
tiṇṇaṉ vīṭu

II.2.1 He's steadfast release, everything else,
virtues beyond thought, my lord
ate earth sky everything
There are no eyes but Kaṇṇaṉ's.

II.2.2 Pity me. Supreme lord.
Who grants grace to end the world's wickedness?
Him who gave Araṉ alms to free him of his curse,
Who else but the lion among cowherds.

II.2.3 The bull-riding god, the lotus-born one
and Śrī are all within him. He stretched
beyond the highest places, claimed the earth
Is there a god greater than Māl?

II.2.4 He created Nāṉmukaṉ
to create the gods and all things,
does anyone but my lord
deserve flowers and worship?

II.2.5 He's the singular cause who created
within himself the great gods and all things
He's my lovely lotus-eyed lord.
Who knows anything beyond this great light?

II.2.6 Everyone and everything
he keeps them within himself easily
his form is light, a flood of pervasive knowledge
he's my lord who rests on the ocean.

II.2.7 He rests on a banyan leaf, he's generous
he holds the seven worlds, the lord with a mighty belly
Who can know what's deep inside him?
Who can know his cunning mysterious mind?

II.2.8 Who else but the mysterious lord
can will the gods and all things into being?
He holds the three worlds in him, protects them
Who else can do this?

II.2.9 Kaṇṇaṉ, our lord protects, it's his nature
He brings them together within himself
He makes Brahmā, Indraṉ, the celestials
and divine worlds for them to live in.

II.2.10 'Thief, you made us and the seven worlds
appear within you' say the one with the white bull
Nāṉmukaṉ, Indraṉ and the celestials.
They bow at the feet of the god who rides the bird.

II.2.11 Kurukūr's Śaṭhakōpaṉ sang
of the lovely dancer who holds the seven worlds
These are ten verses of a thousand
those who master them will lack nothing.

Tiruvāymoḻi II.3 (133–143)
ūṉilvāḻ uyirē

II.3.1 Life dwelling in this body, be well
he's got you. My father,
lord of celestials, Madhusūdaṉ.
Within himself
he and I are mixed
like milk honey ghee sugar nectar.

II.3.2 Incomparable mysterious lord
peerless and supreme,
life of all things, mother
who birthed me, my father too.
You teach me what I don't know, lord
I can't know all you do for me.

II.3.3 In that time when I knew nothing
when I was caught in the great delusion
you came to me, made me love you.
Like an innocent child, you begged three steps
from Mahābali, tricked him.
You're mingled in my breath.

II.3.4 In return for your great gift
of mingling with my breath, I gave you my breath.
Now what's left to return? You're the breath
within my breath, father who ate the seven worlds
Whose breath is this? Who am I
but that which you gave made kept.

II.3.5 My father beyond the wisdom of the wise
you're the sweet ripe pleasure of release
my nectar untouched by the ocean
the sole being in my lonely life
You became a pig to lift the seven worlds
I've joined your feet.

II.3.6 You're poison to the wicked deeds
of those who reach you
Inseparable from those of steadfast minds
a flame that lights their lives
One who cut the demon's nose
I've been with you since before the beginning.

II.3.7 The ripe taste of a finely tuned harp,
supreme lord the learned strive to reach,
pure one sweet as sugar. Nectar,

dark storm cloud, my Kaṇṇā,
I am nothing without you,
Think of me.

II.3.8 What's gained over ages
through wisdom and penance,
I achieved in a matter of days.
In this very birth
my heart followed the thief of butter
I ended the grief of life.

II.3.9 Kaṇṇaṉ wears fragrant cool tuḷasi,
he's the lord of celestials,
supreme peerless pure.
I rooted out this illness tough as weeds
I plunged in, lapped up his goodness
I am drunk.

II.3.10 Free from joy and desire
cut from birth disease age death
when will I merge with that brilliant light?
He protects the sky heavy with rain, this earth.
When will I join his devotees? Mysterious lord
who holds the fiery disc and conch.

II.3.11 Śaṭhakōpaṉ of bustling Kurukūr
sang from experience
this set of ten verses from a thousand
on him who wiped out the great demon's clan.
Crowds of devotees, sing them
join together and dance.

Tiruvāymoḻi II.4 (144–154)
āṭi āṭi akam karaintu

II.4.1 She dances, dances dissolves. Sweetly
she sings, sings. Her tears flow. Everywhere
she searches, searches calling 'Narasiṅkā'
She shrinks, shrivels, this girl with a bright forehead.

II.4.2 This girl weakens, longing to see you
You who cut Bāṇaṉ's mighty arms
won't show yourself.
You have no pity.

II.4.3 Her heart melts, like wax
held too close to a flame. You have no pity.
What can I do, lord
who ruined Laṅkā?

II.4.4 'You raised your banner over ruined Laṅkā'
she says. Her heart swells, her breath
burns, she weeps, bewildered
she stands, hands pressed in worship.

II.4.5 Night and day, she's delirious. Her eyes
wet with tears are like cool dark lilies.
You won't give her the tuḷasi she wants,
perfect lord, is this your compassion?

II.4.6 'You're perfect, the one I desire'
'You're my life's nectar'
she says all this,
dissolves inside.

II.4.7 Her life's parched, she wilts.
'Generous one, Kaṇṇaṉ' she says,
then, 'You rest on the white ocean'
what deceit has touched my clever girl.

II.4.8 'Deceiver' she cries, then joins her hands
to pray. Her cool heart burns, she sighs
says 'You tricked Kaṁsaṉ'
see how she suffers for you.

II.4.9 She knows neither night or day.
but she asks for your cool sweet tuḷasi.
Lord with the sharp flaming disc
what do you intend for this poor girl?

II.4.10 Night and day tears spill
from the bright eyes of this foolish girl.
You ruined Laṅkā, burned its boundless wealth
don't wreck this girl's beauty too.

II.4.11 These ten from the proper thousand,
sung by generous Śaṭhakōpaṉ
on Vāmaṉaṉ of endless fame
are a fitting garland for his feet.

Tiruvāymoḻi II.5 (155–165)
antāmattu

II.5.1 In that place he loved me
fused with my breath.
the lord who wears lovely garlands,
a crown conch disc thread jewels:

His large eyes like a pool of lotuses
his lips red lotuses, his feet too lotuses,
his red-gold body glows.

II.5.2 His body glows like the sun
his eyes and hands bright as red lotus
Śrī rests on his chest
Ayaṉ is in his navel
Araṉ takes every other place.
He's within me, mingled
leaving not a whit of space.

II.5.3 The one who's in me, all mixed in
his mouth a red lotus, his eyes feet hands
all lotuses too,
is a great bright mountain.
The earth, the seven worlds are in his belly
there's nothing not mingled in him
there's nothing outside of him.

II.5.4 He is all things, him
a dark emerald mountain, his eyes
feet hands red lotuses in full bloom.
In every moment, in every day
in every month and year, in every age,
age upon age, for all time
he is my nectar that never sates.

II.5.5 The nectar that never sates
mixed himself with little me.
Kaṇṇaṉ is like a dense dark cloud.

Coral can't equal the redness of his lips
nor lotus the brightness of his eyes feet hands
my lord wears a tall crown, the sacred thread,
and jewels of every kind.

II.5.6 His jewels are many, his names are many
his luminous forms are many.
To think of his nature
is to know the many pleasures
of seeing eating hearing touching smelling
him. Vast is the wisdom
of the one who rests on a serpent.

II.5.7 He rests on a serpent on the ocean of milk
He killed seven bulls for Piṉṉai,
her shoulders slim as bamboo
In a honey-sweet grove, he pierced seven trees
He's a fierce fighting bull, this one
whose radiant crown is circled
with cool tuḷasi.

II.5.8 My lord, a fierce fighting bull
wears a radiant crown and cool tuḷasi
His four shoulders are broad,
He has no end. Thinking nothing
of my lowliness, he mingled with me.
I have no words for him.
What can I say? Tell me.

II.5.9 Tell me about my lord
the spirit of my spirit

my brilliant dark jewel of infinite greatness
sweet nectar,
the release difficult to attain,
fragrant as the alli in bloom
is the one who is neither male nor female.

II.5.10 Not male not female
neither both
the one who can't be seen
neither is nor is not
taking the form you desire
and not that either
how difficult it is to speak of my lord.

II.5.11 Kurukūr's Śaṭhakōpaṉ spoke
of the pot-dancer, the lord
difficult to describe
in these ten verses part of an antāti
of a matchless thousand.
Those who master their recitation
will reach Vaikuṇṭha.

Tiruvāymoḻi II.6 (166–176)
vaikunthā maṇivaṇṇaṉē

II.6.1 Lord of Vaikuṇṭha, glittering dark gem
my cunning little youth, nectar in my heart
great bull who's always within me
You relieve the wickedness of your devotees
destroy the evil of demons
Kuntā, I've caught you.

II.6.2 He swallowed the worlds whole
held them tightly within himself,
nothing could leave. He's entered me.
The nectar that steadies,
The one with eyes like new lotuses,
sees no other place but me.

II.6.3 Celestials praise him of lotus eyes,
a golden mountain garlanded with tuḷasi.
My lord lets us draw near him
to praise and worship him,
dancing in joy, tongues blooming in song
Generosity. It's his nature.

II.6.4 Generous Madhusūdanā
my emerald mountain, father
you gave yourself to me to think on.
I plunge into praising you like into a flood
I dance I sing, sickness flees.
How can I leave you?

II.6.5 I killed my evil deeds that have no end
entered into your ceaseless service
Will I let it go?
Absorbed in yogic sleep on the ocean of milk,
his bed a serpent with five dancing hoods,
my father, I think only of you.

II.6.6 I think only of you. I sing great words.
I dance. I pull out my evil deeds, roots and all.
You ripped the broad chest of Hiraṇyan̲

who slighted you in his thoughts,
my primordial lion
what can't I do now?

II.6.7 What can't I do now?
He ate the seven worlds, happily
entered me and now won't leave.
My kin seven generations before and after me
escape the grief of disease dense as weeds,
they escape forever a fiery eternal hell.

II.6.8 I was born again and again, at last
I've reached your feet. My mind is clear
I drown in a flood of limitless joy.
You swoop down on your eagle
scattering demon hoards.
Father, don't leave me.

II.6.9 Father who dwells in cool Vēṅkaṭam,
Destroyer of Laṅkā, peerless archer
who pierced seven trees with a single arrow
lord adorned with fragrant tuḷasi
my nectar, you've dissolved yourself into me
where will you go now?

II.6.10 In times past, now, in the future,
you're mother father life. Master
of unending fame. Ruler
of the three worlds. Supreme lord
adorned with tuḷasi, abiding in Vēṅkaṭam
I've got you. Will I ever let you go?

II.6.11 Those who sweetly sing these ten
from the thousand wise antāti verses
spoken by Śaṭhakōpaṉ Māṟaṉ of southern Kurukūr
in praise of the one with eyes large as lotuses,
the one who wears garlands of tuḷasi,
they are Keśavaṉ's kin.

Tiruvāymoḻi II.7 (177–189)
keśavaṉ tamar

II.7.1 They are Keśavaṉ's, my kin,
seven generations before and after me
blessed with great good fortune and prosperity
because of him, that god, my dark jewel
my lovely luminous Kaṇṇaṉ, king of celestials
my lord my sovereign, Nārāyaṇa.

II.7.2 Nāraṇaṉ, king of the seven worlds
is the Veda.
He's the cause result source of all action
my father praised by the fortunate immortals
lord who broke the elephant's tusks
he's my Mādhavaṉ.

II.7.3 'Mādhavaṉ' I said, and he caught me
saying 'I take your vanity.'
He entered me simply stayed there,
the nectar that destroys vice
my lotus-eyed mountain-hued lord
Govindaṉ, my perfect taste of sugar.

II.7.4 'Govindaṉ, pot-dancer, Kōvalaṉ'
I say his names, bow before him, sing dance.
He makes me right, ends my evil deeds
awakens in seven generations of kin
desire for him,
Viṣṇu, my mighty lord.

II.7.5 Viṣṇu, a radiant light
his feet, his hands his eyes lotuses
his body a dark brilliant mountain
his conch a luminous moon, his disc a sun
the lord wears a radiant crown,
he's Madhusūdaṉaṉ.

II.7.6 There's no one but Madhusūdaṉaṉ,
my sole refuge. My actions cease
I sing his praise, dance, age upon age
He comes before me, enters me
graces me in every birth
my lord, Trivikramaṉ.

II.7.7 'Trivikramaṉ has eyes bright as lotus,
lips red as fruit, teeth bright as crystal.'
I repeat this, bow down, think of you.
Age after age you gave me a mind
fit to worship your feet,
my lord, my Vāmaṉaṉ.

II.7.8 Vāmaṉaṉ, brilliant emerald
with lotus eyes, father of Kāmaṉ
I repeat this, sing of your feet, bow down.

You killed my evil mind, made it pure
ended the grief of birth.
Śrīdharaṉ, what can I do for you?

II.7.9 'Śrīdharaṉ with eyes bright as lotus'
I said this night and day in a frenzy
my eyes dripping tears my breath hot.
Dread fate's at an end, joy grows day by day
you've placed yourself inside me,
my Hṛṣīkeśaṉ.

II.7.10 'Hṛṣīkeśaṉ, my lord who stopped
the cruelties of Laṅkā's demon clan
my master, king of immortals'
Heart, if you know this worship him
hold firm, even when you're confused,
don't let go of Padmanābhaṉ.

II.7.11 Padmanābhaṉ, higher than the highest
made me his then gave himself to me
mighty lord, my tree of wishes
my nectar, master of the hills of Vēṅkaṭam,
my father dark as storm clouds
lord of the heavens, Dāmodaraṉ.

II.7.12 Dāmodaraṉ, primordial cause
swallows worlds. Who can know him
his devotees wonder.
Even Śivaṉ and Brahmā who dwell
within Dāmodaraṉ's body cannot know him,
my lord dark as the sea.

II.7.13 These twelve songs on his twelve names,
part of a garland of thousand Tamiḻ verses
sung by Śaṭhakōpaṉ of southern Kurukūr
about Neṭumāl, the jewel-bright flame,
king of immortals, that Kaṇṇaṉ,
will bring you to his feet.

Tiruvāymoḻi II.8 (190–200)
aṇaivatu aravaṇaimēl

II.8.1 He reclines on a serpent,
his body merged with Śrī.
He's the source of both
mixed in all things,
the source of release
He's the raft in the sea of birth.

II.8.2 The only end to the grief of birth
and everything else
the only root of griefless release
is to merge with our king
who wears tuḷasi, him
who saved the elephant from pain.

II.8.3 Ayaṉ who creates, rises from his navel.
Araṉ who destroys, lives on his left.
Śrī rests upon his lovely chest,
placed there by him.
He directs everything
his great deeds are everywhere.

II.8.4 Give up the five senses and their objects,
enter the land of incomparable endless good.
He's the killer of evil demons
mired in confusion.
Immerse yourself without end
in his unshakeable ancient greatness.

II.8.5 The primordial source protects
from the endless grief of birth
He guards the three worlds
He became horse tortoise fish man
He's matchless,
the lord of gods.

II.8.6 When Pārthaṉ placed flowers
at the feet of the one who measured worlds
and saw them again on Śivaṉ's head,
he understood his greatness,
him adorned in fresh tuḷasi.
Who can speak of such greatness again?

II.8.7 He reclines sits stands spans
becomes a boar to enter raise up,
caressing with his great broad arms
this earth he eats and spits out.
Who can know all that Māl does
for the earth, his woman?

II.8.8 Who can see Kaṇṇaṉ? How do you see him?
The whole world's but a morsel for him.

His heaven is high above all else.
The life within all things
the great one pervades
everything, is everywhere.

II.8.9 'Kaṇṇaṉ is everywhere' claimed the boy
'He's not here' replied Hiraṇyaṉ
and struck the pillar.
There, right then, to his astonishment
he appeared, my lion.
Who can know his greatness?

II.8.10 He's the highest release, heaven, hell,
abiding amidst the deathless gods
in all things, he's the root the seed
spreading everywhere, standing apart
is my Kaṇṇaṉ dark as storm clouds.
I've seen him.

II.8.11 Those who master these ten verses
from the musical thousand in Tamiḻ
about the black-bodied god with large bright eyes
sung by the master of Vaḻuti,
land of gardens swarming with bees,
will rule heaven and find the great release.

Tiruvāymoḻi II.9 (201–211)
emmā vīṭṭu tiṟamum

II.9.1 I don't ask for that great release.
Place your lotus feet upon my head,

lord who ended the elephant's suffering,
this is all your servant desires.

II.9.2 All I want now and for all time,
my dark jewel-bright lord my father
is wisdom to guide me to your feet
give it to me. Do not delay.

II.9.3 You keep me from wickedness
my Kaṇṇaṉ, lord who holds the disc.
Even when phlegm blocks my throat
grant that I praise your feet without cease.

II.9.4 'Always serve only me' he says
enters my mind, remains forever
takes me for himself
These are Kaṇṇaṉ's greatest gifts.

II.9.5 When I die whether I gain release
find heaven or hell, I'll never forget him
I'll happily praise him of many lives
that birthless lord.

II.9.6 Divine being of joy, blossoming light
filling the worlds, come to me.
Let me always worship you
with blissful mind words deeds.

II.9.7 You haven't let me shelter at your feet
forever. You haven't placed yourself
within me and cooled my desire.
Come now. Be with me always for all time.

II.9.8 If only my father, my sweet fruit
swallowed by the perfect Vedic poets
would live inside me for all time
I'll ask nothing else of him.

II.9.9 I didn't know myself,
thought only of me and mine.
I know I am you, all I own is yours
my bull-like lord praised by the gods.

II.9.10 Tamer of the seven bulls
blaze of light that turned Laṅkā to ash
tie me to your golden feet
let me go nowhere else.

II.9.11 This ten from the faultless thousand
spoken by Śaṭhakōpaṉ of Kurukūr
on the lord with the ruthless disc
ends suffering, grants eternal release.

Tiruvāymoḻi II.10 (212–222)
kiḷaroḷi iḷamai

II.10.1 Before glorious youth is lost
before you fade and grow old,
it's good to reach the temple
of the radiant lord of mystery,
his Māliruñcōlai encircled by gardens.

II.10.2 Turn from the charms of young women
praise Aḻakar with his booming conch

praise his temple in Māliruñcōlai,
its peaks touched by the moon.
This is the purpose of your life.

II.10.3 Heart, all action is futile
except the act of reaching the temple
in Māliruñcōlai thick with gardens,
the hill dear to the one
dark as storm clouds.

II.10.4 He dissolves the bonds of karma,
the one who raised the mountain
His temple is in Māliruñcōlai
its peaks cloaked in clouds,
the only way to live is to get there.

II.10.5 Don't multiply your wickedness,
instead go to the temple
of the one who holds the wheel of justice
he's in the hills of Māliruñcōlai
amidst its gushing springs.

II.10.6 Think. Don't be base. Do the right thing
and take the straight road to Māliruñcōlai
where deer live with their young.
Go to the temple of the one
who ate butter.

II.10.7 Think deeply. Don't sink to hell.
There is virtue in circling Māliruñcōlai
its hills touched by the perfect moon

and worshipping at the temple
of the one who lifted the earth.

II.10.8 Don't waste your life.
Circle Māliruñcōlai worshipped by celestials
circle the temple of the lord of mystery
who roamed with his cows.
Do it every day.

II.10.9 Think about what's right.
Don't drown in wickedness. Resolve
to bow at Māliruñcōlai with its elephant herds
to worship him who killed the demoness.
It's the only good.

II.10.10 Don't cheat and don't gamble
your only goal should be to enter
the temple in Māliruñcōlai
its hills filled with peacocks, the place
dear to the one who revealed the Veda.

II.10.11 These ten verses from a thousand
by Śaṭhakōpaṉ of Kurukūr, praising
the one who created the world
the one full of grace,
will place you at his feet.

The Third Hundred

Tiruvāymoḻi III.1 (223–233)
muṭic cōtiyāy

III.1.1 Does the radiance of your face flare
into the radiance of your crown?
Does the radiance of your feet bloom
into the lotus upon which you rest?
Did your own radiance mingle
with the golden radiance of your silks and jewels?
Tell me, Tirumāl.

III.1.2 In truth, the lotus is no equal
to your eyes your feet your hands.
Pure polished gold is no peer
to your luminous body.
All just insufficient words of praise
uttered by this world,
O supreme light.

III.1.3 Supreme light, highest
supreme light with no equal,
supreme light who made the wide worlds
within yourself,
my supreme light
Govindā
I can't speak of your nature.

III.1.4 This great world won't hold
your form, a blossom of radiance
a treasure, in its mind. It turns

instead to all the other paths
you made, while your heart
rests on the sweet tuḷasi
Won't the world suffer?

III.1.5 Your body glows,
radiant without effort
you are sorrowless wisdom
you are limitless.
Ruler of time
protector of the world
How can I praise you?

III.1.6 All who sing, all that is sung
in any world honours
only you. Nothing else.
You, with a crown of tuḷasi
You, with Śrī on your chest
what words do I have
to praise you?

III.1.7 Let many praise you.
You ordered Nāṉmukaṉ
who is within you
'Make the worlds and oceans'
Glorious Araṉ and the celestials
may praise you, but even they
can't do justice to your ancient fame.

III.1.8 You are faultless light
You are unsullied wisdom

that neither blooms nor withers.
You are everything. You rule it all.
If the king of the beautiful gods
worships you, won't it dim
the radiance of your lotus feet?

III.1.9 You swooped in on your eagle
wielding the strong sharp disc
to rescue that loving elephant.
If you grant undying wisdom
to all who worship you,
won't that diminish
the radiance of your light?

III.1.10 Vast light within the four Veda,
you made spread ate spat out
measured this world.
The god with the moon in his hair,
Nāṉmukaṉ and Indraṉ
know and praise you as the highest god.
Is this a wonder?

III.1.11 These ten from a perfect thousand
spoken by Śaṭhakōpaṉ of Kurukūr,
city of the virtuous,
on the one praised in the Veda
him, both wondrous and not,
will cut the life that rises
from this earth circled by the roaring sea.

Tiruvāymoḻi III.2 (234–244)
munnīr ñālam

III.2.1 My lord dark as storm clouds
creator of world and sea,
I've strayed in this body you gave me
so long ago.
When will I end the pain of cruel days
When will I root out my deeds
When will I join you?

III.2.2 My Vāmanā who measured
this wide world, I drown
in the great delusions of countless births
When will I cut the old wretched deeds
that shadow me,
When will I reach your feet
to remain there forever?

III.2.3 My father, your harmless whip
wiped out the two armies
of the Bharata war.
Tell me how do I cut
the unbreakable ties
to my treacherous body.
Tell me a way to reach you.

III.2.4 You're the infinite bright light
of wisdom, that neither grows
nor subsides. My father
who is everywhere,
how do I shake off my vileness

to shelter at your feet? Come,
show me the way.

III.2.5 Even when you come,
you don't still my mind.
If this is the way it is,
father dark and beautiful
as clusters of kāya blooms
tell me
how will I ever draw close to you?

III.2.6 In days past, I didn't do
good, nor did I not do bad
I lived to savour trivial things
I strayed.
Supreme one, creator of countless lives
when will I reach
your bright golden feet?

III.2.7 Heart, you suffered
without end, devoid of wisdom
drowning in a life doomed by deeds.
How do I reach the flame of wisdom,
the one who is everywhere
the one without end
How do I reach Kaṇṇaṉ?

III.2.8 I haven't abandoned
acts that bring sorrow
I haven't worshipped your feet
without pause
ancient pervasive beautiful Kaṇṇā

my supreme light, I call out to see you.
Where should I call to see you?

III.2.9 I cry out
from the tangle of my wickedness
stumbling through many paths,
growing wretched.
Long ago the lord
cared for his cows, spanned the worlds
When will I draw near him?

III.2.10 When the time comes
and Namaṉ's men tighten the noose
grief dissipates.
I've seen my Kaṇṇaṉ
praised in the books of wisdom
My heart steadies
My life is eternal.

III.2.11 These ten from the perfect garland
of thousand musical verses
on the one who owns all life,
him who holds the worlds
by Śaṭhakōpaṉ of southern Kurukūr,
city of birds and gardens,
will rid you of the body that sheathes life.

Tiruvāymoḻi III.3 (245–255)
oḻivil kālam ellām

III.3.1 For all time in all places
we must serve him faultlessly,

our father's father's father
the gorgeous light
of Tiruvēṅkaṭam, where cascades roar.

III.3.2 He's my father, father to his
father, father even to his father.
Praised endlessly by celestials and their king
the lord dark as storm clouds
is in Tiruvēṅkaṭam, where flowers burst red.

III.3.3 The mysterious lord
has eyes bright as red lotuses
lips red as fruit, a gem-dark body.
The lord of celestials, him of ancient fame
is in Tiruvēṅkaṭam, with its clear cool springs.

III.3.4 If I say 'Lord of celestials'
does it burnish the greatness
of the one in Tiruvēṅkaṭam?
I am small, I am nothing
still that supreme light loves me.

III.3.5 If I say 'Primordial god,
light worshipped by the worlds'
can it really describe
the nectar of the Veda,
the one in perfect Tiruvēṅkaṭam?

III.3.6 Those who worship
him in Vēṅkaṭam
are relieved of the bitter debts,

of their past and future deeds
They do themselves good.

III.3.7 The celestials led by their king
carry flowers water lamps incense
to worship at Tiruvēṅkaṭam,
the great mountain which grants
incomparable release.

III.3.8 He raised a mountain to offer
shelter from bitter rain.
The supreme lord who measured worlds
is in Tiruvēṅkaṭam. Reach his great hill
just once. End your deeds.

III.3.9 Praise his feet lovely as flowers
place him in your mind, and
the cowherd of Tiruvēṅkaṭam
will kill relentless old age
birth death disease.

III.3.10 Before you reach the limit
of your time, before you grow old
reach him who rests under a serpent hood,
reach him in Tiruvēṅkaṭam, hill
filled with forests flowers lakes.

III.3.11 Those who master this ten
from the incomparable thousand
spoken by Śaṭhakōpaṉ of Kurukūr

about the lord who leapt the earth
will gain a worthy life and the world's praise.

Tiruvāymoḻi III.4 (256–266)
pukaḻum nal oruvaṉ

III.4.1 Shall I say
he's the one worthy of praise
he's the fine incomparable earth
the cool wide ocean
he's fire wind vast sky
the towering twin lights
he's all of it.
How should I speak of Kaṇṇaṉ?

III.4.2 I don't know how to speak of him.
Shall I say
he's the mountains, life-giving rain
the brilliant stars
the art of poetry, the soul of wisdom?
How should I speak
of my infinite lord with eyes like lotuses
How should I speak of Kaṇṇaṉ?

III.4.3 Shall I say
his eyes are lotuses, his lips red as coral
his feet beautiful and bright. Should I say
he's black as kohl
his crown glows like a red sun? Shall I say
his chest holds Śrī and that lovely mark
and he has the conch and disc?
How should I speak of my perfect gem?

III.4.4 Shall I say
perfect gem, luminous pearl
flawless diamond, clear light?
Shall I say
primordial flame, primordial Puruṣaṉ?
How should I speak of Acyutaṉ
my father, imperishable and perfect
who was before everything?

III.4.5 Shall I say
he's perfect Acyutaṉ, the great medicine
that cures the deeds of his devotees?
Shall I say, he's an ocean of nectar
sweet sweetness, the six flavours,
ghee and honey, or
shall I say
he's fruit and milk?

III.4.6 Shall I say
he's milk, or that he's the fruit
of the four Veda? Shall I say
he's scripture? Is he music,
the highest good, the reward
for virtue? Shall I call him
Kaṇṇaṉ, Māl, mysterious,
him who is first among celestials?

III.4.7 Shall I say
he's first among celestials, their god
their intoxication, their everything?
Shall I say

he's unsoiled wealth
unspoiled heaven
unsullied mokṣam, him
an incandescent gem.

III.4.8 Shall I say
he's a glittering gem, singular
with a crescent moon in his hair?
Shall I say he's Nāṉmukaṉ?
My lord joyfully made
the worlds he protects,
mysterious Kaṇṇaṉ
adorned with tuḷasi.

III.4.9 Mysterious Kaṇṇaṉ
churned the ocean of its nectar,
great king, imperishable Acyutaṉ
endless Aṉantaṉ asleep
on the endless serpent,
Māl who ate and spat out the worlds
I can't understand him
who is everything and everyone.

III.4.10 He's everything and everyone
yet stands apart from it all, he's
beyond the five senses,
the very form of feeling, life
bound to breath unfettered
from it, he's the self within
to be joined there.

III.4.11 Those who master
these ten from the thousand
sung by generous Śaṭhakōpaṉ
of Kurukūr, city of flowering groves,
on the lord dark as storm clouds
the one wearing sweet-scented garlands,
will find the bliss of release and
a place among the immortals.

Tiruvāymoḻi III.5 (267–277)
moym mām pūm poḻil

III.5.1 When the crocodile ensnared
the elephant in a pond of flowers
the one dark as storm clouds saved it.
Tell me people
who live in this world circled by the sea,
what use are those
who won't speak sing leap dance
in praise of Kaṇṇaṉ?

III.5.2 Tirumāl kills merciless demons
who feast on all who live in this world
circled by the sea.
If you won't sing leap sway wander
praising him,
you'll be born only to be crushed
under the weight of your own deeds.

III.5.3 He raised a mountain
to shield his herd from a hail of stones,

eased their suffering.
Those who won't utter his names
or bow and touch the ground, or
endlessly praise such a lord
will sink into hell
to know only its manifold miseries.

III.5.4 Śrīdharaṉ of ancient fame
and coral-red lips
killed the seven bulls
for the woman with garlands in her hair.
What use is a life among the virtuous
if you won't wander
bowing praying dancing swaying
in his praise?

III.5.5 Just to kill Kaṁsaṉ,
tormentor of the virtuous,
he left his primordial form of light there
and was born here.
Are they even men of learning
if they simply chant
but won't leap in the streets
singing of the source of the Veda?

III.5.6 He became a man, many other things
became everything. Birthless
he was born, the lord asleep
on the wide ocean.
He is ripe fruit, the sweetness
of sugar cane honey nectar

Praise him without rancour
and you'll comprehend all.

III.5.7 As the hundred devoid of virtue
stood defeated, their armies crushed,
he blessed the five.
If you don't think of that great light
don't dance and weep, eyes spilling tears
heart melting,
instead just feed your body and belly,
what use are you to good people?

III.5.8 My father is up north in Vēṅkaṭam
amidst pools and lovely waterfalls.
Speak his many names, and
people may call you mad.
Roam through cities, and
the world will mock you.
Dance, let your passion build, and
even the immortals will bow before you.

III.5.9 Leave aside the ones with still minds
those masters of yoga
who think they are with him.
For the rest of us
the only way is to yell and dance
thinking of the one
the immortals worship
the lord of all worlds.

III.5.10 He is karma its results its cause
He is Māl, lord of gods

his body gem-bright, his eyes lotus red.
Place him in a firm mind
dissolve yourself, dance
shed pride and shame
Shout his praise, put an end
to your stupidity.

III.5.11 This ten from the thousand
on the imperishable Acyutaṉ, our lord
who corrects his devotees and accepts
them into his service,
sung by Śaṭhakōpaṉ of Kurukūr,
city of fields,
will reduce wretched deeds
to ash.

Tiruvāymoḻi III.6 (278–288)
ceyya tāmaraik kaṇṇaṉ

III.6.1 See him
the one with lotus eyes who ate the world
who became earth sky people gods,
who became this this this this
He became luminous wisdom
created everything
He became light fiery and intense
then he became three.

III.6.2 Praise him
the one who became three,
first among them, their creator,
remover of curses, god of gods

asleep on the wide sea, archer
who set Laṅkā ablaze,
vanquisher of vice, him
of lotus eyes.

III.6.3 Sing of him
the supreme one praised by celestials,
supreme light, kuravai dancer,
gem-bright pot-dancer
great lord asleep on a serpent
amidst the sea with it rolling waves
Fix your mind on him
without end through night and day.

III.6.4 Keep him
in your heart. The gods
and their king, Nāṉmukaṉ,
the great lord with matted hair
praise him with love
thinking all day of his lotus feet.
What can I say about the greatness
of that mysterious lord?

III.6.5 He is
the wandering breeze wide sky
firm earth vast sea blazing fire
the twin flames, this this this,
Kaṇṇaṉ, our god of gods
his body dark, his eyes lotus-bright
a glittering crown atop his black curls,
all these forms are his.

III.6.6 He is
beyond birth and death
of matchless form, full of grace
Māl of bright lotus eyes,
at once angry and kind
he is smell form taste sound touch
the bull among celestials
I have none but him through all my lives.

III.6.7 He is
in every life my breath's sweet nectar,
my precious life, a dense brilliant flame,
a gem-bright pot-dancer,
ripe fruit relished
by the great immortals and sages.
Worship him with a pure mind and
your troubles vanish in an instant.

III.6.8 He is
the pain of acts both bad and good,
yet is beyond them,
Acyutaṉ, a towering light
who ate and spat out the seven worlds
a poison to Namaṉ's kin,
son to Daśaratha,
I have no refuge but him.

III.6.9 He is
father mother himself, none of these.
He is first among the faultless immortals.
He is ancient creator of the three gods.

All you frightened folk, don't worry
if he's this or that,
the one dark as the sea
takes the form your heart seeks.

III.6.10 He is
Kaṇṇaṉ dark as the sea,
the celestials' glittering black gem,
my precious light. Long ago
that great light asleep on the serpent
drove a chariot in a terrible war
for the five and destroyed the hundred.
When will I see his feet?

III.6.11 Śaṭhakōpaṉ, king of Kurukūr,
in the lush land of Vaḻuti,
sang these ten from a melodic thousand
on the one difficult to see
but easy to remember,
that lord of gods
who blesses all who dwell in this world.
Learn them and become his devotee.

Tiruvāymoḻi III.7 (289–299)
payilum cuṭaroḷi

III.7.1 His form is radiant light. His eyes are lotuses
He's the supreme one asleep on the ocean of milk.
Those devoted to him, whoever they are
rule me in every life.

III.7.2 The great ruler with four wide shoulders,
him with a disc, is Kaṇṇaṉ my king, bright as a gem.
Those who bow to him, palms folded
are my masters in every life.

III.7.3 Master praised on earth and sky, wise one
wreathed in tuḷasi, lord with the golden disc, my father.
Those who serve the servants who serve his feet
rule me in every blessed birth.

III.7.4 Nāraṇaṉ is draped in fine silks, decked in jewels
a gold thread crosses his chest, a crown rests on his head.
His servants' servants are my kin
through all my endless births.

III.7.5 Great lord of the virtuous, father who fed
that rare nectar to the immortals to end their woes.
Those who praise those who praise his greatness
rule this and every birth to follow.

III.7.6 Great protector wreathed in garlands
lord with a disc, Kaṇṇaṉ my king, bright as a gem.
Those who hold that brilliant flame in their minds
will guard me from grief, birth after birth.

III.7.7 Birth after birth he protects his devotees
refines their nature, shelters them at his feet
Those who praise those who praise his glory
will guide me to the good way.

III.7.8 Steadfast lord, creator of worlds,
inseparable from Śrī, unknowable even to the gods
Even if they praise him from vilest hell
they are my kin in every birth.

III.7.9 Even if they fall outside the four castes,
are outcastes devoid of virtue, if they serve those
who keep him who wields the disc in their heart
They rule me.

III.7.10 He measured the world, ate it,
incomparable child asleep on a banyan leaf.
He's my lord, my father, and his servants' servant,
their servants' servant, their servants' servant are my masters.

III.7.11 Śaṭhakōpaṉ of southern Kurukūr
made this humble offering of ten from a thousand
to praise the lord who killed the hundred, blessed the five.
Master them, and these births so difficult to end will end.

Tiruvāymoḻi III.8 (300–310)
muṭiyāṉē

III.8.1 The three worlds praise your great feet,
you churned the deep ocean, you ride the eagle
fly it as a banner, one dark as storm clouds
towering king, higher than the celestials
my heart says these things, waiting for you.

III.8.2 In the grand city of my heart
you are the safe harbour.

You, a deadly poison to Laṅkā's king
You, a cunning youth who claimed the worlds
these are the ways I praise you. Always.

III.8.3 King of celestials, my words are only for you.
Wearing a smile bright as a young moon,
you who are like a mother to cowherds
snuck into their humble huts to steal butter.
How I long to touch you.

III.8.4 I worship you with my hands over and over
all day in every moment without pause.
Supreme lord asleep on the serpent,
my eyes long to see you
in your true form.

III.8.5 My eyes yearn to see
Vāmaṉaṉ who claimed the earth
joyfully riding his bird.
I imagine the rustle of its wings,
my ears strain to hear that sweet sound.

III.8.6 My ears long only to hear your praise
songs ripe as fruit and sweet as honey,
one who holds the great gold disc
while on this earth, my breath craves you
without end.

III.8.7 My breath, precious nectar, you rule me.
You, on your lovely bird
You, with your fiery disc

my wicked heart calls for you endlessly, and
I still can't see your beautiful form.

III.8.8 Beautiful one, dark as jewel-black kohl
eyes bright as lotus, you cut my life.
Virtuous lord who is past future present,
time itself
When will I see you?

III.8.9 'Great Bali, give me three steps' you said.
Trickster. You cut the thousand arms of Bāṇaṉ
quashed his strength, killer of Kaṁsaṉ
skilled rider of the bird,
when will I join you?

III.8.10 Great one who slid between
two dense maruta trees, I yearn to see
your feet. I string garlands of songs
thinking only of you
how much longer must I grieve?

III.8.11 Those who know these ten verses
from the powerful thousand spoken by
Śaṭhakōpaṉ of wealthy Kurukūr
on the great lord who measured worlds
will rise far into the sky.

Tiruvāymoḻi III.9 (311–321)
coṉṉāl virōtam

III.9.1 Listen, you may disagree when I say
my tongue won't sing sweet songs for anyone

but my father, my elephant, my great lord
who is in Tiruvēṅkaṭam, its hills thrumming
with honey-seeking bees.

III.9.2 They think themselves invincible, count
wealth as their greatest asset.
Why should I sing of such men?
My father Kaṇṇaṉ is in Kuṟuṅkuṭi,
city of pools and rich fields.

III.9.3 Poets, when you can praise
the lord of celestials
who reveals the way out of endless aeons,
why sing of mere men
unworthy of thought?

III.9.4 How long will that wealth last
when you praise puny men?
If you sing of the father of celestials
he'll make you his
and end your births.

III.9.5 Poets, why waste your eloquence
on the glories of wealth, useless garbage.
Sing of the generous one,
bright as a gem, him
who lacks nothing, grants everything.

III.9.6 Come, work your bodies for a living
I've seen no real patrons in this world.
Sing of a god dear to you and

it will still reach my Tirumāl
crowned in light.

III.9.7 I can only praise him of limitless
fame, lord of a thousand names.
'Arms that reach the clouds
strong shoulders like mountains'
I can't utter such lies about the sod of the world.

III.9.8 I've sung the endless glory
of Piṉṉai's beloved. I love him.
I long to cast aside this body,
shelter at his feet.
What words do I have for deluded fools?

III.9.9 I'm not a poet to praise men.
The one who wields the disc
nurtures me, promises me the highest world
slowly sets me free.
He's the only one for me.

III.9.10 For the many days spent in this body
for the many births wasted thinking it will end,
he creates world after world
I am his poet
how can I sing of anyone else?

III.9.11 Śaṭhakōpaṉ of Kurukūr
sang these ten from a thousand of great fame
on glorious Kaṇṇaṉ, lord of celestials.
Those who master these words of praise
will end their births.

Tiruvāymoḻi III.10 (322–332)
caṉmam pala pala

III.10.1 He reveals himself in countless births,
we see him with his conch disc bow
fine club sharp sword and sceptre
He swoops down on his eagle
decimating mighty demon armies
I praise his greatness
I lack nothing.

III.10.2 He climbed atop the fierce serpent
on the vast flawless sea, closed his lotus eyes
in deep yogic sleep. He's my brilliant gem
Kaṇṇaṉ who rides the red-beaked eagle,
lord who fells demons.
I sing and dance praising him
nothing stops me.

III.10.3 The singular lord of unhindered joy,
sugar honey nectar milk fruit sugar cane
to the three worlds
his crown wreathed in sweet fragrant tuḷasi,
I worship him, and
in every moment
my mind is free of pain.

III.10.4 Bāṇaṉ came with his armies,
the destroyer of the three cities, his son and Agni
all ready to fight.
Even then, the mysterious lord who rides the eagle
that cowherd protected him.

When I hold tight to Hari, Acyutaṉ
I am free of grief.

III.10.5 On the same day in the same moment
without the slightest difficulty
he drove a chariot with glorious Pārthaṉ
and the brahmin, and out of his own light
returned from death the brahmin's boys.
I think of him
I am free from despair.

III.10.6 Nothing mars his fiery luminosity,
not even sorrow-filled human births
he endured before our very eyes
They only bared his divinity to the world.
Glorious Kaṇṇaṉ, mysterious lord,
I praise him
and end my pain.

III.10.7 He's all that brings pain and pleasure
He's every world.
He's hot joyless hell, sweet heaven too
He's all these many lives, all
these countless mysterious games are his
When I have him
I need nothing.

III.10.8 He's limitless pleasure unmarred by pain,
a beautiful encompassing light
lord delighting in Śrī
boundless wisdom, wisdom itself

endless mysterious lord who guides all things
I reach Kaṇṇaṉ's feet
I have no sorrow.

III.10.9 Flame of wisdom untouched by sorrow
great lord wreathed in tuḷasi, he changes
form as he desires—how mysterious.
He holds within himself the naked god,
Ayaṉ and everyone else
That master's mine
I don't despair.

III.10.10 He's eternal infinite singular wisdom
devoid of sorrow. Formless god
beyond the five senses. Incandescent light,
the five elements the twin fires,
he's radiant mysterious Kaṇṇaṉ
I clasped his feet
nothing can harm me.

III.10.11 Those who learn these ten
from among the thousand
sung by Kurukūr's Śaṭhakōpaṉ
on Keśavaṉ of flawless fame,
will gain the great release, joyfully
witnessed by cities and countries.
They will rule the three worlds.

The Fourth Hundred

Tiruvāymoḻi IV.1 (333–343)

oru nāyakamāy

IV.1.1 As the world watches
those who once ruled as kings
beg with broken bowl in hand
black dogs nipping at their heels.
Quick, think now of Tirunāraṇaṉ's feet.

IV.1.2 'Give us tribute and live'
said the rulers of the world, now
they've lost their sweet wives to others
and wither in the burning wastelands.
Quick, reach the feet of Tirumāl.

IV.1.3 Kings bowed before them
their crowns at their feet, as drums
thundered in their pavilions, now
they're just dust mingled with earth.
Quick, think of Kaṇṇaṉ's feet.

IV.1.4 More innumerable than grains of sand
are kings who ruled the world through the ages
but still died, not a trace left of them.
Quick, worship him
who killed the rut-mad elephant.

IV.1.5 On beds of flowers they sipped
the sweet nectar of pleasure. Now they wander
dressed in rags, mocked by women.

Quick, sing his names,
the mysterious one bright as a gem. Live.

IV.1.6 All through time, even if they lived
well, they die
like droplets in a great storm of rain.
If you want a good life,
serve him who sleeps on the deep deep sea.

IV.1.7 They gorge on food of six flavours
then eat more beguiled by women, now
they wander begging for a grain of rice.
Quick, think of his nature, him
a primordial light.

IV.1.8 Even good kings, who are generous
and make the world their own, lose
pleasure and wealth if they don't think of him.
Quick, sing the names of him
who rests on the serpent.

IV.1.9 They may give up wealth, master the senses,
punish their bodies, they may even attain heaven,
but they'll just return to earth
if they don't think of him.
Find the feet of the one who flies the eagle-banner.

IV.1.10 Even for the wise who look inward,
who renounce everything, it's still not enough.
The briefest thought binds, then there's no release.
Hold tight to the perfect lord, don't let go,
that is freedom.

IV.1.11 As a humble service,
Śaṭhakōpaṉ of Kurukūr, city of groves,
sang of Kaṇṇaṉ's feet as the path to freedom
in these ten verses from a set of thousand.
Learn them, rise above despair and be free.

Tiruvāymoḻi IV.2 (344–354)
pālaṉāy ēḻ ulaku uṇṭu

IV.2.1 'He's the boy who ate the worlds
then blissfully slept on a banyan leaf
I want the cool tuḷasi from his feet'
My innocent girl says such confused things,
I am doomed.

IV.2.2 My doll-like girl says
'He played with the cowherd women,
danced the kuravai with them
I want the sweet-scented tuḷasi from his feet'
I am doomed.

IV.2.3 My girl says
'I want the red-gold tuḷasi
from the feet of the one
praised by gods and sages singing the Veda'
I am doomed.

IV.2.4 My girl sings
'Different schools praise him
argue their differences about the great lord.
I want the tuḷasi fine as gold from his feet'
I'm doomed for the ages.

IV.2.5 'He killed the seven bulls for Piṉṉai,
that cowherd, pot-dancer
I want the tuḷasi that adorns his feet'
says my girl as she fades a little
every day.

IV.2.6 'Long ago for the great earth goddess
he came as a boar and
pierced this vast space
I want the tuḷasi from his feet' says
my innocent child.

IV.2.7 Friends, my innocent girl is mad
for the cool tuḷasi from the feet
of the one who placed Śrī
a flower herself
among the garlands adorning his broad chest.

IV.2.8 My girl only wants
the tuḷasi from the feet of the one
who for his lovely Sītā
burned Laṅkā with a hail of arrows.
Friends, what shall I do?

IV.2.9 Friends, you too have raised girls with love.
What can I say about my poor girl?
Night and day all she says is
'Conch disc tuḷasi'
What should I do?

IV.2.10 Friends, what should I do?
My silly girl won't listen to me

she only wants the tuḷasi
from Kaṇṇaṉ's feet to adorn her breasts.
She's wasting away.

IV.2.11 Śaṭhakōpaṉ of glorious Kurukūr
sang about our Kaṇṇaṉ's feet
a cure for the disease of love.
Those who master these ten from a thousand
will be fit to join the celestials.

Tiruvāymoḻi IV.3 (355–365)
kōvai vāyāḷ

IV.3.1 You fought seven bulls for the woman
with lips red as ripe kōvai fruit.
You killed the king of fortified Laṅkā
You broke the tusks of the mighty elephant
I don't worship you with flowers and water
My heart is the sweet sandal
for your petal-soft body.

IV.3.2 My heart is sweet sandal
My words are the garlands and silks
that adorn him
My hands folded in prayer
are his brilliant jewels
This is my father of singular form,
lord who ate and spat out the worlds.

IV.3.3 His form is one it's two it's three
it's many.
He's the five elements the twin flames

he's formless.
Nārāyaṇaṉ asleep on a serpent in the midst of the sea
You've filled me with you
My grief ends.

IV.3.4 The devious demoness placed your mouth
to her breast, thinking to kill you.
You drained her life, mysterious cowherd,
Vāmaṉaṉ, Mādhavā
I may not worship you with garlands
of new flowers,
my life adorns your towering crown.

IV.3.5 My life is a garland, my love is
your crown of light your countless jewels
your fine silks.
It is even the songs of praise
chanted in the three worlds
for Kaṇṇaṉ my lord my master
who wields the disc of time.

IV.3.6 'Wielder of the disc of time
and white conch, Nārāyaṇaṉ,
who ate and spat out the world'
I cry out over and over again
but even if you won't come,
your lovely lotus feet
adorn my head.

IV.3.7 Vāmanā who stretched his leg
and took the worlds,
mysterious one who stays close

to those who worship his feet
I may not offer you flowers and water
but your form of words and light
is in my breath.

IV.3.8 You've entered my breath,
radiant light of wisdom
filling the seven beautiful worlds.
My breath is yours
Your breath is mine
I can't describe how this is
I can't describe the way you are.

IV.3.9 I can't describe you,
will I ever find the shore in the flood
that is your endless glory?
I'm rising in love, faultless supreme lord,
supreme light without falseness
When good people roar your praise
I join in too.

IV.3.10 I praise him, the seven worlds praise him
he praises himself,
even if all this praise comes together
can it reach an end?
I praise my lord
sweet as honey milk sugar nectar
I live.

IV.3.11 Those who master these ten
from the truth-filled thousand
on Kaṇṇaṉ's beautiful feet,

the only path of refuge
sung by Śaṭhakōpaṉ of Kurukūr,
city of ponds of red lotuses and paddy fields,
will rule heaven and earth.

Tiruvāymoḻi IV.4 (366–376)
maṇṇai iruntu tuḻāvi

IV.4.1 She feels the earth and says,
'This is Vāmaṉaṉ's'
She bows to the sky and points out
'This is the Vaikuṇṭha he loves'
Tears spill from her eyes as she says
'The one dark as the ocean'
He's bewitched my girl,
friends, what can I do to him?

IV.4.2 She cups her palms and says,
'He sleeps on the ocean'
She points to the red sun and says,
'There's Śrīdharaṉ'
Her tears flow freely, she crumples
crying 'Nāraṇaṉ'
I don't understand anything
my blessed child does.

IV.4.3 She touches red fire and says,
'Acyutaṉ' and is unharmed
She hugs the cool winter breeze and says,
'My Govindaṉ'
My child tender as a fawn

smells of his fragrant tuḷasi
I am doomed, all I see
are the strange things this girl does.

IV.4.4 She points to the bright moon and says,
'Look, it's the gem-bright lord'
She sees the mighty mountain and says,
'Great tall Neṭumāl, come'
She sees the rains pouring down and says,
'Nāraṇaṉ is here'
See all the ways he's bewitched
my sweet tender girl.

IV.4.5 She pets the soft young cows and says,
'Govindaṉ has grazed them.'
She follows a slithering snake and says,
'This is where he sleeps'
He's bewitched my tender girl,
I don't know where his mysterious antics
will end.
I am doomed.

IV.4.6 She runs after the pot-dancers saying,
'It's Govindaṉ'
She hears the flute and says,
'It's the mysterious one'
She sees butter churned by women and says,
'This is the butter he ate'
My girl is mad for the one
who suckled at the ghoul's breast.

IV.4.7 As her madness rises she says
'Kaṇṇaṉ created all these worlds'
She runs after men with a white mark on their brow
calling them Neṭumāl's people
She sees fragrant tuḷasi, declares
'This is Nāraṇaṉ's garland'
Conscious or not, my girl
is crazy for the mysterious one.

IV.4.8 She sees wealthy kings and says,
'I've seen Tirumāl'
She sees bright beautiful things and says,
'He measured worlds'
Every temple with their gods
is home to the one dark as the ocean
whether afraid or fainting from love
she only wants Kaṇṇaṉ's feet.

IV.4.9 She sees sages and says,
'He ate the wide world'
She sees great dark clouds and says,
'It's Kaṇṇaṉ' and tries to catch them
She sees cattle herds and follows them
saying 'He's here'
The mysterious one has made her cry,
this girl of mine, so hard won.

IV.4.10 She faints, she looks around
her eyes search the far distance for him
she sweats, she weeps tears like rain

her breath grows hot, her body fades
still she calls out, 'Kaṇṇā great lord, come'
What can I do for my simple girl
mad with love?
How wretched I am.

IV.4.11 Śaṭhakōpaṉ of wealthy Kurukūr
sang with devotion
these ten verses from a thousand
on Kaṇṇaṉ who ends wicked fate.
Those who learn them as a blessing
destroy their terrible pasts
enter Vaikuṇṭha
and will live worshipped by all.

Tiruvāymoḻi IV.5 (377–387)
viṟṟiruntu ēḻ ulakum

IV.5.1 He rules the seven worlds
with an unbending sceptre, great lord
of imperishable virtue who killed the fierce horse.
I praise him, I worship him palms pressed together
I string garlands of words to adorn him
What can I lack in seven births?

IV.5.2 Śrī her eyes lovely and dark, blooms
on the chest of the great lord of celestials,
him with large bright eyes.
I sing garlands of songs to praise him.
I have him in me and
the fierce burning miseries of the vast world end.

IV.5.3 Our Acyutan̲ abides in the farthest reaches
of endless bliss, the great lord of celestials,
endlessly good, one whose eyes open like flowers.
I praise him endlessly in song
I reach him and
abide in the farthest reaches of endless bliss.

IV.5.4 Draw near him, worship him
he ends your fate, sidles close to you
the lord with the fine-feathered bird and fierce disc.
I string garlands of song for him
I've reached him, but still don't know
how his breath moves within mine.

IV.5.5 The great lord patiently reveals
the right paths, that bull of the immortals
unfurls all things, all meaning.
I praise my lord with garlands of words
I am ecstatic, and my wickedness
turns to dust borne away by the wind.

IV.5.6 He wears a streak of white earth
on his black skin, that great lord of celestials
with eyes large and beautiful.
I've strung garlands of perfect words for him
I've got him now. Can anything be difficult
Is anything beyond my reach?

IV.5.7 Eternally singular peerless beyond compare
sovereign, master of all worlds
he lifted a mountain against the rain

I adorn him with fine garlands of words
I am meant to do this
What do I lack?

IV.5.8 The great lord of earth and sky
the great lord whose feet rest on cool lotuses
is sweetest pleasure for us and Śrī.
I've been vested
to string garlands of words for him
Who in the vast heavens can equal me?

IV.5.9 He fills the heavens, everything beyond
He fills the earth everything beneath
He fills the eight directions, the one
who holds the gently curving conch in his palm
I sing of the pot-dancer, the king of celestials
Who can equal me?

IV.5.10 This earth he ate spat out
spanned dug slept on dwelt in
held court in, embraced, he owns it.
This garland of fine Tamiḻ verses
I've strung for him is a rainstorm
of nectar for those who serve him.

IV.5.11 Kārimāṟaṉ Śaṭhakōpaṉ of Kurukūr
city of lush gardens
sang these ten songs from a thousand
about the lord of Vēṅkaṭam,
that cool mountain where rains never fail
Master them and Śrī will end your deeds.

Tiruvāymoḻi IV.6 (388–398)
tīrppārai yām iṉi

IV.6.1 How do we find a healer?
We know the welcome illness
that fades her bright face is longing
for the charioteer who guided the five to victory
in that astonishing war long ago.
Her mind wanders seeking him.

IV.6.2 This illness that bewilders
is brought on by the great god
not some little god for whom you dance crazily
as though possessed.
If you say 'Conch' 'Disc' so she hears it
she'll recover quickly, you'll see.

IV.6.3 Don't listen to this fortune teller
and do silly things
like offer toddy and meat.
Just praise the feet of the mysterious lord
who wears a crown of honey-sweet tuḷasi,
the only cure for her dread disease.

IV.6.4 'This is the cure' said that cunning woman
and you listened to her, uselessly offering a mix
of black and red rice to some god.
If you speak the names of the great god
who in an instant ate and spat out the seven worlds
you'll get her back.

IV.6.5 Such crazy dancing won't bring back your girl,
her dark eyes now dull, her once red lips pale.
Speak the names of the lord
who killed the rut-mad elephant,
smear her with his white clay
and put an end to this.

IV.6.6 Women, your wild dancing at all hours
won't end her illness, will only make it worse.
Find the dust from the feet
of the devotees of the mysterious one,
brilliant as a dark jewel.
Your girl needs nothing else.

IV.6.7 You think a goat, toddy and wild dancing
are rare precious cures.
Women, it's useless, like
watching an ass eat drying grain.
Praise the devotees of the mysterious lord,
those who've mastered the Veda.

IV.6.8 Approach those firm in the Veda
to worship the feet of the great lord of celestials, and
end her sickness. You won't do this.
Instead, you praise little gods, spill toddy,
beat drums, dance wildly, acting
in low uncouth ways.

IV.6.9 You're uncouth, so you dance wildly
to the drum of some low chap, muttering vain words

I can't watch this.
The only cure for birth after birth in seven lives,
the only cure for this dread disease
is to praise Kaṇṇaṉ's feet.

IV.6.10 She thinks of no god but him
she worships none but him, yet
you dance on wildly, saying what you wish.
Praise the one who is in the Veda
the king of Dvārakā, and she
too will dance in joyous worship.

IV.6.11 Śaṭhakōpaṉ of Kurukūr of ancient fame
worshipped sang danced in praise
of the one brilliant as a flawless gem
and put an end to his disease.
Those who praise dance sing these ten on madness
from his faultless thousand will never know sorrow.

Tiruvāymoḻi IV.7 (399–409)
cīlam illāc ciṟiyēṉum

IV.7.1 I am low. I am small. My misdeeds are legion
I raise my hands above my head, call out all day,
'Eater of worlds, icon of wisdom, Nārāyaṇa'
you still won't reveal your beautiful body
you still won't call me to you.

IV.7.2 'You give a flood of limitless pleasure,
generous one, Vāmanā who claimed the world'
I cry out again and again in the deep dark of night,

and in the bright light of day, cunning mysterious lord
you still won't come so my eyes can see you.

IV.7.3 How much wickedness have I done?
'My father who measured worlds, Dāmodarā'
I cry out as my heart dissolves into streams of tears.
You won't even say 'You poor wretched thing'
You won't show yourself to me.

IV.7.4 'Father, come stand before me
your eyes bright as lotus, your body glowing like gold –
show me this kindness' I cry out stripped of shame.
But what's the point, great one,
when even the gods can't see you.

IV.7.5 'Father who wields the fierce disc
mighty lord who churned the deep sea,
can I ever see your four great shoulders'
I weep, my breath slowly dries, I'm bereft
Still I keep looking for you. Come now.

IV.7.6 I search hoping to see you. I speak
of this deepest desire even when I lack wisdom.
You're within me, in my breath
in everything around me, you exist everywhere.
I know you well.

IV.7.7 I know you well, I see you clearly, deep
within myself as the full perfect form of wisdom,
I've kept you there. I'm done

with the nonsense of birth and death, of being.
Lord adorned in garlands of tuḷasi I've found you.

IV.7.8 When I see you, my hands will overflow
with flowers from everywhere that I'll offer at your feet.
I'll praise and exalt you, sing and dance with your devotees,
so why won't you come to this earth bound by the sea
my king decked in garlands of sweet-scented tuḷasi?

IV.7.9 I haven't fed the hungry nor quenched the thirsty
I've not conquered the five senses, I've not been dutiful
offering flowers as I ought. Still love sharpens
in my silly heart, and this wretch seeks you.
Where will I see the lord with the disc?

IV.7.10 'Lord with a disc' I said and wept,
in despair I searched, but could not see.
He's the very form of wisdom, the light of the Veda
I'll see him with the eye of wisdom
I'll touch him too.

IV.7.11 Māṟaṉ Śaṭhakōpaṉ of Kurukūr, city of mansions
sang with overflowing love for Kaṇṇaṉ
these ten verses from a thousand in flawless Tamiḻ.
Those who sing and dance them with love
will reach Vaikuṇṭha.

Tiruvāymoḻi IV.8 (410–420)
ēṟāḷum iṟaiyōṉum

IV.8.1 The god who rides the bull
the god facing the four directions

the beautiful goddess, all
reign from within his singular form.
He wields his weapons turning clan upon clan
of demons to dust.
My jewel-like lustre is useless
if it can't enchant that mighty lord.

IV.8.2 The goddess of flawless radiance is on his chest
his lovely shoulders are wide as mountains
his broad hand holds the fierce disc.
He's taken me entirely into his service
and made me his.
My innocent heart is useless
if it can't enchant him,
my jewel-bright lord of mystery.

IV.8.3 She came disguised as a perfect mother
with a pure heart,
but you a small child with great wisdom
suckled at her poisoned breast
supreme Puruṣaṉ with shoulders vast as mountains,
asleep on a serpent
My beauty is useless
if it can't enchant that great lord of mystery.

IV.8.4 To hold Piṉṉai full of beauty,
her arms slender as bamboo,
he tamed seven fierce bulls.
He's the one in ochre silk,
holding a flute and
a staff to herd his cows.

My skin glowing like a new leaf is useless
if it can't enchant that cowherd.

IV.8.5 For her, skin glowing like a new leaf
for her, imprisoned and alone
for her, with a parrot-sweet voice
he burnt down the demon's city.
He wears a crown of sweet-scented tuḷasi
my mind is useless
if it can't enchant him
who loves this world bound by the sea.

IV.8.6 So this vast world could know wisdom
he took every form
became every path
him of singular form
came as a tiny man to claim the world
through merciless cunning
My youth is useless
if it can't enchant the king of pranks.

IV.8.7 A flawless lion burst out
fiery with rage and bright as light,
tore open Hiraṇyaṉ's massive chest
and roared with joy.
He holds a disc of fire and the right-turning conch
my pretty bangles are useless
if they can't enchant him
dark and brilliant as a gem.

IV.8.8 His perfect right-turning conch booms
scorching his enemies, ending the earth's grief.

Even Śivaṉ difficult to know,
Brahmā and the king of gods
praise him.
The jewels at my waist are useless
if they can't enchant him
whose fame has spread everywhere.

IV.8.9 He broke the shoulders of mighty Bāṇaṉ,
father to that woman
with a slender waist adorned in jewels.
He lies on his serpent as though asleep,
but thinking only of the world's good.
My body is useless
if it can't enchant him,
so deep in yogic sleep.

IV.8.10 He split life from the bodies
of mighty demons, left them in piles
like shattered mountains,
then felt joy.
The one from whose matted hair a river flows
lives quietly within him.
My breath is useless
if I can't enchant him.

IV.8.11 Those who master these ten verses
from a garland of thousand perfect songs
by Śaṭhakōpaṉ of Kurukūr
about the one who kept with himself
the seven worlds teeming with life,
about him who lapped up curd and butter,
will cut their bonds of endless birth
and will reach Vaikuṇṭha.

Tiruvāymoḻi IV.9 (421–431)
naṇṇātār muṟuvalippa

IV.9.1 Enemies laugh, the virtuous cry
what is this world of countless miseries?
You churned the ocean, kind one
show me the way to your feet
Give me death.

IV.9.2 Death comes, wealth goes,
kin keel over in grief, cheated.
What is this world?
Lord asleep on a serpent, I know no path
Call me to you. Quick.

IV.9.3 Joy family pride wealth wives
all this dies. This world I see
I cannot bear, lord dark as the ocean
don't consider me as I was
Call me to your feet now.

IV.9.4 Wealth begs to be taken, then
like a great fire swallows everything.
What world is this?
Generous gem-bright one, give me the gift
of your feet. Favour me.

IV.9.5 In a world bloomed from water
lives exist, birth, death, illness, suffering
then burning hell. What world is this?
Gem-bright lord accept me
Don't deny me.

IV.9.6 Caught in nets, they destroy, kill, eat
know what's right, but remain in denial.
What world is this?
My precious nectar wreathed in tuḷasi
you've made me yours. Call me to you now.

IV.9.7 You alone are everything
that moves and stays in this world.
Nothing exists without you, so call me to you,
end the sick grief of age death birth
Don't show me this cruel world.

IV.9.8 You show it, hide it, this world
you spat out made of earth water fire sky ether.
When will you break me out of this egg, fortress of the gods?
When will you bring me to your feet, so difficult to reach?
When will you draw me into your light?

IV.9.9 Lord asleep on the serpent, you make it
so even the gods can't worship you. I know this,
stripped of desire, I wander bearing your feet
upon my head. I see now
that you have brought me to your precious feet.

IV.9.10 I saw heard touched smelled tasted
the endless pleasures of the five fickle senses.
I saw you and resplendent Śrī
together inseparable permanent
I've reached your feet.

IV.9.11 Śaṭhakōpaṉ of Kurukūr yearning to reach
Nāraṇaṉ's feet sang these ten verses from the Tamiḻ thousand

in praise of the feet of Keśavaṉ, that supreme light.
They will lead you to his feet
and make you one with them.

Tiruvāymoḻi IV.10 (432–442)
oṉṟum tēvum

IV.10.1 There were no gods no world no life nothing, and
then he made Nāṉmukaṉ, the gods, gave life to the world.
When Ādippirāṉ the primordial lord is in Tirukkurukūr
where mansions rise like jewelled mountains
why seek another?

IV.10.2 He made you and the gods you seek,
Ādippirāṉ of endless fame lovingly dwells
in his temple in Tirukkurukūr, city of soaring mansions.
People, sing its praise, dance, spread the word,
get yourself there.

IV.10.3 He made these gods these many worlds, then quickly
swallowed hid spewed crossed split all of it.
You see this but don't understand.
He's in Tirukkurukūr where the gods bow in worship.
There's no god but him, the highest one. Speak.

IV.10.4 He alone is master of Śivaṉ and Brahmā, and
all these gods of whom you speak.
You know the story of the skull, right?
Ilaṅkiyar, why speak uselessly about the god
in lovely Tirukkurukūr encircled by mighty walls?

IV.10.5 You folks with your Liṅga texts, you Jains
and Buddhists argue fiercely, when he's all your gods.
You see the radiant god in Tirukkurukūr
where red paddy arcs like fans
It's no lie. Praise him.

IV.10.6 You praise these other gods, and he still
teaches you something. If release was for everyone,
no one would be left in the world. He's in Tirukkurukūr
where red rice and lotuses rise from the muck.
You know his mysterious ways. Run to him.

IV.10.7 You run, birth after birth, sing and dance
honour other gods, follow many paths.
The primordial god who flies the eagle-banner
is in Tirukkurukūr praised by celestials
Become his now.

IV.10.8 When Mārkaṇḍeyaṉ took refuge with the naked god,
and lived, that was in fact Nārāyaṇaṉ's grace.
When Ādippirāṉ is in Tirukkurukūr
bordered by flowers white as cranes
how can you speak of other gods?

IV.10.9 Even the six paths and every other way
find him difficult to know, impossible to see.
He's Ādippirāṉ and he's in Tirukkurukūr
encircled by beautiful dense fields.
If you want to live take him deep inside you.

IV.10.10 Inside him, within his faultless form
is every god every world everything.
The pot-tossing acrobat, that tiny ascetic dwells
in Tirukkurukūr amidst fields of red rice and sugar cane.
Serve him alone. It's the only thing.

IV.10.11 Māraṉ Śaṭhakōpaṉ from Kurukūr
who wears a garland of fragrant makiḻ flowers
sang with love these ten verses from a thousand
on the one who rules, him who holds the disc.
Those who learn them reach Vaikuṇṭha, never to return.

The Fifth Hundred

Tiruvāymoḻi V.1 (443–453)
kaiyār cakkarattu

V.1.1 'My dark jewel holding the precious disc' I lied
again and again while still in love with other things
I wandered everywhere, somehow found the truth.
Who would reject your care, Kaṇṇā?
You can't leave me now.

V.1.2 'You slipped between the great trees, my flawless jewel
my sweet sweet honey' I said, praising a few of his deeds,
and he became me, my great lord himself
the sky this great earth everything
is inside me.

V.1.3 Something else was inside me, I still uttered sham words
'Generous one brilliant as a gem' thinking to deceive you.
I turned from my cunning mind. I saw you and lived,
Lord reclining on the ocean,
what's left for me but you?

V.1.4 'What do I have but you' I say such things but can't wrest
my cunning mind, control my tears, turn my heart to you
move closer to you. It's up to you to wipe the filth
off me, call me to you beloved
my only Kaṇṇaṉ.

V.1.5 Kaṇṇaṉ, master, dark jewel of the gods, sweet nectar
I reach you, yet remain far away. You've stranded me
in a body tied down by the hard cords of my actions

you patched up my wounds, hid them
then simply cast me out.

V.1.6 It's done, repeated births into a body bound by fierce fate
I've seen your four broad shoulders your red lips your eyes
bright as lotus, your beautiful hand holding the disc
that turns the law. I've seen your dark body
master, I've seen you at last.

V.1.7 The master, the one with the disc, where is he? Who am I?
'You stopped the elephant's suffering' I said arms raised,
I loved him and my lord encompassed me. See, even if
your wickedness is great, when it's your time
it's time.

V.1.8 The gods in heaven, the gods on earth worship him,
now Māl has settled into my mind. He's become
women with lovely eyes, great wealth, children
my honoured mother and my father,
he alone is all of this.

V.1.9 'Who'll be my friend' I asked sinking like a storm-tossed ship
in the sea of birth. I shivered. He came then a glorious form
holding in his hands the sacred disc and conch
'Come, come' he called to give me a gift
and joined himself to me.

V.1.10 I said he has me, he rules me. Instantly joyous he came to me
himself to become me completely, to give me this sweet gift.
Fish turtle man-lion dwarf wild pig Kalki

still to come, he's all of this, the only one
dark as storm clouds.

V.1.11 Those who recite as food these ten verses from a thousand
in splendid Tamiḻ by Śaṭhakōpaṉ of Kurukūr of well-tilled fields
on Kaṇṇaṉ, dark as storm clouds and eyes bright as lotus,
they will shelter at his feet and
will flourish there.

Tiruvāymoḻi V.2 (454–464)
polika polika

V.2.1 Woohoo, the curse of life is finished, hell is crushed
there's nothing left for Yama, the age of Kali ends
All his people are in this world: him dark as the ocean.
We've seen them singing dancing wandering everywhere.

V.2.2 We've seen, we've seen at last what's sweet to our eyes
friends, let's keep praying, let's make some noise
Mādhavaṉ who loves cool sweet tuḷasi, his people are in this world
We've seen them singing dancing wandering everywhere.

V.2.3 The encroaching age of Kali ends, the gods descend
the great golden age returns, a flood of joy spreads
him dark as storm clouds, dark as the sea, his people are in this world
singing crowding everywhere, making every place their own.

V.2.4 As if to root out every other religion in every place,
the great lord asleep on the vast sea, his people come
to sleep stay move sing songs of many kinds.
They walk fly dance. See all the plays they stage.

V.2.5 I see only one thing. The one in Vaikuṇṭha, his people
are everywhere in this world. Folks, there's no doubt
that if you're demon or monster, there's no escape,
they'll kill you and overturn this dread age.

V.2.6 Illness hate hunger all manner of evil kill life, feed on it
The lord with a disc, his people want only to end them
They spread through the earth singing leaping dancing
Steady your mind, friends, worship him and live.

V.2.7 See, the gods you've placed in your mind aid you
only by his leave. Mārkaṇḍeyaṉ is your example.
Don't let your mind become clouded. There's no god but Kaṇṇaṉ.
All these forms are his. Worship him alone.

V.2.8 He eats everything you give to these other gods.
He is the other gods. He is their king, him with Śrī on his chest.
His people without malice fill the world with song.
Bow to them, join them and find release.

V.2.9 Join in worship find release. People with the Veda
on their lips, who never falter from the path of wisdom
fill the world. They grow close to Acyutaṉ, adorn him
with flowers fragrance flames sandal water.

V.2.10 Through all the worlds the naked god, Ayaṉ,
Indraṉ and the gods praise Kaṇṇaṉ alone. Friends
if you join all the gods everywhere who worship him,
you'll reduce the age of Kali to nothing.

V.2.11 The ten verses from the famous thousand
by Kārimāṟaṉ Śaṭhakōpaṉ of Kurukūr, city of fields,

on the kind lord, destroyer of the Kali age, a radiant light,
mysterious Kaṇṇaṉ, will cut through the faults within you.

Tiruvāymoḻi V.3 (465–475)
mācaṟu cōti

V.3.1 I wanted him
flawless light-red lips great mountain-like form
perfect one who shreds desire, primordial lord.
Can you count the days
since I grew pale and lost my mind?
Friend, what do I care for village gossip?

V.3.2 Friend, what do I care for village gossip?
What can it do? My lord with eyes bright as lotus
has claimed me.
Now I've lost my lustre
my body is thin, my red lips are pale
my dark eyes have lost their light.

V.3.3 He shattered the cart with his feet
He suckled at her poisoned breast
He fills me.
I repeat his name, only his name
nothing else all day
Dear friend, what do I care for village gossip?

V.3.4 Village gossip is the manure
my mother's words water
In the field of my heart he planted a seed
grew a love larger than the sea

Kaṇṇaṉ dark as storm clouds
Friend tell me, is he cruel?

V.3.5 Cruel fierce lofty Māl
holds the earth under his feet
He's mysterious, impossible to know
still my pitiless heart wants
only him.
Gentle friend, what will mother do?

V.3.6 What will mother do?
What will the village say?
Friend, there's no hope for me
the lord of gods, king of fine Dvārakā,
Vāsudevaṉ, brilliant as a gem
has caught me in his net.

V.3.7 He caught me in his net, then
summoned my heart to him,
the lord asleep on the ocean, him who holds the disc.
Beautiful friend
Will I ever see him with these eyes?
Will I ever bow before him in front of these women?

V.3.8 He suckled the demon's breast,
shattered the cart, split the trees,
ripped the bird, killed the elephant.
He has a bright smile and lips red as toṇṭai fruit.
Friend, when will I reach him
and shame these women?

V.3.9 He stole my shyness, called my heart to him
Then went off to rule the gods in heaven
I'll declare our love to the whole world
I'll bend stalks of palm into a horse
and ride the maṭal.
Friend, I swear.

V.3.10 I'll ride the maṭal,
I'll be shameless in every street
Tongues will wag, women will heap abuse
the city will clamour, but
I'll be wearing the cool tuḷasi of the lord
who holds the disc in his beautiful hand.

V.3.11 In these ten verses from a thousand set in antāti
Śaṭhakōpaṉ of Kurukūr, city of lush gardens,
sang about Kaṇṇaṉ dark as the roaring sea
Those who learn them well
will find Vaikuṇṭha
in every city.

Tiruvāymoḻi V.4 (476–486)
ūr ellām tuñci

V.4.1 The city slumbers, the world turns black
the waters still, a single long night stretches
He swallowed the earth, our lord who lies
on his serpent does not come.
My misfortune grows
Who can save my life now?

V.4.2 Who can save my life now?
The deep sea the earth the sky disappear
under a great mercurial night, long and fierce,
and bright beautiful Kaṇṇaṉ does not come.
Such is my misfortune, heart,
that even you aren't with me.

V.4.3 Heart, even you aren't with me
time is still, the long night an aeon
Kākuttaṉ with his fierce frightening bow
does not come.
How do I end this life?
It's my misfortune that I've been born
a woman.

V.4.4 'I cannot witness these women suffer'
says the bright sun and hides.
He measured this world, my dark bull
with large dark eyes and lush red lips.
He does not come, so who's to cure me
of this grand disease of the mind?

V.4.5 Who cares for me? No one asks about me
not my friends, not my mothers
sound asleep through the long night.
Kaṇṇaṉ, dark as storm clouds does not come
My misfortune is such
my name will endure even after death.

V.4.6 This lovesickness is an ambush,
a great torment to my heart
the night stretching to an aeon is before me

hiding everything, I am blind.
My eternal lord with his disc does not come
Now who here can protect this long life of mine?

V.4.7 Who here can protect me? The night is dense
a fine powder of black, an endless aeon, it goes on and on.
With his spotless white conch and his disc
he does not appear,
my misfortune scorches like fire
what can I do?

V.4.8 What can I do?
One night multiplies into seven aeons,
it haunts me, whittles my life.
My Kaṇṇaṉ who wields the disc does not come
the cool breeze burns
worse than the fiercest fire.

V.4.9 Worse than the fiercest fire
is the fine powdered darkness of night
the tall chariot of the beautiful sun doesn't appear,
my beloved, his eyes bright as lotus-blooms, does not come
Who can end my heart's grief?
I dissolve to nothing.

V.4.10 I dissolve to nothing, the wide sky too dissolves
drenching the night
The one who long ago came to measure worlds
won't come now
No one says this, not once.
They just sleep.

V.4.11 The great lord's yoga is like sleep
Śaṭhakōpan̲ of Kurukūr with its fine gardens
sang these ten verses
from a resplendent antāti set of thousand
Sing these and reach Vaikuṇṭha
How can you not?

Tiruvāymoḻi V.5 (487–497)
eṅṅkan̲ēyō

V.5.1 Mothers, why do you scold me?
I saw beautiful Tirukkuṟuṅkuṭi Nambi.
Now my heart can only follow
his conch his disc,
his lovely lotus eyes,
his lush red lips.

V.5.2 See through my heart's eyes,
don't scold me.
I saw the lord of Tirukkuṟuṅkuṭi, city of cool groves.
Now his bright thread, his earrings,
the mark on his chest, his four broad arms,
are everywhere.

V.5.3 Mothers, how you scold me
'She just stands there, she wanders, she fades'
I saw Tirukkuṟuṅkuṭi Nambi in his city of palaces tall as hills.
Now his mighty bow, his mace, his sword, his conch
are everywhere,
in my eyes, in my very heart without end.

V.5.4 Tears fall from my eyes without end
and you scold me, mother
I saw the lord of Tirukkuṟuṅkuṭi, city of honey-rich gardens.
Despite my wickedness
his cool garlands, his sweet tuḷasi, his crown of gold
his form, his silks have come close to me

V.5.5 'Her gaze fixed, standing stock-still, fading'
mothers, this is how you scold me
I saw glorious Tirukkuṟuṅkuṭi Nambi.
Now his lips red as toṇṭai fruit, his slender brows,
his lovely lotus eyes are within me,
touching the breath of this little wretch.

V.5.6 'She's a disgrace to our family' mother says
and makes me hide
I saw the lord of Tirukkuṟuṅkuṭi, city of cool shaded groves.
Now his slender nose, his lotus eyes, his red lips
his dark body, his four great arms
fill my heart.

V.5.7 'She brings great shame to our family' says mother
and makes me hide.
I saw the lord of glorious Tirukkuṟuṅkuṭi.
Now his radiant form a flood of light
fills me. Disc in hand
he lives within me.

V.5.8 'She buries her face in her hands, fades' mother says
and scolds me

I saw the lord of Tirukkuṟuṅkuṭi, city of mansions.
Now his lotus-bright eyes his hips his waist
thick dark curls brushing his broad shoulders his body
appear before me.

V.5.9 'You stick out too much' my friends say
joining mother to scold me
I saw the lord of Tirukkuṟuṅkuṭi, city of mansions.
Now his tall crown his every jewel are before me
He's sugar milk nectar
that will not leave my heart.

V.5.10 'Her impossible love grows every day' mother says
and makes me hide.
I saw glorious Tirukkuṟuṅkuṭi Nambi
Now his form a flood of light worshipped by the gods
has risen in my heart.
It's beyond all understanding.

V.5.11 Those who learn these ten about Tirukkuṟuṅkuṭi
from the thousand sung by Śaṭhakōpaṉ of Kurukūr
who sought out fine flowers and cried out
for the lord difficult to know, for the one who holds the disc.
Master them and become Vaiṣṇavas
on this earth surrounded by deep ocean.

Tiruvāymoḻi V.6 (498–508)
kaṭal ñālam ceytēṉum

V.6.1 I made oceans, I made this earth
I became oceans, I became this earth

I took oceans, I took this earth
I split oceans, I split this earth
I swallowed oceans, I swallowed this earth.
Has the lord of oceans, lord of this earth
taken her?
What else do I say about my daughter
who wanders saying such things?

V.6.2 I am beyond the limits of learning
I am all that is learned
I alone create learning
I alone am its end
I alone am its very essence.
Has the lord of wisdom entered her?
Wise friends, what can I say
about my daughter who claims to know
everything?

V.6.3 I am all the land you see
the sky you see, I am that too
I am the hot flame, this wind that blows
and all the ocean, I am.
Has the one dark as the ocean
the one who sees all entered her?
You stand as witness in this world
seeing everything my girl does
what shall I say?

V.6.4 I am all that is done now
I am all that remains undone
what has been done, I am that as well

the fruit of all that doing is mine
and I make the actors too.
Has the precious lord
with lotus eyes entered her?
what else can I say to this wise world
about my gentle daughter with berry-red lips?

V.6.5 I guard the world, count on me
I lifted the mountain, count on me
I vanquished demons, count on me
I protected the five, churned the ocean
count on me
Has the lord dark as the ocean taken over?
What shall I say to this unforgiving world
about all that my daughter
has attained?

V.6.6 I alone lifted a mountain dense with bamboo
I killed the herd of bulls and
I grazed little calves
I guarded cows and led the cowherds.
Has the king of gods claimed her?
What's left to say about my daughter
with eyes bright as spears?
What's left to say that your sharp spear-like eyes
haven't seen?

V.6.7 I have no kin
everyone here is my kin
I make my own kin
I destroy them too

I am the bond between kin.
Has the mysterious lord
who has no kin claimed her?
What shall I say to you, friends,
about the things my innocent girl utters?

V.6.8 You speak of a three-eyed god. I am him.
You speak of a god who looks in four directions. I am him.
You speak of the immortals. I am them.
You speak of their king. I am him.
You speak of sages. I am them too.
Has the one dark as storm clouds
claimed my daughter?
What shall I say to you who speak too much
about my daughter, fragile as a vine?

V.6.9 I don't act in terrible ways
I become terrible acts
I do terrible things
but I end them too
I killed the terrible lord of Laṅkā.
Has the lord who rides the fierce bird
claimed her?
People who live in this terrible world
what shall I say about my beautiful girl?

V.6.10 I am beautiful heaven
I am hell devoid of beauty
I am bright beautiful mokṣam
and all these beautiful lives too
I am the beautiful singular root.
Has the one dark as storm clouds claimed her?

People of this beautiful world tell me
what shall I say about my daughter
with beautiful flowers in her hair?

V.6.11 Master these ten from the garland of thousand
woven in humble service by Śaṭhakōpaṉ of Kurukūr
from the rich Vaḻuti lands
about the husband
of the goddess with fragrant hair,
the goddess of the earth
and the tender sprout of the cowherd clan, and
gain the great wealth to serve
Tirumāl's devotees even in this world.

Tiruvāymoḻi V.7 (509–519)
nōṟṟa nōṉpu ilēṉ

V.7.1 I've observed no vows, I've no subtle wisdom, still
I can't bear to leave you for even a moment.
Lord asleep on the serpent, my father
who abides in the city of Śrīvaramaṅgala
with its fields of red paddy and blossoming lotus,
I am nothing without you.

V.7.2 I am not there, I am not here
mad to see you, I am nowhere.
Lord who destroyed Laṅkā, you are
in Śrīvaramaṅgala, city of mansions limned by the moon
You who hold conch and disc
I am alone, give me grace.

V.7.3 Your banner bears Garuḍa, your hand holds the disc
my lord dark as storm clouds, I was without meaning,
you gave me meaning, then claimed me as your own.
You favour the many who've mastered the four Veda,
live among them in Śrīvaramaṅgala.
I don't know how to repay you.

V.7.4 For the five you staged a war, razed
the hostile armies of the hundred, reduced them to ash
My father, lord who dug up the earth
you abide in Śrīvaramaṅgala where the wise
perform Vedic sacrifices without pause
Where shall I call out to reach you?

V.7.5 You're in all things, even among enemies
lord of dark body, lord of tricks,
may I call out to reach you?
You live in Śrīvaramaṅgala, where good men worship you,
their sacrifices always complete
I too have seen this.

V.7.6 My father who became a pig to dig up the earth
Kaṇṇā, master who rules me, lord of heaven
brilliant gem of light worshipped by the people
of Śrīvaramaṅgala with its cool honey-sweet groves,
great towering mountain, lord of Vāṉamāmalai,
come grace me, so I too can worship you.

V.7.7 You gave me grace, made my heart your home
lord of celestials, primordial mother, father of the world
who swallowed seven worlds

are praised without end in Śrīvaramaṅgala
by good men who never end their Vedic sacrifices
Don't abandon me.

V.7.8 I know well these five terrible senses
that keep one from you. But you pushed even me
into this dense mud, lord who abides
in Śrīvaramaṅgala with its tall dazzling mansions,
my father who ripped the bird,
you are difficult to enter.

V.7.9 You ripped the bird, squeezed past the maruta trees,
killed seven bulls, my cunning mysterious lord,
my dark glowing flame, you're within cool Śrīvaramaṅgala
where the wise have mastered the four Veda
My father, lift me up
give me grace.

V.7.10 You showed me the way, offered your feet as refuge
I have nothing to offer in return
my life is yours.
You're in Śrīvaramaṅgala, city of sugar cane and paddy
lord crowned in wreaths of sweet tuḷasi
lord of celestials, Deyvanāyakaṉ.

V.7.11 Those who sing these ten verses on Śrīvaramaṅgala
from the thousand by Śaṭhakōpaṉ of Kurukūr,
city of gardens bursting with flowers,
praising the feet of Deyvanāyakaṉ
Nāraṇaṉ, Trivikramaṉ
will be as nectar to the gods.

Tiruvāymoḻi V.8 (520–530)
ārā amutē

V.8.1 Sweet nectar I can't get enough of,
you make my body soften in love,
dissolve, flow like water
Neṭumāl, I've seen you reclining in Kuṭantai
with its arcs of ripe paddy, its rushing waters
I've seen your dazzling form,
lord, you're mine.

V.8.2 My lord, my lord of pure white, you rule me
taking any form at will, my beautiful dark bull
you're in Kuṭantai with its rushing waters
its broad red lotuses that bloom like eyes
your eyes large and lovely as lotuses
closed in sleep.
How shall I endure?

V.8.3 How shall I endure?
Who's to protect me?
What are you doing to me?
I've no one but you.
You're asleep in Kuṭantai with its strong firm walls
let me spend my remaining days at your feet
Make it so.

V.8.4 Your glory goes beyond
what the wise can see
Limitless singular lord
who contains the worlds

You're asleep in Kuṭantai where the good live
I gaze up at the sky seeking you
I weep, I pray.

V.8.5 I'll weep I'll pray I'll dance
I'll sing I'll cry I'll search.
I drop my head in shame
bound by my wretched past,
lord asleep in Kuṭantai with its rich fields
lord with bright lotus eyes
show me how to reach your feet.

V.8.6 Cut through my wicked past
show me how to reach your feet
I cower in this bottomless pit
How much longer will you keep me from you?
King of celestials, sweet music, my nectar,
fruit of all knowledge, bull among lions.
You're asleep in Kuṭantai of ancient fame.

V.8.7 Bull among lions, my precious golden flame
dark storm cloud, bright eyes, mountain of fiery coral
four-armed lord, my father
your grace binds me, your servant forever
Tirumāl of Kuṭantai
I can bear no more.
Give me refuge now. Rid me of my birth.

V.8.8 End my sorrows, don't end it
but I have no one else who can end it

You wield the curved disc as a weapon,
great mysterious lord asleep in Kuṭantai
When my body grows weak
when life slips away
let me hold your feet.

V.8.9 You made me want you, then
placed me at your feet.
My lord, master to the master of eternal immortals,
great primordial being asleep in Kuṭantai,
rich in jewels casting their light everywhere
lord praised by this eternal world
Come, let me see you.

V.8.10 My mysterious lord of many forms
and no form, imperishable
nectar I can't get enough of,
sweet to my spirit, sweetening my life
You've chosen Kuṭantai as your city
You ruled me to end deeds that never end
So why am I still wandering?

V.8.11 Those who stop babbling and master
these ten verses from the thousand
sweeter than a flute's melody
sung by Śaṭhakōpaṉ of Kurukūr
whose only refuge is the feet of the one
who nursed at the demon's breast, drained her of life,
will be adored by lovely doe-eyed women.

Tiruvāymoḻi V.9 (531–541)
māṉēy nōkku

V.9.1 Gentle doe-eyed women, look at me
waste away day by day. I am doomed.
When will I reach the feet of the king
who dwells in Tiruvallavāḻ
with its kamuku trees that touch the sky
and its air sweet with honey and jasmine?
I am his.

V.9.2 Friends, why do you tease me so?
He stands in Tiruvallavāl,
a city to delight the heart,
where the gentle breeze scents the air
with golden puṉṉai, makiḻ and mātavi
When will the dust of his feet touch us
We are his.

V.9.3 Friends adorned in flowers, look at me
grief makes me thin
Will I ever gaze without cease
upon the feet of the lord
who is in cool Tiruvallavāḻ
where the Veda resound like the sea
where fragrant smoke from sacrifices fills the air?

V.9.4 Friends, why torment me?
He's in cool Tiruvallavāḻ
where slender green trees of
kamuku jackfruit coconut
shade the terraces of tall mansions

Our lord reclines on the snake that spits poison
My life is his.

V.9.5 My dear friends, he's in cool Tiruvallavāḻ
where smoke from the sacrifices of the virtuous
rises to veil the sky.
Sweet as sugar, sweet as fruit, sweeter than nectar,
he stole my happiness
When will my eyes see
that radiant light?

V.9.6 Women with lips red as fruit, tell me,
when will I see him? I am wrecked.
He's in Tiruvallavāḻ
where the breeze carries the song of bees
and the groves are dense with trees.
When will I see the lotus feet
of the tiny youth, my Kōlappirāṉ.

V.9.7 Beautiful friends,
he's the master of Tiruvallavāḻ
where lotuses rise from large deep pools
to kiss the bright faces of beautiful women.
When will I worship at the feet
of our lord who ate the world
When will I shower them with flowers every day?

V.9.8 Wise friends, our lord remains
in Tiruvallavāḻ, where the sugar cane sways gently
the rice ripens to gold and pools of flowers
are everywhere.
The lord who measured worlds

when will I worship his feet
when will I stay there forever?

V.9.9 Will I ever again
fill the empty circle of my bangles?
The lord with that swift cutting disc
is in Tiruvallavāḻ
where bees in cool shaded gardens drink honey
and make music sweet as the harp.
Will I ever grow full with his ancient grace?

V.9.10 Friends when will our good deeds
and his ancient grace let us sing
the many names of Nārāyaṇa?
Our great lord is in the sacred city of Tiruvallavāḻ
where earth and heaven worship him
to receive his grace,
where the virtue of thousands is firm.

V.9.11 Those who recite these ten verses
in praise of sacred Tiruvallavāḻ
from the profound thousand spoken
by Śaṭhakōpaṉ of blessed Kurukūr
about the feet of the lord
with a thousand names,
will prosper even in this world.

Tiruvāymoḻi V.10 (542–552)
piṟanta vāṟum

V.10.1 Your mysterious ways:
how you were born, how you grew,

your feats in the great war, your counsel to the brave five,
these have pierced my very core
my breath dissolves, I am devoured.
Bright flame, when will I reach you?

V.10.2 You tamed bulls for your woman
tore apart the jaws of a monstrous horse
danced the kuravai with lovely cowherd women
Can I describe your deeds in this way or that?
You dissolve me, primordial cause of this ancient world
when will I join you?

V.10.3 The demon came with flowers in her hair
still you nursed at her breast, though just a child,
with valour you kicked the cart with your little feet
but when you ate butter, saw your mother with stick in hand,
tears flowed from your eyes, and you were afraid.
I think of these things and dissolve.

V.10.4 You snuck into the city in disguise
entered the demons, tore them apart, consumed their life
The one with a river in his matted hair
is not apart from you, shines brilliantly from within you
These things have entered me, melt me
I am consumed.

V.10.5 You ate the food meant for the king of celestials
then lifted a massive mountain as shelter from the rains
You created ate spat out crossed dug married the earth
I think about your mysterious ways
and my heart grows soft
like wax in a flame.

V.10.6 It's impossible to understand you:
Standing seated reclining
your countless forms your wonders
I think only of you, yet you elude me
Tell this wretch of a single good path,
brilliant flame that consumes the world.

V.10.7 Brilliant flame within deep darkness,
truth within untruth, these are the ways
you come before me, dissolve me
I lose myself thinking of this, my dark jewel
let my eyes gaze on your lovely form
for just a single day.

V.10.8 Look how you slept, how you created the world,
hidden within the god who faces four directions
and rises from your navel, look how you rule.
When I hear these things, my heart dissolves
tears spill like waterfalls
What should I do?

V.10.9 Look how you begged three steps,
then in two strides took the deep sea the earth the heavens.
I hear these important things and
my heart dissolves into you
I am wretched
but when will I join you?

V.10.10 Look how you churned the ocean
fed the nectar to the gods leaving out the demons
what tricks you play.

These things enter my breath, melt me consume me
Tell me how to reach you,
lord asleep on the venomous serpent.

V.10.11 Those who master these ten
from the thousand in a hundred antāti
by Māṟaṉ Śaṭhakōpaṉ of Kurukūr,
who thinks only of our lord's feet as his refuge,
him asleep on the snake,
they will attain the bliss of Vaikuṇṭha.

The Sixth Hundred

Tiruvāymoḻi VI.1 (553–563)
vaikal pūṅkaḻivāy

VI.1.1 Flocks of cranes feeding in flower-filled marshes,
he's in Tiruvaṇvaṇḍūr where the rice grows tall
When you see my great lord
with a disc in his hand and lips red as a fruit
bow before him and speak
of this wretch's love.

VI.1.2 Black cranes seeking food with your mates,
he's in Tiruvaṇvaṇḍūr,
filled with the sounds of Vedic sacrifices
When you see our king, our great lord
who swallowed the whole world
touch his feet and speak well of me.

VI.1.3 Birds flocking to the fields,
he's in prosperous Tiruvaṇvaṇḍūr
When you see the great lord
with the whirling disc and berry-red lips
bow to him humbly
speak of my suffering.

VI.1.4 Innocent geese, drowning in joy unmarred by pain,
he's in cool Tiruvaṇvaṇḍūr
where the Veda echo without cease
When you see Neṭumāl,
Kaṇṇaṉ dark as the sea, tell him
she melts for you.

VI.1.5 Innocent geese, you quarrel you reconcile,
he's in Tiruvaṇvaṇḍūr
where conches cover its sandy shores
When you see our great lord
crowned with cool tuḷasi,
join your hands and praise him for me.

VI.1.6 Sweet kuyil in the puṉṉai tree, I beg you,
he's in Tiruvaṇvaṇḍūr
with its marshes of leaping fish
When you see the great lord, king of immortals
with the powerful disc in his hand,
demand an answer to end this madness.

VI.1.7 Gleaming parrot, just this once go,
speak to him for me
He's in Tiruvaṇvaṇḍūr
with its dense flower groves and red sand.
Dark body red lips radiant eyes hands feet
a shining disc and conch. This is how he is.

VI.1.8 Little bird, go see him then return to me
He's in cool Tiruvaṇvaṇḍūr, city of groves
Large eyes cool and bright as lotuses
a tall crown four broad shoulders
a body like a great dark storm cloud.
This is how he is.

VI.1.9 Geese resting among the lotuses,
worship his feet
he's in Tiruvaṇvaṇḍūr, where conches sound at dawn

When you see fierce mysterious Kaṇṇaṉ, that Neṭumāl,
tell him of this wretch, speak to him in secret
of my pitiful state.

VI.1.10 Great swarm of bees, you're different
He's in Tiruvaṇvaṇḍūr
on the cool Pampā's northern bank,
him who turned to ash the city walls
of the demon peerless in war.
When you see that great bull, tell him I exist.

VI.1.11 Śaṭhakōpaṉ of Kurukūr sang a musical thousand,
of which these ten verses are on Tiruvaṇvaṇḍūr
and the feet of the cunning youth
who wears a thread like lightning
who came and took the world.
Those who sing these well will win the love of women.

Tiruvāymoḻi VI.2 (564–574)
miṉṉiṭai maṭavārkaḷ

VI.2.1 Women with waists thin as lightning
wear your grace. I worry.
Mysterious one who scorched Laṅkā
I know your tricks, so what?
Return my ball and my anklets, and
leave.

VI.2.2 Leave. Your bright lotus eyes
your red lips your smile hurt us.
Is this the fruit of our penance?

Go where women lovely as peacocks
are fit for your love. Leave your herds
and go play your flute for them.

VI.2.3 Leave. Go feed your lies
to someone more gullible,
your lips, your eyes are dangerous
Who are these women with shoulders slim as bamboo?
Lord who churned the vast deep sea,
who are these women who can win your love?

VI.2.4 Long ago you ate the seven worlds, then
lay upon a long banyan leaf
When celestials can't fathom your mysteries,
how can we? Go graze your cows
where women with eyes sharp as spears play.
Don't bother us.

VI.2.5 Don't blabber on. All of earth and heaven
know your lies well.
Master of that ancient dazzling disc,
let me tell you something,
as sweet-voiced women touched by your love
waste away, don't come coo at our birds.

VI.2.6 It's useless to sidle up, take our dolls,
flirt. We're used to it all, so
what's the use of such special favour?
In all the worlds are many beautiful women
fit to be your wife, don't cross into our group.
It's childish, even for you.

VI.2.7 You steal our dolls right from our hands
This isn't right. You ate the sea and earth,
pure one so far above us, a wrong is still a wrong
even for you. Don't utter such lies, don't toy with us
When our brothers hear this, they won't care
about right and wrong. They'll just come to fight.

VI.2.8 You entwine everything and everyone,
divided different yet one, nothing escapes.
Your glory is limitless, you are radiant wisdom
When our friends call us to play,
you scorch us, stop us
What will our enemies say?

VI.2.9 Our hearts dissolve in joy,
we're caught in your lotus-bright gaze
A smile lighting your face, you watched us
making our sandcastles, our little bits of food,
then you came and stomped on it all.
This isn't fair.

VI.2.10 You wear a glorious crown,
your axe cut down generations of kings,
long ago you created this wide world, and now
you're among cowherds to guide their way.
Dark jewel radiant flame, we're cowherd women,
still you make us suffer.

VI.2.11 Śaṭhakōpaṉ of Kurukūr praised
in a garland of thousand Tamiḻ verses
that dancing lord who cried

when scolded by his mother for eating butter.
Those who sing these ten
will not know poverty.

Tiruvāymoḻi VI.3 (575–585)
nalkuravum celvum

VI.3.1 He is poverty and wealth, hell and heaven
He is enmity and friendship, poison and nectar.
The great lord of many forms rules me
I saw him in Tiruviṇṇakar where the wealthy thrive.

VI.3.2 The joys and sorrows we know, confusion and clarity,
punishment and pardon, heat and shade, he's all this.
The great lord so difficult to know is in Tiruviṇṇakar
that fine city circled by clear waters.

VI.3.3 He's city and village, wisdom and idiocy,
incomparable light and darkness, he is earth and sky.
The lord is in Tiruviṇṇakar city of tall mansions
his blazing glory is the only blessing one needs.

VI.3.4 He is virtue vice union separation memory
forgetfulness truth illusion, and he's none of these.
Kaṇṇaṉ is in Tiruviṇṇakar with its strong palaces
find his sweet grace there, this is his way.

VI.3.5 He is deceit and honesty, both black and white
falsity and truth, youth and age, new and old.
The lord is in Tiruviṇṇakar surrounded by strong walls
see the gardens he laid, these three worlds.

VI.3.6 He's the three worlds and not them. Joy and rage,
Śrī and her elder sister, fame and shame, he's those too.
The lord in Tiruviṇṇakar, praised by the gods,
is the matchless flame that glows in my heart.

VI.3.7 He is both matchless flame and filthy body
He's cunning, hiding then revealing himself.
The gods bow before the lord in Tiruviṇṇakar
whose feet fulfil every desire. They are the only refuge.

VI.3.8 He's firm refuge for the gods, dread death for demons
He shelters the worlds beneath his feet, and he does not.
The lord is in Tiruviṇṇakar, shelter of the south
He's my refuge, my Kaṇṇaṉ, father who rules me.

VI.3.9 He's my father, foster mother, woman who birthed me
My father precious as gold, as gems as pearls is the father
in Tiruviṇṇakar encircled by walls of gold, Oppārillappaṉ,
that peerless father, shelters me beneath his feet.

VI.3.10 He's shade and sunshine, small and grand, short and tall
all that moves, all that's still, he's all this and none of it.
The lord is in Tiruviṇṇakar with its sweetly humming bees
his feet alone protect us. Know this.

VI.3.11 'Watch' he said and towered over the world.
Commanded by him, Śaṭhakōpaṉ of Kurukūr sang
a thousand verses. Those who master these ten
on Tiruviṇṇakar will teach even the gods.

Tiruvāymoḻi VI.4 (586–596)
kuravai āycciyarōṭu

VI.4.1 He danced the kuravai with cowherd women,
raised the mountain, crushed the snake
living in the raging waters.
Night and day I sing of the countless mysteries
of the one asleep on the serpent
What do I lack?

VI.4.2 He played sweet songs on the flute,
grazed his herd, embraced Piṉṉai,
his woman of shining eyes and fragrant hair.
I think of all my beautiful mysterious lord does
time passes, my heart melts
What world can equal this?

VI.4.3 He killed the matchless wrestlers,
grazed his herd, crushed the elephant
tall as a mountain.
I spend my time thinking of all he's done
my lord, a glorious light. I weep
What can hurt me now?

VI.4.4 He cried when his mother bound him
he killed the faithless woman who nursed him
he shattered the cart.
I think of all these deeds of the beautiful god of gods
my heart melts, time passes
What more do I need?

VI.4.5 When the pitiful gods begged him
he took birth in deep darkness, leaving
his mother weeping to enter the cowherd clan
to be nurtured in secret, plotting his tricks
he killed Kaṁsaṉ. I cry out these things
Can anything hurt me?

VI.4.6 He tore apart the hateful bird,
killed the humped bulls, felled the kuruntu trees
rising high above the groves, did so much more.
Night and day I sing of the mysterious ways
of my father who measured the wide worlds
Why should I despair?

VI.4.7 Out of kindness, he took birth
in this desperate filthy world of men,
took the form he chose, vented his fury.
I think only of my father's wondrous deeds
him adorned in fresh fragrant tuḷasi
Who can equal me?

VI.4.8 Amazed, the wide earth and heavens
watched the great war he staged
he cut Bāṇaṉ's thousand arms, did so many things.
My heart sees my father's wondrous ways
my mysterious lord who as a youth took the world
What can trouble me?

VI.4.9 He drove a chariot across seven swirling seas
seven mountains seven worlds to the worlds' end
a marvel among his many wondrous deeds.

My tongue sings of the ink-dark lord
with a conch in his left hand and a disc in his right
Who on this earth can harm me?

VI.4.10 To end the earth's heavy burden
he waged the great Bharata war, vanquished armies,
did so many wondrous things, then
entered his realm beyond the sky.
I've drawn close to that great light, I worship his feet
Who can rule me now?

VI.4.11 The master of seven worlds swallowed
those seven worlds, then spat them out
He became them, and wasn't them.
Learn these ten out of a flawless thousand sung
by Śaṭhakōpaṉ of Kurukūr praising Keśavaṉ's feet
and become perfect devotees.

Tiruvāymoḻi VI.5 (597–607)
tuvaḷil māmaṇi māṭam

VI.5.1 She prays to Tolaivillimaṅgalam
with its towering mansions shining like jewels.
Women, let her be, you don't care for her
She whispers, 'Spotless white conch disc lotus eyes'
She just stands there, tears
spilling from her shining eyes
filled to bursting with despair.

VI.5.2 You took her to Tolaivillimaṅgalam
bursting with the din of festivals, and
without a care you left her there,

this sweet-voiced soft-spoken girl
Dazed, she says 'Devapirāṉ, lord of gods'
her lips twist, tears fill her eyes
she softens breaks dissolves.

VI.5.3 You took her to Tolaivillimaṅgalam
city of gardens and rivers, and
without a care you left her there,
this girl of gentle words. Now she babbles
'He sleeps on an ocean, he measured worlds,
he grazed cows' as tears stream
from her long lovely eyes.

VI.5.4 She saw Tolaivillimaṅgalam
where the Veda thrives, and
lost all control went mad
Can't you see, friends?
She delights in saying 'Kaṇṇaṉ dark as the sea
is all there is to know' Devoid of modesty
her joy blooms inside, she melts away.

VI.5.5 You took her to Tolaivillimaṅgalam
and showed this pitiful girl
that blazing light, the lord with bright lotus eyes
From that moment, her eyes wept like clouds,
absorbed, her mind rests in him
she bows, and looks
only in his direction.

VI.5.6 Tolaivillimaṅgalam, everywhere you look
Sugar cane, tall ripening rice red lotuses
flourish along the northern bank of the Porunal

Friends, she saw this and looked
nowhere else, all day every day,
the only words on her lips
the name of him, luminous as a gem.

VI.5.7 Friends, our lovely peahen,
our little doe has slipped our grasp,
all she hears is Tolaivillimaṅgalam
Is this the fruit of her past or
his enchantment, the one dark as storm clouds?
She only wishes to speak
his signs and his names.

VI.5.8 On the Porunal's northern bank
is wealthy Tolaivillimaṅgalam, filled
with the sound of the perfect Veda, sacrifices
and lovely women. She bowed to him there.
From then until now she can only say
'lotus-eyed lord, Aravindalocaṉa'
She weeps melts dissolves.

VI.5.9 She suffers all day, her lips quiver,
tears drip from her eyes, and when she cries out
'Luminous gem' even the trees pity her.
When she learned he lives in Tolaivillimaṅgalam,
that one who ripped open the horse's jaws,
she pressed her palms together and
said only that city's name.

VI.5.10 Is she Piṉṉai, Bhū or Śrī born here?
It's a great mystery.

She calls out 'Neṭumāl' then stands there.
He's in Tolaivillimaṅgalam
she bows before that city,
wants only to hear its name
This is her only thought.

VI.5.11 For Śaṭhakōpaṉ of Kurukūr,
in thought word and deed, Devapirāṉ
the lord of gods is mother and father.
Those who master from his ageless thousand
these ten verses in perfect Tamiḻ
about Tolaivillimaṅgalam
will always serve Tirumāl.

Tiruvāymoḻi VI.6 (608–618)
mālukku vaiyam aḷanta

VI.6.1 My girl, her hair scented with flowers
has lost her conch bangles to Māl,
her beloved who measured worlds, him
dark as dark clouds, him
with eyes bright as lotuses.

VI.6.2 My girl has lost her lustre to him
who wields conch bow sword staff disc,
him with lips red and ripe as fruit, him
with lotus-bright eyes, him
crowned with garlands of honey-sweet tuḷasi.

VI.6.3 My girl with lustrous black hair
has lost her pride because of him

that dark one, the little thief
with a maw fit to swallow the wide world, him
who holds the whirling disc.

VI.6.4 My girl with gently curving hips
has lost all modesty because of him
who made mighty Brahmā, her beloved
who measured this prosperous world, the prince
who served as a messenger for kings.

VI.6.5 This girl precious as my eyes
has lost her chastity because of him
the highest one who taught the Veda, him
the Varāha who dug up the fertile earth, him
our lord of gods asleep on the clear ocean.

VI.6.6 My girl with brows that curve like bows
has lost her body to him
with arms like kalpaka trees, him crowned
in flowers that tower like mountains of gold, him
with hands that bloom like lotuses.

VI.6.7 My lovely girl has lost
her beauty because of him,
adorned in countless jewels, him
asleep on the hooded snake, Kaṇṇaṉ
whose hands and feet glow red.

VI.6.8 My girl with fragrant hair
has lost her beauty because of him
who shattered the kuruntu trees, him

who kicked the cart, the beloved lord
who sucked the demon's milk, made her a corpse.

VI.6.9 My girl, her breasts beautiful with jewels
has lost her radiance because of him,
the cunning little youth, him
who is a mountain of radiance, him
our Kākuttaṉ full of beauty.

VI.6.10 My virtuous girl has lost all
sense of propriety because of him
who wears a tall crown of tuḷasi, him
who locked arms with the wrestlers, him
of so many forms, that mysterious lord.

VI.6.11 Śaṭhakōpaṉ of lovely Kurukūr sang
these ten verses from a beautiful set of thousand
on the lord of Vēṅkaṭam, city of fine gardens
Those who master them
will know pleasure of celestials.

Tiruvāymoḻi VI.7 (619–629)
uṇṇuñ cōṟu

VI.7.1 Everything I eat drink taste is Kaṇṇaṉ,
she says this as her eyes fill with tears
She seeks the city he fills with his greatness,
my little fawn is in Tirukkōḷūr.

VI.7.2 Forgetting herself she cries out his names, his marks
makes cities, towns, the whole world do the same

Tell me cruel black birds, will she ever return
from Tirukkōḷūr with its fertile fields?

VI.7.3 Her black birds parrots balls pots baskets
call out Tirumāl's names, and now she's gone,
off to Tirukkōḷūr with its fertile fields
her lips quiver, her eyes rain tears. What can she do?

VI.7.4 What will they say, the village gossips,
that she's shameless or full of virtue?
My little fawn has gone off
to Tirukkōḷūr, that rich city of his.

VI.7.5 Weak with desire, with no interest in play,
my little goddess has gone to Tirumāl, to his Tirukkōḷūr
Is she soothed by his temple his lakes his gardens in bloom?
Is she happy?

VI.7.6 My little fawn is of no help to me
today she left for Tirukkōḷūr, jewel of the south
She gazes at her Tirumāl's lovely eyes, his red lips,
her long eyes fill with cool tears. She dissolves.

VI.7.7 Eyes filled with tears, heart bewitched
'Neṭumāl' she cries through the night and bright day.
Slowly she goes towards his wealthy Tirukkōḷūr
Will she reach?

VI.7.8 Can she reach Tirukkōḷūr, a hand on her frail waist,
with a heart full of love and eyes full of tears?
My girl abandoned me for Śrī's beloved,
my heart full of love dissolves.

VI.7.9 Saying 'Everything good is for my Kaṇṇaṉ'
my love-mad girl abandoned all this, went to Tirukkōḷūr
The village gossips, still she walks away
not thinking of me.

VI.7.10 Gods, what should I think? My little fawn's gone,
unable to live without him for an instant, him
who rules the world, the lord with lotus eyes
She's gone to his Tirukkōḷūr, uncaring of the family's shame.

VI.7.11 Those who recite these ten on Tirukkōḷūr
from the thousand verses by Śaṭhakōpaṉ of Kurukūr
who cried out for Madhusūdaṉaṉ, Vaittamānidhi,
that precious treasure, will rule this golden world.

Tiruvāymoḻi VI.8 (630–640)
poṉ ulaku āḷīrō

VI.8.1 Fine flocks of birds, you'll rule
this golden world, the whole earth if
you tell the one who created all these worlds
the one dark as storm clouds
the one who stole my well-being,
tell Kaṇṇaṉ of my wretched plight
I beg you.

VI.8.2 In front of women with eyes sharp as swords
I'll feed you sweet milky rice
from the palm of my hand
Parrots, now go to him
the one with berry-red lips, see him

the one with the disc in his hand, tell him
of my love and return to me.

VI.8.3 Come swarm around me, drawn
to the large bright flowers in my hair
your mouths brimming with sweet honey
from the cool tuḷasi he wears,
that lord who steered a mighty chariot
turned armies and horses to ash
for five brothers on a great battlefield.

VI.8.4 Bees nestled in my jasmine
when you next seek sweet honey
go find the king of celestials
crowned with garlands of nectar-rich tuḷasi
See him who deceived me,
left me wrecked.
Ask him if this is right.

VI.8.5 Parrots, I raised you
so listen to all I say.
A great tree of wishes with flashing eyes,
red lips, a body dark as storm clouds
swept in on an eagle, made off with my heart
Wherever he is, find him
ask him if this is right.

VI.8.6 A bright thread rests across his chest,
my Kaṇṇaṉ, my ink-dark lord
At his long slender feet is the cool tuḷasi
meant just for me.

I raised you, taught you words.
Now go, little black birds
repeat those very words to him.

VI.8.7 Dark as pūvai blooms, eyes bright as lotuses,
mysterious, in everything in everyone
is my lord with his disc, Madhusūdaṉaṉ
who ripped open the horse's mouth
Little dolls, take a message to him
I am wrecked, ask him
to end my sickness.

VI.8.8 I turn pale, fade
as the ages pass. How much longer?
Spotless white herons, be kind
One day when you see him
the king of celestials
his hair dark glossy perfect
Tell him 'She has eyes for no one but you.'

VI.8.9 This wretch has no one but you
to protect her. Great flocks of herons
skimming the waves in search of food
go see him, dark as storm clouds
king of celestials, my Kaṇṇaṉ
return to me with his reply, and
repeat it all day long.

VI.8.10 You're with your jewel-like beloveds
happily gliding among the flowers
O geese, go to him

who holds Śrī to his chest,
tell him 'See how she is'
tell him all about me in secret,
then return and repeat what he says.

VI.8.11 Śaṭhakōpaṉ of Kurukūr,
city encircled in fragrant flower gardens,
composed with thought and care
these ten verses from the thousand
on the feet of Madhusūda
Those who master them will dissolve
like soft fine sand in a spring.

Tiruvāymoḻi VI.9 (641–651)
nīrāy nilaṉāy

VI.9.1 You became water earth fire wind vast sky,
two brilliant orbs. You became Śivaṉ, Ayaṉ too.
I am wicked, still stand before me
with your disc and white conch
Come to me for a single day
so earth and heaven rejoice.

VI.9.2 Earth and heaven rejoiced when you came
as a tiny youth, showed your might and
took for yourself earth and heaven
Mysterious lord, let me close to you,
let me see you, let me dance in joy.
Just walk this earth one more time.

VI.9.3 You walk stand recline, you simply are,
a protector through every age
to every life in this world,
Will I never join you and your lovely Śrī?
How many long long days
must I grow weak with waiting?

VI.9.4 You twisted mangled shattered
the demon-cart with a mere kick of your feet
O great lord, let me see you some day
high in the sky, surrounded by the shining gods
Brahmā, Śivaṉ, Indraṉ and all the celestials
Come to me.

VI.9.5 In the sky, atop the mountain,
asleep on the ocean, walking the earth
you live hidden in every place
in worlds far beyond measure, you're there too
You're within me dancing
Why hide yourself from me?

VI.9.6 One foot measured the earth
encircled by sea, the other
took the whole sky.
Mysterious one, I yearn to see you
How long must I wander this earth
grieving, growing soft as wax in fire?

VI.9.7 You're the actions and actors
that wander this world, you're the life

within every life, formless,
you're the ten directions, all that lies beyond
My ignorance is endless. Love me.

VI.9.8 I am ignorant, still grant me your love,
soul of the wise, body of fragrant light,
my towering Neṭumāl, when I know nothing
but you, will you set me aside,
find small ways to destroy me?
My breath seizes.

VI.9.9 You bewilder me, revealing
the small pleasures of the five senses.
Do you think to ruin me?
Isn't it time to summon me
to shelter under the broad lotus feet
that took the world?

VI.9.10 Yes, it's a limitless unchanging joy
to be with you for an endless age, but
mysterious one
can it ever equal serving you
even if for just a moment
and never again?

VI.9.11 These ten verses from the thousand
by Śaṭhakōpaṉ, a servant of servants of servants
of Tirumāl, who is beyond conception
beyond contemplation beyond concentration,
will mould you into the servants of him
who ate the world.

Tiruvāymoḻi VI.10 (652–662)
ulakam uṇṭa peruvāyā

VI.10.1 You took the whole world
into your enormous mouth, towering lord
of undying fame, radiant body of everlasting light,
my precious life, a lovely mark on the brow of the world,
my great master of Tiruvēṅkaṭam
I come from a long line of devotees
show me the way to your feet.

VI.10.2 Your sharp disc spitting fire cuts
turns to ash entire clans of wicked demons.
King of celestials, master of Tiruvēṅkaṭam
where lotuses bloom like red fire
I burn with love for you that will not cool
Show me the way to your feet,
give me this grace.

VI.10.3 Beautiful dark wondrous storm cloud
mysterious one seeping into my thoughts
sweet as nectar, king of celestials,
master of Tiruvēṅkaṭam
where waterfalls spill jewels gold pearls
call me to you, and
bring me to your feet.

VI.10.4 A rain of fire-arrows pierces
the lives of demons who torment this world
Beloved of Śrī, great god of Tiruvēṅkaṭam
dear to celestials and seers

I am a wretch, still take me
to your feet that bloom like flowers
Be with me.

VI.10.5 Masterful archer who pierced seven trees
with a single arrow, primordial lord
who crawled between two giant trees,
master of Tiruvēṅkaṭam
where elephants cluster like storm clouds
lord who holds the Sārṅga-bow
when will I reach your feet?

VI.10.6 Celestials remain unblinking
awaiting the day they'll see
the feet that measured worlds,
in great groups they praise you,
serve you with their body voice mind
Master of Tiruvēṅkaṭam
will the day I'll reach your feet ever come?

VI.10.7 Sweet nectar I love, king of celestials
with the fierce eagle as banner,
great lord with lips red as berries,
cure for sins that multiply like weeds,
my great lord of Tiruvēṅkaṭam
I've kept no vows, but
I can't wait another moment to see your feet.

VI.10.8 'We aren't fit to see your feet' think
the blue-throated god, wise Nāṉmukaṉ, Indraṉ
with women whose eyes dart like carp, still

they surround you, wanting only your feet.
Master of Tiruvēṅkaṭam
Māl who bewitches, come to me
Come as you came before.

VI.10.9 You seem to come, then don't
you seem not to come, yet here you are,
eyes bright as lotus lips red as fruit
four great shoulders, sweet nectar
my precious life, master of Tiruvēṅkaṭam
where brilliant gems turn night into day
I can't be apart from your feet for an instant.

VI.10.10 'I won't part from you for an instant'
says Śrī who rests on your chest,
lord of matchless fame,
holder of the three worlds
my king, master of Vēṅkaṭam
dear to peerless immortals and sages
with nowhere else to go, I've settled at your feet.

VI.10.11 'Devotees, come settle at my feet'
says the incomparable great lord, offering grace
Those who hold fast
to these ten verses on Tiruvēṅkaṭam,
of the thousand
by Śaṭhakōpaṉ of fertile Kurukūr,
will secure a place in the highest heaven.

The Seventh Hundred

Tiruvāymoḻi VII.1 (663–673)
uḷ nilāviya

VII.1.1 You use those five that thrive
within me to make me suffer,
mean to torment me further parting me
from your lotus feet.
My immeasurable lord of mystery
great master praised by the celestials
you who own the three worlds, sweet nectar
my father, you rule me.

VII.1.2 Those five who thrive within me
govern like cruel despots, clashing inside night and day
you ensure that I can't come
close to you.
Sugar, sweet nectar,
guardian of sea and earth
dark as storm clouds, with a disc bright as lightning
I am a wretch, and you the master of the Veda.

VII.1.3 You've set the five as obstacles
to trip me up, to slam into me, to stop
this wretch from reaching your feet.
Why?
Primordial one who made this wide world
only to eat it spit it span it lift it
One who wears a tall radiant crown
Madhusūdanaṉ, I am yours.

VII.1.4 You trapped me, twisted me
distracted me with the five
so I can't even approach
your feet.
You, a child on a long banyan leaf
hiding all things all beings in your belly,
are the only cure
for this wretch full of wretched deeds.

VII.1.5 Five diseases with no cure
toss and squeeze me like an oil press, yet
you block me from every side every angle,
watch as I am crushed.
You routed entire demon clans
with your frightening disc, cutting them
off at their roots, lord of celestials
who's to be my cure now?

VII.1.6 The five senses torment even
the celestials who serve you. What will they do
to me here on earth if you abandon me?
Supreme lord, hidden in song, the secret in poems,
heart of devotion, you
dwell in my eyes, live in my heart
are in my words, come
say something to me.

VII.1.7 These five say anything, stay with nothing
How will I defeat them without your loving aid?
As gods and demons flailed in the ocean
with its rising waves
you looped a serpent around a mountain

my father, I am wicked,
you are the sweet nectar
I drink.

VII.1.8 The five seduce like sweet nectar,
a delusion to everyone. This was your doing.
Now root out your primordial illusion
let me think only of your symbols your form
let me praise only them
let me worship only you
my mother, my Kaṇṇaṉ, lord of celestials
grant me this grace.

VII.1.9 The five fling me into a cruel pit
of wretchedness so awful it destroys entire clans.
Grant me this gift, to blunt their strength
to vanquish them utterly.
You made this earth, all these worlds
within them made matter both still and moving
my Kaṇṇaṉ, my supreme light.

VII.1.10 'My supreme light' I cry out
melt with love over your feet, two lotuses.
Just then you heft a burden on me, and
the five join in with cruel weights, dragging
me this way and that.
Long ago you churned the ocean drew out its nectar
this is your divine form.

VII.1.11 He has three forms, three guṇas
that create keep destroy.
He's my father resting on the waters,

a lotus rising from his navel.
Those who master and sing
these ten verses from a thousand by Śaṭhakōpaṉ,
servant to servants' servant and their servants,
will have their fate destroyed, night and day.

Tiruvāymoḻi VII.2 (674–684)
kaṅkulum pakalum

VII.2.1 Night or day her eyes won't close in sleep
tears pool in the palm of her hands
'Conch disc' she weeps, pressing her hands together
'Eyes-lotus' she cries, growing faint
'How can I live without you?' she says
feeling this vast earth with her hands.
Lord of Tiruvaraṅkam where red fish dart through the water
What have you done to my girl?

VII.2.2 'What are you doing my dear?' she says
as her eyes fill with tears
'What can I do, lord of Tiruvaraṅkam?' she says
as her hot sighs melt her
'My past keeps you from me' she says.
Lord dark as storm clouds, is this fair?
You made this world, ate it spat it measured it
What kind of end awaits her?

VII.2.3 She's become shameless, crying out
'Dazzling gem' staring at the sky, fainting away.
'Singular lord who sucked the life of demons'
she says and dissolves.

'Kākuttā, Kaṇṇaṉ, you're hard to see,
let me see you, give me this grace' she begs
Lord of Tiruvaraṅkam, circled by mighty walls
What have you done to my girl?

VII.2.4 Her hands her feet appear frozen in place
but she gets up wanders about bewildered
She cups her palms, sighs that love is hard
'Cruel one, dark as the ocean,
you with the disc in your right hand, come'
she calls out and faints.
Lord of Tiruvaraṅkam with its rushing waters
What do you intend for her?

VII.2.5 She's lost in thought, faints,
Recovers, cups her hands muttering,
'You're in Tiruvaraṅkam.' Come here
she calls as her eyes rain tears.
As dusk fell you ripped apart the demon
precious nectar who churned the ocean
You've bewitched this girl now wasting away
She only desires to be at your feet.

VII.2.6 'Great trickster who bewitched me and
stole my heart, my jewel in Tiruvaraṅkam,
circled by cool flowing waters, first among celestials,
one who wields sword mace disc bow.'
She calls to you in all these ways.
I know my past deeds are to blame, still
lord asleep on the serpent
Show her grace.

VII.2.7 'You created both pain and pleasure,
you love even those who have no love for you,
you hold the wheel of time, lord dark as the ocean
on which you recline, beloved Kaṇṇaṉ, lord of Tiruvaraṅkam
circled by the cool river with its darting fish, my refuge.'
She calls to you in all these ways, as
tears stream like rain from her large lovely eyes
This little girl frail as a new shoot.

VII.2.8 'Lord of celestials who lifted a mountain
to protect your herds of cows' she says weeping
she prays, her breath hot as fire sears her life
Calling to you, black as kohl,
she searches the sky with unblinking eyes, asks
'Where can I see you?'
Lord of Tiruvaraṅkam with its gardens and deep pools
What can I do for my precious girl?

VII.2.9 'Inseparable from Śrī who rests on your chest,
beloved of the earth you raised up on your tusks,
dear to the cowherd girl for whom you killed seven bulls,
you're my life.'
She calls to you in all these ways,
lord in the temple at Tiruvaraṅkam
what end awaits her
I do not know.

VII.2.10 'I don't know the end that awaits me,
ruler of the three worlds, you're Nāṉmukaṉ
and the god with fragrant koṉṟai in his matted hair,
you're the king of celestials, beautiful lord of Tiruvaraṅkam.'

She calls to you in all these ways
She seemed like she wouldn't reach your feet
but she's reached them
The feet of the one dark as storm clouds.

VII.2.11 Those who master these ten from the thousand
sung on the banks of the sacred Porunal
in praise of the feet of him dark as storm clouds
by Śaṭhakōpaṉ from Kurukūr, who adorned by grace
reached his feet, the one dark as storm clouds,
will be swept up in a flood of bliss and will remain
among celestials who are forever with him
dark as storm clouds.

Tiruvāymoḻi VII.3 (685–695)
veḷḷaic curicaṅkōṭu

VII.3.1 Holding a white conch and disc
riding an eagle, Kaṇṇaṉ with eyes like lotuses
drives into my heart. You don't see this
so what can I say to you?
He lives in Tiruppērai, resounding
with Vedic chants, festival clamour
and the joyous laughter of children
I'm headed there.

VII.3.2 Beautiful friends, my mothers, neighbours
I can't control my stubborn heart,
it slips my hold, roams
night and day, then remains by
the sweet lips of Kaṇṇaṉ, him
dark as a jewel, lord of celestials

who lives in Tiruppērai
surrounded by gardens and cool fields.

VII.3.3 It devours his sweet ripe lips, bends low
before his tall radiant crown, delights seeing
his conch and disc, his bright lotus eyes
Friend, in these ways
my heart shed its reserve, its modesty
before our lord who lives
in Tiruppērai with its endless festivals
that stretch on through night and day.

VII.3.4 My heart set out to retrieve my lustre
ended up remaining there. Now
who's left to comfort me?
I drowned in his wonders, him
who holds the conch, him
who lives in Tiruppērai,
where the Veda roar like the thundering ocean.
Mothers, why scold me?

VII.3.5 I lost my modesty, lost myself to him.
In a fury he smashed the cart, suckled
the breast of the deceitful ghoul, slipped
between the maruta trees, flung
the calf against the trees
Mothers, why scold me? Show me
the quickest way to the lush gardens of Tiruppērai,
Kaṇṇaṉ lives there.

VII.3.6 Greater than the sea is my love
for him dark as storm clouds

He stands before me just beyond my grasp.
Show me the quickest way
to where brahmins perform sacrifices without pause
to where ripe grain sways gently
to where cool waters pool
to Tiruppērai, his home on earth.

VII.3.7 The destroyer of southern Laṅkā
guarded by forts and the sea
lives in Tiruppērai.
My heart left in search of him,
never to return. Friends, I have no one here,
none to call back my heart,
nothing to fight for, now
my eyes follow my heart.

VII.3.8 They gather to share what they've seen
to gossip about my love
for the lord dark as the sea.
Friends, my love only grows,
bigger than the firm earth,
the seven seas the lofty sky
I go where he is, to join him
in Tiruppērai circled by cool streams.

VII.3.9 Friends, let me go
Mothers, don't comfort me
what use are your words?
I've lost my heart and my modesty to him
dark as storm clouds, that swallower of earth and sea
Kaṇṇaṉ lives in the great city of Tiruppērai

with its dense lush fields.
I've gone there.

VII.3.10 Shameless, I search town country
everywhere, friends. He lives in Tiruppērai
with its fine mansions tall as jewelled mountains.
The mysterious Makara Neṭuṅkuḻaik Kātaṉ, him
with dazzling makara earrings
suppressed the hundred brothers, him
dark as rain clouds, the peerless one with the disc
stole my heart long aeons ago.

VII.3.11 Those who master these ten on Tiruppērai
from the thousand verses in incomparable antāti
sung by Śaṭhakōpaṉ of beautiful Kurukūr
on Acyutaṉ dark as the sea
who protects the world age after age
with different forms names deeds
the one with a disc in his lovely hand
will be immersed in his service.

Tiruvāymoḻi VII.4 (696–706)
āḻi eḻa

VII.4.1 The disc grew, the conch and bow too
praise swelled, rising in all directions, the staff
the sword grew, the huge world a bubble pierced by
his head his feet and time grew long,
this is how my father took the earth.

VII.4.2 Rivers that thundered down hills raced up again
the serpent's body scraped against the mountain

the swirling sea lashed back and forth
this is how it sounded
the day my father took the nectar.

VII.4.3 The seven worlds remained in place
the seven mountains rooted in place
the seven seas stayed still in place
on the day my father
raised the earth on his tusks.

VII.4.4 Day died, earth and water tumbled
sky and stars disappeared, fire and wind swelled
mountains heaved, light and sound ceased
time stilled when my father
ate and kept the worlds.

VII.4.5 The sound of well-fed wrestlers falling
the sound of the king's trembling armies
the sound of celestials gathering to witness it all
this was how it was on the day my father
directed the Bharata war.

VII.4.6 Dusk set. The sky turned red
a river of blood flooded the sky, when he came
a lion tearing through a mountain
this is how my father
killed the demon who brought such sorrow.

VII.4.7 Arrows thundered in a dense stream
making a mountain of corpses, blood pooled
into rivers and seas, flooding streams

this was Laṅkā in ashes,
my father's work.

VII.4.8 First the god with a rooster-banner fled
then the god of fire ran
finally the god with three eyes surrendered
this was how it was on the day my father
cut Bāṇaṉ's mighty arms.

VII.4.9 It began with earth water fire wind sky
mountains and two brilliant flames followed
then came rain life gods and all the rest
this is how in primordial time
my father made the worlds.

VII.4.10 Herds of cows huddled
great pools overflowed, waters gushed
animals villagers crowded in pressed together
when my father lifted the mountain
to hold off the fierce rain.

VII.4.11 Śaṭhakōpaṉ, one with the devotees
of the lord who lifted a mountain,
sang these ten verses from the elegant thousand.
Those who learn and recite them well
will be victorious in everything.

Tiruvāymoḻi VII.5 (707–717)
kaṟpār irāma pirāṉai

VII.5.1 If you can learn of great Rāma,
why would you learn anything else?

From a blade of grass to the smallest ant
to things aware and unaware
he blessed everything that lived in Ayodhyā
that fortunate land Nāṉmukaṉ made.

VII.5.2 If you hear of all he did,
can you love anyone but Nāraṇaṉ?
He endured such miseries
for men and kingdoms tormented by demons
He sought and killed them, and in this way
guarded protected saved this world.

VII.5.3 If you hear of Keśavaṉ's glory,
can you listen to anything else?
Śiśupālaṉ's abuse ripened
through long hostility blistered ears,
yet he reached his feet
What else is there to know?

VII.5.4 If you know the nature of things,
can you bow to anyone else?
In that time long ago, when all things were not
he made the fine waters, made Nāṉmukaṉ,
mingled and made everything within himself
Can you think of anything but his marvellous ways?

VII.5.5 Can you consider any path
but the feet of the mysterious one?
The earth sank into vast deep waters,
in an instant, he became a glorious boar
raised her whole and unbroken on his tusks.
Can you listen to this and still seek something else?

VII.5.6 When the gods troubled by Mahābali
of limitless generosity, begged you
to end their sorrow, you came as Vāmaṉaṉ
and stretched out your hands.
If you hear of Keśavaṉ, know of him, see his deeds
how can you submit to anyone else?

VII.5.7 When the god with flowers in his matted hair
brought before you young Mārkaṇḍeya,
you gave him life, and made him one of yours.
If you've heard these things,
considered them, know them
can you serve anyone but Kaṇṇaṉ?

VII.5.8 When Hiraṇyaṉ with power earned
off limitless austerity tormented the gods,
he came as an enormous lion and
mauled his demon-body.
Knowing his mysterious ways,
can you learn of anyone else?

VII.5.9 Destroyer of armies, vanquisher
of the covetous hundred, charioteer
for the peerless five
When you hear these legends and
learn the mysterious ways of the mysterious one
can you serve another?

VII.5.10 He plucks out by their roots
the endless sorrows of endless birth illness age death,
shelters you beneath his feet

If you understand his wise words
If you think of all the good he does
can you serve anyone but the mysterious lord?

VII.5.11 These ten from the lucid thousand
by Śaṭhakōpaṉ of Kurukūr on Kaṇṇaṉ,
giver of the highest bliss to any
who worships him with unshakeable clarity,
grant a clear mind celebrated in the three worlds
to all who master them.

Tiruvāymoḻi VII.6 (718–728)
pāmaru mūvulakum

VII.6.1 A body of lotuses
from your navel, a lotus, emerged three vast worlds
your feet, lotuses, measured the three worlds
your eyes are lotuses, your hands too
Padmanābha, my ruler, I am alone
when will I reach you?

VII.6.2 When will I reach your lovely feet
praised by Araṉ and Nāṉmukaṉ?
My father who is earth water fire wind ether
you're life and everything else
you're my dancer
who lifted a mountain to care for your cows.

VII.6.3 My dancer who lifted a mountain
against a storm of stones
hair adorned in sweet tuḷasi and pretty koṉṟai

four-faced Nāṉmukaṉ, lord of limitless fame
you're my precious life
where do I meet you?

VII.6.4 Where do I meet you?
You're the three beautiful worlds
You're the three-eyed god and great Brahmā
You're Indraṉ who holds the fierce thunderbolt
You're all the gods, and you're my Kōvalaṉ
wearing sweet-scented tuḷasi in your hair.

VII.6.5 My Kōvalaṉ
my perfect dark jewel
the three worlds blossom from your navel
flood of radiance in your realm of radiance
my precious life
how do I reach you?

VII.6.6 I don't know how to reach him
a gem of fire within a flame of blue
radiance sparking from the silk at his waist
his feet navel hands chest eyes lips
glowing red
my lord in whom Śrī resides.

VII.6.7 Śrī is on his chest, Pārvatī's at his side
Nāmakaḷ is on his lips, he's Śacī's beloved
he's within all these gods.
The one who raised the earth, burnt three forts

bound the senses, rules the sky
I can't see him.

VII.6.8 Like horses snorting before a monster,
foxes howling before a lion, the demons wailed,
abandoned Laṅkā, entered the underworld to hide,
when he came on his fierce eagle, killed strong Māli,
made a mountain of corpses.
Can't I see him too?

VII.6.9 Heart, will I see him?
He destroyed the formidable demon clan
of wicked deeds and untold vigour,
then gifted Laṅkā to the demon's brother,
returned to reign, entered into his own light,
that lion among celestials.

VII.6.10 He gifts us precious Vaikuṇṭha
impossible to reach, yet lived among cowherds,
a little child, killer of death-like Kaṁsaṉ,
vanquisher of cruel armies for the five
The wise one's ways are mysterious,
He's the great light. Hari.

VII.6.11 He came as a lion, took pleasure
in mauling the demon,
he's the dear one with the disc
Those who master these ten from the thousand
by Śaṭhakōpaṉ of Kurukūr
will be praised and served by beautiful women.

Tiruvāymoḻi VII.7 (729–739)
ēḻaiyar āvi

VII.7.1 Is it death come in a pair
to devour the life of the wretched or
the beautiful eyes of Kaṇṇaṉ
dark as the sea
I can't tell. They surround me
like lotuses in full bloom
Friends, mothers, I am suffering
What should I do?

VII.7.2 Why push and punish me, mothers?
What's this abuse?
Is it a tendril or a new shoot
from the tree of wishes?
I don't know. His fine nose
mingles with my life
like a strong steady flame.
It's him, the one who stole butter.

VII.7.3 Is it ripe fruit or my wicked fate?
Is it a lovely sliver of rich coral?
I don't know.
His lips red as toṇṭai fruit
fill the directions,
I see them everywhere,
a torment to my sweet life.
He's my lord dark as dense storm clouds.

VII.7.4 Are they two dark bows bent
on wrecking the life of the wretched?

Is it the fine sugar cane bow of Madaṉaṉ,
him of undying beauty. No.
They are the brows of his father,
that great god Kaṇṇaṉ
burning my life
They are my eternal torment.

VII.7.5 Is it white hot lightning
or a string of gorgeous pearls
that take my life?
I don't know.
The lord who lifted a mountain
his smile subdues my life, mothers
I don't know how I'll survive
Where do I go?

VII.7.6 Where can demons and the wretched go?
No place is safe
when even sparkling fish darting
through reeds look like
jewels adorning his beautiful ears.
Don't you see how
the one asleep on the serpent spitting poison
torments me without end.

VII.7.7 Mothers, how do I show you?
Is it the bright waxing crescent or
a poison to lovers? No.
It's his broad beautiful brow
that kills me, takes my life,
him the great lord

with four wide shoulders, and I
full of wickedness.

VII.7.8 Bright beautiful lotuses,
a slender creeper, red coral,
two arched bows, small white pearls,
a curving shoot, the cool white moon
glow in a circle a light,
Kaṇṇaṉ's shining face
steals my life
so full of wickedness.

VII.7.9 Are these skeins of thread
dyed in the shimmering darkness of night?
No. They're his black curls
sweet with the fragrance of tuḷasi
that spreads everywhere,
here to take my life.
He's full of mystery, mothers,
you understand nothing.

VII.7.10 'Why're you out there?' you ask
and wring your hands, then
corner me to spew abuse.
My heart's fixed on his crown of light
him dark as a gem
his radiance filling the three worlds
Mothers, there's no use
scolding me for this.

VII.7.11 Śaṭhakōpaṉ of Kurukūr composed
this ten from the powerful thousand on Kaṇṇaṉ

whom even the invisible gods
Brahmā Śivaṉ Indraṉ
struggle to see.
Those who master these verses
will never die
will find a place among the celestials.

Tiruvāymoḻi VII.8 (740–750)
māyā vāmaṉaṉē

VII.8.1 Mysterious one, Vāmaṉaṉ, Madhusūdā be kind.
You became fire water land sky wind
You became mother father children everything else
You became yourself. How do I make sense of you?

VII.8.2 Acyutaṉ, crowned in sweet-scented tuḷasi, be kind.
You became the moon and sun, the bright stars and dark night
You became pouring rain, you became fame and infamy
You are fierce-eyed death. What magic is this?

VII.8.3 Skilled charioteer who wields the disc, be kind.
You became the many ages, the glittering things within them,
beyond decay, each different,
you are within it all. What mischief is this?

VII.8.4 Your eyes, open lotuses rich in honey, Kaṇṇaṉ, be kind.
You are what is, what isn't, what dies, every thing.
You sleep on the venomous snake in a vast ocean,
deep in yoga. What tricks are these?

VII.8.5 You cut my bonds, took me for yourself,
mysterious one with fragrant tuḷasi in your hair, be kind.

You became body and breath, death and life, so many
wondrous things. How you bewilder me.

VII.8.6 Deceptive Vāmaṉaṉ, be kind. Let me understand.
You became forgetfulness and clarity, heat and cold,
wonder and wondrousness, victory fate fruit fatigue,
creator of grief. What suffering is this?

VII.8.7 Kaṇṇā, adorned in a crown of light, creator of grief,
you became insolence pride joy torturous desire,
you are the boundary, you are stability and mobility,
you create all this pain with your games. Be kind.

VII.8.8 Kaṇṇā, you rule me, so why these games?
Your nature lies beyond understanding,
long ago you became the three worlds, created them
abide within them, yet are outside them. Who are you?

VII.8.9 My Kaṇṇā, how are you so many things?
These arms, these feet stitched together, all other forms
taste sight touch sound smell, you're all this.
There's no end to knowing you, no end to your subtleties.

VII.8.10 There is nothing more subtle than this,
your form your formlessness, so say the ancient books.
My Acyutaṉ wearing garlands of tuḷasi buds,
whatever we think, you are that.

VII.8.11 Those who recite these ten from the thousand
glorious Tamiḻ verses by Śaṭhakōpaṉ of Kurukūr
who knows well elusive Hari, impossible to know,
will be his forever.

Tiruvāymoḻi VII.9 (751–761)
eṉṟaikkum eṉṉai

VII.9.1 He lifts me every day for all time
moulds me into himself with each passing day
in sweet Tamiḻ he sings of himself through me
He is cause of all things, my light. What can I sing?

VII.9.2 What can I sing? He's merged with my sweet life
my words are his sweet songs, his own
words of praise of himself. He's mysterious
he stands before me, three forms, singular.

VII.9.3 He makes it clear 'I am singular cause'
burrows into my tongue to sing sweet songs
of himself for his devotees. He rests on my lips
always first, my father, how can I ever forget him?

VII.9.4 Can I ever forget my father? He's become me
sings perfect songs about himself. I am incomparable
in my wickedness, yet he lifts me up
makes me better. I've seen his brilliance.

VII.9.5 I saw his brilliance, still couldn't sing fine songs.
I'm without distinction, he made me into himself
saw himself through me, sang his own sweet songs
that fill the world with his praise. The highest one.

VII.9.6 He doesn't sing about himself
through the greatest poets and their sweetest songs
Instead he sidled close to me, merged with me
made me sing of himself, my lord of Vaikuṇṭha.

VII.9.7 The lord of Vaikuṇṭha destroys
my wickedness, places himself within me
sings his own praise as Vaikuṇṭha's lord,
Kuntaṉ, will I ever tire thinking of him?

VII.9.8 I am low. Still he made me into himself
to sing of his own greatness, my lord with the disc in his hand.
If his praise on all the earth, sky and waters should mix,
even if I were to lap it all up, can it sate my desire?

VII.9.9 If I were to lap up the joy of him in past and future
Tirumāl's greatness, his wholeness, would it ever sate?
I am dim, still he made me into himself, used me
to sing so many sweet songs of himself.

VII.9.10 I thought to barter my life for his help
only to realize that too is his. My father
sang himself sweet songs through me.
There's nothing I can do for him in heaven or earth.

VII.9.11 Śaṭhakōpaṉ of glorious Kurukūr understood
nothing exists without Tirumāl, who is everywhere.
Sing these ten from his thousand however you will
and know bliss.

Tiruvāymoḻi VII.10 (762–772)
iṉpam payakka

VII.10.1 With his beautiful wife, Śrī,
our lord rules the seven worlds, brings joy.
Full of love he abides in Tiruvāṟaṉviḷai

enfolded in lovely gardens
Will I ever circle this city
Will I worship there with folded hands?

VII.10.2 Tirukkuṟaḷappaṉ, my father stretched out,
the wide expanse beneath his two feet became his.
He's in Tiruvāṟaṉviḷai, where banners snap and flutter
on tall palace walls.
Will I sprinkle fragrant water and circle the city?
Will I ever worship there?

VII.10.3 If I can't see Govindaṉ Madhusūdaṉaṉ,
that fierce lion, if I can't see him on his restless bird,
can I at least worship him at Tiruvāṟaṉviḷai
where the four Veda the five sacrifices the six parts
are cherished by all who live there?
Is this possible?

VII.10.4 Will I keep him in mind always?
He abides in Tiruvāṟaṉviḷai
circled by great fields of sugar cane and red paddy,
master of the three worlds, born in Mathurā,
Kaṇṇaṉ, dark as a gem,
will I be so fortunate to think of his petal-soft feet?

VII.10.5 He's blessed his many devotees,
lord asleep on the serpent, father in Tiruvāṟaṉviḷai,
city of mansions and high walls
If we keep his petal-soft feet in our hearts
always sing his boundless praise in the world
our wicked deeds will wither, nothing will remain.

VII.10.6 All wickedness will wither, leaving nothing behind
when you keep him inside, worship him.
He vanquished enemies for lovely Rukmiṇī
settled into her embrace
He's the same lord who's in my heart for all time
He's here too in this great city of Tiruvāṟaṉviḷai.

VII.10.7 He's in great Tiruvāṟaṉviḷai, city of gardens
Neṭumāl, Kaṇṇaṉ, king of celestials,
he entered Bāṇaṉ's city, waged a fierce war
vanquished the three-eyed god
shattered Bāṇaṉ's thousand arms.
He's our only refuge.

VII.10.8 'You're my only refuge' cried the elephant
lifting his long trunk, and you listened
eased the pain of his heart.
That lord is in Tiruvāṟaṉviḷai, city of gardens
If we ever circle this city
wickedness has no place in our minds.

VII.10.9 Even if I ascend into the clear sky,
heart devoid of wicked deeds,
I'll still want only to circle Tiruvāṟaṉviḷai
city of gardens, worshipped in words
and enshrined in the hearts of devotees
It's all I think of.

VII.10.10 I think of nothing else but him
and the lord of gods knows it.
There are no mysteries the mind conjures

that he doesn't already know.
He's the lord of Tiruvāṟaṉviḷai, the heart's delight
worshipped in every way by the gods of earth.

VII.10.11 Śaṭhakōpaṉ of prosperous Kurukūr
took the pure lord of sacred places into his pure mind
knowing he's the only refuge.
Those who master these ten out of thousand verses
will themselves become sacred
extolled by the gods and their wives.

The Eighth Hundred

Tiruvāymoḻi VIII.1 (773–783)
tēvimār āvār

VIII.1.1 Śrī and Bhū are your goddesses
the celestials bow before you
the three worlds are your domain,
every form you desire is yours.
You devastate me
with your lotus eyes and coral-red lips
You a jewel, and I a wretch.
My breath sweetest nectar
father who churned the ocean
let me see you.

VIII.1.2 'Let me see you' I howl as tears flow
I am a wretch, but I've loved you
in every way that I can love.
Let me speak your names
at least give me this.
Let me see you Kākuttā, my Kaṇṇā
fruit from the tree of wishes, nectar
to those who desire you, great generous one
who raised the vast earth from cool deep waters
I am yours.

VIII.1.3 Generous Nandagōpaṉ's sweet life,
his little child, Yaśodā's great joy,
young elephant of the herd,
my only master.
In a great battle you mauled the demon
tore him in two with your claws,

but now you won't come,
you won't show yourself to me
in the way you see fit.
My ocean, how can we know you?

VIII.1.4 You take the form your devotees love
they rejoice in your feats and
your mysterious ways, but I
with my little knowledge
live in doubt.
Lord who unleashed a great war,
destroyed armies on the vast field of battle
sweet nectar to celestials
poison to demons
you are my precious life.

VIII.1.5 My precious life
you created this vast world
dug it ate it spat it spanned it,
supreme spirit
you made the wide ocean to rest on it
churned it bound it broke it,
great soul
what gods are to men you are to the gods
Singular life of all the worlds
where can I be close to you?

VIII.1.6 Where can I be close to you?
You rule me.
You are the seven worlds
you are the gods you created

to rule those worlds, and
all the ways those gods are worshipped.
If there is anything beyond
you are that too
you are formless and subtle
you are the death of the senses.

VIII.1.7 You alone are past future present
you're this that everything in-between
but fool that I am, I doubt this knowledge.
You are fresh milk
the ghee within milk
the sweetness within that ghee.
You are the sea's nectar
the sweetness of nectar
the bliss of that pleasure
great cowherd who embraces Piṉṉai.

VIII.1.8 Great cowherd who won her with love,
your fine qualities cut me.
I am wretched
You, death to demons
You, atop your fierce eagle
You, resting on a snake with thousand hoods
You, asleep on the ocean of milk
I don't know how to worship you
my mind my words my deeds
they're all you.

VIII.1.9 If it's true I am you, then
every terrible hell is you

so why should I gain the joys of heaven?
And what if one enters hell?
Though I know you
have become me,
I'm afraid
of hells that await.
You're high in heaven abiding in that joy
let me rest at your feet.

VIII.1.10 You gave me the greatest gift, your feet,
in return, I clutch you to me
and give you my priceless life.
My light with a thousand arms
a thousand heads
eyes a thousand blooming flowers
a thousand feet
a thousand names
I am alone, great father
but I have you.

VIII.1.11 Great Śaṭhakōpaṉ of grand Kurukūr
composed these ten, a garland of fine words
among a thousand on the great father,
father to Brahmā
father to Rudraṉ
perfect father to sages
father to gods
singular father to the world
Learn them, devotees,
and you too can be free.

Tiruvāymoḻi VIII.2 (784–794)
naṅkaḷ varivaḷai

VIII.2.1 Dear friends decked in bangles,
I am shamed before my enemies,
I try to find the words, but cannot.
My bangles slip, I've lost my lustre
my full breasts shrivel, I grow pale
I only want my king
who rides the eagle with fierce eyes
I went after the lord of Vēṅkaṭam,
now I am like this.

VIII.2.2 Dear friends who know
how to get what you want,
I can't describe my suffering
even to you.
If I see him, the thief with lotus eyes
the king of the gods
our king
how long will it take him to return
my bangles and my health to me?

VIII.2.3 Time may die, but I won't,
gripped by fate.
Friends, you witness my shame
before the world, what modesty remains?
A blossom-burst of blue, a towering flame
Kaṇṇaṉ, dark as storm clouds
stole my lovely bangles, took my health

a long while ago.
I still await their return.

VIII.2.4 I've set out wanting him,
lost my bangles, my heart, everything else,
stand stripped of even honour
before my friends,
their wrists decked in bangles.
Māyakkūttaṉ, the enchanting dancer,
lives in southern Kuḷantai
atop his restless eagle and wielding the war-disc
What else am I to do?

VIII.2.5 Friends, you're not like me
I want him, the one who holds the disc,
and he will come
is this just for me?
Through the ages the wise
have thought of him, but not known him
Still I'll think of him,
a singular ancient primordial flame
I know it's hard to say anything at all.

VIII.2.6 I think of him an ancient glorious light
and my words fall short.
He bewilders even the celestials
but let that be.
Māl has stolen my beauty,
refuses me his sweet-scented tuḷasi
instead rests in Kuṭantai, circled by fields,
his large lotus eyes closed in sleep.
Tell me, to whom should I complain?

VIII.2.7 'Māl Hari Keśavaṉ Nāraṇaṉ
Śrīmādhavaṉ Govindaṉ Vaikuṇṭhaṉ'
I howl out his names, him
who made me, left me, him
who refuses to reveal even a trace of himself.
Mothers, with hair fragrant with flowers
Friends, what would you have me do?
Time will pass, I'll see him I swear
there's nothing left between us.

VIII.2.8 My parrots mynahs kuyil peacocks
now there's nothing left for you
he's taken everything
my beauty my conch bangles my heart.
He's close by
in Vaikuṇṭha, the ocean of milk,
that black mountain, Vēṅkaṭam,
but he won't let me see him
not until I shred the passions that bind me.

VIII.2.9 He won't let anyone see him.
He showed up as a beautiful little youth, only
to blossom like a flower
filling earth and sky with his glorious arms.
This is his mystery.
To the lord of gods, I gave everything
my dignity my diffidence
tell me friends,
what else is left to give?

VIII.2.10 Friends, what should I do?
'I'm no longer yours' my heart said

and left to join him
who holds the disc and conch in his hands
the brilliant sun and the milk-white moon
rising above a great tall dark mountain
this is how he is
the singular lord.
My heart is at his feet.

VIII.2.11 Śaṭhakōpaṉ of fine Kurukūr
wanting to reach his feet,
cut his other bonds
and praised faultless Kaṇṇaṉ
in a flawless antāti of thousand verses.
Those who masterfully sing
these ten verses
will themselves become flawless
and will have everything here and beyond.

Tiruvāymoḻi VIII.3 (795–805)
aṅkum iṅkum

VIII.3.1 The gods, the dānavās, everyone everywhere
can't fathom you, they take refuge in you,
conch and disc in your hands,
your body one with Śrī Bhū Nīlā.

VIII.3.2 We didn't take refuge in the four Veda
yet vanquished death birth disease,
we've become his, the lord who wields the fearsome disc
that burns down armies of every kind.

VIII.3.3 The king holds the disc and conch on his own,
no one follows carrying his sword and bow,
I want to fill my hands with him, his feet his shoulders
I wander the world looking for him.

VIII.3.4 He took the world for food, him so tiny
asleep on a great banyan leaf, my master.
Time stretches like a dense black aeon,
I long to see your dark beauty.

VIII.3.5 You sleep peacefully and without pause
in Kōḷūr with its mansion and flags, in Puḷiṅkuṭi too
Are you tired from rescuing your many devotees? Or perhaps
it's fatigue from measuring the world. Answer me.

VIII.3.6 The celestials bow to none but him
who holds the lovely conch and disc. See him.
He destroys the cruel ills of this world
he's come into my mind, a glittering black gem.

VIII.3.7 People come and go, see him in Vaṇparicāram
holding Śrī to his breast, but they won't speak of me.
I want to trail you, following your conch and disc.
They won't say these things. What should I do?

VIII.3.8 When are you thinking of bringing me
to your precious beautiful feet? Tell me
Tirumāl who leapt seven hills seven worlds seven seas,
you who wields the disc.

VIII.3.9 Do Nāṉmukaṉ and the red-haired god know you?
Why say these things? I speak from love,
call you Tirumāl, primordial one, lord of time,
your great dark body rules me.

VIII.3.10 Sages with steady minds sight the shore
celestials stand firm in their worship
the vast sea shook when he churned it
how can we praise him? Tell me.

VIII.3.11 Śaṭhakōpaṉ of Kurukūr, with houses like hills,
spoke these ten verses from the thousand strung together
about the one with a tall crown, him who destroys all ills,
those who master them will escape birth in this vast world.

Tiruvāymoḻi VIII.4 (806–816)

vār kaṭā aruvi

VIII.4.1 He snapped the tusks of an elephant,
a mountain, a river of musk, then stole
the life of its fierce mahout, slaughtered
the wrestlers, and as the terrified kings
assembled on the balconies fled, he
leapt at Kaṁsaṉ seated high above in his fine mansion
killed him. That sweet little cowherd boy
lives by the Ciṟṟāṟu in Tirucceṅkuṉṟūr.
He's our only refuge.

VIII.4.2 He's our refuge, our nectar,
Imaiyavarappaṉ, father to celestials,
my father. He takes three forms

to create to protect to destroy the three worlds,
one impossible to know. He's in Tiruccenkuṉṟūr
encircled by honey-sweet paddy, where
red carp dart in the Ciṟṟāṟu.
Apart from him the primordial one
who stands by me always?

VIII.4.3 My lord perfect for me,
great lord of the celestials, my lord
who dug up this vast world, my lord
who destroys my past deeds, rules me.
He stands facing west on the shores
of the Tirucciṟṟāṟu in Tiruccenkuṉṟūr,
jewel of the southern lands
His feet are my only refuge
nothing else will do.

VIII.4.4 He appeared as a tiny man, then grew
to fill the three worlds, my father
a glorious gem who churned the ocean.
My great lord stands in a form
I can know
by the Tiruccirṟāṟu in Tiruccenkuṉṟūr
with its dense cluster of trees ripe with fruit
His feet are my singular refuge.
I want nothing else.

VIII.4.5 He's in every place, he's every refuge
nothing is apart from him. This is true
but my life wants only him, the one
on the shores of the Tiruccirṟāṟu in Tiruccenkuṉṟūr,

where the fragrant smoke
from the brahmins' sacrifices
conceals the sky's light.
That rich city of towering mansions
is my only refuge.

VIII.4.6 My refuge, my precious life
father and mother to celestials
one obscure even to himself
the lord asleep on the vast ocean
lives on the shores of the Tiruccir̲r̲ār̲u
in Tirucceṅkun̲r̲ūr, city of towering mansions,
and enshrined in the minds
of three thousand people equal to Śivan̲ and Ayan̲
I've seen him there.

VIII.4.7 I saw him
by the Tiruccir̲r̲ār̲u in Tirucceṅkun̲r̲ūr,
his bright lotus eyes his red lips
his red feet his red hands
his navel a blossoming red lotus
his chest a lotus in full bloom
his crimson garments his brilliant crown
his jewels his weapons
shimmer in my mind.

VIII.4.8 He glows within me,
the one who lives
by the Tiruccir̲r̲ār̲u in Tirucceṅkun̲r̲ūr,
praised and worshipped by
kings and brahmins everywhere.

He's refuge to luminous celestials
He's cruel death to mighty demons
He creates destroys protects the three worlds.
I don't know how to praise him.

VIII.4.9 He creates destroys protects.
He is the highest one,
Brahmā and Śivaṉ too.
He's in every form without end,
every word of praise is his alone
He alone is himself, the lord
who lives by the Tiruccirrāru in Tiruccenkuṉṟūr
city of the wise the noble the virtuous.

VIII.4.10 The perfect lord becomes all
graces all, the master lives on the shores
of the Tiruccirrāru in Tiruccenkuṉṟūr,
city of cool fertile fields,
home to three thousand brahmins
and those who rule the earth.
He is both three-eyed and four-faced,
I've reached him
that mysterious one.

VIII.4.11 The master who ate the world
is sweet as honey milk sugar nectar
He's the mysterious one who made Nāṉmukaṉ
rise from his navel, a cool blooming lotus.
These ten from the thousand verses
spoken by Śaṭhakōpaṉ of fertile Kurukūr
about his king

will grant you heaven, earn you grace,
will end the great dizzying dance of birth.

Tiruvāymoḻi VIII.5 (817–827)
māyak kūttā

VIII.5.1 Mysterious dancer, Vāmanā
Kaṇṇā, my fated love
your eyes your hands your feet
red lotuses
your lips a red bud
your body a dark new leaf
you a cool fragrant pool of lotuses
let me see you at least once.

VIII.5.2 Let me see you.
I wander the world shameless
eyes dry, mouth parched.
You take no pity, won't show yourself
even for a day,
your crown limned by light
a brilliant black sun, a black jewel
rising over a great dark mountain.

VIII.5.3 A crown limned by light,
garlands of cool tuḷasi and sweet flowers
adorn you, lord.
I long to see you, cry out
to see your earrings
your coral lips your four arms
your slender waist

your body a cool dark storm cloud
come before me, just so.

VIII.5.4 A cloud of cool water
a luminous form
berry-red lips lotus-bright eyes
fill my mind.
Asleep on a vast sea
like a dark storm cloud
cresting a great white mountain
My father
you render me speechless.

VIII.5.5 How can black sorrow touch me?
Your luminous feet
twin suns of limitless light
shine within me.
What can I say, lord
dark as clouds
heavy with rain, lord
who ate the world
circled by the sea.

VIII.5.6 'Kaṇṇā, dark as storm clouds,
pot-dancer, my fated love,
lord of heaven' I call out
Come claim me.
Let me see your feet
in the sky on earth in the vast sea
anywhere.

Show yourself to me
for a single day.

VIII.5.7 Show yourself.
If you won't
then summon me to your feet
that once measured the world.
Let me serve you,
a brilliant black sun
spreading its countless rays,
your eyes hands feet lips
red as lotuses.

VIII.5.8 Every day I see
a great mass of clouds,
think he's here, melt
then dissolve in defeat.
You drove a chariot
into battle for the five
brought the hundred to their knees
but you won't come for me.
Is this fair?

VIII.5.9 Is this fair?
Warrior wielding a disc sharp as lightning,
you who ride a mighty eagle,
fly that soaring bird on your banner
I yearn for you.
You end the sorrows of this wide world,
mysterious one

born in northern Mathurā
what is in your mind?

VIII.5.10 Mysterious in so many ways
there's the mystery of your births,
the Bharata war, another mystery
You're the great lord within
air fire water ether earth, everything
You're like butter hidden in milk,
invisible but everywhere
Great master of mystery
where can I see you?

VIII.5.11 'Where can I see my lord,
sweet as tuḷasi?'
Śaṭhakōpaṉ of beautiful Kurukūr
spoke these simple words.
Those who master the ten
from among a thousand verses
will know bliss,
night and day,
in this very life.

Tiruvāymoḻi VIII.6 (828–838)
elliyum kālaiyum

VIII.6.1 Night and day we think only of him
this is how he blesses us.
Our father wreathed in lilies and tuḷasi
is with his devotees in Tirukkaṭittāṉam.

VIII.6.2 See, that lord merges Tirukkaṭittāṉam
with my mind, dwells inside.
Long ago his rain of arrows left nothing
of the demon's body. Him singular in war.

VIII.6.3 He's One. He's Two. He's Three.
He's hidden he's within. He tastes sweet.
He lives in Tirukkaṭittāṉam with Śrī on his chest,
that mysterious lord.

VIII.6.4 The mysterious one slayed wicked fate
and with love made my heart his home.
He lives amidst the fragrant groves of Tirukkaṭittāṉam,
where even the luminous immortals come to pray.

VIII.6.5 His temple is in Tirukkaṭittāṉam,
he made my heart his palace too, him
worshipped in Vaikuṇṭha by every god,
the king who dances with pots.

VIII.6.6 The dancer ended all that afflicts me,
wicked though I am. Mysterious Madhusūda
lives in cool Tirukkaṭittāṉam amidst gardens in full bloom
worship him and end your grief.

VIII.6.7 Rot your grief, let your heart rest
at Tirukkaṭittāṉam where men and gods worship
the luminous lotus feet of Govindaṉ
who measured earth and sky.

VIII.6.8 The mysterious lord may live
in fine cities in heaven on this earth in the sea,

Yet he's chosen my heart and Tirukkaṭittāṉam
as his home.

VIII.6.9 He's in many fine cities,
yet the king of cowherds, the marvellous one
has chosen to live in Tirukkaṭittāṉam
city favoured by celestials.

VIII.6.10 Wondrous Nārāyaṇaṉ, Hari, Vāmaṉaṉ
lives in my heart and in Tirukkaṭittāṉam
where the sound of the Veda
echo through groves of kalpaka trees.

VIII.6.11 Śaṭhakōpaṉ of Kurukūr spoke these ten
from a honey-sweet thousand on Tirumāl
who lives amidst the gardens of Tirukkaṭittāṉam.
They will take you to Vaikuṇṭha.

Tiruvāymoḻi VIII.7 (839–849)
iruttum viyantu

VIII.7.1 I begged him for days on end
to place me at his radiant feet.
Now Vāmaṉaṉ sees me, has entered
my mind to dwell there with love.

VIII.7.2 He watches over me, destroying
the rowdy five, ruling my impoverished heart.
I know only the grace he gives,
the great lord who saved the elephant.

VIII.7.3 I know nothing but his grace,
him inside me banishing darkness.
He cares for me more than the three worlds
Is this an illusion or one of his tricks?

VIII.7.4 The enthralling lord of mysterious power
tricked me. The lion among celestials, simple cowherd
my master, placed his radiance within me
his grace shines everywhere.

VIII.7.5 His grace touches me, him
praised by the world stands within me
like a mountain of gems.
What does fame mean to me now?

VIII.7.6 If he gifts me a treasure
a lotus blooming on a mountain of dark gems:
chest feet eyes hands coral lips navel,
to whom can he now gift all of himself?

VIII.7.7 He stands before me all radiance
red lips navel white teeth earrings.
When he enters me a smile on his red lips
I know no greater grace.

VIII.7.8 I only know his grace. He rules me
grants his favour as he wishes
the one who holds the three worlds in his belly
dwells in my little mind.

VIII.7.9 Māl holds kings, their subjects
everyone else, the three worlds in his belly

I took him into my belly with my mind
and have held him there.

VIII.7.10 The supreme one sleeps atop a fierce serpent
on the ocean of milk with its roaring waves.
My mind open I placed him deep inside me
I can never tire of him. I'll never let him leave.

VIII.7.11 These ten verses from a thousand
by Śaṭhakōpaṉ of Kurukūr on Tirumāl's feet,
on him asleep on the ocean, coax our lord's fiery glance
that ends the bonds of birth.

Tiruvāymoḻi VIII.8 (850–860)
kaṇkaḷ civantu

VIII.8.1 He's within me,
bright eyes full lips white teeth
dark as storm clouds, earrings a glittering crown
four broad shoulders, a curved bow a shining conch
mace disc sword,
the peerless one is inside little me.

VIII.8.2 He's in me, within my body
he's in the world and in everything
outside it. He's this and he isn't
the highest lord, sweet scent in fragrance
beyond pleasure and pain,
divine awareness, the peerless one.

VIII.8.3 I took him, the king of celestials
the peerless one into my mind. It is his grace.

He stayed, that too is his grace.
He made me realize
mind life body infinite things
are useless,
then he became me.

VIII.8.4 He became me. He was
before everyone and everything. He is
himself, Śivaṉ, Brahmā. He is
peerless, singular. He is
honey milk sugar nectar sweetness. He is
my body my breath my awareness.
He's the only one I know.

VIII.8.5 I've known it, but can't say
its subtle nature is this or that.
You may know it, but it's impossible to see.
Transcendent indescribable unfading
unknowable as either good or evil
it exists beyond all wisdom.

VIII.8.6 If you go beyond wisdom, cut the senses
know that great rare undying ether,
if you rid yourself of joy and sorrow, of attachments,
then at that very moment, in that very moment
you'll be free.
That's freedom, the only real freedom.

VIII.8.7 That's freedom. Having freedom
is the only joy. If you know this, if you want
nothing, if you gain nothing, that is freedom,
the only joy. Those who don't know this

wonder 'What is freedom?' 'What is joy?'
and tire themselves out with searching.

VIII.8.8 'He's gone, he's gone, he's gone' cry
your kin your neighbours pressed together
as a crowd. As you go they'll clutch at you
like drunkards, madness rising, desire flowing.
At that moment remember our lord
place him in your heart. That's the right way.

VIII.8.9 It's good if you can become one,
but to be one is to be the mysterious lord
with the dancing bird and high-flying banner
that's impossible for he's him and we're us.
Still bound to earth, some imagine themselves free,
yogis wandering the earth clutching a fake prize.

VIII.8.10 He exists for those who say he is
even for those who say otherwise.
My peerless one now lives in me
vanquishing death and birth
light and dark, wisdom and ignorance
that wax and wane like the moon.

VIII.8.11 Śaṭhakōpaṉ blessed by Tirumāl
who vanquished wisdom and ignorance
who placed Ayaṉ and Śivaṉ at his glorious feet
sang these ten verses from a thousand,
they reach us to our king
our brilliant black gem.

Tiruvāymoḻi VIII.9 (861–871)
karu māṇikka malai mēl

VIII.9.1 Radiant Tirumāl
is like a mountain of black gems
thick with lotuses,
red chest lips eyes hands navel feet clothes
She has no words
but the names of the mysterious one
who's in Tiruppuliyūr
amidst the lush fields of Kuṭṭanāṭu.
Friends, what can I do?

VIII.9.2 Friends, what can I do?
All she says is
our lord is in Tiruppuliyūr
with its gardens of puṉṉai
wearing his tall glittering crown
and jewels of every kind
he's like glorious Meru
touched by a glowing sun
like countless stars in the sky.

VIII.9.3 Night and day she speaks
only of Tiruppuliyūr
with its tall glittering palaces,
city of the one
who plunges into battle
his fiery disc raised
to cut down demons,
him a blue sea of fire,
a roiling flame.

VIII.9.4 Lush gardens sugar cane ripe paddy
cool sedge the well-tilled earth
proclaim the wealth
of Kuṭṭanāṭu's Tiruppuliyūr,
city of the god of gods
who ate and spat the worlds.
She can only speak his names.
She can only speak his greatness,
this beautiful gem of a girl.

VIII.9.5 If you study her jewels her clothes
note her ethereal lustre
you know she's gone
beyond understanding.
She's submerged in his love,
the lord who rules the three worlds
father who lives in cool Tiruppuliyūr
where lotuses fill lakes.

VIII.9.6 She's submerged
in his love
bears the mark
of that love,
soft lips red as fruit of the betel tree
ripening in cool Tiruppuliyūr
by his grace,
the place that Kaṇṇaṉ dark as water
has kindly made his home.

VIII.9.7 Tender green creepers clutch
the young trunks of betel trees,
cool breezes touch

ripening plantains
rustle the leaves of coconut palms
in Tiruppuliyūr,
home of her dear Kaṇṇaṉ
Our simple little girl
has reached his feet there.

VIII.9.8 Friends, how do I explain?
She can utter nothing
but his names,
the one asleep on a serpent in Tiruppuliyūr,
where wealthy brahmins
recite the northern language
feed the sacrificial fires
and raise clouds of smoke
enough to obscure the heavens.

VIII.9.9 Night and day she speaks
of nothing but his city
encircled by fields,
Tiruppuliyūr
where the Veda thunder like the sea,
where crocodiles live
in ponds blooming with lotuses
bright as flames,
where Kaṇṇaṉ black as water lives.

VIII.9.10 Why does she smell of sweet tuḷasi?
Why else?
She's touched by the love
of Māyappirāṉ, the mysterious lord

of Kuṭṭanāṭu's Tiruppuliyūr,
clustered with jewel-bright mansions
tall as hills,
the crimson dot on the brow
of the southern lands.

VIII.9.11 Śaṭhakōpaṉ,
servant of the servants
of the servants
who serve
the master of the three worlds,
sang a garland of thousand verses
in perfect Tamiḻ
Those who master this decad
will also be bound to serve Neṭumāl.

Tiruvāymoḻi VIII.10 (872–882)
neṭumāṟku aṭimai

VIII.10.1 I pretended to serve Neṭumāl
like his devotees, and even that
rid me of my wicked ways.
Is there an easier path
for a wretch like me
than to serve his servants?
No. Not even if you win the three worlds.

VIII.10.2 If I win the three worlds,
even if I become him
can it equal the joy
of serving at his supplicants' feet?

Their victory is to shelter under his feet
covered in flowers
He's the one dark as storm clouds.

VIII.10.3 He stretched out his tiny form
and took the three worlds
my lord with lotus-bright eyes.
When his great devotees, simple men
who rule me still wander the world,
is it right that I should shelter at his feet,
fragrant with the scent of flowers.

VIII.10.4 Why shouldn't I wander here?
I've been blessed to worship him
with flowers, praise spilling from my lips,
him in my heart, my senses bound to my lord
with eyes bright as lotus
and a coral-red mouth
that ate and spat out the world.

VIII.10.5 If I am so blessed
to worship him, to rest
at the feet of the mysterious one,
to know the swirling pleasure of his light,
could it ever compare to this lowly birth,
learning his greatness with others,
singing of him in a rush of poetry?

VIII.10.6 To sing in praise of my lord
who cut down the raging elephant
with his golden disc, my lord

who crushed the lives of wild-eyed demons,
him who rides the great bird,
can this ever compare
to release from the three worlds?

VIII.10.7 He as himself was Brahmā
the first seed who sprouted
the three worlds
lord of singular eternal fame.
Even if I find shelter under his divine feet,
it can't equal the joy
of being one with his devotees.

VIII.10.8 He made the cool ocean,
spread himself, his feet his shoulders his hair
everywhere,
lay like a forest of wish-fulfilling trees
blanketing a mountain of gems
glowing like a thousand suns.
Still I only want to be among his devotees.

VIII.10.9 He destroys the wickedness
in his devotees with his many weapons
the disc conch sword bow staff
Eternal youth, father of love
I am alone, but
exalted in the company
of his servants' servants' servants.

VIII.10.10 In age after age,
I only want to be in a family

of servants of servants of servants
of the eternal servants
of my father dark as kāya flowers,
with his four large shoulders and golden disc.
They rule me.

VIII.10.11 Śaṭhakōpaṉ of lovely Kurukūr
spoke these ten verses from a thousand
about the one with eyes bright as lotuses,
the one who fills
the three worlds rich in virtue.
Those who master them will live a good life
happy with their wives and children.

The Ninth Hundred

Tiruvāymoḻi IX.1 (883–893)
koṇṭa peṇṭir

IX.1.1 Wives children kin neighbours everyone
love you for what you have. Be bound to the lord
who ate the eight directions, space, everything
He's the only refuge.

IX.1.2 While you have wealth, they'll pretend friendship
only to suck you dry like leeches. The storm-dark one
who pierced seven trees with a single arrow
is the only refuge. There's nothing else.

IX.1.3 When you're rich, they'll sing your praises
when in dark despair, they'll grow mute.
The one born in Mathurā, him a doom to demons,
is your only refuge. Bind yourself to him and earn his grace.

IX.1.4 We think them our refuge, but they're selfish
as moneylenders. Why go on about this?
Think of the glory of the one born in Mathurā,
there's no other way, he's the only refuge.

IX.1.5 They succumb to the pleasures
of sweet-talking women, then feel their rejection.
There's no greater joy than to serve
the one born in Mathurā, him a killer of demons.

IX.1.6 Joy doesn't exist in this world,
unheeding of this, so many just live and die.
Speak of the glory of him born in ancient Mathurā.

To put it simply, there's nothing else.

IX.1.7 I've told you plainly, there's nothing else
for every living thing in this vast wide world.
Think of him, learn to praise him, live to praise
the faultless one born in Mathurā.

IX.1.8 This is the way to spend a lifetime:
praising the one born in Mathurā, a companion
to the guileless who think only of him,
the mysterious lord. There's nothing greater.

IX.1.9 A life wasted, to think there's nothing greater,
is like stretching your lobes till they're useless.
There's no refuge but Kaṇṇaṉ,
born in Mathurā, city of mansions.

IX.1.10 There's no other refuge but Kaṇṇaṉ,
born in Mathurā to ease the world's burden
Surrender what's yours to his feet
everything is his, there's nothing but him.

IX.1.11 Those who sing these ten verses from the
thousand in flawless Tamiḻ by Kurukūr's Śaṭhakōpaṉ,
who bowed with devotion to Kaṇṇaṉ alone,
will rule us forever.

Tiruvāymoḻi IX.2 (894–904)
paṇṭai nāḷālē

IX.2.1 We've served you forever,
by your grace and hers,

coming to your temple
generation after generation,
binding ourselves to you.
Lord asleep in Tiruppuḷiṅkuṭi,
circled by fields and the clear Porunal,
speak to us, look at us.

IX.2.2 We are bound to you
through generations
utterly yours, we serve you
sheltering beneath your feet.
One asleep in Tiruppuḷiṅkuṭi,
circled by golden walls and cool fields,
ornament my head with your feet
that stretched out beyond measure.

IX.2.3 How long did you lie there,
surely your body's now sore.
We are bonded to you in eternal service.
Open your lotus-bright eyes,
rise with Śrī, your lotus-born woman,
lord asleep in Tiruppuḷiṅkuṭi,
where the three worlds gather to pray,
grant us this grace.

IX.2.4 You lie in Tiruppuḷiṅkuṭi,
sit in Varaguṇamaṅgai, stand in Vaikuṇṭha,
you rule my mind without end.
Amaze the three worlds, give me grace,
making them dance and shout
let us see you

your gleaming storm-dark body
your coral-red lips.

IX.2.5 Let us see you,
your coral-red lips your smile,
your teeth bright as pearls,
your lotus-bright eyes.
You rode in on your fierce eagle
to save the elephant, now
you lie in Tiruppuḷiṅkuṭi by the Porunal,
its bed dense with coral and conch.

IX.2.6 You rode in on your fierce eagle
like a gold mountain capped by dark storm clouds,
killed brutal Māli and Sumāli.
Kāyciṉa Vēṉtē, my ferocious king
wearing a crown of rays,
you're in Tiruppuḷiṅkuṭi circled by green fields.
Use your five merciless weapons
end my suffering.

IX.2.7 You end my suffering, you rule me,
do the same for the unblinking celestials.
You recline in Tiruppuḷiṅkuṭi
with its fields of lotus bursting red.
Hear the din of our love
know the joy of our hearts
even if for just a day, show yourself
to the simple people of this world.

IX.2.8 So everyone in this world
worships your feet, their love ripe

vying to praise you with their speech,
lord asleep in Tiruppuḷiṅkuṭi
with its mansions that touch the moon
great god of Tiruvaikuṇṭham,
some day make a place for yourself
somewhere in this vast world too.

IX.2.9 Make a place for yourself
in this vast world too
so we can praise you without pause,
see you without cease
sipping your body like bees at a new bloom.
You're in Tiruppuḷiṅkuṭi with its fields
of darting carp and ripening grain,
lord whose weapons wipe out demon clans.

IX.2.10 With your fierce weapons
you end the gods' grief, bring demons pain.
You are poison to evil, nectar to me,
one in Tiruppuḷiṅkuṭi,
where peerless Śrī and Bhū
caress your tender feet.
Call me to you,
let me hold them just once.

IX.2.11 Śaṭhakōpaṉ from the land of Vaḻuti
where the swollen Porunal flows
sweetly said to him
who churned the ocean
'Come to me or let me come to you'
Those who master these ten from a thousand songs

will keep him in their hearts forever,
the one who measured the three worlds.

Tiruvāymoḻi IX.3 (905–915)
ōr āyiramāy

IX.3.1 He protects the seven worlds in a thousand forms
that great one of a thousand names
his beautiful body dark as storm clouds
is our own Nārāyaṇaṉ.

IX.3.2 He made this wide earth then dug it up
He ate it then spat it out. He measured it too.
He is him is him is he is everything.
We know this.

IX.3.3 Incomprehensible to the wise Veda
incomprehensible to all the wise books
the wise worship Hari as all
the cure to the ills of the wise.

IX.3.4 'You're our bliss' say the gods
he's my lord, the black god Kaṇṇaṉ
who gives you heaven.
My mind, never leave him.

IX.3.5 Mind, I am wretched but I
caṉ say this with conviction, listen well.
Never leave him, the peerless one
adorned in garlands of cool tuḷasi.

IX.3.6 He holds lovely Śrī in an embrace
wages terrible war against demons
churns the ocean for nectar.
My heart is entirely with him.

IX.3.7 He merged two bodies as Narasiṅkaṉ
then split a body with his sharp claws.
To see him in Vaikuṇṭha is all my mind thinks
night and day.

IX.3.8 He destroys both good and bad deeds
so we inhabit no new bodies, are released.
On this vast earth, he's in Vēṅkaṭam
where the gods go to pray.

IX.3.9 It isn't enough to worship you
with flowers water flames fragrance
lord of ancient fame asleep on your snake,
I don't know how to reach your feet.

IX.3.10 He blossoms from your navel.
He is in your body, the one with a polished axe.
Those who worship you are gods
how can my praise ever suffice?

IX.3.11 Śaṭhakōpaṉ of beautiful Kurukūr
sang a garland of thousand verses to adorn
the feet of the one of limitless perfection.
Those who master these ten will reach Vaikuṇṭha.

Tiruvāymoḻi IX.4 (916–926)
maiyār karuṅkaṇṇi

IX.4.1 A lotus blooms on your chest, the goddess
with kohl-black eyes. You're Tirumāl.
You hold the burning disc and spiral conch
my eyes think only to see you.

IX.4.2 You're my eyes. My heart thinks
of all the ways to see you, cries out.
Gods and ascetics may struggle to see you
I won't stop till I reach you.

IX.4.3 I am like a dog wagging its tail. I call for you,
dissolve. Long ago you lifted a mountain
to shield your herds from the rain.
I doubt your grace will find me.

IX.4.4 I became yours, thinking this right,
my simple heart frets for what lies ahead.
Even celestials and demons struggle to know you
elusive lion, my lord.

IX.4.5 Lord, lion, god of gods, great one
primordial creator of the creator
asleep on the serpent, dark one
my only thought is to see your feet.

IX.4.6 You're thought. Longing to see you
I fixed you firmly in my heart.
Primordial leader of the gods, infinite light
I hold you within me. I rejoice.

IX.4.7 I rejoice. You live within me, deep inside
perfect one, you've made your place there.
You ripped the chest of the great Dāṉavaṉ
with your claws, Narasiṅka.

IX.4.8 He stands beyond the six religious paths,
he's the essence of all things, primordial one
womb of the gods, Kaṇṇaṉ,
I've seen him. I've found him.

IX.4.9 I've found him. My eyes drink him in.
All my old deeds are dead, my bonds severed
I made this garland of nectar for his servants
he's the god of gods and I am his servant.

IX.4.10 'This one's mine' he said and gave me grace
the lord who flies the eagle banner, the one
who measured worlds without faltering
I've reached his feet.

IX.4.11 These ten from the thousand in sets of hundred
by Śaṭhakōpaṉ of southern Kurukūr with its fertile fields
brings you to him who killed the mad elephant,
him who is life to the gods.

Tiruvāymoḻi IX.5 (927–937)
iṉuyirc cēvalum

IX.5.1 You and your sweet mate coo at each other
hurting my very life. How much longer, little kuyils?
You won't call Kaṇṇaṉ, dear to me as life
do you really mean to chatter my life away?

IX.5.2 You long for each other, aṉṟil,
you keep calling out in yearning.
Govindaṉ the trickster is unreliable,
yet my life lies in his hands.

IX.5.3 My precious life lies in his hand, aṉṟil,
you coo lovingly, prance and dance around me.
I've done nothing to help me survive. I am wrecked
How long can I live listening to your love talk?

IX.5.4 Even if he hears you, my mysterious Kaṇṇaṉ
won't come. Peacocks, cease your high-pitched calls.
My words my heart my deeds are with him
my body and my life stranded somewhere, stumble.

IX.5.5 Mynahs warbling uselessly, stop chattering
I make no place for you. He, with Śrī on his chest,
He, who took the seven worlds with tricks,
He thinks to consume my life now.

IX.5.6 I thought it a good idea to raise you, little parrots
stop chattering. Your red beak and lustrous body
remind me of Kākuttaṉ precious as life, my Kaṇṇaṉ
who took me devoured me left me.

IX.5.7 He took me devoured me left me,
Kaṇṇaṉ of lovely eyes and red lips, a flawless dark gem.
Storm clouds, flashing like his bow, don't show yourselves
you are death to me.

IX.5.8 This will be my death, I said. Still
silly kuyil, you spoke Kaṇṇaṉ's names.

I pampered you with fine food, taught you speech
and this is the fine character you show.

IX.5.9 Don't sing fine bees. Your sweet song
pierces like a spear prodding a wound.
Kaṇṇaṉ with eyes like full bloomed lotuses
devoured my life, then left.

IX.5.10 I've gone with him to his home in heaven
so why are you still here, cranes of the field?
My lovely body sheds its jewels, slips away,
let the world be happy.

IX.5.11 The mysterious one who grants pervasive eternal joy,
let Kurukūr's Śaṭhakōpaṉ sing in his praise
these nine plus one verses sung from the thousand
that will melt the hearts of the three worlds.

Tiruvāymoḻi IX.6 (938–948)
urukumāl neñcam

IX.6.1 My heart dissolves beyond the limits of life
my desire swells, what can I do?
I think of the mysterious one and his tricks
the one who lives in Tirukkāṭkarai
where flowers perfume the streets.

IX.6.2 My heart splinters, dissolves
with every thought, my precious life burns
with every word of praise, Kāṭkarai Appā,
my father in Tirukkāṭkarai with its fragrant gardens
I can't imagine how to serve you.

IX.6.3 He tricked my heart, it's his nature.
He entered me, became my life, then devoured it
My father dark as storm clouds
is in Kāṭkarai with its lush forests
I don't understand his tricks.

IX.6.4 I don't understand his grace.
The worlds are in him, he's the lord within them
yet my father in Kāṭkarai
city of fragrant groves
devours my precious little life.

IX.6.5 Grace was a pretext to enter me,
to devour my body and my precious life
all at once. These are the tricks
of dark beautiful Kaṇṇaṉ, my father
who lives in Kāṭkarai encircled by gardens.

IX.6.6 My Kaṇṇaṉ's tricks are like an adornment.
He devoured me left my precious life dry.
Foolishly it laments day and night
calling for Kaṇṇaṉ
praising his Kāṭkarai.

IX.6.7 As desire sharpens, I dissolve.
I thought he'll just take me over,
but the mysterious one devoured me.
As my life shrinks I praise Kāṭkarai
Kaṇṇaṉ lives there.

IX.6.8 He didn't ask anything
just devoured my life, day by day

ate me entirely. My father
is in Kāṭkarai with its dark storm clouds
I am his, still see how I suffer.

IX.6.9 Who knows what I've known?
His eyes are large unfurled lotuses
his lips a ripe red fruit
his arms are broad and beautiful
the one in Kāṭkarai with its lovely rain clouds.

IX.6.10 If I see you, I'll swallow you whole
I thought. Before I could,
he drank me completely, my father
in Kāṭkarai, him dark as storm clouds,
is very clever indeed.

IX.6.11 These ten from the beautiful thousand
by Śaṭhakōpaṉ of southern Kurukūr,
encircled by walls covered in creepers,
about the lord who killed cruel Kaṁsaṉ
will end birth, will kill this mirage.

Tiruvāymoḻi IX.7 (949–959)
em kāṉal

IX.7.1 Red-legged cranes, happily feeding
in my marshes, take a message
to the one in Tirumūḻikkaḷam
my pot-dancer, with tuḷasi in his hair
Do this, and you and your friends
may rest your feet on my head.

IX.7.2 Herons, never apart from your mates,
eternally in love, the one in Mūḻikkaḷam
spurns me, my kin here shame me.
Am I not good enough
for him and his people?
Why should I live? Ask him.

IX.7.3 Storks stalking prey in these pools
ask him if I am good enough for him.
He lives in cool Tirumūḻikkaḷam
his eyes blossoming lotuses
his lips a ripe red fruit
his body a dark lustrous lotus leaf.

IX.7.4 Beautiful clouds, go as messengers
to wealthy Tirumūḻikkaḷam.
If you ask him to reveal
his lovely body to me,
will he strip you of your lustre
and chase you from the sky?

IX.7.5 Bright clouds racing across the sky
in swirls of fire, he lives in my heart,
his sacred heavenly city.
Him a flame in Tirumūḻikkaḷam
Him with tuḷasi in his hair
I am a wretch, give him my message anyway.

IX.7.6 Sweet-voiced bees
speak my message to him
He's in Mūḻikkaḷam
lush with honey-rich groves.

Tell him who keeps the goddess on his chest
about the state of my bangles.

IX.7.7 He slipped out of my grasp,
taking my bangles with him. Wild herons,
some day when you see that famous one
in Tirumūḻikkaḷam, when you see
his lotus-bright eyes his coral-red lips
speak well of me.

IX.7.8 Bees and dragonflies
feasting in these gardens,
speak well of me to him
dark as a kāya bloom, to him
with tuḷasi in his hair, to him
who's made Tirumūḻikkaḷam his home.

IX.7.9 Young storks, living in these waters
my breasts are pale, my eyes fill with tears.
Tell him who wears a crown of sweet tuḷasi
and holds a gold disc, tell him
who lives in Tirumūḻikkaḷam,
that he's kept himself from me,
and it isn't fair.

IX.7.10 Pretty geese with your slow gait,
happily feeding in these wide pools,
I've grown so thin jewels slip from my body.
Now go to Tirumūḻikkaḷam
before I lose my life,
tell him this isn't right.

IX.7.11 These ten, a song about a girl,
from the immortal thousand
by Śaṭhakōpaṉ of perfect Kurukūr
about the brilliant light
who always lives in Tirumūḻikkaḷam
will cure all ills.

Tiruvāymoḻi IX.8 (960–970)
aṟukkum viṉaiyāyiṉa

IX.8.1 Fate fades for those who think
only of holding him in their hearts.
How do I reach Tirunāvāy
surrounded by cool fragrant gardens?

IX.8.2 He's husband to her, slender as a vine
dear to Piṉṉai, with eyes sharp as spears
He towers over the gardens of Tirunāvāy
when will I reach him?

IX.8.3 When will I reach him?
I think only of this and weep.
Faultless Tirunāraṇaṉ is in Tirunāvāy
I don't know when I'll get there.

IX.8.4 I've served him without pause,
I don't know when I'll join him.
Dear to Piṉṉai, her eyes sharp as spears,
he lives amidst the lush gardens of Tirunāvāy.

IX.8.5 Husband to Śrī and Bhū,
eye of all the worlds and all the gods.

His home is in the sky but he lives in Tirunāvāy
when will my eyes drink him in?

IX.8.6 When will my eyes drink you in?
I've lived to serve only you without flaw
My king of cowherds lives in Tirunāvāy
surrounded by gardens of flowers and bees.

IX.8.7 You took the world from great Bali,
conqueror of demons, lord of gods, Tirumāl
my prince, my Nāraṇa living in Nāvāy
mark me as your servant, give me this grace.

IX.8.8 You can stop short of offering grace
but make me yours, shelter me beneath your feet,
grant me clarity so you're firmly in my heart,
remove all doubt, my lord in Tirunāvāy.

IX.8.9 Even gods and sages can't see you,
first among three, ruler of the three worlds
you chose to live in Tirunāvāy
who can be close to you?

IX.8.10 When will I be close to you, Tirumāl?
It's all I think of and my heart grows heavy
I call to you, my dark jewel who lives
in Tirunāvāy, surrounded by gardens.

IX.8.11 Śaṭhakōpaṉ of Kurukūr sang these ten
from a thousand in musical Tamiḻ
about him who is in Tirunāvāy, city of mansions.
Those who master them will rule the world.

Tiruvāymoḻi IX.9 (971–981)
mallikai kamaḻ

IX.9.1 The breeze sweet with jasmine cuts
the haunting notes of kuṟiñci pierce
the waning light of dusk bewilders
the red evening clouds destroy me
My lord with eyes bright as lotus
that bull among cowherds,
a lion, the mysterious one
embraced these shoulders, these breasts
Now where has he gone?
Why am I alone?

IX.9.2 Forlorn forsaken, I've nowhere to go
to escape the mournful bells the gentle breeze
water lilies the dying light of day the scent of sandal
keening songs the jasmine filling the air
This wide world created dug up
eaten spat out measured ruled
by that mysterious one, lord of cowherds,
death to demons
He still does not come
who can save me now?

IX.9.3 Who is to save me now?
My soft breasts yielded to his touch, my hips too
when he pushed into me, plunged deep into my self
then he left, abandoned me,
cast me aside, thief.
Now Kaṇṇaṉ that young lion,

my mysterious lord won't return
his lotus eyes his lush lips his cool dark curls
his four wide shoulders torment my heart
this is my wretched fate.

IX.9.4 I am wrecked.
A breeze pierces my heart
one moment cool one moment hot
the moon burns, my soft bed of flowers scalds.
He swooped down on Garuḍa,
came to me,
a divine bee sipped me like a flower
left me drained and depleted
His wicked ways are more than I can bear
my heart is no help at all.

IX.9.5 The heart is no friend.
As evening falls the cows return
and my cowherd's heart
turns to stone.
His flute's sweet song cuts deep
and my friends, my dear companions
filled with worry for me
swoon before my eyes.
Who is to protect my life?
How hard it is to earn his grace.

IX.9.6 How hard it is to earn his grace
but only his grace will suffice
nothing else can save my life.
Evening ends the day,
my heart is lost.

He joins himself to Śivaṉ to Brahmā to Śrī
He cuts into me
Where do I hide?
What can I do?
What is left to be said?

IX.9.7 What is left to be said?
The sharp cold breeze singes my breath
still my stolen heart is with deceitful Kaṇṇaṉ,
dark as storm clouds.
The wind from the north bears down
carrying with it the fine smoke of akil
the harp's haunting melodies
cool red sandal and heady jasmine
with such an army, it wages war against me
I am destroyed.

IX.9.8 I burn.
The young breeze from the north surges
heady with the scent of fresh jasmine,
the red sky fades bringing misery
greater than Kaṇṇaṉ's deceit.
He came. He left.
Crueller still are the sweet jasmine and fresh sandal
but most cruel of all,
the haunting song he plays for his cowherd women
This I cannot bear.

IX.9.9 He slays me with his sweet song
his bright eyes speak secrets

his darting glances toy with me
he makes a sad face
then pretends to be hurt
To ease the pain in my stupid heart
he sings another song.
I know nothing except
evening has come and
he has not.

IX.9.10 Evening has come and
he has not.
Soft cowbells sound like a lament
as the cows nuzzle their mighty bulls
a flute's cruel song fills the air, while
bees hover and hum
over bright clusters of jasmine
the sea's howls rend the sky
How do I console myself
when I cannot live without him?

IX.9.11 The lovely cowherd women
bereft of him, not wanting to live
filled the evening with their wails.
These ten verses from his thousand
are Kurukūr's Māraṉ Śaṭhakōpaṉ's lament,
his songs of yearning
for the one who ate and spat out worlds.
Sing this garland of words and live well
Sing these words and draw near him. Māl.

Tiruvāymoḻi IX.10 (982–992)
mālai naṇṇi

IX.10.1 Draw near Māl,
worship him and end your fate
day and night offer flowers at his feet
He's the one at rest on a banyan leaf,
abiding now in Tirukkaṇṇapuram,
where waves crash against the city's tall walls.

IX.10.2 Worship him
with flowers dripping honey
He abides in Tirukkaṇṇapuram,
protected by tall walls that touch the stars,
a city of fertile fields and ponds teeming with crabs.
Keep his city in mind devotees, and rise up.

IX.10.3 Devotees, if you wish
to end your suffering, love only him,
worship him with fresh flowers.
The ruler of worlds, great lord of celestials
abides in Tirukkaṇṇapuram,
city of gardens where bees sing.

IX.10.4 Worship the beloved
of doe-eyed Piṉṉai with honey-sweet flowers,
the one who of his own volition
lives in Tirukkaṇṇapuram,
city circled by walls that touch the sky.
That great lord is our only refuge.

IX.10.5 He is refuge for anyone
who reaches his feet. At death
he gives you Vaikuṇṭha.
He's in Tirukkaṇṇapuram, circled by mighty walls
He rules the world, is filled with love
for those who love him.

IX.10.6 He loves everyone who reaches his feet,
he mauled the demon's red-gold body.
The one full of love
lives in Tirukkaṇṇapuram,
circled by high golden walls
He is truth to those who are true to him.

IX.10.7 He is all that is true
for those who love him, hidden
to those whose worship is shallow.
He's in Tirukkaṇṇapuram,
where fish thrive in the fields
He's close to those who hold him tight.

IX.10.8 He is dear to anyone
who reaches his feet.
He ends illness death birth
the supreme one in Tirukkaṇṇapuram,
city encircled by glittering walls
Worship his feet every day.

IX.10.9 Worship his feet every day
and nothing can bind you.

What do I lack?
He's in Tirukkaṇṇapuram, city of brahmins.
Suffering can't touch
those who've reached the primordial one.

IX.10.10 I don't suffer any more
what do I lack?
The one with Śrī on his chest
is in Tirukkaṇṇapuram,
city of sturdy stone walls
Just utter its name, banish pain.

IX.10.11 If you want to break
the painful bonds of fate,
sing and dance these ten
from the thousand Tamiḻ songs
by Śaṭhakōpaṉ of Kurukūr.
Worship his feet.

The Tenth Hundred

Tiruvāymoḻi X.1 (993–1003)
tāḷa tāmarai

X.1.1 He's happy in Tirumōkūr, abiding there always
amidst lush fields and lotus ponds.
He's the only way, Kālamegham,
dark as storm clouds,
with flowing hair lotus eyes red lips
whose four strong shoulders vanquish demons.

X.1.2 I've no other way but to shelter
under the cool shade of his feet,
the lord wreathed in sweet tuḷasi
the lord with a thousand names
He's in Tirumōkūr, city of good brahmins
who've mastered the four Veda.

X.1.3 'We have nowhere else to go' cried
Nāṉmukaṉ, Araṉ, all the other gods,
turning to him in need,
he roams the three worlds to protect them.
He is in Tirumōkūr.
Let me reach it and end my suffering.

X.1.4 'End our suffering, rule us'
plead gods and sages
praising that light.
He reclines on a serpent, its hood spread wide.
He's in Tirumōkūr,
let us serve his feet that end all suffering.

X.1.5 We serve our light, the singular cause
who measured the three worlds.
He's in lovely Tirumōkūr,
dense with sugar cane and red paddy
Let us circle his temple
Let us dance there.

X.1.6 Dancer, Kōvalaṉ, death
to disruptive demons, joy
to devotees gods sages,
Āttaṉ, friend in Tirumōkūr
surrounded by cool gardens and rich fields
We have no refuge but your lotus feet.

X.1.7 We have no refuge but you
great primordial creator of the waters,
of the ancient sages, of the gods
maker of worlds.
You're in Tirumōkūr
we circle you there, our grief fades.

X.1.8 Grief fades when you come here
to worship in lovely Tirumōkūr
with its lush gardens and cool pools,
the one who ruined demons
of a thousand names, Daśarathaṉ's son,
a glittering emerald pool.

X.1.9 Luminous feet flower-bright eyes
coral-red lips four broad jewelled shoulders,
a god who overwhelms demons, the king

is amidst the gardens of Tirumōkūr.
We've reached it
our only refuge.

X.1.10 The gods in fear of wicked demons
sought him as their only refuge.
Like so, he assumes the form
we desire to protect us
He is in Tirumōkūr,
speak of this place think of it praise it.

X.1.11 Grief stops
for those who master
these ten verses on Tirumōkūr
from the thousand made in humble service
by Śaṭhakōpaṉ of Kurukūr
in praise of that pot-dancer.

Tiruvāymoḻi X.2 (1004–1014)
keṭum iṭar

X.2.1 We say Keśavā and our grief ends,
death's cruel attendants cannot draw near.
He relishes his rest on the venomous serpent
He's in Aṉantapuram,
city of ponds and fields thrumming with bees
Let us enter there.

X.2.2 If you go there this moment,
pain can never touch you.
The mysterious one in Aṉantapuram,

city of towering mansions and fragrant groves,
his one name is equal to a thousand,
it brings you heaven.

X.2.3 The eagle he rides flutters on his banner,
he ate and spat out entire worlds
Quickly enter his cool Aṉantapuram
to end the illness of wicked deeds
I know this for sure,
utter just one of his thousand names.

X.2.4 Speak. Don't be shy.
Look how they worship him
in the right way, showering him with flowers
the one who resides with love in Aṉantapuram
encircled by fields and the vast ocean.
They are blessed.

X.2.5 Worship him with flowers and water
think of the father's names and end your births.
I speak of what I know well.
Shelter beneath the lotus feet
of the one in Aṉantapuram, city of gardens,
and become a god.

X.2.6 First among the gods, praised
by the king of the gods in Aṉantapuram,
worshipped there by celestials,
listen people, we too must go there, to the one
who ended the grief of Kumaraṉ's father,
we must reach Govindaṉ there.

X.2.7 Govindaṉ, destroyer and creator
of worlds of lives of gods of everything,
is my supreme god, him asleep on a snake
in lovely Aṉantapuram.
Simply sweeping its threshold
will end cruel fate.

X.2.8 Cruel fate will end when you see
Kāma's father in lovely Aṉantapuram,
his chosen abode. He's asleep there
under the serpent's raised hood
See his feet. Go, people,
I've revealed all I know.

X.2.9 Time grows short.
Aṉantapuram, city of gardens,
brims with goodness.
When you offer fresh flowers and incense
at Vāmaṉaṉ's feet
your deeds will simply disappear.

X.2.10 Say Mādhavā and your deeds
will sever themselves.
Offer perfect worship
with fragrance flowers flame
to our father in Aṉantapuram
and earn limitless fame.

X.2.11 Those who master
these five and five verses from the thousand
by Māṟaṉ of Kurukūr about the primordial one

in Aṉantapuram of limitless fame
will embrace beautiful women
in the land of the gods.

Tiruvāymoḻi X.3 (1015–1025)
vēymaru tōḷ iṇai

X.3.1 My shoulders slender as bamboo droop
I grow thin and lonely, still
the pretty cuckoos and flocks of peacocks
don't notice, but dance and coo.
You've gone to graze your cows,
a single day stretches into thousand aeons
Your lotus eyes cut me, still, Kaṇṇā,
you show no mercy.

X.3.2 Kaṇṇā, you show no mercy.
When you cupped my full breasts, at your touch
joy flooded crashing beyond the sky, drowning
thought, washing over me. It ended in a dream.
Desire entered, entered every part of me
I cannot bear it. Don't leave.
Parting kills me. You go
to graze your cows. Don't.

X.3.3 I die when you go
to graze your cows. Breath burns life
and I have no one. I don't know if I'll live
to see your black body dance.
When you leave, the day grows long

and my eyes won't stop their tears.
I'm just a lowly girl from a lowly cowherd clan
end my deadly loneliness now.

X.3.4 Govindā, you don't think
of our loneliness nor the grief
that comes from parting. You choose
to leave us, you choose your cows.
Your honey-sweet words flood me, enter
my heart my mind, infuse my every pore
I think of the lies that spill from your berry-red lips
and burn.

X.3.5 Kaṇṇā, I think of your lies and burn.
All day you're gone to your cows
the jasmine-touched breeze bears down
the evening descends like a rutting elephant.
Press your chest to my breasts, scent them with jasmine
give me the sweetness of your lips
touch your lotus-soft hands
to my head.

X.3.6 Beautiful Kaṇṇā, caress my head
there are many who clasp your feet,
but that's not for me. I cannot practise
such restraint. Tears drip without pause
from the deep pool of my eyes
My heart won't stop. When you go
to graze your cows, you break me and I melt
like wax in a flame.

X.3.7 My life melts like wax in a flame
jewels slip off my body, pearls drip
from my flower-like eyes,
my breasts are pale, my shoulders droop
You brilliant as a dark gem,
your feet soft as red lotuses must hurt
as you follow your cows. Still you go,
what if demons found you there?

X.3.8 What if demons found you there?
I fret, my life shudders. Don't go.
Love and desire mingle inside me
it hurts. Don't slip from my grasp
show your bewitching eyes your lips
your hands your yellow silk
to women with tiny waists. Enjoy them
but don't go.

X.3.9 When you're with these virtuous women
enjoying them, your heart free of sorrow
we are happy too. Our restraint is gone.
Don't go grazing your cows, my lord,
Kaṁsaṉ's goons arrive on his orders
assuming any form they wish
Terrible things will happen
Listen to me. Don't go.

X.3.10 Listen to me, terrible things will happen
when Kaṁsaṉ's goons gather. They wander
frightening even ascetics.
You're always alone, refuse

even Balarāma's company. I think
of all this and fret. My life burns.
Our divine cowherd, lord of berry-red lips,
you love your cows even more than heaven.

X.3.11 Śaṭhakōpaṉ of Kurukūr,
city awash in conches from the Porunal,
sang these ten verses from a thousand
about the feet of the divine cowherd
and his women who despaired at their parting
when he left to graze his cows.
Those who utter these words
will have him too.

Tiruvāymoḻi X.4 (1026–1036)
cārvē tavaneṟi

X.4.1 Dwell only on Dāmodaraṉ's feet, the sole path.
He is dark as the ocean, his eyes lotus-bright
He holds the disc, he is water sky earth fire air,
the glorious one praised by the gods.

X.4.2 Greater than the gods who live in the sky
impossible to see for those distant from themselves
Māl on whose chest Śrī always rests
destroys the twin fates. He rules me.

X.4.3 The one with the disc rules me. What do I lack?
I've shed the grief of birth, I'll never return
I've seen the feet of Piṉṉai's beloved
I adorn my head with his feet.

X.4.4 I adorn my head with his feet, the one
asleep on a banyan leaf, the one in the mountains
where celestials worship him. I cannot move him
from my mind. This is certain, he's inside me.

X.4.5 I'm certain, he's in my heart and won't leave,
the great lord with the disc is full of tricks
untrue to unbelievers, true to those who love him.
He is ours, the one asleep on his serpent.

X.4.6 The lord asleep on his serpent grants grace
to all who hold him in their hearts. I worship his feet,
the one who made a place within himself for the god
who wears a young crescent moon in his matted hair.

X.4.7 Heart, always worship the highest one
and no illness will touch you. Madhusūdaṉaṉ
a flame bright as a jewel, destroys all birth.
My lord with the luminous gold disc rules us.

X.4.8 The one with the disc is beyond even the immortals
primordial creator, lord of time, cowherd, one
who bore a mountain on his gorgeous shoulders,
never forget his feet. Praise them and live, my heart.

X.4.9 I saw his feet bright as lotus, in that instant
all my wretchedness severed at the roots died.
I serve him without pause, I worship the highest one
in all the ways he laid down.

X.4.10 Their minds fixed on him, the gods came
from everywhere to worship Mādhavaṉ

with fragrances and flames, flowers and water
He's the only refuge, his devotees' only bond.

X.4.11 Those who learn these ten from the thousand
in antāti on the highest one, the mighty lord,
composed by the man from the fertile Vaḻuti lands
will gain Kaṇṇaṉ's feet, the only goal, the only bond.

Tiruvāymoḻi X.5 (1037–1047)
kaṇṇaṉ kaḻaliṇai

X.5.1 If you're of a mind to find Kaṇṇaṉ's feet
the only name worth holding on to is the Nāraṇam.

X.5.2 My lord Nārāyaṇa, the earth's beloved,
that elephant-killer, is the only cause.

X.5.3 He's the whole world. He created it split it
ate it spat it out. He alone rules it.

X.5.4 Our ruler rests on his serpent in the deep ocean,
offer flowers at his feet, seek him always.

X.5.5 Seek him always offering fresh flowers
sing his names. Be free.

X.5.6 The one dark as a kāya bloom is in Vēṅkaṭam
he's Mādhavaṉ who nursed at the demon's breast.

X.5.7 'Mādhavaṉ Mādhavaṉ' repeat it repeat it
neither evil nor grief can touch you.

X.5.8 Grief can't touch you, you'll live like gods
when you repeat the names of the storm-dark lord.

X.5.9 Inscrutable to the gods, a friend to his kin
worship him and wretched fate can't touch you.

X.5.10 Dark wretched fate will flee in fear
when you offer flowers and think of the supreme one.

X.5.11 These ten from the thousand by Śaṭhakōpaṉ, adorned
in the supreme one's grace will grant grace to devotees.

Tiruvāymoḻi X.6 (1048–1058)
aruḷperuvār

X.6.1 I serve his devotees who receive his grace, so
the one with the disc gives me grace too. This is destiny.
I refuse birth into this dark world. Shed your confusion
my heart. Worship at the feet of the one in Vāṭṭāṟu.

X.6.2 Worship at the feet of the one in Vāṭṭāṟu, he'll
end birth into this great world. Innocent heart, sing
of my lord Keśavaṉ, cut your wretched deeds. Break
with worldly people and reach Nāraṇaṉ.

X.6.3 We spoke his many names, reached Nārāyaṇaṉ.
He's in this world in fertile Vāṭṭāṟu, ready to give
us the heavens. This is destiny. My heart,
everything I wished for has come to pass.

X.6.4 He's in my heart speaking fine Tamiḻ poems,
the one in Vāṭṭāṟu mauled strong-hearted Hiraṇyaṉ,

hearts quaked in fear when he fought a war for the Pāṇḍava
good heart, our lord will only ever give us grace.

X.6.5 The one in Vāṭṭāṟu showed me the path to heaven.
I've begun my ascent there on his command. Laugh at hell,
heart. He wanders the world on his eagle. His feet
adorned with honey-sweet tuḷasi rest on my head.

X.6.6 His feet rest on my head. My lord of lotus-bright eyes
never leaves my heart. He's asleep on a serpent in Vāṭṭāṟu,
where mansions rise like mountains. He broke the tusk
of the rut-mad elephant. We are by his feet.

X.6.7 We're at his feet, my Govindaṉ lives in me. He's
in Vāṭṭāṟu, jewel of the south limned by the sea, city
of mansions that rise like mountains. The tuḷasi
at his feet has seeped into my body. It perfumes me.

X.6.8 Tuḷasi perfumes him, his body his crown. He
bends the disc to his will. He's in Vāṭṭāṟu, his form
rising like a mountain. He's luminous in my heart.
What good did I do for grace like this?

X.6.9 Śrī rests on his glorious chest. Luminous Tirumāl
is in cool Vāṭṭāṟu. He roams on his noble eagle
destroying demon clans. He gladly lives in my heart,
he's always there. He never leaves.

X.6.10 'Be bound to me forever. Never leave' he said
and cut my births. Then, as a lion he tore open Hiraṇyaṉ.
Serve the virtuous to gain the impossible. To prove this
he's in Vāṭṭāṟu on a serpent with fangs sharp as swords.

X.6.11 The one in Vāṭṭāṟu reveals his feet, ends cruel hell,
Śaṭhakōpaṉ of fertile Kurukūr sang about our lord
in these ten from a garland of thousand Tamiḻ songs,
sweet even to the gods.

Tiruvāymoḻi X.7 (1059–1069)
ceñcoṟ kavikāḷ

X.7.1 Poets of fine words, take care. The cunning thief
the great trickster of Tirumāliruñcōlai
stole into my heart and into my life, a magical poet
he dissolved into me, remained there unknown
devoured my heart and my life
then filled me with himself.

X.7.2 He filled me with himself, filled everything
every world every life. He became me,
called himself me to sing of himself.
The king of Tirumāliruñcōlai, sweet
as honey milk sugar nectar
has devoured me entirely.

X.7.3 He devoured me entirely, snuck
into this fading body, made me fully into himself.
The mysterious one is in the south,
in Tirumāliruñcōlai. I worship him there.
Where else can I go?
What grace this is.

X.7.4 What grace this is. He became worlds, all life
he holds me tight, won't let me go even a little.
He wanders the world vanquishing demons

who spurn him. He's settled forever
in the hills of Tirumāliruñcōlai,
auspicious gem of the south.

X.7.5 To vanquish demons who spurn him
to make the virtuous gods prosper
to kindle joy in sages who think unthinkable things,
he became me, sang of himself
such sweet songs,
my lord who lives in Tirumāliruñcōlai.

X.7.6 The one in Tirumāliruñcōlai
took the three worlds into this vast belly,
Tirumāl protects them, age after age.
Invisible to Śivaṉ and Brahmā
who sought his feet, he blessed them
He's my lord, Māl who rules me.

X.7.7 'Lord give me grace' implored Śivaṉ
wise Brahmā, the king of celestials, gods
and sages who defeat darkness,
they praise his sacred hill, the hill of gems
the hill that defeats delusion
lovely Tirumāliruñcōlai.

X.7.8 My head, the hills of Tirumāliruñcōlai
and the ocean of milk. My body, Tirumāl's Vaikuṇṭha
and his cool Tiruvēṅkaṭam. He won't leave me,
my ordinary life my mind my speech my karma,
not for an instant will he stay away. Him
the singular primordial cause of time.

X.7.9 Singular primordial cause of time, incomparable
one who keeps the worlds within him, creating
protecting destroying them age after age, my lord
dark as the deep sea. Heart, hold firm
to lovely Tirumāliruñcōlai, never leave.
Let body and breath fade.

X.7.10 My king who lives in Tirumāliruñcōlai,
you became me to protect me.
The surging senses, their instruments,
karmas the five elements this life matter
greatness ego mind,
let these grand delusions die.

X.7.11 So greatness ego mind may die,
and the five senses too, he entered as I
to become me to become himself.
Śaṭhakōpaṉ of Kurukūr, city of gardens,
sang these ten verses from a thousand on greatness
and I-ness, and the hills of Tirumāliruñcōlai.

Tiruvāymoḻi X.8 (1070–1080)
tirumāliruñcōlai malai

X.8.1 The moment I said Tirumāliruñcōlai
Tirumāl entered and filled my heart. He's in
Tiruppēr on the southern bank of the Poṉṉi
its waters glittering with dark gems.

X.8.2 Today the lord who lives in Tiruppēr entered
and filled my heart. He won't leave. The insatiable lord

ate worlds clouds oceans mountains, still wanted more
I've caught him. I hold him tightly inside me.

X.8.3 I hold him tightly. I've destroyed my births
escaped disease, ended the singular delusion of worldly life
He's in Tiruppēr city of towering mansions
it's become easy for me to reach his feet.

X.8.4 My path is now easy.
My eyes delight, my heart too. I rejoice.
He's in Tiruppēr amidst gardens full of parrots
He'll give me clear vast luminous heaven.

X.8.5 To give me heaven, he's stuck to me
inside the nest of my body, has ended
my bewildering deeds himself.
He's in Tiruppēr, city of gardens.

X.8.6 He's in Tiruppēr, the lord in the hills
of Tirumāliruñcōlai. Today he entered me
insisted he would stay, filling my heart.
I've got my desire. I taste the nectar. I rejoice.

X.8.7 I've tasted the joy. Why do I need heaven?
I've served him, earned the final syllable
I see him in Tiruppēr, surrounded by dense groves
He's in my eyes. He won't ever leave.

X.8.8 He's in my eyes. He won't ever leave.
Beyond thought, subtle, essence of the seven notes

the one in Tiruppēr, city of glittering mansions,
is now in my mind.

X.8.9 Today he made me mean something
placed himself inside me. Why then did he
turn from me all these many days?
Lord in Tiruppēr, answer me.

X.8.10 I've got you. I served you, reached
your feet. My father, what else do I need?
He's in Tiruppēr, where those wise in the Veda live.
Grief cannot touch his devotees.

X.8.11 Those who master these ten from the thousand
Tamil̲ songs on Tiruppēr, where grief does not last,
by Śaṭhakōpan̲ of Kurukūr, city of the virtuous,
are his devotees. They will rule heaven.

Tiruvāymol̲i X.9 (1081–1091)
cūl̲ vicumpu

X.9.1 Lovely clouds filling the vast sky
thunder like drums, waves resound
like clapping hands and dancing feet,
the seven worlds offer up gifts, rejoice
when they see the devotees
of Nāraṇan̲, my father.

X.9.2 They see Nāraṇan̲'s devotees
and the clouds fill to brimming
like golden pots high in the sky,

the seas crash and thunder,
and people the world over fly banners
tall as mountains everywhere.

X.9.3 Everyone worshipped them
with incense and a shower of flowers,
they are his, the one who measured worlds.
Sages gathered on either side
ushered them in, saying
'This way to Vaikuṇṭha.'

X.9.4 Celestials set up places to rest
along the way, each sun raises
his arms to light the path,
drums roar like the thundering sea,
all for the devotees of Mādhavaṉ
who wears a crown of sweet tuḷasi.

X.9.5 At the door of heaven
the gods usher Mādhavaṉ's devotees
'Enter our home' they say
as the kiṇṇaras and garuḍas sing,
masters of the Veda
perform their sacrifices.

X.9.6 Sacrificial smoke rose
spreading its sweet smell everywhere,
trumpets and conches mingled to make music
'Devotees of the one with the disc
you rule the heavens'
decreed women with eyes bright as swords.

X.9.7 Women sang, the maruts, the vasus
filled every place with their praise
of those bound to him for generations,
our Keśavaṉ, asleep on a sea, him
adorned in a crown of brilliant light,
our Kōvalaṉ of Kuṭantai.

X.9.8 'They've been his for generations'
said the celestials arrayed in rows
welcoming Govindaṉ's devotees
as they neared
the towering walls and tall towers
of beautiful Mādhavaṉ's Vaikuṇṭha.

X.9.9 As they cross into Vaikuṇṭha
celestials at the threshold declared
'Enter our home, devotees of Vaikuṇṭha's lord'
Gods and sages are wonderstruck
that all of earth's people
are destined for Vaikuṇṭha.

X.9.10 'It's their destiny to enter here'
understood those who've mastered the Veda
and washed the feet of devotees
as women with faces bright as the full moon
welcomed them with precious things
footrests fragrances and pots of cool water.

X.9.11 Śaṭhakōpaṉ of Kurukūr, city of gardens,
sang of himself and devotees
brimming with infinite joy, welcomed

into a great jewelled hall by him.
Any who masters these ten from a thousand
will become a sage.

Tiruvāymoḻi X.10 (1092–1102)
muṉiyē nāṉmukaṉē

X.10.1 Silent sage four-faced one three-eyed father
my perfect dark jewel
with berry-red lips and lotus-bright eyes,
my cunning thief.
I am alone and you are my precious life
at last you're here resting on my head.
I won't let you go now
Please, no more tricks.

X.10.2 Don't trick me. Śrī, her hair fragrant with flowers
rests like a garland on your lovely chest,
I swear on her, I bind you
to this oath, see.
You loved me, mixed my life with yours
barring all others.
Don't draw back now.
Come, call me to you.

X.10.3 Call me to you. Make me yours,
my perfect dark jewel
My breath leans on you, it knows nothing else.
From the lotus rising from your navel
came Brahmā Śivaṉ Indraṉ who worship you.
You are the root,

the primordial one
Sole goal of the gods.

X.10.4 You're the cool expanse
of the celestial world and everything within it.
You're sky and light,
Brahmā and Araṉ within it.
You're the silent sage
who made the world above and everyone.
You were to do right by me,
Instead you've left me here.

X.10.5 If you simply leave me out here
what then? Whom shall I rely on?
What is mine?
What am I?
To quench my precious life
like hot iron in water
You became nectar that never sates.

X.10.6 You became my nectar that never sates
devouring my breath my sweet life
still your heart hungered for more.
Don't stop.
Dark as a kāya bloom
with lotus-bright eyes and berry-red lips
dear to the lovely woman perfect for you
You are my love.

X.10.7 My love, dear to lovely Śrī,
like a black mountain touched by two moons

you rose as lovely Varāha
with the earth between your tusks,
My father, lord
who churned the dark ocean
I finally have you
Will I ever let you go?

X.10.8 I finally have you
Will I let you go?
You are my singular life
You are the twin fates
You are life and its fruits
You are the vast multitudes of the three worlds
You lie hidden within them
You are my primordial seed.

X.10.9 Primordial seed, sole cause
of the three worlds and everything else
when will I join you?
Singular source of life
that fills the vastness
Primordial one
swirling spreading deep and high
You have no end.

X.10.10 Swirling spreading deep high endless vastness
Swirling growing beyond that
a great blossoming light
Swirling growing beyond even that
the luminous bliss of wisdom

Swirling growing beyond even that
my love for you. You cut that too
and engulfed me.

X.10.11 Calling on Hari who ends desire
who engulfs Ayaṉ Araṉ engulfs all,
Śaṭhakōpaṉ of Kurukūr
who cut desire and found release
ended the thousand flawless antāti verse
with these ten that cut desire.
Those who know them will earn a birth
Most high.

Annotations to Nammāḻvār's *Tiruvāymoḻi*

Tiruvāymoḻi First Hundred (I.1–I.10)

I.1.1–I.1.11: *The text opens with a description of the transcendence of god, and an imperative to the poet's mind to fix itself on a contemplation of this transcendence. God is not named in the first decad, but he is described as pervading all things and all beings.*

I.1.1: In the traditional commentaries, the opening verse is understood as distilling three principles—the truth (*tattva*), the path (upāya) and the goal (puruṣārtha). The truth is the supremacy of Viṣṇu (not yet unnamed), the path is devotion to his feet and union with those feet is the goal.

I.1.7: The god who has eaten everything refers to the myth of Viṣṇu swallowing the worlds in the end times. He floats as an infant on a banyan leaf on the waters that dissolve the world. During this time, he keeps and protects the world in his stomach. He creates the world by then spitting them out. The first reference in the *Tiruvāymoḻi* to Viṣṇu on the banyan leaf occurs in I.9.4, while the action of both destruction/protection and creation (swallowing and spitting out) of the worlds is found in I.5.8.

Śruti: Literally that which is heard. It refers to the Veda, which Brahmanical Hinduism regards as revealed.

I.1.8: Araṉ is Śiva; Ayaṉ is Brahmā.

In the line, as Araṉ and Ayaṉ he unmakes and remakes the world, the poet refers to Viṣṇu (as yet unnamed in the poem) as both the creator and destroyer of the world. Later in the poem, he will also be praised as the world's protector.

'He burned the three cities' refers to the myth of the three cities destroyed by Śiva as Tripurāntaka. In the most well-known versions of the myth, Śiva fires an arrow (Viṣṇu) from a bow that is Mount Meru. Here the myth is used to assert Viṣṇu's pre-eminence as he dwells within Śiva and thus directs his actions.

I.1.11: Kurukur is identified with present-day Alvar Tirunagari, along the banks of the Tamiraparani, in the deep south of peninsular India. The town appears in almost every concluding verse of the *Tiruvāymoḻi*'s cycle of Tens. In addition, an entire decad (IV.10) is also dedicated to the place.

Śaṭhakōpaṉ is the name by which the poet refers to himself in the final verse of each Ten.

I.2.1–I.2.10: *This decad describes the goal of devotion to Viṣṇu, which is mokṣa, or complete and total release out of the cycle of saṁsāra. It also reveals the path to that goal, which is taking refuge in Viṣṇu. Thus, this decad may be seen as explicating the crucial Śrīvaiṣṇava notion that Viṣṇu is both the way (upāya) and the goal (upeya).*

I.2.1: This verse repeats the word vīṭu (to let go) in multiple forms. Vīṭu also refers to the final release, mokṣa. In the verse's second line, Viṣṇu, (who has yet to be named), is described as *vīṭu uṭaiyāṉ* (the one who possesses vīṭu). The commentaries read this to mean the site of vīṭu, i.e. heaven/mokṣa. That is, surrendering to him who is the site of mokṣa/heaven will grant one final, eternal release. In other words, he is the path to release, the one who grants release, and the final destination of that release. I have chosen not to translate vīṭu as release or mokṣa, and have instead privileged the hypnotic rhythm and repetition in the Tamiḻ.

I.2.10: The poet finally names his deity as Nārāyaṇa (Nāraṇaṉ), an appropriate choice, for the name signifies that he is the resting place of the primordial waters, and the resting place of men.

I.3.1: Śrī is Viṣṇu's primary consort. She is the goddess of fortune, sovereignty and auspiciousness, and is never apart from him, resting perpetually on his chest.

The goddess is referred to here as *malarmakaḷ* (literally, the lady in the flower), referring to Śrī's association with the lotus, a sign of auspiciousness and good fortune.

'He filched butter . . .' refers to an incident in Viṣṇu's avatāra as Kṛṣṇa. As a child, Kṛṣṇa would frequently steal butter. On one occasion, when his foster mother Yaśodā found out, she tied him to a mortar as a punishment. However, the rope she sought to tie him with was never long enough. Ultimately, Kṛṣṇa allowed himself to be bound by her. It is on account of this incident that he earns the name Dāmodara (one tied around the waist with a rope). The name Dāmodara appears for the first time in II.7.11, while the myth occurs frequently.

The story is narrated in Book 10, Chapter 9 of the *Bhāgavata Purāṇa*. While the *Bhāgavata Purāṇa* is compiled after the lifetime of the āḻvār poets, they were no doubt aware of these stories.

The poet uses this incident to illustrate the quality of god's accessibility (*eḷimai*), and his ease with devotees. The same god, who is transcendent, unknowable, pervasive, unbounded, takes birth and allows those who love him to know him and to bind him.

According to traditional commentaries, when the Āḻvār contemplated god's paradoxical qualities expressed in this verse, he fell into a deep swoon for several months.

I.3.1, I.3.2: In both these verses, god is characterized as having the quality of eḷimai (ease, accessibility, availability), particularly to his devotees. I have translated this as friend (*eḷiyavaṉ*, I.3.1), simple (*eḷivē*, I.3.1) and open (*eḷivarum*, I.3.2) to capture the many shades of the word.

I.3.4: Two kinds of people (*yārum*, those who) are referenced in this verse. In the first category, are the learned, who cannot know god, because they do not love him. In the second instance, are the lowly, who do not have wisdom but know god because they love him.

I.3.5: Here, the right path is not just the path of devotion and loving surrender, but in the *Īṭu* is seen as making a reference to the *Bhagavad Gītā*.

The poet uses the phrase *āti am pakavan* (primordial Bhagavan), in an echo of the opening couplet of the *Tirukkuṟaḷ*.

I.3.7: Nāṉmukaṉ, literally the four-faced one, refers to Brahmā.

I.3.9: The one who razed the three cities is Śiva. Refer to I.1.8 for the myth.

The one in his navel is Brahmā.

'Creating Brahmā from his navel' records another creation myth. Viṣṇu contains everything inside his body. While Viṣṇu is deep in yogic sleep upon the multi-headed serpent, Ananta, on the cosmic ocean, Brahmā emerges from within him, rising out of his navel on a lotus. Viṣṇu then directs him to create the forms of the universe.

I.3.10: 'Measuring the world' refers to the story of Viṣṇu when he assumed the form of Vāmana, a diminutive, beautiful brahmin youth to attend the sacrifice of Bali. Bali, the king of the asuras, controlled the universe, and the gods appealed to Viṣṇu to restore their portion to them. When the king distributed gifts after the sacrifice, Vāmana approached him and asked him for three measures of land—what he can measure with his feet. The prideful king, seeing the tiny feet of the young man, acceded. Vāmana immediately shed his form, grew to gargantuan proportions, and measured earth and sky with two strides. When Bali observed that Viṣṇu had nothing else left to measure, Bali offered his head for the third stride. Viṣṇu placed his foot on Bali's head and pushed him into hell. In this large form, Viṣṇu is called Trivikrama, the conqueror of the three worlds.

Viṣṇu spanning the three worlds is one of the few Viṣṇu-myths found in the Vedic corpus. In that context, this act is connected with creation, for to measure is also to create. In later versions, it is an expression of his sovereignty over the universe, as its protector. The myth is also used (in the *Tiruvāymoḻi*) as a way to speak about god's cunning nature. He is a trickster, hidden in plain sight, but invisible to those, like Bali, who cannot see. Nammāḻvār deploys the myth in both ways. This myth, particularly the Trivikrama aspect, is invoked most frequently in the *Tiruvāymoḻi*.

I.3.11: 'Him who churned the sea' refers to Viṣṇu's avatāra as Kūrma (tortoise), and the churning of the cosmic ocean for the nectar of immortality (*amṛta*) by the gods and demons. In the story, the mountain Mandara is used as a churning rod and the serpent Vāsuki as the churning rope. As the churning begins, the mountain begins to sink. Viṣṇu takes the form of a giant tortoise and lifts up the mountain, so the churning can continue.

I.4.1–I.4.10: *This decad introduces the female voice (talaivi). It is also the first of four messenger poems in the Tiruvāymoḻi.*

I.4.1: The mighty eagle is Garuḍa, Viṣṇu's cosmic vehicle. He both rides the bird and also uses the bird as an emblem on a banner.

I.4.3: The youth who stole three steps, refer to the note on I.3.10.

I.4.4: Aṉṟil is a type of lovebird.

I.4.10: 'Sleeps on the ocean he made himself' refers to the ocean of milk, also called *pārkaṭal*. This is Viṣṇu's *vyūha* form (first emanation). It is the second of his five forms. The other four are *paratva* (transcendent), *vibhava* (incarnation), *arcā* (iconic) and *antaryāmin* (in-dwelling).

Viṣṇu holds a war-disc (signifying the sun) in his right hand and a white conch (signifying the moon) in his left. In this verse, only the former is referenced.

I.5.1: The king of cowherds refers to Viṣṇu's avatāra as Kṛṣṇa. In this avatāra, he is born as a prince to Devakī and Vasudeva. Because of a threat to his life, he is spirited away as an infant to the cowherding community of Nanda and his wife, Yaśodā. He spends his boyhood with them, having many adventures, which comprise some of the most well-known Kṛṣṇa stories.

Piṉṉai, also called Nappiṉṉai, is the cowherd wife of Kṛṣṇa. She is a distinctly Tamiḻ figure, and does not appear in the later, Sanskrit *Bhāgavata Purāṇa*. She is referenced in the *Cilappatikāram*, in the 'Madurai Kāṇṭam', in the section describing the dance of the cowherd women (*āycciyar kuravai*). For further discussion on the identity of Piṉṉai, see Dennis Hudson. 'Pinnai: Krishna's Cowherd Wife'.

The verse references Kṛṣṇa killing seven bulls in order to win her. The seven bulls are seven demons in disguise. We do not know much else about this myth, but it appears to have been popular in the Tamiḻ-speaking regions in the period of the āḻvār poets. Bull-fighting continues to be an important expression of Tamiḻ cultural identity.

'Thief of butter' see I.3.1. The myth is referenced again in I.5.8.

I.5.3: 'Birth the worlds' refer to the note on I.3.9.

'Spanning the directions' refer to the note on I.3.10.

I.5.4: Vaikuṇṭha is Viṣṇu's heaven, the highest realm in which he exists in his transcendent form.

I.5.5: 'With your bow you unbent her back' can either refer to an episode in the Rāma or Kṛṣṇa avatāras. There is no extant story of Rāma straightening a woman's curved back, and the received story of Kṛṣṇa straightening the back of Trivakrā does not involve a bow. Thus, the mythic reference here is ambiguous. It is possible that Nammāḻvār has deliberately conjoined two myths, or that there is a local, Tamiḻ variant of either myth that is now lost to us.

In the former, it could refer to Rāma pelting the curved back of Mantarā, the loyal attendant to Rāma's stepmother, Kaikeyī. In the Kṛṣṇa story, it refers to the incident with Trivakrā, whose back he straightened, transforming her into a beautiful woman. The story is narrated in *Bhāgavata Purāṇa*, Book 10, Chapter 48.

I.5.6: 'Pierced seven trees with a single arrow' refers to an episode in which Rāma demonstrated his skill to the monkey-king, Sugrīva. Sugrīva was doubtful of Rāma's strength and wonders if he can defeat his brother and enemy, Vāli. To prove his might, Rāma first kicked a demon skeleton far into the distance, by flicking it with his toe. Sūgriva was still not convinced, and asked him to cut down trees with a single weapon. Rāma did so easily, not just felling the trees, but piercing the earth, and eventually having the arrow return to his quiver. This episode is described in the twelfth chapter of 'Kiṣkindhā Kāṇḍa' of the *Vālmīki Rāmāyaṇa*.

I.5.8: 'To eat and spit out the worlds' refers to Viṣṇu's actions as destroyer and creator of the world. In the end times, he absorbs the world back into himself (eating it), and keeps it within himself, until he regurgitates it during creation. In the *Tiruvāymoḻi*, the poet uses either both parts of the story or just one part. Refer to I.1.7 for a discussion of the myth.

I.5.9: 'Turning poison to milk' is a reference to an episode in Kṛṣṇa's childhood, when Pūtanā was sent by king Kaṁsa of Mathura to kill Kṛṣṇa. She arrives in disguise, and suckles the infant Kṛṣṇa at her poisoned breast. Kṛṣṇa, aware of her treachery, drains her of her life-breath as he nurses at her breast. The episode is narrated in the *Bhāgavata Purāṇa*, Book 10, Chapter 6.

I.5.10: 'Warded off the twin deeds' (*iru val viṉai*) refers to actions both good *(puṇya)* and bad *(pāpa)*, that as the *Īṭu* says, are inherent in one as oil is hidden in a sesame seed, or fire within a tree. It may also refer to actions that one does and does not do.

I.6.2: Veda refers to a collection of texts considered to be revealed. They are also referred to as the śruti.

I.6.6: 'Giving nectar to immortals' refers to the second part of the churning of the cosmic ocean, mentioned in I.3.11. At the end of the churning, the nectar of immortality (amṛta) appears, and the gods (deva) and demons (asura) fight over it. Viṣṇu takes the form of the enchantress, Mohinī, and assumes control over the amṛta, distributing it entirely to the deva, with nothing left for the asura. The episode is narrated in the *Bhāgavata Purāṇa*, Book 8, Chapter 6.

I.6.7: 'He slashed the arms of Laṅkā's king' refers to the defeat of Rāvaṇa in the great battle that concluded the *Rāmāyaṇa*. Rāma is a prince of Ayodhyā, who is exiled to the forest; his wife, Sītā, and brother, Lakṣmaṇa, accompany him. Rāvaṇa abducts Sītā and takes her to his kingdom, Laṅkā. Rāma wages a terrible battle against Rāvaṇa, killing him and rescuing Sītā.

The Rāma story was well known to the āḻvār poets, and it is cited frequently in their poetry. The āḻvār also offer several unique approaches to the story, and include what appears to be local variations of the Rāma narrative. For a brief discussion of these, see Vasudha Narayanan. *The Way and the Goal.* pp. 26–30.

I.6.11: One of the few concluding verses in a decad that does not make mention of the poet's city, Kurukur.

I.7.2: Child of cowherds, see the note on I.5.1.

I.7.3: 'Yielded to a beating' is another part of the butter-stealing antics of Kṛṣṇa. He is beaten by his mother, Yaśodā for stealing butter. God's acquiescence of his mother's scolding and his acceptance of her punishment is exemplary of his accessibility, particularly to those who love him. For a fuller account of the myth, see the note on I.3.1.

I.7.5: 'Making eyes at the cowherd girls' refers to Kṛṣṇa's boyhood with the cowherds. During this time, Kṛṣṇa would play with, dance, tease and flirt with the young cowherd girls (*gopī*). The gopis' love for Kṛṣṇa is the subject of two moving decads in the *Tiruvāymoḻi* (IX.9 and X.3), while VI.2 describes a lovers' quarrel.

I.7.6: 'Lifting the earth' refers to the third of Viṣṇu's avatāras, as Varāha, the boar. In this form, Viṣṇu dove under the waters to rescue the abducted earth from the clutches of the demon, Hiraṇyākṣa.

'Piercing the trees' refer to the note on I.5.6.

I.7.9: 'Giving the nectar to the immortals' refer to the note on I.3.11 and I.6.6.

I.7.8: 'Embracing Piṉṉai' refer to the note on I.5.1.

I.8.2: 'Tearing the horse's jaws' is a reference to Kṛṣṇa killing the horse demon, Keśī (long-haired one), another demon dispatched by Kaṁsa. According to the *Bhāgavata Purāṇa*, Kṛṣṇa kills the demon by thrusting his arm down his throat. The arm expands until the horse, unable to breathe, falls dead. *Bhāgavata Purāṇa*, Book 10, Chapter 37. This version of the story—with Kṛṣṇa's arm in Keśī's throat—is depicted in a famous Gupta-period sculpture (321–500 CE), now held at the Metropolitan Museum of Art. It is on account of this deed that Kṛṣṇa earns the name Keśava.

I.8.3: Vēṅkaṭam is one of the 108 sacred sites (Divya Deśa), popularly called Tirumala-Tirupati. It comprises seven peaks, which are understood to be the seven heads of Ādiśeṣa, the serpent upon which Viṣṇu reclines. The temple is located in the modern-day Indian state of Andhra Pradesh, and is one of two Divya Deśas located there (the other is Ahobilam). It is well attested to in Tamiḻ Saṅgam works (see for instance, *Akanāṉūṟu* 61, 83, 393), where it is described as a wild and hilly terrain, the territory of a king named Pulli. In classical and medieval Tamiḻ works, the hills of Venkatam were often used to mark the northern boundary of the Tamiḻ-speaking regions (for example, *Akanāṉūṟu* 211 or the epilogue of the *Cilappatikāram*). While the Saṅgam works do not explicitly connect Venkatam to the worship of Māl/Viṣṇu, this association is provided in the *Cilappatikāram* ('Madurai Kāṇṭam', First Canto), where it is linked definitively to Viṣṇu; the other two sites are Srirangam and Tirumaliruncolai.

If one brackets out the references to Kurukur in a Ten's concluding verses, Venkatam is the most lauded site in the *Tiruvāymoḻi*, with two entire decads dedicated to it (III.3; VI.10) in addition to several allusions and references, such as this one. While Srirangam receives the most number of verses from the āḻvār poets, Venkatam comes in second. It is praised by ten of the twelve āḻvār poets, with a total of 202 verses in its honour (the site is not praised in the works of Madurakavi and Toṇṭaraṭippoṭi). It holds a place of special significance within Śrīvaiṣṇavism, for

Nammāḻvār is believed to surrender to the deity enshrined here (prapatti) in VI.10, the second entire cycle in the *Tiruvāymoḻi* in praise of Venkatam.

I.8.4: In this story, Kṛṣṇa dissuades the cowherds from worshipping Indra and redirects them to worship the mountain, Govardhana. In retaliation, Indra sends a cataclysmic thunderstorm to destroy the cowherds. In the *Bhāgavata Purāṇa*, Kṛṣṇa states that the cowherds accept him as their shelter (Chapter 25, verse 18), and then easily raises Govardhana hill to protect the residents of Vrindāvan from Indra's wrath. Indra is subdued and withdraws the rains. The episode is described in *Bhāgavata Purāṇa*, Book 10, Chapters 24 and 25.

I.8.5: 'Stirred butter' refer to the note on I.3.1.

I.8.6: 'Youth who took the world' refer to the note on I.3.10. The myth is referenced again in I.8.10.

I.8.7: 'Subdued seven bulls' refer to the note on I.5.1.
'Ate seven worlds,' refer to I.1.7.

I.8.8: 'He became cowherd' refers to Viṣṇu's avatāra as Kṛṣṇa. In this avatāra, although he was born into a royal family, he had to be raised by cowherds. Kṛṣṇa spent his childhood among the cowherds, and several of his most well-known adventures occur during this period. The *Tiruvāymoḻi* is rich in references to Kṛṣṇa's mythic deeds.

Taking the form of the fish refers to Viṣṇu's first avatāra. In the earliest versions of this myth, Viṣṇu is not explicitly connected to the fish (*matsya*). In this version, such as recorded in the Śatapatha *Brāhmaṇa* (c.700 BCE), a magical, ever-expanding fish comes into the care of Manu, the first man, asking him to care for it until the prophesied time of dissolution. At the fish's command, Manu builds a ship, and when the apocalyptic flood arrives, ties the ship to the now gigantic fish's horn. In this way, he is saved from the final deluge. In later versions, as in the *Matsya Purāṇa* (250–500 CE), the connection of the fish to Viṣṇu is explicit, and Manu saves plants, animals, the seven seers (ṛṣi) and the Veda.

For Viṣṇu as Varāha, the boar, refer to the note on I.7.6. In the Tamil̲, the poet uses several words for Viṣṇu in this form. In some cases, as here, he uses *ēn̲am* (pig) as opposed to *kēḻal* (wild boar). The choice is always deliberate, driven by melody and internal rhymes (as in this verse) as well as a need to make a theological point about god's unfathomable accessibility. It is a wondrous thing that a transcendent deity would assume a base form like that of a pig to aid those dependent on him. This is what makes him special. I follow the poet's lead in my translation—wherever he uses a Tamil̲ word that obviously means pig, swine or hog, I use pig, while in other instances, such as when he employs kēḻal, I use boar.

I.8.11: Here, god is compared to water (*nīrpurai vaṇṇan̲*). As the *Īṭu* suggests, he has the quality of water, which can be directed as a human wants. God too, goes where his devotees are. Thus, this analogy expresses god's straightforwardness, non-hypocrisy, his simplicity and open-heartedness (*ārjava guṇa*).

I.9.2: 'Breaking the tusks of the elephant' refers to Kṛṣṇa killing the elephant, Kuvalayāpīḍa, who guarded the gates of Mathura. Kṛṣṇa and his brother Balarāma meet the elephant and his keeper when they arrive in Mathura. When they refuse to step aside, Kṛṣṇa fights the elephant, eventually killing him by throwing him to the ground, and then ripping out his tusk. He then stabs the mahout with the tusk, killing him as well. The story marks a shift from Kṛṣṇa's youthful adventures in Gokula to taking on the mantle of the slayer of Kaṁsa. The episode is recounted in *Bhāgavata Purāṇa*, Book 10, Chapter 43.

I.9.4: The innocent cowherd girl is Nappiṉṉai. In this verse, Śrī and Bhū are referred to by their epithets malarmakaḷ (lady in the flower/lotus) and *nilamakaḷ* (lady of the earth/earth goddess).

'The lord resting on the banyan leaf' is a reference to the end times, when Kṛṣṇa in the form of a child, is carried on a banyan leaf on the cosmic deluge. In this form, he has absorbed all of the worlds into his belly, keeping them safe until the time of creation. Also see the note on I.1.7.

I.9.5: Indraṉ is the king of the celestials, and also the god of rain and thunder.

'Drank her milk' refer to the note on I.5.9.

I.10.1: 'Youth who took the world' refer to the note on I.3.10. The myth is referenced again in I.10.5.

I.10.5: 'He ate the world' refer to the note on I.1.7.

I.10.9: Kuṟuṅkuṭi, present-day Tirukkurungudi, is one of the 108 Divya Deśas. It is located in the Tamiraparani region, in the deep south of peninsular India. See the opening note on V.5 for a fuller description of the site.

Tiruvāymoḻi Second Hundred (II.1–II.10)

II.1.1–II.1.10: *This decad is in the heroine's voice.*

II.1.1: The phrase *amar ulakum* that occurs in the verse's second line is translated as immortals, instead of world of immortals.

II.1.3: The heroine ends the verse with the blessing, *vāḻi* (live long, may you prosper), which is repeated in II.1.7. The blessing can be read sarcastically (i.e. you care nothing for me, may you prosper), or as an expression of sympathy (you are like me—at least, may you live well).

'The one who burned Laṅkā' refers to Rāma's destruction of the kingdom of the demon king, Rāvaṇa. He had imprisoned the abducted Sītā in a forest in that city. In the great war Rāma wages against Rāvaṇa, he destroys the city and kills its king.

II.1.6: The verse describes Viṣṇu as reclining on the serpent. While this implies that he is asleep on the ocean of milk, as the place is not mentioned specifically, I have not listed it in the Index of Sites.

II.1.8: 'The one who kicked the rolling cart' refers to Kṛṣṇa's defeat of the cart-demon, Śakaṭāsura. In the episode described in the *Bhāgavata Purāṇa*, Book 10, Chapter 7, or in the earlier *Harivaṁśa* (1–2 BCE), the cart is neither explicitly linked to a demon nor described as Kaṁsa's henchman. In both stories, Yaśodā leaves the baby Kṛṣṇa under a cart that he dismantles when he playfully kicks his feet as babies are wont to do.

II.1.10: 'Crawled between the maruta trees' links to the incident when Yaśodā tied Kṛṣṇa to a grinding stone (see, I.3.1). He began to crawl, dragging the stone behind him. Eventually, he crawled between two trees, causing them to break. The trees were two celestials who had been cursed. When the trees crashed, the celestials were released from their curse. The story is narrated in *Bhāgavata Purāṇa*, Book 10, Chapters 9 and 10.

Maruta is the Arjuna tree.

'Ripped the horse's mouth' refer to the note on I.8.2.

'Measured worlds' refer to the note on I.3.10.

II.2.1: The word vīṭu is used once again, here to refer to both release (mokṣa) and the site of that release, which is heaven (Vaikuṇṭha).

The verse's last line offers up a range of possibilities through its play on the word *kaṇ* (eye) and Kaṇṇaṉ, which the *Īṭu* interprets beautifully. His are the eyes by which you see the world, which is his own form. Everything we see, with our eyes, is also Kṛṣṇa. He is knowledge; he is the sole protector.

The phrase *allatu illai* echoes the penultimate verse of Nammāḻvār's *Tiruviruttam* (99) in which he declares that there is no one but the god of wisdom *(jñāna-p-piṛāṉ allāl illai)*. In the *Tiruviruttam*, jñāna-p-pirāṉ is Varāha.

'Ate the world' refer to the note on I.1.7.

II.2.2: The word *pāvam* (Sanskrit: pāpa) is the accumulation of negative action, or can also refer to the negative action itself. It is also used as an interjection of sympathy or self-pity. It is in the latter sense that I have translated the first pāvam that opens the verse ('Pity me'). The word occurs once again in the third line, which I have translated as wickedness, rather than as the more common, sin. I have avoided this choice primarily because of the Christian sense it evokes.

The word occurs numerous times in the *Tiruvāymoḻi*. I have translated it differently based on the context.

'Who gave Araṉ alms . . .' refers to Viṣṇu releasing Śiva in his form as Bhikṣāṭaṇa, the wandering beggar. Śiva assumes this form because of a curse for pinching off Brahmā's fifth head. The head sticks to the palm of his hand. He wanders the world, until he finally reaches Viṣṇu's abode. There, he battles Viṣvaksena, and kills him. According to the *Kūrma Purāṇa*, when Śiva enters Viṣṇu's abode carrying Viṣvaksena's body, he cuts an artery in his forehead, letting the blood flow out into the skull of Brahmā. Even after a thousand years, the skull remains unfilled. Viṣṇu then directs Śiva to the holy city of Varanasi to expiate his sin. *Kūrma Purāṇa*, Chapter 31.

II.2.3: The bull-riding god is Śiva. The lotus-born one is Brahmā. As there is no explicit mention of Brahmā rising from Viṣṇu's navel, this verse is not listed under the Index of Myths.

'Stretched beyond' refer to the note on I.3.10.

II.2.5: The final line of the verse *mikum cōti mēl aṟivār evarē* (Who can you know beyond this great light?) implies that no gods exist beyond Viṣṇu. Is there anyone who knows of such a god (aṟivār evarē)? The answer is of course, no.

II.2.7: 'Rests on a banyan leaf' refer to the note on I.9.4 and I.1.7.

II.2.9: The second line of this verse reads: *cērkkai ceytu taṉ untiyuḷḷē* (having gathered together, from within his navel). The *Īṭu* reads this line as implying god's power to destroy and then create the world. Thus cērkkai ceytu is taken as destroying the world, which he then absorbs into his body *(tirumēṉi)*, only to recreate it once again.

In this verse, Brahmā is referred to as Ticaimukaṉ (one facing the directions). I've not rendered this epithet literally in the translation.

II.2.10: The one with the white bull is Śiva.

The god who rides the bird is Viṣṇu. The bird is Garuḍa.

II.3.1: As per the *Īṭu*, the word uyir (life) which resides in the body, can also be taken as maṉam (heart-mind) or as the ātman (Self).

'Destroying the demon clan' refers to Rāma's destruction of Rāvaṇa and the kingdom of Laṅkā. Refer to the note on I.6.7.

II.3.2: The poet uses the phrase *aṭiyēṉ aṟiyēṉ* (literally, I, who am your servant, do not know) in the final line of this verse. The word aṭiyēṉ signifies subservience and submission; he is one who is at god's feet. It also has implications of bonded labour and servitude, for you are owned entirely by Viṣṇu. Śrīvaiṣṇavas often greet each other with the word aṭiyēṉ which is reciprocated with *aṭiyēṉ tācaṉ* (I am the servant's servant), to signify both humility and the primacy of submission before god and his devotees.

I have translated aṭiyēṉ with just the first person singular pronoun.

II.3.3: Mahābali is the king vanquished by Viṣṇu-Trivikrama when he is sent into the netherworld. See the note on I.3.10 for a fuller description of the myth.

II.3.4: 'Eating the world' refer to the note on I.1.7.

II.3.5: 'My nectar untouched by the ocean' is the nectar (amṛta) that did not emerge from the churning of the ocean. See the note on I.3.11 for a fuller description of the myth.

'Lifting the seven worlds' refer to the note on Varāha, I.7.6.

II.3.6: 'One who cut the demon's nose' refers to an episode that occurs in the 'Āraṇya Kāṇḍa' of the *Rāmāyaṇa*. Śūrpanakhā, the sister of Rāvāṇa, attempts to seduce the exiled Rāma. When she persists, Rāma's brother, Lakṣmaṇa, slices off her nose and ears. In south Indian versions, he also cuts off the tips of her breasts. Several fifteenth-century temples in Tamil Nadu, such as the Srivilliputtur Āṇḍāḷ temple, depict this local version of the mutilation of Śūrpaṇakhā. This myth is referenced only once in the entire *Tiruvāymoḻi*.

II.3.11: 'Wiped out the demon's clan' refers to the destruction of Rāvaṇa and Laṅkā. See the note on I.6.7.

II.4.1–II.4.10: *This decad is in the mother's voice.*

II.4.1: Narasiṅka is Viṣṇu in his man-lion form. This links to the myth in which he kills the demon Hiraṇyakaśipu. The myth is explicitly referenced in II.6.6. See the note on that verse for an explication of the myth.

II.4.2: Cutting the arms of Bāṇa refers to Kṛṣṇa's defeat of Bāṇāsura, one of the sons of Bali. Bāṇa, who had a thousand arms, was Śiva's devotee. He is overcome with arrogance over his power, thinking that Śiva alone is his equal. His daughter, Uṣā, dreams of Aniruddha, Kṛṣṇa's grandson, and desires him. Uṣā's friend, Citralekhā, uses her magical powers to bring the young prince to Uṣā. The two spend time in secret, and fall in love. Kṛṣṇa, accompanied by Balarāma, wages a war against Bāṇa, thinking to rescue Aniruddha. In the ensuing battle, Bāṇa, supported by Śiva and his armies, is defeated. At the end of the battle, Kṛṣṇa cuts off Bāṇa's arms, save four. The story is recounted in *Bhāgavata Purāṇa*, Book 10, Chapter 62.

II.4.3: 'Ruined Laṅkā' refer to the note on I.6.7. Also referenced in II.4.4 and II.4.10.

II.4.4: The banner has an eagle (Garuḍa) on it. It is both Viṣṇu's vehicle as well as his emblem. The verse mentions the eagle, but I have left this out in the translation.

II.4.8: Kaṁsa was Kṛṣṇa's maternal uncle and the king of Mathura. A prophecy had predicted that the eighth child of his sister, Devakī, would kill him and assume the throne of Mathura. He imprisoned Devakī and her husband, Vasudeva, killing each child that was born to them. Kṛṣṇa was the eighth child. Through divine intervention (Viṣṇu's power), Vasudeva spirited Kṛṣṇa to be raised in secret among the cowherds of Gokula. He is raised as the child of Yaśodā and Nanda. Kaṁsa ferrets out Kṛṣṇa's hiding place and sends several demon-assassins to kill the boy. None is successful. Eventually, he and his older brother, Balarāma, travel to Mathura, where Kṛṣṇa confronts Kaṁsa, and kills him. The episode is narrated in *Bhāgavata Purāṇa*, Book 10, Chapter 44.

II.4.11: This phala-śruti does not explicitly lay out the benefits to be accrued by learning, reciting or hearing this decad of verses, but it is implied. The *Īṭu* fleshes out the merits in terms of eternal service *(kaiṅkarya)* at the feet of Viṣṇu.

It is significant that Nammāḻvār ends the decad by using the name Vāmaṉaṉ. As the *Īṭu* explicates, this avatāra was about his reclaiming what belonged to him—the world. Will he respond to the mother's entreaties and claim the girl too? Here, Nammāḻvār does not invoke any element of the myth, but simply uses the name of the avatāra. I have therefore not listed it in the Index of Myths, but it is listed in the Index of Names.

II.5.1: The verse begins with the phrase *am-tāmattu* (in a beautiful place), which the *Īṭu* reads as referring to Vaikuṇṭha. That is, the Āḻvār desired to be with Viṣṇu in his paradise (Vaikuṇṭha), but god wished him to remain here on earth for a little while longer. Therefore, he came to him and merged with him, such that this world was equal to the eternal realm in the bliss it conferred.

II.5.2: 'Ayaṉ is in his navel' refer to note I.3.9.

II.5.7: 'Kills seven bulls' refer to note I.5.1.
'Pierced seven trees' refer to note I.5.6.

II.5.9: *Alli* is a red water lily.

II.5.11: Kṛṣṇa as the pot-dancer is an obscure mythic reference. The āḻvār corpus does not provide further details to flesh out the story. In the *Īṭu* it is taken to signify his accessibility, and as the means to entice and capture the Āḻvār. F. Hardy suggests it connects to Kṛṣṇa's defeat of Bāṇa. He is said to have danced with pots as he entered the defeated demon-king's city. He bases this on a reference in the Āycciyar Kuravai (Dance of the Herdswoman) in the 'Madurai Kāṇṭam' of the *Cilappatikāram*. He also suggests, based on the *Gopālaviṁśati*, that Kṛṣṇa danced with pots while stealing butter to attract Yaśodā's attention. Friedhelm Hardy, *Viraha Bhakti*. pp. 180–181, fn. 206. Vasudha Narayanan, following the lead of the commentators, suggests that pot-dancing may be related to the myth of Kṛṣṇa as the butter-thief. Vasudha Narayanan. *The Way and the Goal*. p. 174.

This phala-śruti contains the first self-conscious reference to the poem as an antāti.

II.6.1: Kunta is an unusual name for Viṣṇu. It refers to a kind of white flower, *kuntam*. Through a secondary derivation, it thus implies god's purity.

The phrase *eṉ pollā-t-tirukkuṟaḷā* is translated as cunning little youth. It refers to the Vāmana avatāra. It is not listed in the myths as it is used as an epithet here, rather than describing the action of the narrative.

II.6.2: 'The nectar that steadies (*tuḷakku aṟṟu amutam āy*)': The *Īṭu* connects this to the first verse of II.4.1 in which the Āḻvār (as the heroine) quivers with longing. With Viṣṇu having now entered him, as nectar (amṛta/amutam), the unsteadiness of longing settles.

'Swallowed the world' refer to the note on I.1.7.

II.6.5: The phrase used in this verse is *yōka nittirai* (*yoga nidrā*), which refers to a meditative sleep.

II.6.6: Hiraṇya is a demon who refused to acknowledge Viṣṇu's supremacy, as he had received a boon from Brahmā that made him nearly invincible. His boon decreed that he could not be killed by man or beast, during day or night, neither inside nor outside, and by no weapon. He had a son, Prahlāda, who was a great devotee of Viṣṇu. Hiraṇyakaśipu, enraged by his son's refusal to accept his sole sovereignty, ordered him to be tormented in various ways. When Hiraṇya, attempting to prove to Prahlāda that Viṣṇu was not all pervasive, kicked a pillar, Viṣṇu emerged in a half-man/half-lion (Narasiṁha) form. It was dusk—neither day nor night—when Viṣṇu placed Hiraṇya on his lap at a threshold—neither inside nor outside—and disembowelled him with his claws, thus using no weapons. This is a popular and well-attested myth, and is recounted in several important *Purāṇas*, including the *Brahmāṇda*, *Matsya* and *Padma Purāṇas*. The name, Narasiṅka, a variation of Narasiṁha, is used for the first time in *Tiruvāymoḻi* II.4.1.

Hiraṇyakaśipu (gold-clothed one) is the older brother of Hiraṇyākṣa (gold-eyed one), who was killed by Viṣṇu in the Varāha myth, referenced for the first time in I.7.6.

II.6.9: 'Destroyer of Laṅkā' refer to the note on I.6.7.

'Piercing the seven trees' refer to the note on I.5.6.

II.6.11: The title or name Māṟaṉ appears for the first time in this concluding verse. It is a title frequently used by Pāṇṭiya kings and their functionaries. Śaṭhakōpaṉ's use of the epithet signals a connection to local Pāṇṭiya kings.

II.7.1–II.7.13: *Unusually, this set consists of thirteen verses instead of the usual eleven verses (ten plus the phala-śruti). This is because it incorporates the twelve names of Viṣṇu in the order in which they are recited: Keśava, Nārāyaṇa, Mādhava, Govinda, Viṣṇu, Madhusūdana, Trivikrama, Vāmana, Śrīdhara, Hṛṣīkeśa, Padmanābha and Dāmodara. Each name is repeated twice (except for Keśava) to form the antāti, giving the sense of a garland of names. For example, Nārāyaṇa is the last word in the first verse (*II.7.1*), and also the first word of the verse that follows (*II.7.2*). The remaining names follow the same pattern. Keśava is linked to the last verse of the previous set (*II.6*), and therefore occurs only once in this set of thirteen verses. The name Dāmodara occurs three times, once in* II.7.11 *and twice in* II.7.12. *The name Kaṇṇaṉ occurs twice, in the set's opening verse (*II.7.1*) and in the final phala-śruti as well (*II.7.13*).*

Although the names Trivikrama and Vāmana relate to the myth of world-striding, as it is not evoked explicitly, it is not listed in the Index of Myths. This is also true of the name Dāmodara, which is related to Kṛṣṇa as butter-thief. All three names are listed in the Index of Names.

II.7.2: The third line of this verse employs the phrase *cīr aṇaṅku*, which can be read as referring to the goddess Śrī (the woman of fortune). Thus, the line could be translated as '[one] praised by Śrī and the immortals'. The *Īṭu* presents this reading as one possibility among others. The phrase can also be used to describe the immortals *(amarar)* as possessed of fortune, excellence and divinity.

'Broke the tusk of the elephant', see the note on I.9.2.

II.7.4: Kōvalaṉ is Gopāla, the protector of cows.

'Pot-dancer' refer to the note on II.5.11.

II.7.6: The poet uses the phrase *viti cuḻantatāl* in the verse's penultimate line. Here, the *Īṭu* directs us to take viti (literally, fate) as god's grace and *cuḻal (*cuḻantatāl) as his avatāra. The verse is interpreted thus: in every birth that the Āḻvār takes, god too is born with him, to remain close to him, to find a chance to grant him grace.

II.7.8: Kāma is the god of love.

After Śiva burns Kāma for disturbing his austerities, he promises Kāmā's wife, Ratī that the two will eventually be united. Kāma is then born as the son of Kṛṣṇa and Rukmiṇī, destined to kill the demon Śambara. Thus, Viṣṇu is called Kāma's father. There are several versions of this narrative, including in the *Harivamśa*, *Brahmāṇḍa Purāṇa*, *Viṣṇu Purāṇa* and the *Bhāgavata Purāṇa*.

In the later Vaiṣṇava traditions, particularly in the Pāñcarātra tradition, Pradyumna is one of Viṣṇu's four emanations (vyūha): Vāsudeva (creator), Saṁkarśana (destroyer), Pradyumna (protector) and Aniruddha (spiritual knowledge).

II.7.10: 'Destruction of Laṅkā's demon clan' refer to the note on I.6.7.

II.7.11: The first line of this verse quotes directly from the *Tiruvāymoḻi*'s opening phrase (I.1.1), using the phrase *uyarvu ayar uyar(um)*.

II.7.12: 'Swallower of worlds' refer to the note on I.1.7.

II.8.1: 'He's the source of both (*iruvar avar mutalum tāṉē*)' refers to Śiva and Brahmā.

II.8.2: 'Who saved the elephant from pain' refers to Viṣṇu's rescue of the elephant, Gajendra. While plucking lotuses from a pond to offer in worship to Viṣṇu, a crocodile trapped the elephant. When Gajendra called out to Viṣṇu for his assistance, he appeared on Garuḍa, and killed the crocodile. Gajendra achieved mokṣa.

II.8.3: 'Ayaṉ rises from his navel' refer to the note on I.3.9.

II.8.4: The verse exhorts the devotee to think without pause on the virtues (*kalyāṇa guṇa*) of Viṣṇu. This is translated as 'immerse yourself without pause/in his unshakeable ancient greatness'.

II.8.5: This verse presents a list of avatāras. The reference to the horse in the list is a reference to Viṣṇu as Hayagrīva. This deity's inclusion in the list suggests that there continued to be considerable flexibility in the list of Viṣṇu's ten avatāras even as late as the ninth century. Today, Hayagrīva is worshipped as the embodiment of knowledge. The famous Śrīvaiṣṇava poet and theologian, Vedānta Deśika's (1268–1369) *Hayagrīva Stotram* is an important liturgical praise-poem on the deity.

'Tortoise' refers to Kūrma—refer to the note on I.3.11. 'Fish' refers to Matsya—see the note on I.8.8. The human avatāras are Paraśurāma, Rāma, Balarāma, Kṛṣṇa, and Buddha. The last of these is an instance of Hindu traditions absorbing another competing religious tradition, and is attested to in several of the Sanskrit *Purāṇa*s, including the *Bhāgavata Purāṇa*, 1.3.24, in a section that recounts Viṣṇu's avatāras. Here, he is described as being born in the Kali age, the last of the four great ages to distract the enemies of the gods.

II.8.6: Pārtha is Arjuna, one of the heroes of the *Mahābhārata*. He is the third Pāṇḍava brother, and in the narrative, a close associate of Kṛṣṇa, who is also his maternal cousin. Kṛṣṇa charioteers Arjuna during the great Bharata war, and also delivers the *Bhagavad Gītā* to him, on the eve of that same war.

'Pārthaṉ placing flowers at the feet' refers to Arjuna's quest for Śiva's bow. Kṛṣṇa advised him to offer flowers to his feet. He did so, and when Śiva appeared before him, Arjuna saw the very same flowers adorning his hair.

'Measured worlds' refer to the note on I.3.10. The myth is referenced again in II.8.7.

II.8.7: 'Becomes a boar' refer to the note on I.7.6.

'Eats and spits out the world' refer to the note on I.5.8 and I.1.7.

II.8.9: The boy referenced here is Hiraṇyakaśipu's son, Prahlāda, a great devotee of Viṣṇu. Hiraṇya challenged Prahlāda's assertion that Viṣṇu existed everywhere and in all things. Thinking to disprove the boy, Hiraṇya kicked a pillar. To his surprise, Viṣṇu emerged from within the pillar, in his man-lion avatāra. See the note on II.6.6, for a fuller discussion of the myth.

II.8.11: One of the few phala-śruti verses in which neither the name of the poet (Śaṭhakōpaṉ) nor his place is mentioned. Instead, the poet refers to himself by the epithet Vaḻuti Vaḷa Nāṭaṉ—the man/master of the Vaḻuti land, which refers to the Pāṇṭiya region.

II.9.1: 'Ending the elephant's suffering' refer to the note on II.8.2.

II.9.2: 'The wisdom to guide me to your feet (*eytā niṉ kaḻal yāṉ eyta ñaṉak kai tā*)': effort alone cannot guarantee that one reaches Viṣṇu's feet. One needs his aid (*kai tā*, literally, helping hand).

II.9.4: The verse speaks to the complete dependence of the poet on god. In the final line, the poet speaks of the *ciṟappu* (superiority, wealth, esteem) that he desired and has received from Kṛṣṇa. The sense is of a blessing, indeed, the only blessing that the poets wants from god. I've translated this as gift.

II.9.5: God is beyond the effects of karma, and therefore cannot be born. Yet, he chooses to take birth, through his avatāras.

II.9.6: Blossoming light is read in the *Īṭu* as referring to the sun and the moon. The implication is that he pervades all.

II.9.10: 'Tie me to your feet': here, the poet asks to be bound to Viṣṇu's feet, so he doesn't return to worldly ways and worldly distractions. He is to tame the poet just as surely as he did the seven wild bulls. For a discussion of the seven-bulls myth, see the note on I.5.1.

'Turning Laṅkā to ash' see the note on I.6.7.

II.10.1–II.10.10: *This is the first cycle of songs in the Tiruvāymoḻi dedicated to a single site—Māliruñcōlai. It is one of four important pilgrimage sites for Vaiṣṇavas. The other three are Venkatam, Srirangam and Kāñci. Classical Tamiḻ texts attest to its pre-eminence as a place sacred to devotees of Māl. It is one of three sites mentioned in the Cilappatikāram (see the note on Venkatam,* I.8.3*).*

The temple is located in the foothills of the Aḻakar Malai (Beautiful Mountains), twelve kilometres north-west of Madurai. It is one of two sites in the Tiruvāymoḻi to receive two entire cycles of songs in its praise; the other site is Tiruvenkatam, first mentioned in I.8.3, *but receiving extended treatment only in* III.3.

It is praised by six of the twelve āḻvār poets, for a total of 128 verses, placing it third on the list, after Srirangam and Tiruvenkatam. Nammāḻvār has contributed the most number of verses (46), followed by Periyāḻvār (34) and Tirumaṅkai (33). Āṇḍāḷ's contribution is 11 verses, while Pūtam and Pēy have composed 3 verses and 1 verse respectively.

The second line of every verse in this set describes Viṣṇu and ends with the word kōyil (temple) to mark the sacrality of the site and to place god there. Similarly, the third line of every verse offers a description of the place and ends with the name of the site, Maliruncolai. The juxtaposition creates an iterative effect that affirms the equation of kōyil (temple) with a specific place (Maliruncolai). This pattern does not apply to the eleventh verse in the set, which is the phala-śruti.

II.10.2: The poet refers to Viṣṇu in this verse as Aḻakar (the Beautiful One). While this could well be an epithet or a simple description, I have treated it as a proper name because it is the name by which the deity of Maliruncolai is known. Thus, the temple at Maliruncolai is called Aḻakar Kōyil (the Temple of the Beautiful One).

II.10.4: The reference is to the myth of Kṛṣṇa raising the mountain Govardhana. Refer to the note on I.8.4.

II.10.5: 'Take the straight road' is not a navigational instruction in the verse. The path here is metaphoric, and refers to the path of virtue, goodness, servitude and devotion that leads one to Viṣṇu.

II.10.6: 'One who ate butter' refer to the note on I.3.1.

II.10.7: 'Lifted the earth' refer to the note on I.7.6.

II.10.8: Kṛṣṇa roaming with cows refers to his time among the cowherds of Gokula. See the note on I.5.1.

II.10.9: The demoness referred to here is Pūtanā. Refer to the note on I.5.9.

Tiruvāymoḻi Third Hundred (III.1–III.10)

III.1.3: In this verse, the word *parañcōti* (*param-jyoti*), highest light/flame, is repeated at the beginning of each line of the verse.

It is also the final word of the previous verse, III.1.2, thus making the antāti.

III.1.4: The *Īṭu* reads the first two lines of this verse, which describe the body of god as a blossom (*malar puraiyum tiruvuruvam*) as describing the lotus that rises from Viṣṇu's navel. That is, the poet says that although the world emerges from Viṣṇu's body, it still won't think about him.

The verse is not included in the Index of Myths, as the reference to the lotus emerging from his body is inferred only in the commentary.

III.1.5: According to the *Īṭu*, this verse should be read as a continuation of the third verse, which too praises the greatness of god and the poet's inability to praise that greatness. The previous verse should be read in isolation, as the poet digresses to lament the world's shortcomings.

III.1.7: 'The king of the gods' (*amarar kōṉ*) is taken in the *Īṭu* to be Brahmā and not Indra.

In this, and the previous verse, the poet argues that any attempt to praise Viṣṇu, whose qualities and virtues are limitless, is a failure, even if undertaken by wise deities like Śiva and Brahmā. Indeed, such attempts may actually diminish Viṣṇu's fame.

'Make the worlds' refer to the note on I.5.3.

III.1.9: 'Rescue the elephant' refer to the note II.8.2.

III.1.10: The god with the moon in his hair is Śiva.

'Ate and spat out the worlds' refer to the note on I.5.8.

III.1.11: Viṣṇu is described as both wondrous and not (*viyappu āy viyappu illā*). He and his deeds are wondrous to his devotees, but to himself he simply is. This is his nature.

III.2.2: The poet addresses Viṣṇu as Vāmana, using the name for the diminutive form he took when he first approached Bali. The poet then describes Vāmana as measuring the world. This expansive form is referred to as Trivikrama. This verse is thus noted twice in the Index of Myths, as it refers to both forms that Viṣṇu assumed in this myth. Viṣṇu measuring the world is referred to again in III.2.9. Refer to the note on I.3.10 for a discussion of the myth.

III.2.3: The Bharata war refers to the great eighteen-day internecine war between the hundred Kaurava brothers and their five Pāṇḍava cousins. Kṛṣṇa is allied with the Pāṇḍavas, who are his maternal cousins. The narrative of the Sanskrit epic, the *Mahābhārata*, builds towards this great catastrophic war. Here, the poet alludes to Kṛṣṇa's role as Arjuna's charioteer in that war.

For a note on Arjuna, see II.8.6.

III.2.5: *Kāya* flower is a flower of deep-purple hue.

III.2.6: The word for supreme one here is Paramā in vocative form.

III.2.8: The phrase used for supreme light is *param cuṭar* (highest flame/light).

III.2.9: 'Caring for cows' refers to Kṛṣṇa as a cowherd. See the note on I.5.1.

III.2.10: Life is eternal (*nīṭu uyir*), here refers to the undying soul (ātman). The poet recognizes his servitude before god.

Namaṉ: Yama, the god of death

III.3.1–III.3.10: *The second full set of verses in praise of a single site, that of Tiruvenkatam. Here, Viṣṇu invites the devotee (Nammāḻvār) to enjoy him in his arcā (iconic) form. The arcā is one of Viṣṇu's five forms. For a discussion on the site, see* I.8.3.

III.3.5: The third line of the verse reads *vētiyar muḻu vētattu amuttattai* (the nectar known by the scholars of the Vedas). I've distilled this in the translation as 'the nectar of the Vedas'.

III.3.8: 'Raised a mountain' refer to the note on I.8.4.

'Measured worlds' refer to the note on I.3.10. This myth is referenced again in III.3.11.

III.3.9: Kṛṣṇa as cowherd, refer to the note on I.5.1.

III.3.10: This verse echoes the opening verse on Tirumaliruncolai (II.10.1), in which the poet urges devotees to reach the site before they have lost their youth.

III.3.11: He does not mention Tiruvenkatam in the concluding verse of this decad.

III.4.1–III.4.10: *In this set of ten, the poet's query 'eṉkō' (shall I say?) is a refrain, appearing at the end of every line of verses one through eight. I have not translated the refrain at the end of each line, but have used different approaches to capture the rhythmic and insistent quality that the refrain produces.*

III.4.1: The towering twin lights (*nīḷ cuṭar iraṇṭum*) refers to the sun and moon.

III.4.3: The lovely mark (*maṟu*) refers to the Śrīvatsa, the mole/curl of hair on Viṣṇu's chest.

III.4.4: Puruṣa, the cosmic man, whose body is the universe.

III.4.5: The six flavours (*aṟu cuvai*)—bitter, sweet, sour, heat, acid, salt.

III.4.7: Mōkkam (Sanskrit: mokṣa): eternal release from the eternal cycle of rebirth and redeath.

III.4.9: The word *aṉantaṉ* (endless) appears twice in this verse. In the first instance, it is used to refer to Viṣṇu, and in the second it is used as a proper noun, to refer to the serpent on which Viṣṇu reclines. I have used Aṉantaṉ as an epithet for Viṣṇu, for it is one, and have also qualified it with the descriptive endless. To avoid confusion, I have not used it as a proper name for Viṣṇu's serpent, but have repeated the word endless to qualify it.

'Churning the ocean' refer to the note on I.3.11.

'Ate and spat out worlds' refer to the note on I.5.8.

III.5.1: 'Saving the elephant' refer to the note on II.8.2.

III.5.3: 'Raising the mountain' refer to the note on I.8.4.

III.5.4: The woman with garlands in her hair is Nappiṉṉai.

'Killing the seven bulls' see the note on I.5.1.

III.5.5: 'Left . . . there/was born here' refers to Viṣṇu leaving Vaikuṇṭha to take birth on earth as Kṛṣṇa. He does so in order to kill Kaṁsa. Refer to the note on II.4.8.

III.5.6: 'He became a man . . .' refers to Viṣṇu's avatāras, that although he is birthless and beyond the effects of karma, he still took birth to aid his devotees.

In this verse the poet offers an odd piece of advice to fellow devotees, counselling them to praise Viṣṇu without rancour (*muṉivu iṉṟi*). If one is a devotee, wouldn't praise be full-hearted and come from a place without envy or jealousy? The verse implies that this is not the case, and the Āḻvār himself tells us in the poem that he sometimes simply mouthed praise and pretended his love. As the *Īṭu* clarifies, one must be moved by a recitation of Viṣṇu's auspicious qualities. If one speaks of his greatness, then one can't immediately look for a fault. One may see his avatāras as examples of a fault, for they are not in keeping with his kingly qualities. In fact the avatāras illustrate his greatest attribute, that of accessibility (*saulabhya*).

III.5.7: Defeat of the hundred and blessing of the five refers to the great internecine Bharata war between the Kaurava (the hundred) and the Pāṇḍava (the five). Refer to the note on III.2.3.

III.5.9: The poet uses the word yoga (*yōku*) to refer to those who tread the ascetic, contemplative path, who immerse themselves in the Self, and mistake this for an apprehension of Viṣṇu. The true bliss is service to Viṣṇu, like that which the gods render to him.

III.6.1: He became light, fiery and intense (*moy koḷ cōtiyoṭu*), is understood in the *Īṭu* commentary as his transcendent (paratva) form in Vaikuṇṭha.

The three forms referred to in this verse's final line are Brahmā, Śiva and Indra.

'Ate the worlds' see the note on I.1.7.

III.6.2: 'The one who became three . . .' refers to Brahmā, Śiva and Indra (and the other gods). As the *Īṭu* points out, Viṣṇu is the cause/creator (*kāraṇam*) of Brahmā and Śiva. Just so, he is his own cause. He is his own leader.

'Vanquisher of vice' is a translation of the phrase *pāva nācaṉai* (the one who destroys pāpa).

'Set Laṅkā ablaze' refer to note II.1.3. For the killing of Rāvaṇa, see I.6.7.

III.6.3: Kuravai is a dance performed in a circle, similar to the formation of the *rāsa*-dance. The dance is described in the *Cilappatikāram*, in the Āycciyar Kuravai section of the 'Madurai Kāṇṭam'. It is also referenced in the *Kalittokai*, a late Saṅgam anthology. In the former, cowherds dance the kuravai while recounting various stories from Kṛṣṇa's time in Gokula. The stories include the love affair between Kṛṣṇa and Nappiṉṉai. In the *Kalittokai*, the dance is connected to bull-fighting, an element obscure in the *Cilappatikāram*'s description. However, this link is consistent with the distinctly Tamiḻ myth of Kṛṣṇa defeating seven bulls to win the hand of Nappiṉṉai. Anne Monius suggests that the kuravai dance is a dance of doom, anticipating the dreadful events that immediately follow it, namely, the unjust execution of Kōvalaṉ, the epic's hero. Anne Monius. 'Dance before Doom:

Krishna in the Non-Hindu Literature of Early Medieval South India'.

III.6.4: The lord with matted hair is Śiva.

III.6.6: 'Giver of grace/Māl of bright lotus eyes/at once angry and kind (*ciṟratōṭu aruḷ peṟravaṉ aṭikkīḻ-p-puka niṉṟa ceṅkaṇmāl*)' is a reference to Narasiṁha. He appeared with anger (ciṟratōṭu) towards Hiraṇyakaśipu, but gave grace (aruḷ) to the one who took refuge at his feet (Prahlāda). The reference to the myth is oblique in the verse, and I have retained this quality in the translation. However, the reference to this story is noted in the Index of Myths. For a discussion of the myth, see II.6.6.

III.6.7: 'Pot-dancer' refer to the note II.5.11.

III.6.8: Son of Daśaratha is Rāma, the hero of the *Rāmāyaṇa*.

'Ate and spat out worlds' refer to the note on I.5.8.

III.6.10: The Five are the Pāṇḍava brothers and the Hundred are their Kaurava cousins.

'Drove a chariot in a terrible war' see the note on III.2.3.

III.7.1: Supreme one is Paramaṉ.

III.7.4: The verse provides a list of specific ornaments that Viṣṇu wears. Rather than translate each of these, which do not have English equivalents, I have grouped them together and translated it as 'decked in jewels'.

III.7.5: 'Fed nectar to the immortals' refers to the churning of the ocean of milk in the quest for the nectar of immortality (amṛta) undertaken by the gods and demons. Once the nectar emerges from the ocean, Viṣṇu intervenes to ensure that the gods alone receive the nectar. Refer to the note on I.3.11.

III.7.6: The first two lines of this verse echo the opening two lines of III.7.2. In III.7.2, god is described as the supreme ruler (*āḷum paramaṉ*) while in III.7.6 he is the supreme protector (*aḷikkum paramaṉ*). In III.7.2, he is described in the first half of the second line as having four broad shoulders (*tōḷum ōr nāṉku*) and in III.7.6 as draped in honey-drenched garlands (*tuḷikkum naṟum kaṇṇi*). Common to both verses are the phrases *kaṇṇaṉai, āḻi-p-pirāṉ taṉṉai* (line 1) and *tūmaṇi vaṇṇaṉ emmāṉ taṉṉai* (line 2).

III.7.7: 'They will guide me to the good way (*naṉmai peṟuttu emmai nāḷ uyyakkoḷkiṉṟa namparē*)': Those who are devotees of devotees are his friends (*naṉpar*), who will guide the poet in a way that he attains virtue (naṉmai peṟuttu) and help him be exalted/saved (uyyakkoḷkiṉṟa).

III.7.8: Viṣṇu is described in this verse as *tiru mārpaṉ* (one who has Śrī on his chest). I have translated this as 'inseparable from Śrī' for this is the implication of the phrase.

III.7.10: 'Measured the world' refer to the note on I.3.10.

'Ate the world' see the note on I.1.7.

'Child on a banyan leaf' see the notes on I.9.4 and I.1.7.

III.7.11: 'Killed the Hundred, blessed the Five' see the notes on III.2.3 and III.6.10.

III.8.1: *Muṭiyāṉē*: literally, the one who wears a crown. I have translated this as king, bringing out an implied meaning. I have also moved the opening phrase to the Tamiḻ text's final line, where it is married to the epithet *neṭiyāṉē* (lofty/tall one). However, this interpretation is in keeping with the understanding in the commentary that the crown signifies his sovereignty over all.

In the verse, there is a juxtaposition of the feet (*aṭi*) and *muṭi* (head/crown) to indicate god's all-encompassing qualities.

'Churning the ocean' refer to the note on I.3.11.

III.8.2: 'Poison to Laṅkā's king' refers to Rāma's defeat of Rāvaṇa, the king of Laṅkā. Refer to I.6.7 for a more detailed exposition of the enmity between Rāma and Rāvaṇa.

'Cunning youth taking the world' refer to the note on I.3.10. The myth is referenced again in III.8.5, III.8.9 and III.8.11.

III.8.3: 'Mother to cowherds' see the note on I.5.1.

'Stealing butter' refers to the note on I.3.1.

III.8.4: The poet longs to see Viṣṇu in an embodied form, not just through a practice of mental visualization. This is similar to the request that opens Nammāḻvār's *Tiruviruttam*, in which he asks Viṣṇu to listen to his petition in a true, embodied form.

There is a long tradition within Hinduism that asserts the tactility of vision. Here that connection is made explicit. The poet is unsatisfied with the intimacy of touch (I worship you with my hands), and instead demands the additional intimacy that is brought by sight, which is itself akin to touch.

III.8.8: Kohl is black eyeliner made from organic materials, usually soot.

III.8.9: 'Killer of Kaṁsaṉ' see the note on II.4.8.

III.8.10: 'Felling the Maruta trees' see the note on II.1.10.

III.9.1: The bees of Tiruvenkatam are described using an onomatopoeia—*tēṉṉā tēṉā*—which also suggests their intoxication from the honey. I've translated this as 'honey-seeking bees'.

III.9.4: The men are described as *maṉṉā maṉicar* (ephemeral men). That is, men die and the wealth they bestow is equally fleeting. We are thus to deduce that the only thing of fixity is Viṣṇu and the only permanent wealth is mokṣa.

III.9.8: 'Piṉṉai's beloved' see the note on I.5.1.

III.9.9: The highest world promised is Vaikuṇṭha, along with the joy of eternal service to Viṣṇu there. The verse asserts that the release (vīṭu) promised is not immediate, but gradual (*niṉṟu niṉṟē*).

III.9.10: Viṣṇu creates world after world as a way to cultivate devotion and to end birth. That is, each world represents an opportunity to break free of the cycle of birth and death.

III.10.2: The phrase used to describe yogic sleep is *yōku puṇarnta* (the one who did yoga). The phrase qualifies the epithet *oḷi maṇivaṇṇaṉ* (luminous jewel-hued one).

III.10.4: The destroyer of the three cities is Śiva as Tripurāntaka, and his son is Skanda. Refer to the note on I.1.8.

Bāṇa was a great devotee of Śiva, and appealed to him for assistance in his fight against Kṛṣṇa. The various gods, including Śiva and Agni, fought on Bāṇa's side. Kṛṣṇa defeated them all, and sent his war-disc to cut off Bāṇa's arms as punishment. Śiva had promised Bāṇa his protection, and petitioned Kṛṣṇa on his devotee's behalf. Kṛṣṇa acceded to Śiva's request and arrested the fury of the disc. For further details on this myth, see the note on II.4.2.

III.10.5: 'From his own light (*cuṭar ōḷiyāy niṉrā taṉuṭaiyac cōtiyil*)' can also be taken to refer to Vaikuṇṭha, the land of light.

In this myth, a brahmin loses his three sons as soon as they are born. When the fourth child is about to be born, the brahmin prays to Kṛṣṇa for protection. Not wanting Kṛṣṇa to interrupt his ritual obligations, Arjuna [Pārthan] promises to stand guard during the birth. However, he fails, and the fourth child too dies as soon as he is born. Kṛṣṇa then takes Arjuna and the brahmin to heaven in a chariot, retrieves the boys, and restores them to the father. The episode is described in the *Bhāgavata Purāṇa*, Book 10, Chapter 89.

III.10.9: The naked god is Śiva.

Tiruvāymoḻi Fourth Hundred (IV.1–IV.10)

IV.1.1–IV.1.11: *This decad describes the ephemerality of mortal kings.*

IV.1.1: Viṣṇu is referred to in this verse by the name Tirunāraṇaṉ (Śrīman Nārāyaṇa). This signifies his inseparability from Śrī.

IV.1.4: 'Killed the rut-mad elephant' refer to the note on I.9.2.

IV.1.8: The verse suggests that even good kings will lose their wealth, their kingdoms and all their attendant pleasures, if they think that all of this is of their own making, rather than because of his grace (*tiruvaruḷ*).

IV.1.10: This verse pits the path of inward contemplation against loving service to god. The former always has the possibility of failure, for the mind is unsteady and unreliable. Loving service to god and the relationship it engenders ensures the mokṣa (vīṭu).

IV.1.11: The *Īṭu* tells us that those who master these ten verses will reject the minor fruits of life (puruṣārtha), and will instead achieve the pleasure of service (kaiṅkarya) to Viṣṇu as the ultimate goal and fruit of that life (puruṣārtha).

IV.2.1–IV.2.10: *This decad is in the voice of the mother. The final verse (*IV.2.11*) does not make a reference to the change in persona.*

IV.2.1, IV.2.2, IV.2.3: The speaker of these three verses (the mother) refers to herself as one who is ill-fated, bound by karma. She uses two phrases to convey this idea, *valviṉaiyēṉ* (IV.2.1), *viṉaiyāṭṭiyēṉ* (IV.2.2, IV.2.3). I have translated this, not as a participial noun (I who am ill-fated), but as I am doomed. In IV.2.4, she uses the word, *ūḻi viṉaiyēṉ*, which I have rendered, doomed through the ages.

IV.2.1: 'Ate the world' refer to the note on I.1.7.

'Slept on a banyan leaf' refer to the note on I.9.4.

IV.2.2: 'Dancing the kuravai' see the note on III.6.3.

IV.2.3: The verse makes an implicit reference to Viṣṇu spanning the worlds (*tēvarkaḷ mā muṉivarkaḷ iṟaiñca niṉṟa cēvaṭi*). The *Īṭu* tells us that the gods in heaven and the sages on earth praised the feet that took the world. The verse though simply says that the girl desires the tuḷasi from the feet praised/revered by the gods and sages. As the reference to the myth is oblique, it is not listed in the Index of Myths.

IV.2.5: 'Killing the seven bulls' see the note on I.5.1.

'Pot-dancer' see the note on I.5.11.

IV.2.6: 'Came as a pig' refer to note I.7.6.

IV.2.8: Sītā is Rāma's wife in the *Rāmāyaṇa*. Rāvaṇa, the king of Laṅkā, abducts her. In the battle Rāma wages to retrieve his wife, he devastates Laṅkā.

IV.3.1: Kōvai is a common creeper that produces a bright-red fruit.

IV.3.3: According to the *Īṭu*, his one form (*eka mūrtti*) is god before creation, where only he exists, with everything contained within him. In his two forms (*iru mūrtti*), he is Prakṛtī (primordial matter) and Mahān (intellect). In his three forms (*mūṉṟu mūrtti*), he is the three *ahaṁkāras* (egos), Sattva (luminous), Rajas (activity) and Tamas (inertia).

This is a classic Sāṁkhya elucidation of the creation of the universe.

IV.3.4: 'Devious demoness' is Pūtanā. See the note on I.5.9.

Kṛṣṇa as cowherd, see the note on I.5.1.

IV.3.7: The form of word and light (*urai koḷ cōti tiru uruvam*), here the word urai (words) can be understood in multiple ways. As per the *Īṭu*, it can refer to Viṣṇu's name, which infuses every word uttered. It can refer to the inability of words to describe Viṣṇu's beauty, which the *Tiruvāymoḻi*, the Tamiḻ Veda (Tamiḻ Maṟai), asserts in III.1.2.

'Took the earth' refer to the note on I.3.10.

IV.3.8: 'My breath is yours/Yours is mine': The Tamiḻ word used here is *āvi* (literally, breath). It also means self or soul. The commentary glosses it as ātman (self/soul). I have chosen to use breath, for it signifies something ethereal and intangible, but essential to life. The mingling of breath, like in a kiss, suggests an experiential, perhaps even somatic intimacy, which the words soul or spirit do not convey.

IV.4.1–IV.4.10: *The mother's voice returns in the decad. We also hear the heroine's voice through the mother. Neither change in voice is noted in the concluding eleventh verse.*

IV.4.1: The mother addresses the other women as *vaḷayīr* (women wearing bangles). This signifies their auspicious state. I have not translated the phrase, and have simply rendered the phrase as friends.

IV.4.6: Kṛṣṇa as the flute-player refers to Kṛṣṇa's ability to entrance the hearts of the gopī women with the melodious music from his flute. So intoxicating is the music that it makes them forget themselves and their surroundings. The description of Kṛṣṇa's flute-playing and its effects is described in *Bhāgavata Purāṇa*, Book 10, Chapter 21.

IV.4.8: 'He measured worlds' refer to the note on I.3.10.

IV.4.9: 'Ate the world' refer to the note on I.1.7.

IV.5.1–IV.5.10: *In this decad, the poet describes the task of stringing a garland of songs for Viṣṇu.*

IV.5.1: 'Killed the horse' refer to the note on I.8.2.

IV.5.6: 'Streak of white earth (*veḷiya nīr*)' refers to the *nāmam*, the Vaiṣṇava insignia.

IV.5.7: The poet uses the word viti (fate/destiny) to describe the act of singing songs of praise. I have translated this as 'I am meant to do this'. The *Īṭu* understands viti in this context as a blessing (*kṛpā*) of Viṣṇu, which enables the poet to sing of him (or alternately, the god singing of himself through the poet).

'Lifted the mountain' see the note on I.8.4.

IV.5.9: The gently curving conch refers to Viṣṇu's right turning white conch (Valampuri/Pāñcajanya), which he holds in his left hand.

'Pot-dancer' see the note on II.5.11.

IV.5.10: This verse recounts a series of myths that express Viṣṇu's relationship to the world—as creator, destroyer, protector, and as sovereign.

'Eating and spitting out the worlds' refers to the notes on I.5.8 and I.1.7.

'Digging the world' refers to the note on I.7.6.

'Spanning the world' refers to the note on I.3.10.

Although the verse itself makes no explicit mention of Rāma, the *Īṭu* reads the second and third lines of the verse as referring to the Rāma avatāra. He lies facing the ocean (*kiṭantu*) right before he sets out for Laṅkā. He stands holding his bow, ready for the fight (niṉṟu), holds court after his triumphant return and coronation (*koṇṭa kōlattōṭu vīṟṟiruntu*), and rules over the earth for eleven thousand years, protecting it, and thus holding it close (*maṇam kūṭiyum*). Since there is no explicit mention, or indeed an explicit allusion to the story of Rāma in this verse, I have not included the Rāma references in the myth index.

IV.5.11: In this verse, Śrī appears to have the authority to end one's deeds and their effects (karma). The issue of Śrī's independence and ability to grant grace on her own becomes one of the main points of contention between the two branches of the Śrīvaiṣṇava tradition.

It is also of interest that the verse concludes with an assertion that it is in praise of Viṣṇu at Venkatam, although none of the ten preceding verses mention the site. For a discussion of the site of Venkatam, refer to the note on I.8.3.

In this verse, the poet refers to himself by the epithet Kārimāṟaṉ. Kāri is generally understood to be his father's name. Thus Māṟaṉ, son of Kāri, would be an appropriate translation of the epithet.

IV.6.1–IV.6.10: *These verses describe the young woman's love for god as an illness. They are addressed to mothers (aṉṉaimīr), which includes the girl's birth parent, foster parent, aunts and other older women. The speaker of these verses can be assumed to be the girl's friend(s). I have not included a translation of aṉṉaimīr in the English. This decad also introduces the character of the kaṭṭuvicci, the fortune teller* (IV.6.3).

The decad follows a familiar conceit from the classical Tamiḻ poetic tradition. The girl is in love, and is exhibiting the symptoms of lovesickness, growing pale, listless, distracted. In the classical tradition, the mothers mistake lovesickness for god possession. Here, the object of love is Viṣṇu, and her suffering is caused by separation.

Several of the verses reference dancing the aṇaṅku/dancing with aṇaṅku (aṇaṅku āṭum). Here, it refers to a dance of possession, usually for/of Murukaṉ. This Ten mounts a sustained critique of what appear to be non-Vaiṣṇava ritual practices (for instance, sacrificing animals, drinking liquor, offering mixed rice grains) and the worship of any deity other than Viṣṇu. This deity could well be Murukaṉ, although the poet does not name any other god explicitly.

IV.6.1: 'The charioteer who guided the victory of the five' refers to Kṛṣṇa as Arjuna's charioteer in the great eighteen-day Mahābhārata war.

The five refers to the five Pāṇḍava brothers. Refer to the note on III.2.3.

IV.6.4: 'Ate and spat the worlds' refer to the note on I.5.8.

IV.6.5: 'Killing the rut-mad elephant' see the note on I.9.2.

IV.6.10: King of Dvāraka refers to Kṛṣṇa, who built a divine city called Dvārakā, and transported Mathura's citizens to it, to protect them. Dvārakā is also a Divya Deśa, the only one located in western India. It is in the present-day state of Gujarat. It has been praised by five āḻvār poets, including Nammāḻvār for a total of 13 verses. Nammāḻvār makes two references to the site, here in this verse, where it is used as a way to describe Kṛṣṇa, and again, in V.3.6, where the place itself is praised.

IV.7.1: 'Eater of worlds' refer to the note on I.1.7.

IV.7.2, IV.7.3: In this verse, Viṣṇu is referred to by the name Vāmana, but the act attributed to him is the claiming of the universe in his form as Trivikrama. I have therefore listed the name Vāmana in the Index of Names, but this verse is listed under Trivikrama (took the world) in the Index of Myths. For a discussion of the myth, see the note on I.3.10.

IV.7.5: 'Churning the ocean' refer to the note on I.3.11.

IV.8.1–IV.8.10: *This Ten is in the voice of the heroine.*

IV.8.1: 'The god who rides the bull' refers to Śiva, the one facing the four directions is Brahmā and the beautiful goddess is Śrī.

IV.8.3: 'Perfect mother with a pure heart' refers to the devious Pūtanā. For the myth, see I.5.9.

IV.8.4: 'Taming seven bulls' see the note on I.5.1.

IV.8.5: The woman referred to in this verse is Sītā, the heroine of the *Rāmāyaṇa*, who was abducted and imprisoned in a grove in the island city of Laṅkā.

IV.8.6 and IV.8.7: The antāti that links both verses here are the words *kiḷar oḷi* (bright light/shining light). In the first case (IV.8.6), it refers to the heroine's bright, youthful beauty. In the second case, it is used to describe Narasiṁha. The phrase also alludes to the important decad (II.10) that begins with the phrase kiḷar oḷi. In that case, it refers to the impermanence of the youthful beauty. That Ten is also significant for being the first on a single site (Tirumaliruncolai).

IV.8.6: 'Claim the world' see the note on I.3.10.

IV.8.7: 'Flawless lion' refers to Narasiṁha. See the note on II.6.6.

IV.8.8: 'The king of gods' refers to Indra.

IV.8.9: The woman referred to in this verse is Bāṇaṉ's daughter, Uṣā, who falls in love with Kṛṣṇa's grandson, Aniruddha. See the note on II.4.2.

IV.8.10: The one from whose matted hair a river flows is Śiva. The river is the Gaṅgā.

IV.8.11: 'Lapped up curd and butter' see the note on I.3.1.

IV.9.1: The poet asks for death so that he may more quickly approach Viṣṇu's feet.

IV.9.8: The egg that is the fortress of the gods refers to the conception of the world as an egg.

IV.9.8: Spitting out the worlds, refer to the note on I.1.7 and I.5.8.

IV.10.1–IV.10.11: *This Ten is devoted to the site of Tirukkurukūr, present-day Alvar Tirunagari, to which the poet closely links himself in the phala-śruti verses. As such, this decad is accorded attention during recitation, particularly during the annual Adhyayanotsavam (Festival of Recitation). It is also worth noting that this decad is among the most explicitly polemical—aggressive and forceful in its denunciation and rejection of other gods and other paths.*

The Tirukkurukur temple comprises an east-facing Viṣṇu shrine. To the north of that shrine, are the shrines to the tamarind tree under which Nammāḻvār is said to have meditated, and that of Nammāḻvār, who faces south.

Tirukkurukur is part of a pilgrimage circuit called the Nava Tirupati. These are nine temples located on the banks of the Tamiraparani. Nammāḻvār has praised all of them in the Tiruvāymoḻi. Save three sites, the remaining six have been lauded in entire decads. Kurukur appears in almost every Ten's concluding verse, and in this Tiruvāymoḻi is the focus of sustained elaboration. Therefore, this can be regarded as the first of the Nava Tirupati sites singled out for praise.

*The other sites are the twin-sites of Tolaivillimaṅgalam (*VI.5*), Tirukkōḷūr (*VI.7*), Tiruppērai (*VII.3*), Kuḷantai/Peruṅkulam (*VIII.2.4*), Puḷiṅkuṭi (*VIII.3.5, IX.2*), Varaguṇamaṅgai (*IX.2.4*) and Śrīvaikuṇṭham (*IX.2.4, IX.2.8*).*

Of these, the following decads are in the female voice: VI.5, VI.7, VII.3 *and* VIII.2.

IV.10.1: In this verse, the poet uses the epithet Ādippirāṉ to address Viṣṇu. He localizes him as dwelling in Kurukur (*ataṉ uḷ niṉṟa*: the one who abides/dwells within). The name of the deity at the temple at Kurukur (Alvar Tirunagari) is Ādippirāṉ. For this reason, I have left it as a name, while also providing a gloss (primordial lord). It is also listed in the Index of Names.

IV.10.3: The verse groups a set of myths that often appear together. They speak to Viṣṇu's creative, destructive, protective attributes, and his role as sovereign.

'Swallowed, hid, spewed the world' see the notes on I.1.7 and I.5.8.

'Crossed the world' as Trivikrama see the note on I.3.10.

'Split the world' as Varāha see the note on I.7.6.

IV.10.4: Viṣṇu relieves the curse of Śiva, refer to the note on II.2.2.

Ilaṅkiyar is taken to mean devotees of Śiva (i.e. those associated with the Liṅga). The *Īṭu* reads the phrase *avam paṟaital* (useless speech) as referring to baseless arguments made by Śiva's worshippers about the primacy of their god.

IV.10.5: The poet uses the word *camaṇar* (*śramaṇa*) for Jains and *cākkiyar* (*śākya*) for the Buddhists.

In this verse, Viṣṇu is described as *polintu niṉṟa pirāṉ* (the radiant/shining god). This is also the name by which the festival icon at Alvar Tirunagari is known. I have therefore included it in the Index of Names, but I have not retained the epithet in translation as it would have necessitated simply replicating the entire Tamiḻ phrase. I have translated the phrase as 'radiant god'. It must be noted that all translations of 'radiant god/radiant lord' in the *Tiruvāymoḻi* do not reverse translate into Tamiḻ as *polintu niṉṟa pirāṉ*. There are many places in the *Tiruvāymoḻi* where the word pirāṉ (lord/god/master) is qualified in some manner. These instances are not taken as proper names, and included in the Index of Names. IV.10.5 presents a unique case, for the epithet comes to refer specifically to the festival icon at the Viṣṇu temple of Alvar Tirunagari. I made a similar translation decision in the verse on Tirumaliruncolai (II.10.2), where Viṣṇu is referred to as Aḻakar (The Beautiful One), the name by which the deity of that temple is also known.

IV.10.8: Mārkaṇḍeya saved by Śiva: In dominant versions of this myth, the young boy Mārkaṇḍeya was destined for death at the age of sixteen. He prayed to Śiva, and when Yama appeared to take him, Mārkaṇḍeya clung to the Śiva Liṅga. Yama's noose was unable to capture the boy's soul, and he thus escaped death. Nammāḻvār offers a different take, attributing Śiva's actions to Viṣṇu's grace (aruḷ). That is, as the *Īṭu* suggests, Śiva merely acts as the mediator (*puruṣakāra*) of Viṣṇu's grace, to ensure that Mārkaṇḍeya escapes death.

Mārkaṇḍeya also plays a significant role in the end-time myth of Viṣṇu as a child on a banyan leaf. In this story, recounted in *Mahābhārata*, Āraṇya Parva 186, Mārkaṇḍeya wandering afraid at the time of dissolution, finds a child resting under a banyan tree. The child invites him to rest inside his body, and Mārkaṇḍeya is drawn in. There he sees the whole universe contained within, and seeks refuge with this deity. He is expelled from within, and is blessed with renewed insight and vision. He then takes the child's feet and places them upon his head. The episode is also narrated in the *Bhāgavata Purāṇa*, Book 12, Chapter 9.

IV.10.10: Viṣṇu as a tiny ascetic refer to the note on I.3.10.

'Pot-tossing acrobat' see the note on II.5.11.

IV.10.11: Makiḻ is a small fragrant white flower. It is also known as the *Vakula* flower in Sanskrit. Thus, the poet, Śaṭhakōpaṉ is also known by the Sanskrit epithet Vakulābharaṇa (the one adorned in Vakula flowers).

Tiruvāymoḻi Fifth Hundred (V.1–V.10)

V.1.2: 'Slipped between the maruta trees' see the note on II.1.10.

V.1.7: The poet says that the simple act of praising Viṣṇu as the protector is sufficient to earn his love that has turned him into a true devotee. Thus, even past transgressions and wicked people (*pāviyar*) can be redeemed when their time is right *(viti vāykkiṉṟu vāykkum)*.

'Stopped the elephant's suffering' see the note on II.8.2.

V.1.9: Viṣṇu is described as calling to the poet, appearing before him holding the conch and disc. The poet characterizes this as *aruḷceytu* (giving grace/bestowing favour, being gracious). I have translated this as 'gift', to capture the sense of gracious favour that characterizes god's sovereignty, as well as the intimacy that exists between god and devotee.

V.1.10: This verse provides a list of Viṣṇu's avatāras, although they do not appear in regular order; his third avatāra as the pig/boar is placed as the penultimate one here. It also introduces the avatāra of Kalki for the first time.

The fish avatāra: refer to the note on I.8.8; the turtle avatāra: refer to the note on I.3.11; man-lion avatāra: refer to II.6.6; dwarf avatāra: refer to I.3.10; boar avatāra: refer to I.7.6.

Kalki(n) is the last of ten avatāras, and is yet to manifest. He is said to come at the end of Kali age, the last of the four ages, to end it, and to then begin the universe again. He is imagined as appearing on a white horse wielding a sword. There are several versions of the Kalki avatāra, including in the *Mahābhārata*, the *Viṣṇu Purāṇa* and the *Bhāgavata Purāṇa.*

V.2.1–V.2.11: *This Ten describes the Kali age, the terrible last cycle of time, and the ways in which devotion to Viṣṇu provides a path out of it. Kali refers to the last of the four ages (yuga) in the cycle of time. It is characterized by strife, chaos, and a devolution of law and morality. This decad links neatly to the first and only mention of the Kalki avatāra in the tenth verse of the previous decad (*V.1.10*) that is meant to end the immorality of this last age.*

V.2.7: The poet only mentions Mārkaṇḍeya by name, and does not provide any further detail, as he does in IV.10.8. As in that verse, the implication here is the same: that even when other gods respond to devotees' petitions, Viṣṇu is always the true actor. Thus, although we may think that it was Śiva who saved Mārkaṇḍeya from his preordained early death, it was really Viṣṇu who ensured his survival.

This idea is further emphasized in the next verse, V.2.8—all of the offerings made to other gods ultimately go to Viṣṇu (he eats everything you give the other gods).

V.2.9: 'People with the Veda on their lips' refers to brahmins.

V.3.1–V.3.10: *This Ten is spoken in the voice of the heroine.*

V.3.3: 'Shattered the cart' refer to the note on II.1.8.

'Suckling at the demon's breast' see the note on I.5.9. The myth is referenced in V.3.8 as well.

V.3.5: 'Holds the earth with his feet' see the note on I.3.10.

V.3.6: 'As king of Dvârakã' see the note on IV.6.10.

V.3.8: 'Ripped the bird' refers to an incident from Kṛṣṇa's childhood. He killed the demon named Bakāsura. He came in the form of a crane and swallowed Kṛṣṇa. Kṛṣṇa burnt in the bird's belly like a fire, that it vomited him out. Kṛṣṇa, furious, killed the demon by tearing open his beak. The episode is described in the *Bhāgavata Purāṇa*, Book 10, Chapter 11.

'Killed the elephant' refer to the note on I.9.2.

Toṇṭai refers to the fruit of a perennial thorny hedge with a red-skinned fruit.

V.3.9: Riding the maṭal is a practice described in the classical Tamiḻ corpus of love poems. It was a public declaration of love by a man, undertaken when his love is unrequited. The practice involved wearing a wreath and garland of the poisonous *datura*, carrying a picture of the girl, and riding a horse created out of thorny palmyra stems in the public square, while declaring one's love. It is impossible to know if riding the maṭal was simply a literary convention, or if it was ever undertaken. Apart from the two references in Nammāḻvār's poem (V.3.9 and V.3.10), Tirumaṅkai composed two poems on the theme, called the *Ciṟiya Tirumaṭal*

(The Short Maṭal) and the *Periya Tirumaṭal* (The Long Maṭal). In both poems, it is the heroine who wants to ride the maṭal.

V.4.1–V.4.10: *This Ten is spoken in the voice of the heroine.*

V.4.1: 'Swallowed the earth' see the note on I.1.7.

V.4.3: Kākuttaṉ (Kākutstha): Rāma as the descendant of Kakutstha, hence Kākutstha in Sanskrit and Kākuttaṉ in Tamiḻ.

V.4.4, V.4.10: 'Measured the world' see the note on I.3.10.

V.5.1–V.5.10: *This Ten is on the sacred site of Tirukkuṟuṅkuṭi (Tirukkurungudi), in the southern Pāṇṭiya region, close to the Nava Tirupati pilgrimage circuit. It is an important site, linked to two of the most important āḻvār poets. Nammāḻvār's parents are believed to have petitioned the Viṣṇu enshrined here (called Nambi) for a child. They were blessed with said child, who was none other than this very Viṣṇu. It is also revered as the place of Tirumaṅkai Āḻvār's mokṣa. Tirukkurungudi is also associated with Rāmānuja, the Śrīvaiṣṇavas' most important teacher. According to the site's local history, Rāmānuja initiated Nambi, who appeared to him in disguise, earning the deity the epithet, Śrīvaiṣṇava Nambi.*

The temple is a magnificent example of Pāṇṭiya-period architecture (fifteenth century and on), particularly the small-scale, detailed sculpture on the Chitra Gōpuram. The temple is unusual in that it features three Viṣṇu shrines, with Nambi in each of his three postures—standing, reclining and seated—in a lateral arrangement. While the vertical arrangement of Viṣṇu in three tiers in three postures is well known (for example, Tirukkoshtiyur, Mannar Koyil, Ramaswami temple in Cheran Mahadevi and Kudal Alakar, all in the Pāṇṭiya region, and Uttaramerur and Vaikuntha Perumal in Pallava territory), this is the only known example of three shrines in a lateral arrangement.

The deity at the temple is called Aḻakiya Nambi (the beautiful prince/the beautiful lord). The Tiruvāymoḻi (like other poems in the Divya Prabandham) employs Nambi as a common description of Viṣṇu. In this decad, Nambi is used repeatedly (e.g. Tirukkuṟuṅkuṭi Nambi), giving the impression of particularity. I have alternated between translating the epithet as lord of Tirukkuṟuṅkuṭi and leaving it as such. The decision to translate depended on whether or not the verse included a description of the town.

This Tiruvāymoḻi is in the voice of the heroine.

V.5.6, V.5.7, V.5.10: The girl says that her mother makes her hide, or more literally, won't let her see (*kāṇakkoṭāḷ*). The implication is that having noted that the girl is madly in love with the lord of Tirukkuṟuṅkuṭi, the mother forbids her from seeing him (presumably in a temple). The girl responds by saying that this has no effect, for Nambi lives in her heart.

V.5.11: Vaiṣṇavas are devotees of Viṣṇu.

V.6.1–V.6.10: *This decad is in the female voice, and its verses are among the most significant in the Tiruvāymoḻi. Each verse begins in the heroine's voice, and concludes in the mother's voice. The girl is completely taken over by god, and asserts that she does all that he does. The mother, speaking to her friends, expresses concern and bewilderment about her daughter's state and her unorthodox claims. For a discussion of the Śrīvaiṣṇava commentaries on this verse, see Frank Clooney. '"I Created Land and Sea": A Tamil Case of God-Consciousness and Its Śrīvaiṣṇava Interpretation'.*

V.6.1: 'I took this earth' refers to Trivikrama. See the note on I.3.10.

'I split this earth' refers to Varāha. See the note on I.7.6.

'I swallowed oceans' refers to eating the worlds. See the note on I.1.7.

V.6.5: 'I lifted the mountain' refers to Kṛṣṇa. See the note on I.8.4. Referenced again V.6.6.

'I protected the five' refers to Kṛṣṇa. See the note on III.2.3.

'I churned the ocean' refers to Kūrma. See the note on I.3.11.

V.6.6: 'I killed the bulls' refers to Kṛṣṇa. See the note on I.5.1.

'Grazed calves' refers to Kṛṣṇa. See the note on I.8.8.

V.6.8: The three-eyed god is Śiva; the god who looks in four directions is Brahmā; the king of immortals is Indra.

V.6.11: The three goddesses mentioned here are Śrī (goddess with fragrant hair), Bhū (earth goddess) and Nappiṉṉai (sprout of the cowherd clan).

V.7.1–V.7.11: *This Ten in praise of the site of Śrīvaramaṅgalam (Vanamamalai/Nanguneri), located in the southern Pāṇṭiya region. It is close to the Nava Tirupati pilgrimage circuit. The temple is located beside a large lake, which lends the name to the site (Nanguneri, Four Lakes). The east-facing seated image of Viṣṇu here is believed to have self-manifested, and it is thus, considered one of the eight Vaiṣṇava svayam vyakta kṣetra (sites of self-manifestation). Of the eight shrines, Nammāḻvār has sung in praise of three—Srirangam, Tiruvenkatam and Nanguneri. The site is also home to the Vanamamalai Maṭha, one of the most important Teṅkalai Śrīvaiṣṇava administrative/monastic institutions. The Maṭha administers the temple.*

Nanguneri is also revered as the site of Nammāḻvār's śaraṇāgati (surrender). It is also famous for its beautiful śaṭhāri (the crown that is placed on devotees' heads in Śrīvaiṣṇava temples) which carries an image of Nammāḻvār upon it.

V.7.1: In the final line of this verse in which the poet declares that he is nothing without Viṣṇu (*uṉakku mikai allēṉ*), the implication is that he cannot be outside or beyond his protection, especially in this town. The particularity of site is emphasized by the use of the word *aṅkē* (there), which is to be taken along with the first phrase of the final line (*aṅkē vīṟṟirunta eṉtāy*), father who abides/ is seated there in Srivaramangalam.

V.7.2: 'Lord who destroyed Laṅkā' see the note on II.1.3.

V.7.3: Those 'who've mastered the four Veda' refers to brahmins. In the poet's description, the presence of brahmins reciting the Veda (V.7.3; V.7.9) and the performance of Vedic sacrifices (V.7.5; V.7.7) signal the site's sanctity and sacrality, and the goodness of its denizens.

V.7.4: 'The Five' are the Pāṇḍavas. See the note on III.2.3.

'Dug up the earth' see the note on I.7.6. This myth is referenced again in V.7.6.

V.7.6: In this verse, the word Vanamamalai is both an epithet of the god as well as the name of the sacred site. In the verse, I provide both readings, translating the epithet, Vanamamalai (literally, the mountain that touches the sky) as great towering mountain, and retaining it as the sacred site, rendering it as lord of Vanamamalai.

Vanamamalai is listed both in the Index of Names and in the Index of Places.

V.7.7: 'Swallowing the worlds' see the note on I.1.7.

V.7.8, V.7.9: 'Ripping the bird' see the note on V.3.8.

V.7.10, V.7.11: The name of the deity at the temple of Vanamamalai is Deyvanāyakaṉ (king of gods/leader of the gods). It is therefore left untranslated in the verse, and is also included in the Index of Names.

V.8.1–V.8.11: *This cycle of songs on Kuṭantai (Kumbakonam) is believed to be the verses that lead Nāthamuni to rediscover the Tiruvāymoḻi. From the eleventh verse, Nāthamuni learnt that the cycle was part of a song of one thousand verses (ōr āyirattuḷ ip pattum), and was composed by a man named Śaṭhakōpaṉ from the town of Kurukur (Kurukur-c-caṭakōpaṉ).*

The temple associated with this site is the Sāraṅgapāṇi temple in present-day Kumbakonam, in the state of Tamil Nadu. Although the poet does not mention a deity name (as he does in other decads dedicated to specific sites), he does consistently describe the god of Kudanthai as reclining, which is the posture in which the main deity is enshrined. The main deity is also known as Ārāmudaṉ (the nectar that doesn't sate), which is the opening line of this decad.

V.8.6: The *tūrākkuḻi* (bottomless pit) refers to the pit of the five senses.

V.8.9: According to the *Īṭu*, the master of the master of the eternal immortals (*amarar talaivar talaivā*) refers to Viṣvaksena (Cēṉaimutalvar), and not to Indra.

V.8.11: 'Nursed at the demon's breast' see the note on I.5.9.

V.9.1–V.9.11: *The Ten is dedicated to the temple site of Tiruvallavāḻ, which is located in present-day Kerala. Nammāḻvār is the only āḻvār to have sung in praise of this site. This Ten is in the heroine's voice and is addressed to her friends. The site is mentioned in the phala-śruti verse* (V.9.11), *but this verse makes no mention of the use of the female voice.*

See Frank Clooney's essay for a discussion of the Śrīvaiṣṇava commentaries on this Ten. 'Nammāḻvār's Glorious Tiruvallavāḻ: An Exploration in the Methods and Goals of Śrīvaiṣṇava Commentary'.

V.9.1: Kamuku is the areca palm.

V.9.1, V.9.2: In both verses the poet uses the word aṭiyēṉ (servant/slave, singula) and *aṭiyōm* (servant/slave, plural). The word evokes the complete dependency of the devotee on god, and that the devotee's self is entirely owned by Viṣṇu. I have translated the word in this instance as 'I am his/We are his' to convey the sense of ownership, avoiding the complicated and negative associations that come with the word slave.

V.9.2: Puṉṉai: Alexandrian Laurel tree, native to southern coastal India. It is an evergreen tree that produces a fragrant white flower.

Mātavi: An evergreen liana, native to India that produces fragrant pinkish-white flowers.

V.9.6: Kōlappirāṉ (the beautiful lord) is the name of the deity of Tiruvallaval. Hence, it is left untranslated in this verse, and is also listed in the Index of Names.

The little youth refers to Vāmana. Refer to I.3.10 for a discussion of the myth.

V.9.7: 'The lotuses rise up to kiss the faces of the women'—the conceit is that if the lotus and the faces of women were placed beside each other, it would be impossible to distinguish one from the other.

'The lord who ate the world' refer to the note on I.1.7.

V.9.8: 'The lord who measured worlds' refer to the note on I.3.10.

V.10.1: 'How you were born and how you grew' refers to Viṣṇu's avatāra as Kṛṣṇa. The first five verses describe several incidents from Kṛṣṇa's life—fighting the great war (V.10.1), taming of the bulls (V.10.2), the killing of the horse, dancing with cowherd women (V.10.2), Pūtanā and the kicking of the cart (V.10.3), lifting the mountain (V.10.5). The remaining verses describe other avatāras and other acts of protection and creation undertaken by Viṣṇu.

V.10.1: The feats in the great war/counsel to the five, refer to the note on III.2.3 and III.5.7.

V.10.2: 'Taming the bulls' refer to the note on I.5.1.

'Tearing the horse's jaws' refer to the note on I.8.2.

'Dancing the kuravai' refer to the note on III.6.3.

V.10.3: 'Nursing at the breast of the demon' refer to the note on I.5.9.

'Kicking the cart' see the note on II.1.8.

'Eating butter' see the note on I.3.1.

V.10.4: This verse makes oblique reference to a myth in which Viṣṇu comes in disguise to destroy demons. The *Īṭu* reads this as a reference to Viṣṇu coming as the Buddha, who is characterized as an atheist. The story is mentioned in the *Viṣṇu Purāṇa*, but in this version, Viṣṇu (as the Buddha) does not kill the demons directly; he simply misleads them, ensuring that they turn from the Vedic path. Without the protection that the Vedic path gives them, the demons are defeated by the gods.

Given that the verse later mentions that Śiva shines as part of Viṣṇu, it is also possible that the myth alluded to here is the destruction of the three cities, where Viṣṇu served as the arrow. This myth is first referenced in *Tiruvāymoḻi* I.1.8, and in I.3.9, the poet declares that Viṣṇu acted as Śiva to destroy the three cities. As the reference to the myth is unclear, I have noted it against both Viṣṇu as Buddha and Viṣṇu as the destroyer of the three cities in the myth index.

V.10.5: 'Eating the food/raising the mountain' refer to the note on I.8.4.

'Ate and spat out the world' refer to the note on I.1.7.

'Crossed the earth' refer to the note on I.3.10. The myth is also referenced in V.10.9.

'Dug and married the earth' refer to the note on I.7.6.

V.10.8: God rising from navel, refer to the note on I.3.9.

V.10.10: 'Churned the ocean' refer to the note on I.3.11.

V.10.11: In this phala-śruti, the poet explicitly characterizes his poem as a *nūṟṟantāti* (an antāti of hundred)—*nūrrantāti āyirattuḷ ivaiyum ōr pattum* (these ten too are from the thousand of a hundred antāti). The Nūṟṟantāti will eventually become a formal poetic category, such as the *Rāmānuja Nūṟṟantāti* or the *Tiruvāymoḻi Nūṟṟantāti*. We could take this verse as an indication that the poet too intended each Hundred to be read as thematically coherent and a cycle unto its own. This is certainly consistent with the approach of the Śrīvaiṣṇava ācāryas.

Tiruvāymoḻi Sixth Hundred (VI.1–VI.10)

VI.1.1–VI.1.11: *This Ten, including the concluding eleventh verse, is in praise of the site of Tiruvaṇvaṇḍūr. It is located in the present-day state of Kerala. The traditional list of Divya Deśas classify it as in the mountainous region or Malai Nāḍu. It is also assigned to the Cēra region (the region once controlled by the Cēra kings), which roughly overlaps with the boundaries of the present-day state of Kerala. It is part of a group of five Kerala temples believed to have been built by the Pāṇḍava brothers. The temple of Tiruvanvandur is attributed to the Pāṇḍava, Nakula. The other sites are Tiruvāṟaṉviḷai, Tiruccenkuṉṟūr, Tirukkaṭṭitāṉam and Tiruppuliyūr. They are praised in* VII.10, VIII.4, VIII.6 *and* VIII.9. *Nammāḻvār is the only āḻvār to sing in praise of this site.*

This Ten is in the heroine's voice. It is one of two messenger decads in this Tiruvāymoḻi and one of four in the entire text.

VI.1.2: 'Swallowing the world' refer to the note on I.1.7.

VI.1.6: Kuyil: Indian cuckoo.

VI.1.7: In this verse, Viṣṇu is described as being black (*karu vaṇṇam*) with red lips (*ceyya vāy*) and similarly hued eyes, hands and feet (*ceyya kaṇ, ceyyakai, ceyyakāl*). I have not translated these phrases as red eyes, red hands and red feet, and instead have drawn forth the implicit contrast of red against black. Therefore, I have translated *karu vaṇṇam* as dark body and the descriptions of the eyes, hands and feet as radiant. I have retained red lips, providing an aural echo to radiant.

VI.1.8: The verse provides a list of trees in the groves of Tiruvanvandur. I have not translated these individual trees.

In this verse, the heroine describes the deity at Tiruvanvandur to the bird, which is her messenger. She then asks it to go see the god (the one she has described), and then to return to her to describe what she saw.

VI.1.10: The Pampa is a river that originates in the Western Ghats. The temple is located on the Pampa's banks.

VI.1.11: 'Who wears a thread like lightning' refers to the brahmins' thread—the *yajñopavīta*—which is worn by upper-caste men over the left shoulder and rests across the chest.

The cunning youth refers to Vāmana. Refer to the note on I.3.10 for a discussion of the myth.

VI.2.1–VI.2.10: *This set of verses is in the female voice, but unlike preceding verses shifts between the first person singular and plural (for instance,* VI.2.6, VI.2.7*). The decad is also unusual in that it describes a separation caused by a quarrel between god and the heroine. In other words, god has arrived for their assignation, but the heroine refuses to see him because she accuses him of dallying with other women.*

In this decad, several allusions to Kṛṣṇa's antics suggest that it is set in the imaginal world of Gokula (for instance, VI.2.2, VI.2.4, VI.2.9, VI.2.10*), and the female speakers in the poem are cowherd women (āycci,* VI.2.10*).*

VI.2.1: This verse is used in the Quarrel Festival (*Praṇaya Kalaka Utsavam*) celebrated at many Śrivaiṣṇava temples. The festival enacts a playful quarrel between Viṣṇu and his consorts. The consorts, believing that Viṣṇu has spent the night with other women, bar the temple doors to him. During the extended dialogue, this verse, along with *Tiruvāymoḻi* VI.9.3, Tirumaṅkai's *Periya Tirumoḻi* X.8.1, X.8.2, and Kulaśekhara Āḻvār's *Perumāḷ Tirumoḻi* VI.5, is used by the goddesses as evidence of the god's dalliance.

VI.2.1: 'The one who scorched Laṅkā' refer to the note on II.1.3.

VI.2.2: 'Flute-player' refer to the note on IV.4.6.

VI.2.3: 'Churning the deep sea' refer to the note I.3.11.

VI.2.4: 'Eating the worlds' refer to the note I.1.7.
'Lying on a banyan leaf' refer to the note I.9.4.
'Graze your cows' refer to the note on I.8.8.

VI.2.7: 'Ate sea and earth' refer to the note on I.1.7.

VI.2.8: The verse offers a contrast between god's play and the play of the girls. God's play is the dissolution and creation of the universe. The verse's first line speaks of dissolution—all things, sentient and insentient are intertwined (*piṇakki*)—and the second line addresses creation, where all things are different, yet without difference (*pēttitum pētiyāttu*). The play of the girls, on the other hand, is simple.

VI.2.10: Your axe cut down generations of kings, refers to Viṣṇu's avatāra as Paraśurāma, the Rāma with the axe. He is born as the son of the sage, Jamadagni and his wife, Reṇukā to bring the power of the *kṣatriya* (the kingly class) under control. In this avatāra he wipes out the kṣatriyas in either eighteen or twenty-one battles. The *Tiruvāymoḻi*'s first allusion to Paraśurāma is in II.8.5, which lists Viṣṇu's avatāras—horse, tortoise, fish, man. Paraśurāma comes under the umbrella of the human avatāras. This verse is the only explicit allusion to the myth and this avatāra in the *Tiruvāymoḻi*.

VI.2.11: 'Scolded for eating butter' see the note on I.3.1.

VI.3.1–VI.3.11: *This cycle of verses is on the site of Tiruviṇṇakar, located near the city of Kumbakonam (Kudanthai) in the state of Tamil Nadu. It is in erstwhile Cōḻa country, in a region made fertile by the river, Kaveri. Three āḻvār poets—Periyāḻvār, Nammāḻvār and Tirumaṅkai Āḻvār—have sung in praise of this site.*

VI.3.4: In the verse's final line, the poet exhorts the audience to go to Tiruvinnakar to secure Kaṇṇaṉ's grace. He uses the word *kaitavam* (cunning and craftiness). As the *Īṭu* makes clear, the poet assures the listener that it is perfectly all right to seek him in this way—that is, there is no subterfuge involved—for, after all, the sweet grace (*iṉ aruḷ*) that god bestows is of his own volition.

VI.3.6: The verse does not use the name Śrī or its Tamiḻ equivalent Tiru. Instead, the goddess of wealth and auspiciousness is described as the woman/goddess who dwells in the flower (*pūvil vāḻ makaḷ*). The elder sister (*tavvai*) referred to in this verse is Jyeṣṭhā, the goddess of poverty and ill fortune.

VI.3.7: In the second line of the verse, Viṣṇu is described as hiding himself and then appearing (*karantum tōṉṟiyum*), which is understood as the avatāras through which he reveals himself.

VI.3.9: The poet refers to Viṣṇu as Oppārillappaṉ (the peerless father), which is the name of the deity (Oppillāppaṉ) at the temple of Tiruvinnakar. I have therefore included both the proper name and a translation, and Oppārillappaṉ is listed in the Index of Names.

VI.4.1: 'Dancing the kuravai' refer to the note on III.6.3.

'Raising the mountain' refer to the note on I.8.4.

'Crushed the snake' refers to Kṛṣṇa's defeat of the water-dwelling snake, Kāliya. The serpent lived in the Yamunā and poisoned its waters. When the unsuspecting cowherd boys drank from the river, they immediately fell lifeless. Kṛṣṇa then leapt into the Yamunā, wrestled with the snake, and subdued it by dancing on its many hoods. The episode in narrated in the *Bhāgavata Purāṇa*, Book 10, Chapter 16. This is the only reference to the myth in the *Tiruvāymoḻi*.

VI.4.2: In this verse, Viṣṇu is described with the epithet Kōlappirāṉ, the name of the deity at Tiruvallaval (V.9). As the poet does not use the epithet in relation to that site, I have translated it as beautiful lord, and not retained the Tamiḻ.

'Playing songs on the flute' refer to the note on IV.4.6.

'Grazing his herd' refer to the note on I.8.8.

'Embracing Piṉṉai' refer to the note on I.5.1.

VI.4.3: 'Killing the wrestlers' refers to Kṛṣṇa and his brother, Balarāma, killing two wrestlers, Cāṇūra and Muṣṭika, in Kaṁsa's court in Mathura. This incident occurs immediately prior to the slaying of Kaṁsa. In the *Bhāgavata Purāṇa*, the wrestling contest is proposed at the end of Chapter 43, with the actual match and the wrestlers' death occurring in Chapter 44. Kṛṣṇa kills Kaṁsa immediately after he vanquishes Cāṇūra, and Balarāma does the same to Muṣṭika. *Bhāgavata Purāṇa*, Book 10, Chapters 43 and 44.

'Crushing the elephant' refers to the note on I.9.2.

VI.4.4: 'Bound by his mother' refer to the note on I.3.1.

'Killed by the woman who nursed him' refer to the note on I.5.9.

'Shattering the cart' refer to the note on II.1.8.

VI.4.5: The myth referenced here is the birth of Kṛṣṇa. He is born to Devakī and Vasudeva in Mathura, as their eighth child. As a prophecy declared that Kaṁsa will be killed by Devakī's child, he kills their prior children. To save the eighth child—Kṛṣṇa—Vasudeva spirits him away, across the Yamunā to be raised by the cowherd chief, Nanda, and his wife, Yaśodā. Kṛṣṇa's birth is described in the *Bhāgavata Purāṇa*, Book 10, Chapter 3.

'Killing of Kaṁsa' refer to the note on II.4.8.

VI.4.6: 'He tore apart the bird' refer to the note on V.3.8.

'Killed the bulls' refer to the note on I.5.1.

The myth regarding the felling of the *kuruntu* trees is unclear. The most common association would be Kṛṣṇa crawling between the two maruta trees, but the verse names a different tree. The other possibility is the tale of Kapittāsura and Vatsāsura, two demons who took the form of a tree and calf respectively. In that case, the tree was a Viḷā tree. A third possibility, suggested in the *Īṭu*, is of Kṛṣṇa shattering the tree because it grew too tall, and by implication, too arrogant.

'One who measured the worlds' refer to the note on I.3.10.

VI.4.7: Viṣṇu takes birth in this world in order to protect his devotees. This offers a contrast between the kindness that he displays in descending to earth and venting his anger. As the *Īṭu* points out, he is like a mother, roused to anger when her child suffers at the hands of someone.

VI.4.8: 'Waged a great war' refer to the note on III.2.3. This myth is referenced again in VI.4.10.

'Cut Bāṇa's arms' refer to the note on II.4.2.

'Youth who took the world' refer to the note on I.3.10.

VI.4.9: 'Driving the chariot across seven seas' is a reference to the myth of Kṛṣṇa retrieving the brahmin's dead sons. Refer to the note on III.10.5.

VI.4.10: 'Entered his realm' refers to Kṛṣṇa returning to Vaikuṇṭha at the end of the avatāra. Although this episode is described in the *Bhāgavata Purāṇa* as the death of Kṛṣṇa (Book 11, Chapter 30), the verse seems to indicate that once the purpose of the avatāra was completed, Kṛṣṇa simply returned to his transcendent form.

VI.4.11: 'Swallowing the seven worlds' refer to the note on I.1.7 and I.5.8.

VI.5.1–VI.5.10: *This Ten is in the voice of the friend, who explain the heroine's plight to the older women in the village, including the heroine's mother and foster mother(s).*

This cycle of songs (1–11) is in praise of the site of Tolaivillimaṅgalam, which is today part of the Nava Tirupati temple pilgrimage circuit. It refers to paired temples, and is known in local parlance as Iraṭṭai Tirupati (Paired Sacred Site). Only Nammāḻvār has sung in praise of this site.

For a fuller discussion on the Nava Tirupati, see the general opening note on IV.10, *the cycle on Kurukur.*

VI.5.2: The Irattai Tirupati comprise two separate temples with two separate deities. One of these deities is known by the name Devapirāṉ, while the other is called Aravindalocaṉaṉ. Both of these names occur in the decad, and they are both left as is in the verses, but are either preceded or followed by a translation of the epithet. Both names are included in the Index of Names.

VI.5.3: 'He measured worlds' refer to the note on I.3.10.

'He grazed cows' refer to the note on I.8.8.

VI.5.5: In this verse, Viṣṇu is described as *iḻai koḷ cōti* (jewelled light). This both describes his resplendence, but also implicitly suggests that he is an ornament to himself.

VI.5.8: The name of the other deity at Irattai Tirupati is Aravindalocaṉa(ṉ) and occurs in this verse.

VI.5.9: 'Open the horse's jaws' refer to the note on I.8.2.

VI.6.1–VI.6.10: *This cycle of verses is spoken in the mother's voice.*

VI.6.1: 'The one who measured worlds' refer to the note on I.3.10. The myth is referenced once again in VI.6.4 and in VI.6.9 (Vāmana).

VI.6.3: 'The one who swallowed the world' refer to the note on I.1.7.

VI.6.4: 'Making Brahmā' refer to the note on I.3.9.

'Messenger between kings,' refers to Kṛṣṇa's role as the Pāṇḍavās' emissary to the Kaurava court just prior to the start of the great Bharata war. In this verse, the Pāṇḍavas are referred to as *Nāḍuṭai maṉṉar* (literally, landed kings/i.e. with a kingdom) although when Kṛṣṇa approached the Kauravas as their messenger, they were in exile with neither land nor kingdom to their name. As Kṛṣṇa was on their side (that is, god was on their side), they are referred to as the ones with property.

VI.6.5: Varāha (boar) is the name by which Viṣṇu in known in his third avatāra. See the note on I.7.6.

VI.6.6: Kalpaka tree is the wish-fulfilling tree. It is also sometimes described as a creeper.

VI.6.8: 'Shattering the kuruntu trees' refer to the note on VI.4.6.

'Kicking the cart' refer to the note on II.1.8.

'Sucking the demon's milk' refer to the note on I.5.9.

VI.6.10: 'Locked arms with the wrestlers' refer to the note on VI.4.3.

VI.6.11: The poet mentions the site name of Venkatam only in the final song. This concluding verse suggests that the entire cycle is on the deity enshrined there, but apart from the mention in the phala-śruti, Śaṭhakōpaṉ offers no other references to the sacred site within the decad.

VI.7.1–VI.7.11: *This cycle of songs is on the site of Tirukkōḷūr, which is part of the Nava Tirupati pilgrimage circuit. It is revered as the birthplace of Madurakavi, Nammāḻvār's disciple. For a fuller discussion of the Nava Tirupati pilgrimage circuit, see the opening note on* IV.10.

This Ten is spoken in the mother's voice. In two verses, the mother's longing echoes that of her daughter's desire for Viṣṇu. In VI.7.2, *she asks the birds if her daughter will ever return to her. In* VI.7.8, *the mother's heart dissolves as she contemplates the loss of her daughter, who herself dissolves in* VI.7.6.

The eleventh verse mentions the site, but does not include a reference to the female voice.

VI.7.11: The only mention of the deity enshrined at Tirukkolur is in this final verse. He is called Vaittamānidhi (the precious treasure that one holds/keeps). The epithet is listed in the Index of Names.

VI.8.1–VI.8.10: *This Tiruvāymoḻi is in the heroine's voice. They are messenger verses, the third of four such cycles in the Tiruvāymoḻi, and the second in this Hundred. The other three decads are* I.4, VI.1 *and* IX.7.

VI.8.3: 'The lord who steered a chariot/Five brothers' see the note on III.2.3.

VI.8.5: 'Tree of wishes' see note on VI.6.6.

VI.8.6: The bright thread is the yajñopavīta, worn by upper-caste men. See the note on VI.1.11.

VI.8.7: 'Ripping the horse's mouth' see the note on I.8.2.

VI.9.1: The two brilliant orbs refers to the sun and moon.

VI.9.2: 'Viṣṇu as a youth' refers to the note on I.3.10. The myth is referred to again in VI.9.6 and VI.9.9.

VI.9.4: 'Shattering the cart' refers to the note on II.1.8.

VI.9.5: In this verse, the poet describes Viṣṇu in his five forms. Transcendent (paratva), in heaven, in iconic form (arcā) atop the mountain, in his first manifestation (vyūha) on the ocean of milk, and in incarnate form (vibhava) when he wanders the earth. As the in-dwelling one (antaryāmin), he resides inside the poet.

The commentary interprets the mountain in the verse as Tiruvenkatam.

VI.9.11: 'One who ate the world' refer to the note on I.1.7.

VI.10.1–VI.10.11: *This is the second complete cycle of Ten on the sacred site of Venkatam. The first cycle is* III.3. *For a fuller note on the site, see the opening note on* I.8.3.

This cycle is of particular significance in the Śrīvaiṣṇava tradition, for it is regarded as describing Nammāḻvār's prapatti (self-surrender) to Viṣṇu at the shrine of Venkatam. The tenth verse in this decad is singled out as expressing the very moment of prapatti. While the Tiruvāymoḻi is filled with instances in which Nammāḻvār takes refuge at the feet of Viṣṇu (see for instance, V.7 *on Vanamamalai), in this decad, the explicit presence of the goddess, who serves as the mediator, is what is seen to make the crucial difference. This is expressed clearly and forcefully in* VI.10.10.

Every verse in this decad mentions god's feet. The poet asks to be shown the path to his feet and to be brought to his feet, to reach god's feet, and to see them. He moves between being an active agent in seeking god's feet (i.e. his grace), and being the recipient of that grace—that is, he cannot reach god's feet on his own, but needs Māl to show him the path, call him, and then shelter him under his feet.

VI.10.1: 'Eating the world' refer to the note on I.1.7.

VI.10.5: 'Masterful archer/piercing the seven trees' refer to the note on I.5.6.

'Crawling between the maruta trees' refer to the note on II.1.10.

Sārṅga-bow, the name of Viṣṇu's celestial bow.

VI.10.6: 'Feet measuring the world' refer to the note on I.3.10.

VI.10.8: The one with the blue throat is Śiva.

In the *Īṭu*, the final line of the verse (*mālāy mayakki aṭiyēṉpāl vantāy pōlē vārāy*/bewitching Māl, come as you came before) is taken to refer to the Kṛṣṇa avatāra. As Māl means black/dark, it is taken as a description of Kṛṣṇa (the black one). Thus, the poet asks for Viṣṇu to come before him as he was in that form.

VI.10.10: This is the climactic verse, in which the Āḻvār formally does prapatti. For a discussion of this verse and the decad as a whole in the major commentaries, see Srilata Raman's *Self-surrender (Prapatti) to God in Śrīvaiṣṇavism*.

Tiruvāymoḻi Seventh Hundred (VII.1–VII.10)

VII.1.1–VII.1.10: *This cycle of Ten is on the five senses.*

VII.1.1: 'Those five that thrive within me' refers to the five senses.

VII.1.3: 'Eating and spitting out the worlds' refer to the note on I.5.8.
'Spanning the world' refer to the note on I.3.10.
'Lifting the earth' refer to the note on I.7.6.

VII.1.4: 'Child on a banyan leaf' refer to the note on I.9.4.

VII.1.7: 'Looped a serpent around a mountain' refers to the churning of the ocean of milk. See the note on I.3.11. The myth is again referenced in VII.1.10.

VII.1.10: The burden hefted on the poet is the body.

VII.1.11: The three referred to here are Brahmā as the creator, Śiva as the destroyer and Viṣṇu himself as the protector of the worlds. The poet uses the word guṇa (virtue or quality) to describe the attributes inherent in the three deities (*kuṇaṅkaḷ koṇṭa mūrtti ōr mūvarāy*). He stands within each of the three gods as an antaryāmin (in-dwelling), and stands as himself within Viṣṇu.

There are three guṇas—rajas (passion), tamas (darkness) and sattva (lucidity). As the creator (Brahmā), he has rajas, as the destroyer (Śiva), he has tamas, and as the protector (Viṣṇu), he has sattva.

'Lotus rising from his navel' refer to the note on I.3.9.

VII.2.1–VII.2.10: *The only decad in the entire* Tiruvāymoḻi *dedicated to the pre-eminent Śrīvaiṣṇava site of Tiruvaraṅkam/ Sṛirangam. The poet does not mention the name of the site in the concluding eleventh verse. Srirangam is the only Divya Deśa to be praised by all twelve āḻvār poets, for a total of 247 verses. It is an ancient site, mentioned in the Cilappatikāram as one of three major Vaiṣṇava sites in the Tamiḻ region. It is one of eight self-manifested shrines (svayaṁ vyakta) and among the five Pañcaraṅga temples (five shrines with reclining images located along the Kaveri).*

The temple houses a large reclining image of Viṣṇu as Raṅganātha (the lord of the stage). The image faces south. According to the temple's legendary history, Vibhīṣaṇa, Rāvāṇa's brother and Rāma's friend, received the image as a gift. He intended to take it with him to Laṅkā, but the image wanted to remain in Cōḻa country. Raṅganātha declared that although he could not be moved, he would face south, forever casting his benevolent gaze upon Laṅkā.

Srirangam has long been the pre-eminent Śrīvaiṣṇava temple, and all of the Śrīvaiṣṇava tradition's most important teachers—Nāthamuni, Rāmānuja, Parāśara Bhaṭṭar, Nañjīyar, Nampiḷḷai, to name just a few—have been connected to it.

Each verse in this Ten (except the phala-śruti) is in two parts. The first is the voice of the heroine (as reported by the mother), and the second is the mother's direct address to the lord of Srirangam. Although both female voices occur in this Ten, it is catalogued as spoken in the mother's voice, for this is how the commentators interpret it. Tiruvāymoḻi *V.6 follows a similar pattern. In that decad, the first part of the verse records the daughter's outsized claims—I made land and sea, I am the wind that blows. In the verse's latter half, the mother addresses an audience (and perhaps indirectly, Perumāḷ), wondering what to make of her daughter.*

VII.2.2: 'Eating and spitting out the world' refer to the note on I.5.8.

'Measuring the world' refer to the note on I.5.8.

VII.2.5: 'Ripping apart the demon at dusk' refer to the note on II.6.6.

'Churning the ocean' refer to the note on I.3.11.

VII.2.7: The poet makes reference to the river that encircles the sacred site. Srirangam is an island, encircled by the Kaveri and the Kollidam rivers. As Vaikuṇṭha too is bounded by a river, the Virajā, Srirangam is known as the Bhūloka Vaikuṇṭha (earthly Vaikuṇṭha).

VII.2.8: 'Lifting the mountain' refer to the note on I.8.4.

VII.2.9: 'Raising the earth' refer to the note on I.7.6.

'Killing the seven bulls' refer to the note on I.5.1.

The cowherd girl is Nappiṉṉai.

VII.2.10: The god with *koṉṟai* in his hair is Śiva.

VII.3.1–VII.3.11: *This Tiruvāymoḻi is on the site of Tiruppērai, which is part of the Nava Tirupati pilgrimage circuit. For a more detailed description of the Nava Tirupati, refer to the opening note on* IV.10.

These ten verses are in the heroine's voice.

VII.3.5: 'Suckled the breast of the ghoul' refer to the note on I.5.9.

'Smashed the cart' refer to the note on II.1.8

'Slipped between maruta trees' refer to the note on II.1.10.

'Throwing the calf against the tree' refers to Kṛṣṇa's killing the demon Vatsāsura, who had been sent by Kaṁsa. The demon took the form of a calf, and insinuated himself into the herd. Kṛṣṇa, recognizing its true nature, grabbed it by the hind legs, twirled it around, flung it against the tree, killing it. The story is recounted in the *Bhāgavata Purāṇa*, Book 10, Chapter 11.

VII.3.7: 'Destroyer of southern Laṅkā' refer to the note on II.1.3.

VII.3.9: 'Swallower of earth and sea' refer to the note on I.1.7.

VII.3.10: The name of the deity at Tirupperai is Makara Neṭuṅkuḻaik kātaṉ, the one who wears dazzling earrings in the shape of a *makara*, or fish. According to the temple's legend, the goddess discovered a pair of makara-shaped earrings while bathing in the Tamiraparani. She offered the jewels to the Viṣṇu there, who accepted them, thus earning the name Makara Neṭuṅkuḻaik kātaṉ.

VII.3.10: 'Suppressing the hundred brothers' refer to the note on III.2.3.

VII.4.1–VII.4.11: *This Ten describes Viṣṇu's various acts to protect the world. It asserts his sovereignty over the worlds, as well as his compassion and care for those very worlds.*

Below, I indicate which myth or act is referenced.

VII.4.1: 'Viṣṇu as Trivikrama' refer to the note on I.3.10.

VII.4.2: 'Churning of the cosmic sea' refer to the note on I.3.11.

VII.4.3: 'Viṣṇu as Varāha, rescuing the earth' refer to the note on I.7.6.

VII.4.4: 'Eating and keeping the worlds' refer to the note on I.1.7.

This verse describes the end of the world, when Viṣṇu eats the world. Externally, everything disappears, relinquishing their positions. Yet, they are all safe and protected in the god's belly, and will re-emerge intact at the time of creation.

VII.4.5: Two myths are invoked in this verse, both relating to Viṣṇu's avatāra as Kṛṣṇa.

Kṛṣṇa's encounter with the wrestlers: refer to the note on VI.4.3.

Kṛṣṇa directing the Bharata war refer to the note on III.2.3.

VII.4.6: 'Killing Hiraṇya' refer to the note on II.6.6.

This marvellous verse turns on a simile—the mountain is the body of the demon Hiraṇyaṉ, the lion is Viṣṇu in his avatāra as Narasiṁha, and the sky turns red from the blood that gushes out, when Narasiṁha disembowels the demon. Narasiṁha kills the demon at dusk, so the red of the setting sun echoes this moment.

VII.4.7: 'Laṅkā in ashes' refers to Viṣṇu as Rāma. Refer to the note on II.1.3.

VII.4.8: 'Defeat of Bāṇa' refer to the note on II.4.2.

The god with the rooster-banner is Murukaṉ, the younger son of Śiva.

VII.4.9: This verse describes Viṣṇu as creator.

VII.4.10, VII.4.11: Viṣṇu as Kṛṣṇa, lifting Govardhana refer to the note on I.8.4.

VII.5.1–V.5.11: *This Ten continues in the same vein as the previous one, with two differences. In* VII.4, *each verse focuses on a single act (except* VII.4.5, *in which two myths are evoked). In this decad, the invocation of myths and acts is not systematic. Second, here the description of the praise is directed at an audience, often framed as a rhetorical question: If you hear these wondrous acts, how can you worship anyone but Viṣṇu?*

VII.5.1: Ayodhyā is the capital of the legendary Ikśvāku dynasty, into which Rāma was born. It is also a Divya Deśa, categorized as belonging to Vaḍa Nāḍu (the northern region). It has been praised by five āḻvār poets (Nammāḻvār, Kulaśekharaṉ, Periyāḻvār, Toṇṭaraṭippoṭi and Tirumaṅkai), in a total of thirteen verses.

VII.5.2: This verse references the Rāma avatāra. Viṣṇu took birth as a human prince, and suffered untold difficulties, including forest exile and the abduction of his wife, Sītā.

VII.5.3: 'Śiśupāla's long hostility' refers to an incident in Kṛṣṇa's life. Śiśupāla was Kṛṣṇa's cousin. Śiśupāla was born with extraneous limbs and a third eye. It was prophesied that these would disappear when the child was placed in the lap of the person who would kill him. This person was Kṛṣṇa. However, Kṛṣṇa promised Śiśupāla's mother that he would forgive the boy one hundred offences. Śiśupāla both committed and exceeded his hundredth offence at the Pāṇḍava, Yudhiṣṭhira's coronation. The moment he crossed one hundred errors, Kṛṣṇa killed him. This is the only mention of the myth in the *Tiruvāymoḻi*. The story is recounted in the *Bhāgavata Purāṇa*, Book 10, Chapter 74.

VII.5.4: 'Made Nāṉmukaṉ (Brahmā)' refer to the note on I.3.9.

VII.5.5: 'He became a glorious boar' refer to the note on I.7.6.

VII.5.6: 'You came as Vāmaṉaṉ' refer to the note on I.3.10.

VII.5.7: The god with flowers in his hair is Śiva.

'Saving Mārkaṇḍeya' refers to the note on IV.10.8.

VII.5.8: 'He came as an enormous lion' refer to the note on II.6.6.

VII.5.9: 'Destruction of the Hundred' refer to the note on II.8.6 and III.2.3.

VII.5.10: The wise words referred to in this verse is taken to mean the *Bhagavad Gītā*, specifically verse 18.66. This verse is the third of the three secret Śrīvaiṣṇava mantras, known as the rahasya traya. In this verse, also called the carama śloka, Kṛṣṇa advises total surrender to him. The verse is as follows:

sarva dharmān partiyajya mām ekam śaraṇam vṛaja
ahaṃ tvām sarva pāpebhyo mokṣayiṣyāmi mā śucaḥ

Abandoning all other paths, take refuge with me
I will make you free from all sins. Do not despair.

VII.6.1: In this verse, Padmanābha (the one with a lotus navel) is both a name and a descriptor. I've used it in both ways in the translation. The myth is referenced again in VII.6.5.

'Brahmā rising from a lotus' refer to the note on I.3.9.

'Measuring the three worlds' refer to the note on I.3.10.

VII.6.2, VII.6.3: 'Lifting a mountain' refer to the note on I.8.4.

VII.6.3: The one with koṉṟai in his hair is Śiva. While the Tamiḻ verse gives us two descriptive phrases—he is the one wearing a crown of tuḷasi (Viṣṇu), and also the one adorned in his matted hair with koṉṟai (Śiva). For the purposes of the translation, I have combined the two identifiers. The thrust of the verse is that the one who lifted the mountain (Kṛṣṇa) is Viṣṇu, Śiva and Brahmā.

VII.6.4: The three-eyed god is Śiva.

VII.6.5: The realm of radiance is Vaikuṇṭha.

The tension in this verse emerges from the poet's inability to attain Viṣṇu in Vaikuṇṭha, as he is subject to the body and the senses.

'Worlds blossom from your navel' see the note on I.3.9.

VII.6.7: Viṣṇu is Śiva (the one with Pārvatī at his side); Brahmā (with Sarasvatī in him), and is also Indra (the beloved of Śacī).

Nāmakaḷ: the goddess of speech, Sarasvatī.

Śacī: the wife of Indra.

'Raised the earth' refer to the note on I.7.6.

'Burnt three forts' refer to the note on I.1.8.

VII.6.8: 'The killing of Māli' refers to the defeat of one of Rāvaṇa's ancestors. Māli and his two brothers, Mālyavān and Sumāli acquired great power, and settled in Laṅkā. They attacked the realm of the gods, and were met there by Viṣṇu. Māli was killed in the battle, and the other two brothers fled to hide in the underworld. Sumāli's daughter gave birth to Rāvaṇa.

The Laṅkā referenced in this verse is to the kingdom when ruled by Mālyavan, Māli and Sumāli, and not to the city under the reign of Rāvaṇa.

VII.6.9: 'The gifting of Laṅkā' to the brother refers to Rāma crowning Rāvaṇa's younger brother, Vibhīṣaṇa after Rāvaṇa's death.

VII.6.10: 'Living among cowherds' refer to the note on I.8.8.

'Killer of Kaṁsa' refer to the note on II.4.8.

'Supporter of the five' refer to the note on III.2.3.

VII.6.11: 'He came as a lion' refer to the note on II.6.6.

VII.7.1–VII.7.10: *Spoken in the voice of the heroine, this Ten provides a description of the beauty of Viṣṇu's face.*

VII.7.2: 'The one who stole butter' refer to the note on I.3.1.

VII.7.4: Madaṇaṉ is Kāma, the god of love. He wields a sugar cane bow and arrows of flowers.

VII.7.5: 'One who lifted the mountain' refer to the note on I.8.4.

VII.7.8: Kṛṣṇa's face is described in terms of a series of metaphors. The lotuses are his eyes, the creeper his nose, the coral his lips, the bow his brows, the shoot his ears, pearls his smile and the moon is his face.

VII.8.3: 'Skilled charioteer' refer to the note on III.2.3.

VII.8.5: The poet complains that although Viṣṇu has cut his bonds and taken him as his servant, he continues to keep him in a body. This mystery bewilders the poet.

VII.8.6: The grief here is that of the body and the experience of the world, which is filled with these dualities—forgetfulness, memory, heat, cold, etc.

VII.8.10: The ancient books mentioned here are the Veda.

VII.9.1–VII.9.11: *This set of Ten is a sustained reflection on how god speaks through the poet. Here, the poet repeatedly insists that god has merged with him and uses the poet to sing of himself (see for instance,* VII.9.6, VII.9.8*).*

These verses are also seen as an expression of god's benevolence, his gracious condescension, bestowing on the poet the honour of singing his praise. As the Īṭu frames it in the introduction to this decad, when god had the option of choosing poets like Vālmīki, Parāśara and the first three āḻvār, who sang in perfect Tamiḻ, to fulfil his desire for song, he still chose the Āḻvār, who considers himself an unworthy, lowly poet.

VII.9.2: The three forms referred to here are Brahmā, Śiva and Viṣṇu. He stands within all of them. The *Īṭu* has a lovely reading of this verse. He stays within Brahmā and Śiva, but when they create and destroy the worlds, we attribute these acts to them—Brahmā created the world; Śiva destroyed the world. Just so, the poet says, that Māl created these poems through the Āḻvār, made it appear as though they were his work, and bestowed on him this great honour.

VII.10.1–VII.10.10: *This set of Ten is on the site of Tiruvāraṉviḷai, located on the banks of the Pampa river in the modern state of Kerala. The site is not mentioned in the eleventh verse of the decad. The traditional list of Divya Deśas classifies it as in the mountainous region or Malai Nāḍu. It is also assigned to the Cēra region (the region once controlled by the Cēra kings). It is one of the five Pāṇḍava temples in that state, and is attributed to Arjuna. Legend has it that Arjuna built this temple to assuage his guilt over killing the unarmed Karṇa during the great Bharata war. The other Pāṇḍava sites are praised in* VI.1, VIII.4, VIII.6 *and* VIII.9.

VII.10.2: The name of the deity at Tiruvaranvilai is Tirukkuṟaḷappaṉ (the father who is the dwarf), referencing Viṣṇu's avatāra as

Vāmana. It is thus left untranslated in the verse, and is also included in the Index of Names.

'My father stretched out' refer to the note on I.3.10.

VII.10.3: Here the fierce lion (*kōḷari*) is not an epithet, but is a reference to Viṣṇu's avatāra as Narasiṁha.

The four Veda refer to the Ṛg, Sāma, Yajur and Atharva texts. The five sacrifices are the *pañca mahā yajña*, and the six parts are the six Vedāṅgas, connected to the study of the Veda. These include prosody, grammar and ritual instruction.

VII.10.4: Born in Mathura refers to Kṛṣṇa's birth. Refer to the note on VI.4.5 for further detail on the myth.

Mathura is the place of Kṛṣṇa's birth and is counted as a Divya Deśa. Five āḻvār poets—Nammāḻvār, Periyāḻvār, Āṇṭāḷ, Toṇṭaraṭippoṭi and Tirumaṅkai—have praised the site. Their verses total fifty verses.

VII.10.6: Against her wishes, Rukmiṇī was betrothed to Kṛṣṇa's cousin Śiśupāla. She sent a secret message to Kṛṣṇa through a trusted brahmin, and asked him to intervene and marry her. Kṛṣṇa acceded to her request, abducting her on the eve of her marriage. In the process, he defeated Śiśupāla. Kṛṣṇa and Rukmiṇi's epistolary courtship and marriage are described in the *Bhāgavata Purāṇa*, Book 10, Chapters 52–54.

VII.10.7: 'Shattered Bāṇa's arms' refer to the note on II.4.2.

The three-eyed god is Śiva.

VII.10.8: 'Aid to the elephant' refer to the note on II.8.2.

VII.10.10: The verse refers to *nilattēvar* (literally, gods on earth, i.e. brahmins) who worship the deity in thought, with words and in deeds (*cintaiyiṉāl*, *colliṉāl*, *ceykaiyiṉāl*). In the commentary, nilattēvar is glossed as devotees or Bhāgavata—that is those who are equal to the *nityasūri*, and who are desirous of mokṣa. In the translation, I have collapsed all the ways they worship Viṣṇu into the phrase 'in every way.'

VII.10.11: Viṣṇu is characterized in this verse as Tīrttaṉ, which I have translated as 'pure lord of sacred places', as a *tīrtha* designates a sacred place of crossing.

In the *Īṭu*, Tīrttaṉ is interpreted as one who is pure, perfect and immaculate. He cleanses all things that come in contact with him. As an illustration, the commentator provides the example of the water that Brahmā pours over Viṣṇu's feet when he measured the world. This water thus purified, descended as the Gaṅgā, and came to adorn Śiva's matted locks. In this way, Śiva too is purified. This retelling subordinates Śiva to Viṣṇu.

Tiruvāymoḻi Eighth Hundred (VIII.1–VIII.10)

VIII.1.1: 'Churning the ocean' refer to the note on I.3.11. This myth is referenced again in VIII.1.5.

VIII.1.2: 'Raising the earth' refer to the note on I.7.6.

Tree of wishes is the kalpaka tree.

VIII.1.3: Nandagopaṉ, the cowherd chief, is Kṛṣṇa's foster father. Yaśodā is Kṛṣṇa's foster mother.

'Mauling the demon' refer to the note on II.6.6.

VIII.1.4: 'Unleashing the war' refer to the note on III.2.3.

VIII.1.5: This verse alludes to several myths that often come clustered together.

'Digging the world' refer to the note on I.7.6.

'Eating and spitting out the world' refer to the note on I.5.8.

'Spanning the world' refer to the note on I.3.10.

It also includes a reference to binding and breaking the ocean. This is an allusion to Rāma building the bridge to Laṅkā.

VIII.1.7: 'Embracing Piṉṉai' refer to the note on I.5.1.

VIII.1.8: Nappiṉṉai is not mentioned directly in this verse. The verse simply begins with the phrase *maṇanta pēr āya* (the great cowherd who wed). It is clear, both from the way the previous verse ends (*piṉṉai tōḷ maṇanta pēr āya*, the great cowherd who embraced Piṉṉai) that she is the figure referenced in this verse as well.

VIII.1.10: The description of Viṣṇu as having a thousand arms, feet and eyes can be read as echoing the description of Puruṣa in the *Puruṣa Sūkta*.

VIII.1.11: Rudraṉ is Śiva

VIII.2.1–VIII.2.10: *This Ten is spoken in the heroine's voice as she addresses her friends.*

The cycle mentions three different terrestrial sites, and the two non-terrestrial ones. The poet mentions Venkatam in the northern country twice, and once each, Kudanthai (Kumbakonam) in the middle/Cōḻa country and Kuḷantai, in the southern region, which is Pāṇṭiya territory. The two non-terrestrial sites are the cosmic ocean and Vaikuṇṭha.

VIII.2.1: The enemies (*ētalar*) referred to here are the mothers.

The verse turns on a contrast between the heroine and the heroine's bedecked friends. The heroine's bangles slip off her wrists because of lovesickness—she has grown thin. The bangles on her friends' wrists remain, to signify that they are with their lovers, or that they are not similarly afflicted.

VIII.2.4: Kuḷantai, the site referenced here, is part of the Nava Tirupati pilgrimage circuit. It is known popularly as Perungulam, as it is located on the banks of a large lake. The deity enshrined at the site is known as Māyakkūttaṉ. For a fuller description of the Nava Tirupati sites, refer to the opening note on IV.10.

VIII.2.8: This verse mentions three sites and by extension, the three forms of Viṣṇu. In Vaikuṇṭha he is in his transcendent form (paratva); in the ocean of milk, he is in his first emanation (vyūha); in Venkatam, he assumes an iconic form (arcā). As in several other instances that evoke Venkatam, this sacred place is situated on par with Vaikuṇṭha and the cosmic ocean.

VIII.2.9: Here both parts of the Vāmana-Trivikrama myth are mentioned. Refer to the note on I.3.10.

VIII.3.1: Dānavas the sons of Danu, are frequent antagonists of the devas (the gods).

VIII.3.3: The conceit here is that god carries his own weapons, despite his lofty status.

VIII.3.4: 'He took the world for food' refer to the note on I.1.7.

'Asleep on the banyan leaf' refer to the note on I.9.4.

VIII.3.5: Both the sites mentioned here—Kolur and Pulinkuṭi—are part of the Nava Tirupati pilgrimage circuit. Each of these sites has a cycle of songs dedicated to them in the *Tiruvāymoḻi*. The cycle on Kolur is VI.7, while the one on Pulinkuti appears in the next Hundred (IX.2). For a fuller discussion of the Nava Tirupati sites, see the opening note on IV.10.

'Measuring the world' refer to the note on I.3.10. The myth is mentioned again in VIII.3.8 as the one who leaps seven hills.

VIII.3.7: Vaṇparicāram, also known as Tiruppatticāram, is deep in southern Tamil Nadu. In the Divya Deśa list it is categorized as one of the thirteen sites in Malai Nāḍu/Cēra country. It is regarded as the birth site of Nammāḻvār's mother, Uṭaya Nāyakī. The deity at this site is called Tiruvāḻmārpaṉ (the one upon whose chest Śrī lives). Only Nammāḻvār has sung in praise of this sacred site.

VIII.3.9: The red-haired god refers to Śiva.

VIII.3.10: 'Churning the sea' refer to the note on I.3.11.

VIII.4.1–VIII.4.10: *This Ten is on the site of Tiruccenkunrur, located in the present-day state of Kerala. It is classified as a site in Malai*

Nāḍu/Cēra country. It is one of the five Pāṇḍava temples. Legend attributes it to Yudhisṭhira. He built the temple to assuage his guilt over the death of his teacher Droṇa during the great Bharata war. The other temples in this network are praised in VI.1, VI.10, VIII.6 *and* VIII.9. *Only Nammāḻvār has sung in praise of this site, but he does not mention the site in the decad's concluding phala-śruti verse.*

For further details on these temples, see the opening note on VI.1 *(Tiruvanvandur). It is the first in this network mentioned.*

VIII.4.1: This verse describes the sequence of events that lead to Kṛṣṇa killing Kaṁsa. He kills the elephant guarding the arena, then he and Balarāma kill the wrestlers, Cāṇūra and Muṣṭika, and finally Kṛṣṇa kills Kaṁsa.

'Snapping the tusks of the elephant' refer to the note on I.9.2.

'Killing the wrestlers' refer to the note on VI.4.3.

'Killing Kaṁsa' refer to the note on II.4.8.

The Ciṟṟaṟu (Little River/Stream) is the river that flows by the site.

VIII.4.2: Imaiyavarappaṉ (father of celestials) is the name of the deity at Tiruccenkunrur. I have included that name, followed by a translation of it. It is also included in the Index of Names.

VIII.4.3: The deity enshrined at Tiruccenkunrur is in the standing posture and faces west.

In the first line of the verse, Viṣṇu is described as *amar perumāṉ*, which is glossed in the *Īṭu* as the great god (perumāṉ) of the celestials is his (the Āḻvār's) god. That is, he is the supreme being both to gods and devotees alike.

'Dug up the vast world' refer to the note on I.7.6.

VIII.4.4: Both parts of the Vāmana-Trivikrama myth are referenced here. For further detail, refer to the note on I.3.10.

'Churned the ocean' refer to the note on I.3.11.

VIII.4.5: The three thousand people referred to here are taken in the *Īṭu* to mean brahmins.

VIII.4.7: 'The lotus-navel' refers to Brahmā rising from it to create the world. The myth is explicitly referenced in this decad in VIII.4.11. For a discussion of the myth, refer to the note on I.3.9.

The lotus on Viṣṇu's chest is Śrī.

VIII.4.8: The verse uses the word *nilatēvar* (gods on earth/rulers of the land), which I have translated as kings. In the *Īṭu*, this word is glossed as Vaiṣṇavas.

VIII.4.10: The verse uses the word *avaṉitēvar* (gods on earth/ rulers of the land), which is once again interpreted in the *Īṭu* as Vaiṣṇava.

The three-eyed [god] is Śiva and the four-faced [god] is Brahmā.

VIII.4.11: 'Eating the world' refer to the note on I.1.7.

VIII.5.1: Here, Viṣṇu is addressed as *viṉaiyēṉ kaṇṇā* (literally, the beloved/Kaṇṇā of I who have deeds/karma). In the *Īṭu*, kaṇṇā is taken as an endearment—my love—and also as the proper name for Kṛṣṇa. The poet says that he is bound by *viṉai* (the fruits of karma), because Kṛṣṇa took that particular avatāra just for him. Thus, I have translated this phrase as 'Kaṇṇā, my fated love'.

VIII.5.5: 'Lord who ate the world' refer to the note on I.1.7.

VIII.5.6: 'Pot-dancer' refer to the note on II.5.11.

VIII.5.7: 'Feet that measured the world' refer to the note on I.3.10.

VIII.5.8: 'Drove a chariot' refer to the note on III.2.3.

VIII.5.9: 'Born in Mathura' refer to the note on VI.4.5.

VIII.5.10: The mystery (*māyā*) of birth refers to the avatāras, through which Viṣṇu demonstrates his accessibility and ease (eḷimai). He is also referred to as māyā (mysterious one/wondrous one) for the ways in which he conducted the great Bharata war. On the war, refer to the note on III.2.3.

VIII.6.1–VIII.6.11: *This Ten is on the site of Tirukkaṭittāṉam, located in the present-day state of Kerala. In the list of the Divya Deśas, it is categorized as located in Malai Nāḍu/Cēra Nāḍu. It is one of the five Pāṇḍava temples, and is associated with Sahādeva. The other Pāṇḍava sites are praised in the following cycles:* VI.1, VI.10, VIII.4 *and* VIII.9. *For a full note, see the note to* VI.1 *on the site of Tiruvanvandur. Nammāḻvār is the only āḻvār to praise this site.*

VIII.6.2: The demon referred to in this verse is Rāvaṇa. See the note on I.6.7.

VIII.6.5: 'Pot-dancer' refer to the note on II.5.11.

VIII.6.7: 'One who measured earth and sky' refer to the note on I.3.10.

VIII.6.9: 'King of cowherds' refer to the note on I.5.1.

VIII.6.10: The name of the deity at Tirukkatittanam is Aṟputa Nārāyaṇaṉ (wondrous Nārāyaṇa). Unlike in other site-cycles in the *Tiruvāymoḻi*, the name does not appear as such. Instead, we have an epithet (*aṟputan*: wondrous one) and a name, Nārāyaṇaṉ. For this reason, I have not listed the name in the index, or followed the practice of leaving the name in place in the translation.

The kalpaka tree is the tree of wishes.

VIII.7.1–VII.7.10: *Several of the verses in this Ten describe Viṣṇu entering the poet.*

VIII.7.1: The rowdy five are the senses.

'Saving the elephant' refer to the note on II.8.2.

VIII.7.4: 'Simple cowherd' refer to the note on I.5.1 and I.8.8.

VIII.8.1–VIII.8.4: *The opening four verses in this Ten continue the theme from the previous set, and describe how Viṣṇu exists within the poet. In the remaining six verses (*VIII.8.5–VIII.8.10*), the Āḻvār describes the self and the nature of freedom/release (vīṭu). The Tiruvāymoḻi's eleventh verse does not make direct reference to either of these themes.*

VIII.8.5: Here the 'it' (*niṉṟa oṉṟai*) refers to the eternal consciousness/self (ātman). In this verse and the five verses that follow, the focus is on this self. While the self is an attribute of god (Viṣṇu) and is owned by him, in these verses, the self is its own entity, with its own specific characteristics. It is not precisely independent, but has a separate identity.

VIII.8.8: The moment of leaving described here is death, and not renunciation.

VIII.9.1–VIII.9.10: *This Ten is in the voice of the heroine's friend. There are three decads in this mode—*IV.6, VI.5 *and this set—in the Tiruvāymoḻi.*

This decad is on the site of Tiruppuliyur, one of the five Pāṇḍava temples in the present-day state of Kerala. This site is associated with Bhīma. The poet specifies that the temple is located in Kuṭṭanāṭu, which is in Kerala. It is classified as a Malai Nāḍu/Cēra region Divya Deśa. This is the last cycle in praise of the Pāṇḍava temples. The other cycles are VI.1, VI.10, VIII.4 *and* VIII.6. *For further information on the network, refer to the opening note on* VI.1. *Nammāḻvār is the only āḻvār to praise this site.*

VIII.9.2: Meru refers to the sacred five-peaked mountain that is believed by Hindus to exist at the centre of the universe.

VIII.9.4: 'Eating and spitting out the worlds' refer to the note on I.5.8.

VIII.9.8: The northern language (*vaṭamoḻi*) is Sanskrit, but in this context, it refers to the recitation of the Veda.

VIII.9.10: The name of the deity at Tiruppuliyur is Māyappirāṉ. Māyappirāṉ (mysterious/wondrous lord) occurs several times in the *Tiruvāymoḻi*, but here it signifies the name of the deity enshrined at the site, and therefore is included as is, and is followed by a translation. It is also included in the Index of Names.

The city is praised as the *tilatam/tilakam* of the southern lands. Men and women adorn their foreheads with a mark (tilakam) to signify well-being and auspiciousness. Women usually wear a red dot. The tilakam by extension implies that an object is cherished and of very fine quality. Here, Tiruppuliyur is described as the tilakam of the southern lands (*teṉ ticai*), to signify both its auspicious character and its pre-eminence.

VIII.10.1–VIII.10.10: *This decad is in praise of Viṣṇu's servants and service to them, a common theme in the Tiruvāymoḻi.*

VIII.10.3: Both parts of the Vāmana-Trivikrama myth are alluded to here. Refer to the note on I.3.10.

VIII.10.4: The way the Āḻvār worships and praises Viṣṇu is in accordance to the ways laid out by devotees. That is, why would the Āḻvār seek heaven if he can continue to worship and praise Viṣṇu here on earth, alongside like-minded devotees.

'The one who ate and spat out the world' refer to the note on I.5.8.

VIII.10.6: 'Killing the raging elephant' refer to the note on I.9.2.

VIII.10.7: 'Making Brahmā to make the worlds' refer to the note on I.5.3.

VIII.10.9: Father of love here refers to Viṣṇu as Kāma's father. In the verse, Kāma is described as the one (*vēḷ*, desire, love) with five kinds of lovely arrows (*kōla aiṅkaṇai*). For a discussion of the relationship between Viṣṇu and Kāma, see II.7.8.

Tiruvāymoḻi Ninth Hundred (IX.1–IX.10)

IX.1.1–IX.1.11: *In this set of verses, the poet presents god as the only refuge. It contrasts the ephemerality of the world and contingent relationships to the permanence and freedom that comes from surrendering to Viṣṇu.*

In this set, verses 3–10 mention the sacred site of Mathura, praising it as the place of Kṛṣṇa's birth. These verses do not allude to any of Kṛṣṇa's childhood heroics. For a brief discussion on the site of Mathura, see the note on VII.10.4.

IX.1.1: 'The god who ate the directions' refer to the note on I.1.7.

IX.1.2: 'Piercing of the seven trees' refer to the note on I.5.6.

IX.2.1–IX.2.10: *This Ten is on the site of Tirupuliṅkuṭi, which is part of the Nava Tirupati pilgrimage circuit. See the opening note on* IV.10 *for more information on the Nava Tirupati. The deity enshrined at this site is in the reclining posture. The poem describes the deity as reclining as a refrain in the opening three verses: tiruppuḷiṅkuṭi kiṭantāṉē (the one who lay in Tiruppuḷiṅkuṭi). Pulinkuti is first mentioned in* VIII.3.5.

In this cycle, the poet counts himself as one among god's many servants, and speaks as part of a community, rather than in the singular as an individual.

IX.2.2: 'Measured the world' refer to the note on I.3.10.

IX.2.4: This verse makes mention of three sites in the Nava Tirupati pilgrimage circuit, and mentions three different postures. Viṣṇu is reclining in Pulinkuti, seated in Varagunamangai and standing in Vaikuntham. Here, Vaikuntham is taken to refer to the site of Srivaikuntham, located on the north bank of the Tamiraparani, going downstream, and not the non-terrestrial Vaikuṇṭha.

As the verse simply indicates the name of the site as Vaikuntham, I have indexed it twice, first as the non-terrestrial Vaikuṇṭha, and again as the terrestrial pilgrimage site.

IX.2.5: 'Save the elephant' refer to the note on II.8.2.

IX.2.6: 'Killing of Māli and Sumāli' refer to the note on VII.6.8.

The name of the deity at Pulinkuti is Kāycin̲a Vēn̲tan̲ (ferocious/angry king). I have retained that name in the verse, and offered an immediate translation of it as well. It is listed in the Index of Names.

IX.2.8: Tiruvaikuntham mentioned here is the terrestrial site on the banks of the Tamiraparani. As it is referred to with the prefix Tiru (Śrī), and is known by that name, I have not listed it under the heavenly Vaikuṇṭha in the Index of Places. Most people know the site's name in its Sanskrit form, Srivaikuntham. Throughout the translation, I have retained the Tamil̲ version for place names, not converting the Tamil̲ Tiru to the Sanskrit Śrī, and do so here as well.

IX.2.11: 'One who churned the ocean' refer to the note on I.3.11.

'One who measured the world' refer to the note on I.3.10.

IX.3.2: 'Digging up the earth' refer to the note on I.7.6.

'Eating and spitting out the earth' refer to the note on I.5.8.

'Measuring the earth' refer to the note on I.3.10.

IX.3.6: 'Churning the ocean' refer to the note on I.3.11.

IX.3.7: Viṣṇu manifests in a hybrid body of a man and lion, reflected in the name, Narasiṅkan̲. The body he splits is that of the demon, Hiraṇyan̲. Refer to the note on II.6.6.

IX.3.8: In the previous verse, the poet asks to see Viṣṇu in distant Vaikuṇṭha. In this verse, he says that he can be seen, right here on earth, in Venkatam. As the *Īṭu* explicates, even Venkatam is far away, but those, like the gods, who can worship there, are blessed.

IX.3.10: 'The one rising from the navel' refer to the note on I.3.9.

The one with the polished axe is Śiva.

IX.4.3: 'Lifting the mountain' refer to the note on I.8.4.

IX.4.4: The lion (*ari*) here is glossed as Narasiṁha in the commentaries, although no element of the myth is mentioned. It can also be taken as a metaphor for Viṣṇu. For this reason, it is not listed in the Index of Myths, but for a discussion of the myth, refer to the note on II.6.6. The myth is referred to explicitly in IX.4.7.

IX.4.5: Here too, the lion referred to is Narasiṁha.

IX.4.7: The Dānavas are the sons of Danu, and are often antagonists of the gods (devas). Here, the great Dāṉavaṉ is Hiraṇyaṉ. For a discussion of the myth, refer to II.6.6.

IX.4.10: 'The one who measured worlds' refer to the note on I.3.10.

IX.4.11: 'Killing the elephant' refer to the note on I.9.2.

This phala-śruti is unique for it provides a fuller explication of the structure of the poem. While most concluding verses simply indicate that the cycle is ten verses out of a thousand (*āyirattuḷ pattu*), here, the poet tells us the poem comes in sets of hundred (*nūṟē coṉṉa ōr āyirattuḷ ippattu*). Other instances, where the text's structure is elaborated occur in II.7.11, where the poet acknowledges twelve verses, instead of the usual ten, and again later in X.2.11, in which he describes the poem as consisting of five and five (i.e.) ten verses, and in IX.5.11, in which he describes the set as consisting of nine plus one verses. In V.10.11, Nammāḻvār specifically uses the phrase nūṟṟantāti (an antāti of hundred) to describe the structure of his poem. In X.10.11, the phala-śruti reflects on itself as the poem's conclusion.

IX.5.1–IX.5.10: *This decad is in the heroine's voice. In it, she addresses the natural world, which to her mind is conspiring against her. Everything reminds her of the beloved—the clouds are dark as he is, the inseparable lovebirds stand as a contrast to her loneliness.*

Only the first verse in this Ten returns to the motif of birds as love messengers.

IX.5.3: The heroine has done no austerities (*tavam/tapas*) and is bound by her past deeds (viṉaiyāṭṭiyēṉ).

IX.5.5: 'He took the seven worlds' refer to the note on I.3.10.

IX.5.10: The heroine makes the claim that she is with Viṣṇu in heaven (*nāmum nam vāṉa nāṭaṉōṭu oṉṟiṉōm*), while her jewels slip off her body, and the body itself slips away (*iḻai nalla ākkaiyum paiyavē puyakku aṟṟatu*). The *Īṭu* glosses the phrase as follows—that the body beautified with jewels fades, showing the typical signs of lovesickness. The *Īṭu* also summarizes and records interpretations of the final line of the verse offered by three luminaries of the Śrīvaiṣṇava tradition—Yāmunācārya, Rāmānuja and Parāśara Bhaṭṭar. Yāmuna says that those who ascend to heaven wish those left behind, well. Rāmānuja suggests that the heroine (the Āḻvār) wishes to spare the world the suffering she experienced. Bhaṭṭar said that the world sympathized with the heroine's (the Āḻvār's) suffering, but he responded that he was at the end of his journey, and wished them well.

IX.6.1–IX.6.10: *This Ten is on the site of Tirukkātkarai, which the poet designates as teṉ kātkarai (southern Kātkarai). It is located in the present-day state of Kerala, and in the list of Divya Dēśas is categorized as belonging to Malai Nāḍu/Cēra region. The site is associated with the Vāmana avatāra, and is the legendary home of Mahābali, the king Viṣṇu vanquished in that form. The Tiruvāymoḻi verses on this site do not reveal any connection to the above myth. Instead, they focus on Kṛṣṇa, and the sole mythic reference in the Ten is to the killing of Kaṁsa in* IX.6.11. *Nammāḻvār is the only āḻvār poet to have sung in praise of this site. The site is not mentioned in the decad's concluding eleventh verse.*

IX.6.2: The name of the deity at the site is Tirukātkarai Appaṉ, and hence is included as is in the Tamiḻ verse, followed by a translation of the epithet. The epithet is repeated across several verses in this decad, but I only offer the dual version in the first instance. In the remaining verses, the epithet is signalled by the use of the word father. All instances of the epithet Kāṭkarai Appaṉ in the Tamiḻ are included in the Index of Names.

IX.6.11: 'Killing of Kaṁsa' refer to the note on II.4.8.

IX.7.1–IX.7.11: *This Ten is in the heroine's voice, and the last of the four messenger cycles in the Tiruvāymoḻi. The decad is in praise of the site of Tirumūḻikkaḷam, located in the present-day state of Kerala, and categorized in the Divya Deśa list as in the Malai Nāḍu/Cēra region. According to the site-legend, four icons—Rāma, Lakṣmaṇa, Bharata and Śatrugña—were entangled in a fisherman's net. The fisherman entrusted the icons to priests, who established four temples, one to each of the brothers. The Tirumulikkalam temple is dedicated to Lakṣmaṇa, and is called the Lakṣmaṇa Perumāḷ temple. The other three temples are Triprayar (Rāma), Kūṭalmāṇikyam (Bharata) and Payyammāḷ (Śatrugña). Tirumulikkalam is the only Divya Deśa in this set of four temples. It has been praised by Nammāḻvār (11) and Tirumaṅkai (3).*

Despite the temple's connection to the Rāmāyaṇa in legend, there are no references to that text or to Rāma in this Ten.

IX.7.1: 'Pot-dancer' refer to the note on II.5.11.

IX.7.11: One of the few instances that a decad's final verse directly addresses the contents of the preceding verses; here, the poet acknowledges his use of the female voice.

IX.8.1–IX.8.11: *The Tirunāvāy temple is located in the present-day state of Kerala, and in the Divya Deśa list is categorized as a Malai Nāḍu/Cēra region. It is located on the banks of the Bharata river.*

Nammāḻvār (11) and Tirumaṅkai (2) have sung in praise of this site.

IX.8.2: 'Husband to Piṉṉai' refers to Kṛṣṇa, refer to the note on I.7.8.

IX.8.3: The deity enshrined at Tirunāvāy is known by two names, Tirunāvāy Mukundaṉ and Tirunārāyaṇaṉ. In this verse, he is referred to by the latter name.

IX.8.4: I don't know when I'll join him (*nāḷēl aṟiyēṉ eṉakku uḷḷēṉ*) begins the verse. The phrase may be literally translated as I don't know how much longer I have. However, the *Īṭu* suggests that we take this to mean, 'I don't know how much longer I have to be apart,' or 'how much longer it will take for my desire (to join you) to be fulfilled'.

IX.8.5: Viṣṇu is described as the eye (*kaṇṇāḷaṉ*) of the worlds and the gods. This can be interpreted in two ways—that he is as precious and dear as eyes to the world and the gods; that he is the one who controls all things.

IX.8.6: 'King of cowherds' refer to the note on I.5.1.

IX.8.7: 'Taking the world from Bali' refer to the note on I.3.10.

IX.9.1–IX.9.11: *These Ten are in the heroine's voice, but they are not an anonymous heroine, such as in* VII.2 *(the song on Srirangam) or in the previous decad. Here, the voices are those of the gopīs, similar to those who speak in* VI.2. *That cycle describes a quarrel (ūṭal) between the gopīs and Kṛṣṇa. In* VI.2, *the speakers self-identify in* VI.2.10, *that is, within the decad itself. In this cycle, the speakers' identity is revealed in the meta-verse,* IX.9.11. *It is hinted at in* IX.9.8, *when the speaker accuses Kṛṣṇa of playing haunting songs for his cowherd women.*

IX.9 *is to be taken in dialogue with* X.3, *which is the last Tiruvāymoḻi in the female voice. While this Ten focuses on the evening, and the absence of the lover at the time, the later decad explores the agony of parting as day breaks. Both decads are rendered in the gopīs' voice.*

IX.9.1: *Kuṟiñci* is one of four old melodic modes in the Tamiḻ tradition.

IX.9.2: 'Digging up the earth' refer to the note on I.7.6.

'Eating and spitting out the world' refer to the note on I.1.7. The myth is referenced again in IX.9.11.

'Measured the worlds' refer to the note on I.3.10.

'Lord of cowherds' refer to the note on I.5.1.

IX.9.5: The flute-player is Kṛṣṇa. Refer to the note on IV.4.6. It is referenced again in IX.9.8 and IX.9.10.

IX.9.7: *Akil* is the aromatic resin produced from the heartwood of the Eaglewood tree.

IX.10.1–IX.10.10: *This decad is on the site of Tirukkaṇṇapuram, located in the Cōḻa region. Although the verses here describe it as a coastal city, it is about twenty kilometres west of the coast. The closest coastal city is Nagappattinam. Legend has it that Tirumaṅkai Āḻvār received his initiation of the sacred eight-syllable mantra from Viṣṇu at this site. The deity at this site is called Nīlamegha Perumāḷ (the god dark as storm clouds), but the epithet does not occur in this Ten. Five āḻvār poets have praised the site. They are Nammāḻvār, Kulaśekhara Āḻvār, Periyāḻvār, Āṇḍāḷ and Tirumaṅkai. Tirumaṅkai has contributed a prodigious 104 verses on Tirukkannapuram.*

IX.10.1: 'The one at rest on a banyan leaf' refer to the note on I.9.4.

IX.10.4: 'Beloved of Piṉṉai' refer to the note on I.7.8.

IX.10.6: 'Mauling the demon's body' refer to the note on II.6.6.

Here, the reference to the killing of Hiraṇya is meant to illustrate Viṣṇu's love for his devotees. Prahlāda belonged to the clan of demons, and his father, Hiraṇya, was antagonistic to Viṣṇu. Nonetheless Prahlāda's devotion to Viṣṇu ensured that he received his grace.

Reaching his feet signifies that a devotee has sought (and found) refuge at Viṣṇu's feet.

Tiruvāymoḻi Tenth Hundred (X.1–X.10)

X.1.1–X.1.11: *This decad is on the site of Tirumōkūr, located in the erstwhile Pāṇṭiya region, and in the present state of Tamil Nadu. It is approximately 70 kilometres to the north of the city of Madurai, which was the capital of the Pāṇṭiyas and Nāyaka kings. The site is associated with the myth of the churning of the ocean of milk, although this narrative is not alluded to in the decad. Nammāḻvār (11) and Tirumaṅkai (1) have praised this site.*

X.1.1: The final Hundred of the *Tiruvāymoḻi* begins by evoking the lotus, with its associations of auspiciousness and beauty. The *Īṭu* tells us the lotus grows from the muck, held up by its sturdy stalk. To show itself, it rises up just like Viṣṇu's feet that measured the world.

The name of the deity enshrined at Tirumōkūr is Kālamegha Perumāḷ. In the verse *kālamēkam* is used as a metonymy (that storm cloud), but I have rendered it as a simile (one dark as storm clouds) as well as a proper name. Viṣṇu is called Kālamēkam for he is generous like a cloud. That is, it is not just his appearance that is cloud-like, but also his very nature.

X.1.2: The poet concludes X.1.1 with the word *kati* (Sanskrit, *gati*), which also opens X.1.2, thus providing the antāti. Gati is understood both as path and as the sole site of refuge, both of which are Viṣṇu. While in X.1.1, I chose to translate it as way, in X.1.2, I offer a translation that accommodates both readings of the word.

X.1.5: 'Measured the worlds' refer to the note on I.3.10.

X.1.6: The name of the processional icon at Tirumokur is Tirumōkūr Āptaṉ, but he is simply referred to as Āptaṉ, friend. In this verse, Nammāḻvār refers to Viṣṇu as Āttaṉ, the Tamiḻ form of the Sanskrit, Āpta. It is listed in the Index of Names.

X.1.8: Daśaratha's son is Rāma.

Here Rāma is compared to an emerald pool (*marataka maṇittaṭam*). The *Īṭu* explicates the analogy. Viṣṇu (Rāma) is akin to trees and ponds that line a path, providing aid and comfort to all. Just so, he (Viṣṇu) takes care of all. He does not seek out enmity, but destroys those like Rāvaṇa, who seek enmity with him. In contrast, he grants Jaṭāyu, who intervened to rescue Sītā from Rāvaṇa, and was mortally wounded in the fight, the higher realm.

X.1.11: 'The pot-dancer' refer to the note on II.5.11.

X.2.1–X.2.11: *This Ten is on the site of Tiruvaṉantapuram, located in the Malai Nāḍu/Cēra region, and the present-day state of Kerala. It is the state's capital. Viṣṇu is enshrined in a reclining posture, facing east. The site of Tiruvāṭṭāṟu, where Viṣṇu reclines facing west, is believed to be a pair to this site. Both sites require the devotee to see the enshrined image in three parts—the head/arm, the torso and the feet—via three doorways. Viṣṇu rests his hand atop a Liṅga, this is seen through the first door; Brahmā sprouts from Viṣṇu's navel, and this is seen through the second doorway. Tiruvattaru is praised later in this Hundred, in Tiruvāymoḻi* X.6.

The name of the deity, Anantapadmanābhaṉ, is not referenced in this Ten.

X.2.3: 'Eating and spitting out the worlds' refer to the note on I.5.8.

X.2.4: Tiruvanantapuram is located on the south-western coast of the Indian peninsula, and the poet describes it as encircled by the ocean.

X.2.6: Kumaraṉ's father refers to Śiva. The myth referred to here is that of Bhīkṣāṭaṇa. Refer to the note on II.2.2.

X.2.8: Kāma's father is Viṣṇu. Refer to the note on II.7.8.

X.3.1–X.3.11: *This Ten is in the female voice, specifically that of the gopī. It can be read in dialogue with the female-voiced decad in the Ninth Hundred (*IX.9*). Whereas that Ten focuses on the separation that dusk brings, this decad explores the pain that comes when dawn breaks. As in* IX.9, *the gopī's voice is acknowledged in the eleventh verse. Although each verse is spoken in the first person singular, we can read each verse as the voice of a different woman. Such a reading would be supported by the phala-śruti, in which the gopīs (maṅkaiyar āycciyar) are referred to in the plural. This is the last set in the female voice, and it is fitting that it is set in Vṛindāvan, and is spoken by the gopīs. In this, it is similar to Kōtai-Āṇṭāḷ's Nācciyār Tirumoḻi, which concludes in Kṛṣṇa's land, and the promise of union achieved communally.*

X.3.6: 'Grazing cows' refer to the note on I.8.8.

X.3.7: The gopī seeks to keep Kṛṣṇa by her side by warning against the demons in disguise who would wish him harm.

X.3.9, X.3.10: These two verses reiterate the theme set out in X.3.7. The gopī(s) understand the threat posed by Kaṁsa, and worry that his henchmen, demons disguised as trees and cows, may assault Kṛṣṇa. See the note on II.4.8 on the killing of Kaṁsa.

X.3.10: Balarāma is Kṛṣṇa's older brother, and they are inseparable.

X.4.1–X.4.11: *The decad speaks of the fruits of devotion (bhakti), and the path of bhakti (bhakti mārga), which the Āḻvār posits as the path to Viṣṇu. This reiterates an idea first introduced in the* I.2 *(vīṭumiṉ muṟṟavum), which was followed by* I.3 *(pattuṭaiya aṭiyavar), in which he described god's accessibility (saulabhya).*

X.4.1: The sole path (*tava neṟi*) refers to the path of devotion (bhakti mārga).

Viṣṇu is referred to in this verse as Dāmodara, the one bound by a thread. Thus, this verse returns us to I.3.1, which describes Kṛṣṇa tied to the grinding stone as punishment for stealing butter. This incident is exemplary of god's accessibility. The poet juxtaposes god's immanent accessibility (Dāmodara) with his transcendence (the glorious one, *perumaiyaṉ*), and the two worlds he inhabits, his paradise Vaikuṇṭha, and this terrestrial realm, as both arcā and avatāra.

X.4.2: The twin fates (*irumai viṉai*) refer to deeds that are both good and bad.

X.4.3: 'Piṉṉai's beloved' refer to the note on I.5.1.

X.4.4: 'The one asleep on the banyan leaf' refer to the note on I.9.4.

The mountain referred to here is taken to be Tiruvenkatam.

X.4.6: The god with the crescent moon in his hair is Śiva.

X.4.8: The cowherd refers to Kṛṣṇa. Refer to the note on I.5.1 and I.8.8.

'Bearing the mountain' refers to Kṛṣṇa lifting Govardhana. Refer to the note on I.8.4.

X.4.11: One of the few phala-śruti verses in which Śaṭhakōpaṉ is not mentioned by name. He is instead simply called *vaḻuti vaḷanāṭaṉ* (the esteemed man from Vaḻuti).

X.5.1–X.5.11: *While* X.4 *returns us to* I.3 *in theme, this Ten returns us to* I.2 *in form; they are both couplets. It also reminds us that the first time we hear the name Nārayaṇa is in that decad* (I.2.10). *The name occurs twice in this decad, first as the eight-syllable mantra and then as the name itself.*

X.5.1: The Nāraṇam refers to the name Nārāyaṇa, and to the eight-syllabled mantra, *om namo nārāyaṇāya*, the first of the three secret mantras, called the rahasya traya.

X.5.2: 'Killer of the elephant' refer to the note on I.9.2.

X.5.3: 'Splitting the world' refers to Viṣṇu as Varāha when he raises the earth from the waters. Refer to the note on I.7.6.

'Eating and spitting out the worlds' refer to the note on I.5.8.

X.5.6: 'Nursing at the demon's breast' refer to the note on I.5.9.

X.5.7: In the Tamil̲, the name Mādhavan̲ is used only once. However, I have repeated it to replicate the mantic quality of what the poet advocates in this verse.

Here, the Āl̲vār is seen as offering an easy way for devotees to demonstrate their devotion, enjoining them to speak the name Mādhava along with the Nārāyaṇa (that is both as name as well as the Tirumantra). The *Īṭu* says that not only will no new suffering touch you, but all old deeds too will be destroyed. As the Āl̲vār recommends repeating Mādhava along with Nārāyaṇa, he is directing devotees to the Tirumantra and the Dvayam. The latter speaks to the role of the goddess as the mediator. The name Mādhava is seen to evoke the goddess (Mā).

X.6.1–X.6.11: *This Ten is in praise of the site of Tiruvāṭṭār̲u. Although it is in the present-day state of Tamil Nadu, it is designated as a site belonging to Malai Nāḍu/Cēra Nāḍu. Nammāl̲vār is the only āl̲vār to sing in praise of this site.*

The temple is located in a bend in the Paraliyaru river. It thus mimics the topography of Vaikuṇṭha, which is surrounded by the Virajā, and of Srirangam, which is bound by the Kollidam and Kaveri rivers. Tiruvattaru is called the Dakṣiṇa Vaikuṇṭham (southern Vaikuṇṭha). The site of Vattaru is mentioned in the Tamil̲ Saṅgam work, the Pur̲anān̲ūr̲u, as the capital of a chieftain named El̲in̲i Ātan̲ (Pur̲anān̲ūr̲u 396). This poem makes no mention of a temple at this site, but it does include a tantalizing reference to the kuravai dance.

X.6.2: The name of the deity enshrined at Tiruvattaru is Ādikeśava Perumāl. In this verse, he is simply referred to as Keśavaṉ.

X.6.4: Here, the poet refers to the god speaking a Tamil̲ *nūl*, or Tamil̲ book. This is taken to refer to the *Tiruvāymoli̲*.

'Mauling of Hiraṇyaṉ' refer to the note on II.6.6. This myth is referenced again in X.6.10.

'Fighting a war for the Pāṇḍava' refer to the note on III.2.3.

X.6.6: The image at the temple in Tiruvattaru is a reclining Viṣṇu, facing west. It is a pair to the Viṣṇu at Tiruvanantapuram (X.2). This image too is seen through three doorways. Unlike at Tiruvanantapuram, the Śiva Liṅga is placed at Viṣṇu's feet.

'Broke the tusk of the elephant' refer to the note on I.9.2.

X.6.7: The site is described as coastal (*tirai kul̲avu kaṭal*), but it is slightly interior, about thirty kilometres north-west of the city of Nagarkoyil.

X.7.1–X.7.11: *This Ten is the second set in praise of Tirumaliruncolai* (II.10). *For details on the site, see the opening note on* II.10.

While in II.10, *the poet urges the devotee to visit and pray at Tirumaliruncolai, here, the god of that sacred site has made a home for himself within the poet. In other words, if that earlier decad speaks of distance, this decad speaks of intimacy. This is in keeping with the traditional commentaries, which read the first half of the Tiruvāymoli̲ as the Āl̲vār seeking Viṣṇu, and the poem's latter half as god seeking out his devotee.*

The theme of the Ten is god's inseparability from the devotee. This is expressed in what appear to be two mutually exclusive actions, both of which are encapsulated in the opening verse. The first is a reversal, where god dissolves into the poet, rather than the other way round. Simultaneously, god devours the poet. It is in the interplay between dissolution and devouring that poetry as revelation is produced. The poet explicitly states that Viṣṇu speaks through him only twice (X.7.2, X.7.5), he asserts numerous times that god fills him (X.7.1, X.7.2, X.7.3, X.7.8, X.7.11), implicitly making an assertion of revelation.

X.7.6: 'Took the worlds into his belly' refer to the note on I.1.7.

X.7.8: In an unusual move, the poet maps sacred sites on to his body—two non-terrestrial sites (Vaikuṇṭha and Tiruppāṟkaṭal), and two terrestrial sites (Tirumaliruncolai and Tiruvenkatam). In doing so, he also evokes three forms of Viṣṇu—paratva (transcendent in Vaikuṇṭha), vyūha (first emanation, cosmic ocean) and the arcā (iconic form, the two terrestrial sites).

In the *Īṭu*, this mapping is read as Viṣṇu relishing the Āḻvār's head as much as he does Tirumaliruncolai and Tiruppāṟkaṭal, and his body is loved as much as Vaikuṇṭha and Tiruvenkatam. The presence of the goddess is asserted through the use of the name Tirumāl (Māl with Śrī).

It is worth reading this Ten in dialogue with I.9, in which the poet visualizes and places god within his body.

X.8.1–X.8.11: *This cycle of Ten is on the site of Tiruppēr in the present-day state of Tamil Nadu. It is located on the banks of the Kaveri, in the region once controlled by the Cōḻa kings. In the opening verse, Nammāḻvār locates the sites on the banks of the Kaveri, providing a salient topographical indicator.*

This site has been praised by Tirumaḻicai Āḻvār (1 verse), Periyāḻvār (2 verses), Nammāḻvār (11 verses) and Tirumaṅkai Āḻvār (19 verses).

In addition to being classified as a Divya Deśa, the site is also categorized as a Pañcaraṅga Kṣetra, five sites located on the banks of the Kaveri, all of which are associated with the deity, Raṅganātha. Of the five sites, three are Divya Deśas (Srirangam, Indalūr and

Tirupper). Some lists swap the site of Vaḍaraṅgam with the temple in Kudanthai (Kumbakonam), which brings the number of Divya Deśas to four. Of the sites on the traditional list, Nammāḻvār has sung in praise of Srirangam and Tiruppēr.

This is the last cycle of verses on a single site.

X.8.1: The Poṉṉi is another name for the Kaveri.

X.8.2: 'Eating the worlds' refer to the note on I.1.7.

X.8.7: The final syllable referred to here is *namaḥ* (to bow down/to pay obeisance), signalling subordination before Viṣṇu.

X.8.9: The central question that the poet poses in this verse is this—why did Viṣṇu who showers me with grace today, turn away from me before?—may be seen as a recurring theme of the text as a whole. The question can be understood in three ways—as a question posed to himself, as a question posed to god, and finally, as uncertainty that the poet experiences within himself. Theologically, the question asserts god's independence (*svātantriya*), that his grace is spontaneous and causeless.

X.9.1–X.9.11: *This Ten describes the ascent to Vaikuṇṭha (arccirāti gati). The poet does not describe this as a first-person account. Rather, it describes what Vaiṣṇavas can expect, should they dutifully practise surrender to Viṣṇu. The process that is understood to have begun in the poet's first work, Tiruviruttam, comes to its conclusion here, with the poet attaining supreme wisdom.*

The Īṭu in its introduction to this Ten tells us that as prapatti is born in the Āḻvār, and along with it, all the attendant qualities, he wishes to ascend to Vaikuṇṭha. Īśvaraṉ (Viṣṇu) wants to fulfil the desire immediately, and displays his qualities and his realm to the Āḻvār.

X.9.2: This is the last time the name Nārāyaṇa or a variation thereof, occurs in the text.

X.9.1 and X.9.2: The emphasis is not on Nārāyaṇa as a deity, but his relationship to his devotees (*nāraṇaṉ tamar*). It echoes the phrase *keśavaṉ tamar* (Keśava's people/devotees), which begins II.7.1. The phrase is echoed in X.9.5 (*mātavaṉ tamar*), X.9.6 (*āḻiyāṉ tamar*), X.9.9 (*vaikuntaṉ tamar*). The iteration of Viṣṇu's multiple names, which evoke his various qualities, echoes the systematic meditation of names in II.7, where the twelve names of Viṣṇu are used.

X.9.3: 'Feet that measured the worlds' refer to the note on I.3.10.

X.9.4: The text simply says '*katiravar avar avar*' (each sun . . .). Although it is not explicitly stated in the verse, the multiple suns could allude to the twelve suns (the twelve Ādityas), who are understood as emanations of Viṣṇu. Each Āditya rules a particular month.

The path referred to here is the arccirāti gati.

Here, Viṣṇu is referred to by the name Mādhava. The *Īṭu* reads this name as signalling the presence of the goddess, for Mādhava is understood as Śrī's beloved. It casts her in the role of the mediator (puruṣakāra). It is therefore significant that the name is used multiple times in this decad, in X.9.4, X.9.5 and X.9.8.

X.9.5: Kiṇṇara is a mythological, celestial creature, who is half man and half horse.

Garuḍa, here, is not Viṣṇu's mount; rather it refers to a class of celestial beings.

The *Īṭu* reads the final line (*vēta nal vāyvar vēḷvi uḷamaṭuttē*) as the brahmins who perform the sacrifices, surrendering any benefit or merit accrued from the sacrifice to the devotees.

X.9.7: Maruts are the gods of wind and breeze, while the Vasus are a class of deities.

The verse replicates the opening phrase kiḷar oḷi (brilliant light) of II.1.1 in its third line. Here, it is used to describe Viṣṇu's crown, while in II.1, it describes the fleeting beauty of youth. God's radiance is permanent, an inherent, inviolable attribute, while the beauty of youth is transitory. The *Tiruvāymoḻi* is filled with repurposed phrases that creates a complex, multilayered intratextuality.

Kudanthai is the last terrestrial site mentioned in the *Tiruvāymoḻi*. An entire decad, V.8, is dedicated to this site.

X.9.10: Once the devotees reach Vaikuṇṭha, god is simply referred to as avar (that him), rather than by a specific name. This returns us to the poem's opening decad in which Viṣṇu is simply referred to as avar (respective form) or avaṉ (him, intimate).

In the *Īṭu*, the avar is glossed as referring to both Viṣṇu and Śrī. This gloss is signalled by the earlier interpretation of the name Mādhava as expressing the presence of Śrī (Mā) within Mādhava.

X.10.1–X.10.11: *This final Ten culminates in the final, irreversible union between Viṣṇu and the Āḻvār. It comes on the heels of complete surrender, which the Īṭu compares to the monkeys seeking refuge at Rāma's feet, under the onslaught of Rāvaṇa's arrows. The* Īṭu *continues, that witnessing this surrender and the Āḻvār's pain, Viṣṇu felt this sorrow of parting even more keenly. He instantly appeared before the Āḻvār, riding Garuḍa and accompanied by Śrī. Viṣṇu cut the body that binds, and in the end even cut his overwhelming desire (avā) to grant him mokṣa (vīṭu).*

At the conclusion of the introduction to the final Ten, the Īṭu offers this pithy summary of the entire text—the hero/subject of this text is god; it's an antāti of endless longing (avāvil antāti) that culminates his love, and one sung by him who cuts delusion and grants one a discriminating mind (mayarvaṟa matinilam aruḷap peṟṟavar kavi pāṭiṉār). The Āḻvār's avatāra is equal to that of god's, and is the fruit of the meritorious deeds of good people.

*As this Ten progresses, we see a shift from the poet's longing for god to god's longing for the devotee, which again replicates the larger structure of the work as perceived by the ācārayas. In verses 1–4, the poet says that he won't let go, binds Viṣṇu, and demands to be united with him. Beginning in verse 5, god's overwhelming love becomes the focus. God hungers for the poet, and in the end it is that love that subsumes the poet entirely (*X.10.10*). In the final sum, god's love for the devotee is seen to be even greater than the devotee's love for god.*

Traditionally, the Tiruvāymoḻi is interpreted as the Āḻvār's journey through the three states of bhakti—para-bhakti, para-jñāna and parama bhakti. In the state of para bhakti (high bhakti), one has a consistent mental vision of god. The Āḻvār exists in this state for the majority of the Tiruvāymoḻi. His longing is for a physical experience and to see god—this is the next stage, that of para-jñāna (high wisdom), in which the devotee sees god, but it is an unsustainable vision. Traditionally, Nammāḻvār is understood to attain this stage in X.9. The final stage is of disembodiment and total immersion in god, leading to mokṣa. This is parama bhakti (supreme bhakti), which he reaches in the final text's decad. The progress is laid out in the concluding aphorism of the Ācārya Hṛdayam, Cūrṇikai 229–232.

X.10.1: The four-faced one is Brahmā and the three-eyed father is Śiva.

X.10.3: 'Lotus rising from navel' refer to the note on I.3.9.

X.10.7: 'Rising as Varāha' refer to the note on I.7.6.

'Churning the ocean' refer to the note on I.3.11. This is the final myth referenced in the *Tiruvāymoḻi.*

This verse has the last two myths referred to in the text—the rescue of the earth as the cosmic boar, Varāha, and the churning of the ocean. Both myths are referenced early in the poem, in the First Hundred. The use of the Varāha myth is particularly significant, for Nammāḻvār uses it in a dramatic fashion in *Tiruviruttam*'s penultimate verse. In that verse, he characterizes Varāha as jñāna-p-pirāṉ the lord of wisdom, and says that nothing exists beyond him (jñāna-p-pirāṉ allāl illai, *Tiruviruttam* 99). Periyavāccaṉ Piḷḷai in the commentary on that verse argues that a devotee should rely only on one who can protect him, such as when Viṣṇu rescued Bhū from the waters, even without being asked.

X.10.11: The last name referenced in the *Tiruvāymoḻi* is Hari. It also invokes the deities, Brahmā and Śiva, asserting that Viṣṇu is the one who creates, protects and destroys the world.

This final phala-śruti explicitly states that this Ten concludes the poem—*antātikalāl ivai āyirmum muṭinta . . . ip pattu*—this ten which conclude the thousand antāti verses.

The verse ends with the word uyar (high), and repeats the verb, *aṟa*, to cut. Both of these return us to I.1.1, which begins with the memorable phrase, *uyarvu aṟa.*

Notes to the Introduction

1. For example, in I.1.5, the poet suggests that all paths ultimately lead to Viṣṇu, whom he has not yet named. However, later in the poem, in perhaps one of the most explicitly polemical sections (IV.10), he condemns those who follow other paths without understanding that Viṣṇu stands behind everything (IV.10.5). In a similar vein, IV.6 offers a critique of alternative religious practices, such as offering meat and toddy to other deities. Although Śaṭhakōpaṉ does not integrate the condemnation of Jains and Buddhists into his poetry like the Tamiḻ Śaiva poet Sambandar, he is keenly aware of the competition among various religious groups. He is consistent in subordinating Śiva to Viṣṇu, appropriating several key Śaiva myths and remaking them to assert Viṣṇu's supremacy. These include the myth of Tripurāntaka, first evoked in I.1.8 and the myth of Mārkaṇḍeya, first mentioned in IV.10.8.
2. The exception to this structure is II.7, which consists of twelve plus one verses. This decad lists Viṣṇu's twelve names.
3. In the translation, each decad is identified in three ways—according to Hundred and decad (VII.1.10–VII.1-11), its corresponding number in the 1102 verses (663–673) and by its opening line. Most Śrīvaiṣṇavas who know the text, refer to a decad by its opening phrase. Thus, decad VII.1 is simply called *uḷ nilāviya*, the opening decad (I.1) is *uyarvaṟa*, the final decad (X.10) is *muṉiyē* and so forth. In addition, I have also individually numbered each verse: I.1.1, VII.1.6, X.10.9, etc.

4. The poem explicitly signals its conclusion in X.10.11, saying that the thousand verses ended with the poet's final release.
5. If we start the poem at V.4.1 and end at V.3.11, we would begin and end on a note of separation, spoken in the intimacy of the female voice. Such a reading would offer its own insights into the text, particularly because the sheer number of successive female-voiced poems distinguishes the Fifth Pattu. V.3.11 ends with the phrase *ūr ellām* (the city entire), and V.4.1 opens with the same phrase. In the context of V.3.11, the phala-śruti, ūr ellām blesses every town as a Vaikuṇṭha for Viṣṇu's devotees. In V.4.1, the city entire (ūr ellām) is insensate with sleep, and the heroine is alone. This is no Vaikuṇṭha, and she is in the company of people dead to the value of a devotional life.
6. Frank Clooney. *Seeing through Texts*. pp. 93–95.
7. Frank Clooney. *Seeing through Texts*. p. 95.
8. Tirukkōnēri Dāsyai, a female commentator on the *Tiruvāymoḻi*, reads the entire text through the lens of the first verse. See Vasudha Narayanan. 'Casting Light on the Sounds of the Tamil Veda'.
9. For a discussion of the commentaries and the arthapañcaka, see Srilata Raman. *Self-surrender (Prapatti) to God in Śrīvaiṣṇavism*. pp. 112–114. For a translation of Piḷḷāṉ's commentary on I.1.1 see, John Carman and Vasudha Narayanan. *The Tamil Veda*. p. 195.
10. While there has always been debate around the authenticity of the phala-śrutis, most scholars accept their validity, and recognize that they form a core part of the text. Norman Cutler provides an excellent analysis of the value of the phala-śruti. Norman Cutler. *Songs of Experience*. pp. 27–29.
11. See for instance, Kurukur as a city of lakes (I.2.11), as wealthy (I.3.11), fertile (I.4.11), city of the virtuous (III.1.11) and of gardens (VI.8.11).
12. For a detailed discussion of the dating of the poet, refer to Archana Venkatesan. *A Hundred Measures of Time*. pp. 83–88.
13. Some examples: Śaṭhakōpaṉ as a poet (III.9.10, VI.4.9), as poet through whom god speaks (VII.9), adviser to poets (III.9, X.7), adviser to fellow devotees (IV.1), a young woman in love (V.5), her

mother (VI.7), self-effacement (IV.7.1, VII.9.8), as god's servant (II.9.1) and as a servant to god's servants (III.7).

14. See Appendix 2 for a translation of *Kaṇṇinuṇ ciṟu tāmpu*. Verses 8 and 9 are especially significant.
15. See Appendix 3 for a translation of all six taṉiyaṉ appended to the *Tiruvāymoḻi*.
16. Maṇipravāḷa (gems and coral) is a specialized language that combines Tamiḻ and Sanskrit vocabulary. Śrīvaiṣṇava Maṇipravāḷa uses Sanskrit vocabulary with Tamiḻ endings, and the occasional Sanskrit ending. The percentage of Tamiḻ and Sanskrit varies depending on the period and the writer. It was primarily the language of Śrīvaiṣṇava written commentary and oral discourse, although a few writers like Vedānta Deśika, composed poetry in it. For an analysis of Maṇipravāḷa in Śrīvaiṣṇava discourse, see K.K.A. Venkatachari. *The Maṇipravāḷa Literature of the Śrīvaiṣṇava Ācāryas.*
17. There is some debate on the dating of the hagiographies. Śrīvaiṣṇavas consider the Sanskrit *Divyasūricaritam* the earlier hagiography, with the Maṇipravāḷa *Guruparamparās* emerging later. Scholars generally agree with this dating. However, I have argued that the Sanskrit *Divyasūricaritam* is the later text. My argument is summarized in Archana Venkatesan. 'A Different Kind of Āṇṭāḷ Story'.
18. The riddle refers to the relationship of the soul to the body. Madurakavi's question can be translated as: How does the embodied soul subsist? Śaṭhakōpaṉ's response is interpreted variously to mean: in an earthly body, it will subsist on food. Alternatively, it can read as abiding in god, it (the ātman), will subsist on god. John Carman and Vasudha Narayanan. *The Tamil Veda.* p. 18.
19. The four compositions are *Tiruviruttam* (100 verses), *Tiruvāciriyam* (7 verses), *Periya Tiruvantāti* (87 verses) and *Tiruvāymoḻi* (1102 verses). Given their odd number and the lack of phala-śrutis, the middle two texts are likely incomplete.
20. The decad that Nāthamuni is said to have heard is V.8 (Fifth Hundred, Eighth Decad). It is in praise of the sacred site of Kudanthai (present-day Kumbakonam).

21. The *Nālāyira Divya Prabandham* is divided into four books comprising a thousand verses each. Śaṭhakōpaṉ's *Tiruvāymoḻi* is either the Third or the Fourth Thousand. His remaining three works are included in the Iyaṟpā section of the *Divya Prabandham*, which is either its third or fourth book, depending on the placement of the *Tiruvāymoḻi*.
22. In the *Guruparamparaprabhāvam* 6000, Madurakavi installs an image (arcā) of Nammāḻvār, which he worships in ritually sanctioned ways. 'Nammāḻvār Maturakavi Vaipavaṅkaḷ'. *Guruparamparaprabhāvam* 6000. pp. 75–87.
23. For a substantive discussion of Nammāḻvār's hagiography see, Friedhelm Hardy. 'The Tamil Veda of a *Śūdra* Saint'.

    The Nammāḻvār story is rich with familiar motifs of Indic storytelling, of which the most striking is textual loss and recovery. The Tamiḻ Śaivas produce a similar narrative about the loss of the poems of Appar, Sambandar and Sundarar. While legend tells us that the *Divya Prabandham* is recovered in its entirety, the parallel Śaiva narratives reveal that their corpus is only partially retrieved.
24. See Ranjeeta Dutta on Rāmānuja as social reformer and Śrīvaiṣṇava self-presentation as a socially open community. Ranjeeta Dutta. *From Hagiographies to Biographies: Rāmānuja in Tradition and History*.
25. For example, see III.7.9, a verse in which the poet affirms that he bows to anyone who is a servant of a servant of god, even those who fall outside the four castes.
26. As Nammāḻvār is the most important of the twelve āḻvār poets, Śrīvaiṣṇavas often simply call him Āḻvār. I occasionally replicate this style in the introduction, using an upper case to denote that it refers to our poet, and lower case when it refers to the group of twelve poets.
27. Vasudha Narayanan provides a detailed reading of the Śrīvaiṣṇava arguments about the equivalence of the *Tiruvāymoḻi* and the Sanskrit Vedas. Vasudha Narayanan. *The Vernacular Veda*. pp. 14–30.
28. Tirumaṅkai is believed to have institutionalized the recitation of the *Tiruvāymoḻi* in Srirangam, prior to Nāthamuni.

29. The *Tiruvāymoḻi* commentaries add another layer to the development of the Nammāḻvār story, particularly as the commentarial tradition matures. Later commentaries, beginning with that of Nañjīyar in the twelfth century, are keen to assert Nammāḻvār's divine descent, and to represent him as a *jñāni* (sage) on par with divinely inspired authors like Vālmīki. For a thorough discussion of the hagiographical mode in the *Tiruvāymoḻi* commentaries, see Srilata Raman. *Self-surrender (Prapatti) to God in Śrīvaiṣṇavism*. pp. 101–106.
30. Legend has it that the Tamiḻ Saṅgam of poets tested the value of works by placing them on a wooden plank. If the work floated, it was deemed acceptable by the high standards of the poets' collective. Several famous works are tested in similar ways—some are thrown into a fire, but are unscathed; some are thrown into water and rise up undamaged. In this narrative, the *Tiruvāymoḻi* is placed on the plank along with other Tamiḻ works, and it alone remains above water, demonstrating that it has no peers.
31. 'Nammāḻvār Maturakavi Vaipavaṅkaḷ'. *Guruparamparaprabhāvam* 6000. p. 86.
32. For a discussion of the move from orality to writing in the transmission of the *Tiruvāymoḻi*, see Vasudha Narayanan. *The Vernacular Veda*. pp. 33–35.
33. I thank Anna Seastrand for alerting me to the significance of Madurakavi's stylus in visual depictions of Nammāḻvār. Her essay, 'Tracing a Line: Guruparamparā in the Murals of Āḻvār Tirunakari', provides a nuanced analysis of the significance of the visual representation of texts in the transmission story of the *Tiruvāymoḻi*.

    The depictions of Nammāḻvār flanked by Nāthamuni and Madurakavi are numerous, particularly in the Tamiraparani region. They also appear in older printed editions of the *Tiruvāymoḻi*. One can find several examples in stone as well as in painting. Examples of stone representations can be found at the temples of Vanamamalai, Alvar Tirunagari, Srivaikuntham, Tirukkurungudi, among others. Painted examples can be found in the murals located in the circumambulatory passage of the Nammāḻvār shrine at Alvar

Tirunagari, and in local maṭhas within the town. Anna Seastrand discusses the Alvar Tirunagari murals in her essay cited above.

34. I offer a brief overview of some of the ways in which Nammāḻvār conceptualizes god in the *Tiruvāymoḻi*. This is a vast topic, and one of great concern to Śrīvaiṣṇava commentators. John Carman and Vasudha Narayanan's *The Tamil Veda* is a methodical study of the first commentary of the *Tiruvāymoḻi*, with substantial portions of the commentary translated. In addition, see Vasudha Narayanan. *The Way and the Goal*. pp. 14–26; Frank Clooney. *Seeing through Texts*. pp. 59–78; Frank Clooney. *The Art and Theology of the Śrīvaiṣṇava Thinkers*. pp.14–19; R.D. Kaylor and K.K.A. Venkatachari. *God Far, God Near*. pp. 15–37.

35. A.K. Ramanujan refers to this crucial, recurring motif in the *Tiruvāymoḻi* as mutual cannibalism. A.K. Ramanujan. *Hymns for the Drowning*. pp. 150–152. John Carman and Vasudha Narayanan provide a comprehensive discussion of the metaphor of swallowing, and what they term, mutual inclusiveness in relation to the Śrīvaiṣṇava commentarial tradition. John Carman and Vasudha Narayanan. *The Tamil Veda*. pp. 159–179.

36. The citations of verses here are intended to be illustrative and not exhaustive.

37. For Nammāḻvār and his fellow poets, god (whether Śiva or Viṣṇu) is full of aruḷ, which he can bestow on those he favours. Viṣṇu's actions, his speech, his deeds are all filled with this aruḷ. It is a capacious word that means favour, compassion, love, kindness, mercy, benevolence. In the Tamiḻ tradition, aruḷ is dynamic and liquid, what David Shulman describes as 'shimmering fullness, marked by shifting, unpredictable intensities'. David Shulman. '*Tirukkōvaiyār*: Downstream into God'. p. 134. In the Śrīvaiṣṇava tradition, the nature of god's grace (aruḷ in Tamiḻ, kṛpā, *dayā*, or prasāda in Sanskrit) becomes one of the key issues of debate between its two sects. In my translation, I employ different words to capture the marvellous quality of this word aruḷ. In some instances, it is grace, in other cases as in VI.2.2 and VI.2.3, it is love; in VII.1.7, it is loving aid, in VII.8

it is 'be kind', a phrase that is repeated throughout the decad, and in I.4.6, I translate it three different ways—as ocean of mercy, as favour and as grace. For a brief discussion of the relationship between aruḷ and grace, see Archana Venkatesan. *A Hundred Measures of Time.* p. 175.

38. Nammāḻvār is heir to the rich Saṅgam literary tradition, in which the natural world is used to comment on and reflect the inner worlds of poetic characters. Nammāḻvār is clearly aware of this legacy, for his poems are replete with allusions and adaptations of verses from the Saṅgam corpus. In the *Tiruviruttam*, he makes explicit mention of the concept of the five landscapes (*aintiṇai*) in verse 26, while verse 68 is an adaptation of *Kuṟuntokai* 68, while *Tiruvāymoḻi* VII.3.8 is perhaps the most obvious evocation of a Saṅgam poem, *Kuṟuntokai* 3. For a discussion of Nammāḻvār's use of the natural world in the *Tiruvāymoḻi*, see G. Damodaran. 'Treatment of Nature'. *The Literary Value of the Tiruvāymoḻi.* pp. 185–201. Eva Wilden discusses the mixing of landscapes in the love-themed verses of the *Tiruvāymoḻi*. Eva Wilden. 'Nammāḻvār as a Master of *Tiṇaimayakkam*—Transposition Techniques in the *Akam* Songs of the *Tiruvāymoḻi*'. pp. 317–335.

39. For example, see II.1.4, II.5.3, II.5.4, III.4.2, IV.4.3, IV.4.4, V.3.1, VI.6.6.

40. For a discussion of the experiential dimensions of Nammāḻvār's bhakti as articulated by the commentators, see John Carman and Vasudha Narayanan. *The Tamil Veda.* pp. 70–110.

41. For a discussion of the female voice (nāyikā) in the *Tiruvāymoḻi*, see Frank Clooney's *His Hiding Place Is Darkness.* I have discussed Nammāḻvār's multiple female voices (heroine, friend, mother and fortune teller) in *A Hundred Measures of Time.* pp. 124–134.

42. While a tone of fierce, desperate melancholy is a hallmark of the female-voiced Tiruvāymoḻis, it is not confined to them. There are several instances when Śaṭhakōpaṉ purportedly speaks in his own voice, which easily match the emotional weight of the woman-Tens. See, for example, the beautiful and moving Tiruvāymoḻi IV.7.

43. See for example, V.6.11 (Vaḻuti Nāḍaṉ) and V.10.11 (Māṟaṉ).
44. False wisdom, wicked conduct, dirty bodies
let's not draw near such things now.
To protect life, you took birth from many wombs
O master of the unblinking ones
stand before me embodied
listen graciously to a servant's plea. (*Tiruviruttam* 1)
Archana Venkatesan. *A Hundred Measures of Time*. p. 25.

45. See Frank Clooney's brief discussion of the Śrīvaiṣṇava understanding of the poem's authorship in *Seeing through Texts*, pp. 22–25. Also see, Vasudha Narayanan. *The Vernacular Veda*. pp. 28–31.
46. The Śrīvaiṣṇava commentators theorize the female voice as the voice of separation and longing (*prema*), while the Āḻvār's own voice is read as that of union and wisdom (jñāna). This is summarized in the Cūrṇikai 118 of the *Ācārya Hṛdayam*. For a discussion of this Cūrṇikai, see Archana Venkatesan. *A Hundred Measures of Time*. pp. 126–128. The āḻvār poets, both male and female, employ female voices masterfully, to index a variety of emotional registers. For a discussion of the use of the female lament in the *Tiruviruttam*, see Archana Venkatesan. *A Hundred Measures of Time*. pp. 124–134. For a discussion of Āṇṭāḷ's female voice(s) in the *Tiruppāvai* and *Nācciyār Tirumoḻi*, see Archana Venkatesan. *The Secret Garland*. pp. 14–30. For a preliminary overview of the female voices of various āḻvār poets, see Archana Venkatesan. 'How to Love God like a Woman'. Friedhelm Hardy's *Viraha Bhakti* explores the theme exhaustively.
47. Following poetic precedent, Nammāḻvār too gives his heroine many mothers. In the Saṅgam poems, the heroine generally has a biological mother and a foster mother, in addition to other maternal figures, perhaps representing a wide kinship circle. In Nammāḻvār's poem, these mothers are referred to in the plural as aṉṉaimīr.
48. A similar observation can be made about the Tens in the mother's voice. See for example, IV.4 (cited above) or V.6.

49. In the section on sacred places, I focus on the terrestrial sites. The references to Vaikuṇṭha and the Ocean of Milk (Pārkaṭal) are plentiful in the *Tiruvāymoḻi*. As discussed above, the *Tiruvāymoḻi*'s penultimate Ten describes an ascent to Vaikuṇṭha. Apart from this, Viṣṇu's heaven is frequently invoked in the phala-śruti, as the reward for those who master a particular decad, and by extension, the text as a whole. Tiruvāymoḻi IV.7.11 is illustrative:

Māṟaṉ Śaṭhakōpaṉ of Kurukūr, city of mansions
sang with overflowing love for Kaṇṇaṉ
these ten verses from a thousand in flawless Tamiḻ.
Those who sing and dance them with love
will reach Vaikuṇṭha.

50. For instance, Nammāḻvār will provide the name of a river, the direction in which the deity faces, or the posture of the deity enshrined in a temple. In the cycle on Tirupper (X.10.1), he places the shrine on the banks of the Ponni, while in the Ten on Tiruvanvandur, he describes it as located on the Pampa's northern bank (VI.1.10). An example in which he describes the posture of the deity, the direction in which he faces, and provides topographical detail is the cycle on Tiruccenkunrur (VIII.4). Here, he describes the city on the banks of the Cirraru, and the deity as standing facing west (VIII.4.3). In IX.2.4 he describes the three postures (standing, seated and reclining) of three linked sites—standing in Srivaikuntham, seated in Varagunamangai and reclining in Pulinkuti.

In several instances, he will also provide a specific name for the deity, such as Tirukkurungudi Nambi (Tirukkurungudi), Deyvanāyakaṉ (Vanamamalai), Oppārillappaṉ (Tiruvinnakar). It is difficult to ascertain if the deities at these shrines were already known by these names, or if they came to be addressed as such *because* Nammāḻvār used them. In some cases, the names are specific—like Makara Neṭuṅkuḻaik Kātaṉ (Tentirupperai)—and in other instances, more generic, like Aḻakar (Tirumaliruncolai). He does not use a specific name for the deity at Venkatam.

51. He sees god in Tirukkurungudi, Kudanthai, enters Tiruvenkatam, reaches Tirumokur. Damodaran provides an excellent list of several examples in support of this argument. See *The Literary Value of Tiruvāymoḻi*. pp. 40–42.
52. In a few verses, Nammāḻvār simply mentions a mountain. In these cases, the commentators gloss it as Venkatam. An example is the verse X.4.4, which opens this section.
53. These are Tirukkurungudi (V.5), Tiruvallaval (V.9), Tiruvanvandur (VI.1), Tolaivillimangalam (VI.5), Tirukkolur (VI.7), Tiruvarankam (VII.2), Tirupperai (VII.3), Tiruppuliyur (VII.9) and Tirumulikkalam (IX.7).
54. Nancy Ann Nayar. *Poetry as Theology*. pp. 41–49.
55. Below I offer some observations on the Śrīvaiṣṇava commentarial tradition, but do not provide an analysis of the commentary. There are many excellent studies of Śrīvaiṣṇava commentaries by K.K.A. Venkatachari, Frank Clooney, John Carman and Vasudha Narayanan (all on the *Tiruvāymoḻi*), and Suganya Anandakichenin on Periyavāccāṉ Piḷḷai's commentary on Kulaśekhara Āḻvār's *Perumāḷ Tirumoḻi*.
56. Frank Clooney suggests that these accounts of the ācāryas' engagement with the *Tiruvāymoḻi* presented the Śrīvaiṣṇava community a way for Nammāḻvār's story to become contiguous with that of the ācāryas, and to provide them with an 'imaginative moral access to the *Tiruvāymoḻi*'. *Seeing through Texts*. p. 241.
57. In *Seeing through Texts*, Frank Clooney offers synopses and an analysis of several episodes involving the ācāryas recorded in the written commentaries. These include instances of one teacher, Nañjīyar, offering multiple interpretations of a single verse (I.2.1); of several ācāryas offering competing explications for the transition between decads (IV.2–IV.3), and the deep feeling that performers of the *Tiruvāymoḻi* would experience while reciting it (IV.7.1). While Clooney offers many more examples, each of the above is sufficient

to illustrate the Śrīvaiṣṇava textual community, the reading and interpretive practices it nurtured and the affective values that it cherished. Frank Clooney. *Seeing through Texts.* pp. 227–242.

58. John Carman and Vasudha Narayanan. *The Tamil Veda.* pp. 8–9.
59. Srilata Raman, citing the linguistic analysis of scholars like Gnansundaram, suggests the Maṇipravāḷa deployed by the Śrīvaiṣṇavas was unique to them, enlivened by colloquialisms and rare vocabulary not attested to in earlier Maṇipravāḷa works. The decision to use Maṇipravāḷa reflected the ācāryas' commitment to both Tamiḻ and Sanskrit. Yet, their decision to adopt this synthetic language, inaccessible to outsiders, reveals their understanding of the *Tiruvāymoḻi* as a sacred text that therefore necessitated secrecy. Secrecy ensured that the community's teachers could properly regulate access to it. Srilata Raman. *Self-surrender (Prapatti) to God in Śrīvaiṣṇavism.* pp. 63–64.

    John Carman and Vasudha Narayanan also discuss the Śrīvaiṣṇava use of Maṇipravāḷa in commentaries. They posit that the language helped strengthen the doctrine of Ubhaya Vedānta (Dual Vedānta). The commentaries do not simply use Sanskrit vocabulary (Sanskrit words with Tamiḻ grammatical endings), but also quote extensively from a range of Sanskrit sources. The commentators' knowledge of Tamiḻ grammar and its literary past is also considerable. Both author/speaker and audience were essentially bilingual, comfortable in both languages, making Maṇipravāḷa an ideal vehicle to declare the equivalency of Tamiḻ and Sanskrit. John Carman and Vasudha Narayanan. *The Tamil Veda.* pp. 9–11.
60. Vasudha Narayanan. 'Oral and Written Commentaries on the *Tiruvāymoḻi*'. pp. 88–89.
61. The dates of the commentators are as follows: Nañjīyar (1182–1287), Vaṭakkutiruvītippiḷḷai (1217–1312), Periyavāccāṉ Piḷḷai's (b.1228), Vātikesari Aḻakiya Maṇavāḷa Perumāḷ Jīyar (1242–1350).
62. See the opening note on the *Bhagavat Viṣayam* commentaries in Appendix 4 for further details on the commentaries and their transmission.

63. A *paṭi* is a unit of 32 syllabic units. Thus, a commentary of 6000 paṭis consisted of 6000x32 syllables.
64. As Māmuṉikaḷ's poem is also an antāti, he begins by directly quoting the opening phrase of the decad he is summarizing, and closes by quoting the opening phrase of the next decad.
65. Frank Clooney offers a close reading of Māmuṉikaḷ's *Tiruvāymoḻi Nūṟṟantāti* in the latter half of the fifth chapter of his forthcoming book, *Reading the Hindu and Christian Classics*. The chapter includes translations from the *Tiruvāymoḻi* as well as of the *Nūṟṟantāti*. I am grateful to Frank for sharing the chapter proofs with me.
66. Vasudha Narayanan is the only scholar to have written on Dāsyai. See Vasudha Narayanan. 'Casting Light on the Sounds of the Tamil Veda' for a thorough and thoughtful discussion about Dāsyai's commentary and of the woman herself. She provides us with a hypothesis on Dāsyai's date (likely thirteenth century), the area from where she hailed (Tirumala), and notes her interest in the performing arts. My discussion of Dāsyai is based on Vasudha Narayanan's work.
67. Hari Rao. Trans. *Kōil Oḻugu*. p. 37.
68. In this version of the story, Nammāḻvār travels to Śrīraṅgam accompanied by Madurakavi. Madurakavi, representing the Āḻvār, recites the *Tiruvāymoḻi* to the accompaniment of gestures. Hari Rao. Trans. *Kōil Oḻugu*. pp. 8–13.
69. Bharati Jagannathan. *Approaching the Divine*. pp. 35–38.
70. Leslie Orr, personal communication, 1 February 2019. Leslie Orr directs us to *South India Inscriptions*, ARE 1923/298.
71. Nilakantha Sastri. *Development of Religion in South India*. p. 123.
72. Leslie Orr, personal communication, 23 July 2018.
73. K.V. Raman discusses the fifteenth-century donor, Kantāṭai Rāmānuja Ayyaṉ, and his donative work at the Viṣṇu temple at Tirumala. These include, popularizing the Adhyayanotsavam at the site, and interestingly, arranging for the recitation of the *Divya Prabandham* by Śāttāda Vaiṣṇavas. K.V. Raman. *Srī Varadarājaswāmi Temple—Kāñci*. p. 79. A sixteenth-century

inscription from the Varadarāja Perumāḷ temple mentions the performance of the Adhyayanotsavam in relation to the Tātācārya family, an important clan of Śrīvaiṣṇavas. Ibid., p. 83. Valerie Stoker discusses the patronage of the Adhyayanotsavam at Tirumala-Tirupati by the Mādhva ācārya Vyāsatīrtha (1460–1539) in his bid to build an alliance with the Śrīvaiṣṇavas at that temple. Valerie Stoker. *Polemics and Patronage in the City of Victory*. p. 94.

74. The *Tiruvāymoḻi* is recited on other festival occasions as well; the Adhyayanotsavam is simply the most elaborate of these recitations. The Śrīvaiṣṇavas also have a summary *Tiruvāymoḻi*, called the *Kōyil Tiruvāymoḻi*, consisting of 143 verses, that they use in domestic and temple ritual. For a discussion of the *Kōyil Tiruvāymoḻi* see Vasudha Narayanan. *The Vernacular Veda*. pp. 59–60.

75. Vasudha Narayanan provides a detailed description of the Adhyayanotsavam at Srirangam in her *Vernacular Veda*. pp. 115–135. Paul Younger's essay 'Singing the Tamil Hymnbook in the Tradition of Rāmānuja' offers another analysis of the Adhyayanotsavam also at Srirangam. Norman Cutler has a brief description of the contemporary recitation practices of the *Divya Prabandham*, with a focus on Alvar Tirunagari in *Songs of Experience*. pp. 187–190.

76. In several temples, particularly in the Pāṇṭiya regions, the Iyaṟpā section of the *Divya Prabandham* is also recited during Irā Pattu. It is generally recited during procession, while the *Tiruvāymoḻi*, which has the status of Veda, is always recited seated. In some temples, like in Srirangam, the entire Iyaṟpā is recited on the concluding day of the festival.

77. Vaikuṇṭha Ekādaśī is the eleventh day of the waxing moon (*śukla pakṣa*) in the month of Mārkaḻi. The *Kōyil Oḻuku* mentions that Tirumaṅkai instituted the *Tiruvāymoḻi* recitation on the Ekādaśī day.

78. At the temples of Srirangam, Srivilliputtur and Alvar Tirunagari, certain verses in the *Tiruvāymoḻi* are selected for gestural interpretation and commentarial comment. These are performed by the Araiyar, ritual performers, who trace their lineage to

Nāthamuni's two nephews. The performance called Araiyar Cēvai survives only at these three temples, and in a truncated form at the temple in Melkote.

79. This brief description of the Irā Pattu Utsavam is based on my observations of the festival at the Nava Tirupati temples, at Tirukkurungudi and at Nanguneri between 2007 and 2018. There are important differences in the celebration of the Adhyayanotsavam at each of these sites. One important difference is the addition of an eleventh day called *Vīṭu Viṭai* (Goodbye, Mokṣa) at the conclusion of Āḻvār Mokṣam (the Tenth Day of Irā Pattu). Celebrated only at Alvar Tirunagari and Tirukkurungudi, Vīṭu Viṭai marks the return of the Āḻvār from mokṣa, to serve as a guide to devotees. Other temples mark this event as well, but celebrate it immediately after Āḻvār Mokṣam. Another important difference is that none of the Nava Tirupati temples, except Alvar Tirunagari has an icon of Nammāḻvār. Therefore, his role is taken by other āḻvārs, most frequently, Tirumaṅkai. Beyond these differences, there is considerable regional and sub-sectarian variation as well. It is beyond the scope of this introduction to catalogue and analyse these differences.

80. Roberto De Nobili. *On Indian Customs.* Trans. S. Rajamanickam, S.J. Palayamkottai: St Xavier's College, De Nobili Research Institute, 1972. p. 38.

81. Ellis was based in the Madras Presidency. He was the first scholar to develop the hypothesis of the Dravidian languages as constituting a separate language family. His ideas were further developed by Robert Caldwell (1814–1891), who credits Ellis's work on Dravidian linguistics in *A Comparative Grammar of the Dravidian or the South Indian Family of Languages* (1856).

82. Sethu Pillai, R.P. ed. *Tirukkuraḷ: Ellis' Commentary.* Madras: Madras University Press, 1955. p. 29

83. Ibid., pp. 30–32.

84. I thank Frank Clooney for drawing my attention to both of these early references to the *Tiruvāymoḻi*. Email communication, 22 June 2019.

85. I thank Frank Clooney for directing me to this source. Although ten volumes have been published, UC Davis's Interlibrary Loan service was only able to acquire four volumes—the First, Fourth, Sixth and Tenth Hundreds. Frank Clooney received a scan of the first Three Hundreds from Harvard's interlibrary service, which he shared with Vasudha Narayanan and me. However, these scans did not include the cover pages for volumes 2 and 3, and the back covers for none of the volumes. Francis X. Clooney. Email communication, 13 July 2013.
86. Kurratalvar Ayyangar. 'Foreword'. *A Free Translation of Tiruvoymoli of Sathakopa: First Hundred.* 1925. pp. i–ii.

    The book begins with a prose translation of all eleven verses of the *Kaṇṇinuṇ ciṟu tāmpu,* and the Sanskrit taṉiyaṉ appended to the *Tiruvāymoḻi.* He does not translate all six of the text's laudatory verses. pp. ii–iii; p. 1.
87. N. Kurattalvar Ayyangar. *A Free Translation of Tiruvoymoli of Sathakopa: Tenth Hundred.* 1926. p. 25.
88. N. Kurratalvar Ayyangar. *A Free Translation of Tiruvaymoli of Sathakopa: Sixth Hundred.* 1927.
89. N. Kurratvalar Ayyangar. Back-flap. *A Free Translation of Tiruvaymoli of Sathakopa: Sixth Hundred.* 1927.

    Ayyangar also acknowledges Ms Pitt in his foreword, crediting her with editorial advice as well. He attributes the publication of the book to her. Kurratalvar Ayyangar. *A Free Translation of Tiruvoymoli of Sathakopa: First Hundred,* 1925. p. i.

    On the back-flap of the translated volume of the Fourth Hundred, published in 1927, Ayyangar gives us an additional reason for this project. He informs us that the volumes, of which nine were ready in 1927, could be purchased directly from him. The proceeds from the book sale were directed to support a school for Śāttāda Śrīvaiṣṇava boys that was based in his home.
90. A.K. Ramanujan. *Hymns for the Drowning.* p. xvi.
91. Doniger's volume also includes several verses translated by John Carman and Vasudha Narayanan, excerpted from their book, *The Tamil Veda.*

92. For a fine analysis and review of *Hymns for the Drowning*, see M.R. Parameswaran and Uma Parameswaran's 'Singing to the Feet of the Lord: On A.K. Ramanujan's Translations of Nammalvar's Poetry'.
93. John Carman and Vasudha Narayanan. *The Tamil Veda.* p. xv.

Appendix 1

Content of Tiruvāymoḻi Hundreds

Tiruvāymoḻi Section	First Line	Summary of Content
The First Hundred I.1–I.10	uyarvaṟa uyar nalam: I.1 vīṭumiṉ muṟṟavum: I.2 pattuṭai aṭiyārkku: I.3 añciṟaiya maṭa nārāy: I.4 vaḷvēḻ ulakiṉ: I.5 parivatu ilīcaṉai: I.6 piṟavittuyar aṟa: I.7 ōṭum puḷ: I.8 ivaiyum avaiyum: I.9 porumā nīḷpaṭai: I.10	• God's transcendence (paratva), his immanence and accessibility (saulabhya), his qualities (kalyāṇa guṇa), the path to him, him as both the way (upāya) and goal (upeya), loving service to god (kaiṅkarya) • First myth mentioned is Viṣṇu eating the worlds (I.1.7) • First mention of the name Nārāyaṇa (Nāraṇa)—I.2.10 • First mention of Śrī (I.3.1) • First avatāra mentioned is that of Kṛṣṇa (I.3.1)

		• First and only mention of Bhagavan (I.3.5) • First mention of the non-terrestrial sacred abodes of the cosmic sea and (I.4.10) Vaikuṇṭha (I.5.4) • First mention of the name Kaṇṇaṉ (I.4.11) • First terrestrial sacred abode mentioned is Venkatam (I.8.3) • The introduction of the female voice, here the heroine (talaivi) in *Tiruvāymoḷi* I.4.1–I.4.11 • The first of four messenger songs I.4.1–I.4.11
The Second Hundred II.1–II.10	vāyum tiraiukaḷum: II.1 tiṇṇaṉ vīṭu: II.2 ūṉilvāḻ uyirē: II.3 āṭi āṭi akam karaintu: II.4 antāmattu: II.5 vaikunthā maṇivaṇṇaṉē: II.6 keśavaṉ tamar: II.7 aṇaivatu aravaṇaimēl: II.8 emmā vīṭṭu tiṟamum: II.9 kiḻaroḷi iḷamai: II.10	• Opens with the female voice, to signify separation from Viṣṇu (II.1.1–II.1.11) • Viṣṇu as the giver of release/heaven (vīṭu) mentioned in II.2. It is also mentioned in I.2 • The supremacy of Viṣṇu as relating to the other deities, specifically, Śiva and Brahmā (II.2.1–II.2.11) • Introduction of the mother's voice (II.4.1–II.4.11) • Generational attachment to Viṣṇu (II.6.7; II.7.1; II.7.4)

		• Singing of the twelve names of Viṣṇu (II.7.1–II.7.13) • The final line of the phala-śruti quotes the opening phrase of the *Tiruvāymoḷi*: uyarvu aṟa uyar • Showing the way out of the path of grief (II.8.1–II.8.11) • The importance of service and Viṣṇu's grace (II.9.1–II.9.11) • First cycle of songs on a specific site—Tirumaliruncolai (II.10.1–II.10.11) • Two phala-śrutis (II.6.11, II.8.11) do not mention Kurukur • II.8.11 mentions neither Kurukur nor the name Śaṭhakōpaṉ
Third Hundred III.1–III.10	muṭic cōtiyāy: III.1 munnīr ñālam: III.2 oḻivil kālam ellām: III.3 pukaḻum nal oruvaṉ: III.4 moym mām pūm poḻil: III.5 ceyya tāmarai kaṇṇaṉ: III.6 payilum cuṭaroḷī: III.7 muṭiyāṉē: III.8	• Opens with the description of Viṣṇu (III.1.1–III.1.11) • The poet feels loss and disconnected from Viṣṇu, and seeks a path to him (III.2.1–III.2.11) • This path leads to Tiruvenkatam, where god invites him to enjoy his iconic form (III.3.1–III.3.11)

	coṉṉāl virōtam: III.9 caṉmam pala pala: III.10	• Complete cycle of songs on Tiruvenkatam (III.3.1–III.3.11) • The first use of the Sanskrit word mokṣa transliterated in Tamiḻ as mōkkam (III.4.7) • He describes devotion and service to god as embodied and all-encompassing (III.5.1–III.5.11) • Juxtaposes god's supremacy and his accessibility (III.6.1–III.6.11) • Extols the value of service to the devotees' devotees, which commentaries see as the crux of this Hundred (III.7.1–III.7.11) • Chastising of poets who sing of ordinary men (III.9.1–III.9.11) • The benefits that the poet gains from total devotion to Viṣṇu (III.10.1–III.10.11) • This Hundred does not have any verses in the female voice • Explicit connection of Viṣṇu to Puruṣa (III.4.4)

Fourth Hundred IV.1–IV.10	oru nāyakamāy: IV.1 pālaṉāy ēḻ ulaku uṇṭu: IV.2 kōvai vāyāḷ: IV.3 maṉṉai iruntu tuḻāvi: IV.4 vīṟṟiruntu ēḻ ulakum: IV.5 tīrppārai yām iṉi: IV.6 cīlam illāc ciṟiyēṉum: IV.7 ēṟāḷum iṟaiyōṉum: IV.8 naṇṇātār muṟuvalippa: IV.9 oṉṟum tēvum: IV.10	• Transience of worldly life and earthly kings (IV.1, IV.9) • Return of the voice of the mother (IV.2, IV.4) • The poet's words as adornment for Viṣṇu (IV.5) • Introduction of the character of the fortune teller (IV.6) • Introduction of the voice of the heroine's friend (IV.6) • Return of the heroine's voice (IV.8) • Rejection of other paths and other gods (IV.6, IV.10) • Complete cycle of songs on Tirukkurukur, the poet's town (IV.10.1–IV.10.11) • All three female voices are featured in this Hundred
Fifth Hundred V.1–V.10	kaiyār cakkarattu: V.1 polika polika: V.2 macaṟu cōti: V.3 ūr ellām tuñci: V.4 eṅṅkaṉēyō: V.5 kaṭal ñālam ceytēṉum: V.6 nōṟṟa nōṉpu ilēṉ: V.7	• Complete cycle on the Kali age (V.2.1–V.2.11) • Return of the heroine's voice (V.3–V.6; V.9) • First mention of the name Vāsudeva (V.3.6) • Mention of riding the maṭal (V.3.9; V.3.10)

	ārā amutē: V.8 māṉ ēy nōkku: V.9 piṟantavāṟum: V.10	• Complete cycle of songs on Tirukkurungudi (V.5.1–V.5.11) • Complete cycle of songs on Srivaramangalanakar (V.7.1–V.7.11) • Complete cycle of songs on Kudanthai (V.8.1–V.8.11) • Complete cycle of songs on Tiruvallaval (V.9.1–V.9.11) • We reach the midpoint of the *Tiruvāymoḻi* with V.10.10 • The sole means to gain what one desires are the feet of Viṣṇu (V.7.10) • Four successive decads, nearly half the Fifth Hundred, is in the female voice (V.3, V.4, V.5 and V.6)
Sixth Hundred VI.1–VI.10	vaikal pūṅkaḻivāy: VI.1 miṉṉiṭai maṭavārkaḷ: VI.2 nalkuravam celvum: VI.3 kuravai āycciyarōṭu: VI.4 tuvaḷil māmaṇi māṭam: VI.5 mālukku vaiyam aḷanta: VI.6	• Complete cycle of songs on Tiruvanvandur (VI.1.1–VI.1.11) • Complete cycle in the voice of gopī (VI.2.1–VI.2.10) • Complete cycle of songs on Tiruvinnakar (VI.3.1–VI.3.11) • Complete cycle of songs on Tolaivillimangalam (VI.5.1–VI.5.11)

	uṇṇuñ cōṟu: VI.7 poṉ ulaku āḷirō: VI.8 nīrāy nilaṉāy: VI.9 ulakam uṇṭa peruvāyā: VI.10	• Complete cycle of songs on Tirukkolur (VI.7.1–VI.7.11) • Complete cycle of songs on Venkatam (VI.10.1–VI.10.11) • The Āḻvār's prapatti in VI.10.10 • Two of four messenger songs appear in this Hundred (VI.1 and VI.8) • Return of the heroine's friend (VI.5) • Return of the mother's voice (VI.6 and VI.7) • All three female voices (heroine, mother and friend) are featured in this Hundred, similar to the Fourth Hundred
Seventh Hundred VII.1–VII.10	uḷ nilāviya: VII.1 kaṅkulum pakalum: VII.2 veḷḷaic curicaṅkōṭu: VII.3 āḻi eḻa: VII.4 kaṟpār irāma pirāṉai: VII.5 pāmaru mūvulakum: VII.6 ēḻaiyar āvi: VII.7 māyā vāmaṉaṉē: VII.8 eṉṟaikkum eṉṉai: VII.9 iṉpam payakka: VII.10	• Cycle of songs on the five senses (VII.1.1–VII.1.10) • Complete cycle of songs on Srirangam (VII.2.1–VII.2.10) • Return of the mother's voice (VII.2) • Complete cycle of songs on Tirupperai (VII.3.1–VII.3.11) • Complete cycle of songs of the poem as god's words (VII.9.1–VII.9.11) • Complete cycle of songs on Tiruvaranvilai (VII.10.1–VII.10.11)

Eighth Hundred VIII.1–VIII.10	tēvimār āvār: VIII.1 naṅkaḷ varivaḷai: VIII.2 aṅkum iṅkum: VIII.3 vār kaṭā aruvi: VIII.4 māyak kūttā: VIII.5 elliyum kālaiyum: VIII.6 iruttum viyantu: VIII.7 kaṇkaḷ civantu: VIII.8 karu māṇikka malai mēl: VIII.9 neṭumāṟku aṭimai: VIII.10	• Return of the female voice (VIII.2.1–VIII.2.10) • Complete cycle of songs on Tiruccenkunrur (VIII.4.1–VIII.4.11) • Complete cycle of songs on Tirukkatittanam (VIII.6.1–VIII.6.11) • On the beauty of the self/soul and its relationship to god (VIII.8.6–VIII.8.10) • Complete cycle of songs on Tiruppuliyur (VIII.9.1–VIII.9.11) • Return of the female friend (VIII.9.1–VIII.9.10); this is the last decad in that mode • In praise of service to the servants of Viṣṇu (VIII.10.1–VIII.10.11)
Ninth Hundred IX.1–IX.10	koṇṭa peṇṭir: IX.1 paṇṭai nāḷālē: IX.2 ōr āyiramāy: IX.3 maiyār karuṅkaṇṇi: IX.4 iṇuyirc cēvalum: IX.5 urukumāl neñcam: IX.6 em kāṉal: IX.7 aṟukkum viṉaiyāyiṉa: IX.8 mallikai kamaḻ: IX.9 mālai naṇṇi: IX.10	• God as the only refuge (IX.1.1–IX.1.11) • Mathura praised as the site of Kṛṣṇa's birth (IX.1.3–IX.1.10) • Complete cycle of songs on Tiruppulinkuti (IX.2.1–IX.2.11) • Return of the heroine's voice (IX.5.1–IX.5.10; IX.7.1–IX.7.10; IX.9.1–IX.9.10) • Complete cycle of songs on Tirukkatkarai (IX.6.1–IX.6.11)

		• Complete cycle of songs on Tirumulikkalam (IX.7.1–IX.7.11) • Last of the messenger poem cycle (IX.7.1–IX.7.10) • Complete cycle of songs on Tirunavay (IX.8.1–IX.8.11) • Complete cycle of songs on Tirukkannapuram (IX.10.1–IX.10.11) • The use of the gopī voice (IX.9.1–IX.9.11)
Tenth Hundred X.1–X.10	tāḷa tāmarai: X.1 keṭum iṭar: X.2 vēymaru tōḷ iṇai: X.3 cārvē tavaneṟi: X.4 kaṇṇaṉ kaḻaliṇai: X.5 aruḷperuvār: X.6 ceñcoṟ kavikāḷ: X.7 tirumāliruñcōlai malai: X.8 cūḻ vicumpu: X.9 muṉiyē nāṉmukaṉē: X.10	• Complete cycle of songs on Tirumokur (X.1.1–X.1.11) • Complete cycle of songs on Anantapuram (X.2.1–X.2.11) • Return of the heroine's voice as a gopī/final decad using the female voice (X.3.1–X.3.11) • Complete cycle of songs on Tiruvattaru (X.6.1–X.6.11) • Complete cycle of songs on Tirumaliruncolai (X.7.1–X.7.11) • Complete cycle of songs on Tirupper (X.8.1–X.8.11) • Description of the ascent to Vaikuṇṭha (X.9.1–X.9.11)

Appendix 2

kaṇṇinuṇ ciṟu tāmpu

Madurakavi Āḻvār

The *Kaṇṇinuṇ ciṟu tāmpu* (The Short Knotted String) is Madurakavi's short poem of eleven verses in praise of his teacher, Śaṭhakōpaṉ-Nammāḻvār and the *Tiruvāymoḻi.* Following in the footsteps of his teacher, this poem also uses the antāti format. The last entry in the First Thousand (Mutal Āyiram) of the *Nālāyira Divya Prabandham,* it is the only work composed by an āḻvār poet in praise of a figure other than Viṣṇu. For this reason, Madurakavi is sometimes not included in the list of twelve āḻvār poets, for he directed his devotion to his teacher, rather than to god. If we accept the traditional relationship assigned to the two poets, and there is no reason not to, this poem represents the first attempt to iconicize and canonize Nammāḻvār and the *Tiruvāymoḻi,* perhaps during or just after his lifetime. Nammāḻvār's poem is not named in the poem; it is simply referred to as sweet song (*iṉ icai*) and as distilling the inscrutable Veda (*aru maṟai*) into Tamiḻ. According to legend, Nāthamuni recited Madurakavi's composition twelve thousand times before receiving a vision of Nammāḻvār, and with that vision therevelation of the *Tiruvāymoḻi* and the remaining three thousand verses of the *Nālāyira Divya Prabandham.*

My father let himself be tied
with a soft short knotted string
Instead of that great mysterious one,
I edge close to the king of southern Kurukūr
I utter his name and nectar seeps from my tongue. (1)

My tongue uttered his name, bliss filled me
I dwell at his golden feet, this is the truth.
I know no other gods, I sing the sweet songs
of Kurukūr's king, and wander. (2)

Even as I wander, I see the dark lovely body
of the god of gods,
this servant ruled by the king of great Kurukūr
has earned this great good. (3)

The holders of the Veda full of goodness
consider me low,
Śaṭhakōpaṉ who rules me
as mother and father, is my king. (4)

Before, I believed in good things others had,
I trusted beautiful women, now
this servant is burnished by love
for the king of Kurukūr, city of golden mansions. (5)

From today and for all time, my lord
has blessed me to sing his praise

He is the king of Tirukkurukūr,
city of mountain-like mansions
he'll never turn me away. You'll see. (6)

Lord Kārimāṟaṉ found me, blessed me
cut all my old terrible deeds
I sing to reveal to the eight directions
Śaṭhakōpaṉ's grace,
the one who uttered beautiful Tamiḻ. (7)

He graced his devotees by blessing them
with the meaning of the difficult Veda,
benevolently singing them
in a thousand sweet Tamiḻ verses,
you can find no greater grace in this world. (8)

He sang the deep meaning of the Veda,
known only to great brahmins,
and set it firmly in my heart.
The moment I was filled with love to serve
Śaṭhakōpaṉ, my king
in that very instant, I received
the gift of service to him. (9)

Even though he has no use for it,
Even though they are unfit
he corrects their ways and accepts them,
that king of Kurukūr,
city of gardens filled with the birds.
I strive only to love his feet. (10)

Those who trust the words
of Madurakavi devoted
to the king of southern Kurukūr
full of love for the devotees
of that lord of love
Vaikuṇṭha is their abode. (11)

Annotations on Kaṇṇinuṇ ciṟu tāmpu

Verse 1

In this verse, the poet turns from worship of Viṣṇu to revering his teacher, Nammāḻvār. He does not refer to him by name, but instead as the king of southern Kurukūr (*teṉ kurukūr nampi*). It is also significant that in this verse, Madurakavi evokes Viṣṇu in his Kṛṣṇa avatāra, particularly to the moment that he is tied to the grinding stone by Yaśodā as a punishment for stealing butter. Nammāḻvār invokes the myth in Tiruvāymoḻi I.3.1 to assert god's inconceivable accessibility. Just thinking about this incident is said to have sent Nammāḻvār into a deep trance.

Verse 2

Madurakavi introduces Nammāḻvār not just as his teacher, but also as the composer of poems. They are simply characterized sweet songs (*pāviṉ iṉicai*). In this verse, he points to taking refuge at Nammāḻvār's feet (*mēviṉēṉ avaṉ poṉṉaṭi*). Nammāḻvār is simply addressed, rather informally, as avaṉ, him. This recalls the opening decads of the *Tiruvāymoḻi* in which Nammāḻvār invokes Viṣṇu as avaṉ and avar. Again, he does not refer to his teacher by name, and simply calls him the king of Kurukūr (kurukūr nampi).

Verse 3

The god of gods (*tevapirāṉ*) is Viṣṇu.

Nammāḻvār's devotion is to Viṣṇu, and Madurakavi's devotion is to Nammāḻvār. Madurakavi is also devoted to Viṣṇu but will find grace through his teacher.

Verse 4

The poet assumes a typical posture here, speaking of his own unworthiness and lowliness. Nammāḻvār makes similar assertions in the *Tiruvāymoḻi* (for instance, VII.9.8), where despite his less than stalwart character, god seeks him out, enters him, or speaks through him. Here, Nammāḻvār assumes that role in relation to Madurakavi. All kinship relationships resolve into the singular relationship between the disciple and the teacher.

Verse 5

The poet explicates the reasons for his lowliness—he coveted the wealth and wives of others. He recognizes Nammāḻvār as the true treasure.

Verse 6

Just as Viṣṇu made Nammāḻvār sing his praise, here Nammāḻvār makes Madurakavi sing his praise (*taṉ pukaḻ ētta aruḷiṉāṉ*).

Even if Madurakavi were to leave Nammāḻvār and return to his previous, base life, Nammāḻvār's grace is such that he would never let him go.

Verse 7

For the first time, Madurakavi refers to Nammāḻvār by a title (Kārimāṟaṉ) and his name, Śaṭhakopaṉ. He also characterizes him as one possessed of shining, beautiful Tamiḻ (*oṇtamiḻ-c-caṭakōpaṉ*). The splendid Tamiḻ is taken to mean the *Tiruvāymoḻi*.

Madurakavi asserts that he is not content simply worshipping Nammāḻvār, but is moved to spread his fame and his words everywhere.

Verse 8

Madurakavi explicitly asserts that Nammāḻvār's poem is a distillation of the Veda. He also tells us that the poem he composed is a thousand verses.

Verse 9

Madurakavi reiterates the statement made in the previous verse, that the *Tiruvāymoḻi* is a distillation of the Veda, which are obscure and difficult to understand.

Verse 10

Nammāḻvār offers grace and refuge although it gains him nothing (*payaṉ aṉṟu*) and people may be unfit *(pāṅku alar)*. His works and his example offer the correct path of devotion.

Verse 11

This is the concluding phala-śruti verse. As is typical in these verses, we get the poet's name Madurakavi. The name—the poet of honey-sweet words—links us back to the first verse, in which he states that just speaking about Nammāḻvār is akin to nectar on his tongue.

Appendix 3

Taṉiyaṉ

Six laudatory verses (taṉiyaṉ) precede the *Tiruvāymoḻi*. They praise the text and its composer, and frame the *Tiruvāymoḻi* as a revealed text. They characterize Nammāḻvār's poem as the Drāviḍa Veda or the Tamiḻ Maṟai, but nowhere in these verses is the poem named as the *Tiruvāymoḻi*. The closest we get to this title is in the Sanskrit taṉiyaṉ, which describes it as the eloquence of Śaṭhakopa (*śaṭhakopa vāṅgmayam*). The later taṉiyaṉs place the *Tiruvāymoḻi* and Nammāḻvār within an emergent ethos of devotion to the teacher, with Rāmānuja being pre-eminent among them.

These taṉiyaṉ are recited before the liturgical recitation of the *Tiruvāymoḻi*. The significance of this text is not only indicated by the number of laudatory verses that precede it—the most of any in the *Divya Prabandham*—but also by their authors. Each of them is a luminary within the Śrīvaiṣṇava sampradāya. The first taṉiyaṉ in Sanskrit is attributed to Nāthamuni, the first Śrīvaiṣṇava preceptor, who is also responsible for rediscovering the text and compiling the *Divya Prabandham*. The remaining five are in Tamiḻ. Taṉiyaṉ 2 is attributed to Nāthamuni's son, Īśvaramuni, who was the father of Yāmuna, the tradition's second teacher. Taṉiyaṉ 3 is believed to have been authored by Yāmuna's son, Coṭṭai Nambi. The fourth taṉiyaṉ is attributed to Rāmānuja's student, while the final two are assigned to Parāśara Bhaṭṭar, the son of Kūrattāḻvāṉ, one of Rāmānuja's foremost disciples. If we accept the traditional authorship of the taṉiyaṉs, they would have been composed between the tenth and twelfth centuries, coinciding with the most productive period of Śrīvaiṣṇava commentarial writing.

Taṉiyaṉ 1: Bhaktāmṛtam

Attributed to Nāthamuni

ca. 10th century

I bow to the ocean of the Drāviḍa Veda,
Śaṭhakopa's eloquent speech,
nectar to devotees, a delight to all the world,
that fulfils the needs of all,
the sum of the meanings
of the thousand branches of the Upaniṣad.

Taṉiyaṉ 2: Tiruvaḻuti

Attributed to Īśvaramuni

ca. 10th/11th century

O mind, be clear and always think
of the feet of the one
who wove the precious Veda
into the endless Tamiḻ antāti,
lauding the auspicious Vaḻuti lands,
and Tirukkurukūr touched by the lovely Porunal.

Taṉiyan 3: Maṉattālum

Attributed to Coṭṭainampi

ca. 11th century

I will not bow before anyone
who does not in thought and word
cherish splendid Kurukūr.
Wealth is nothing
The feet of my father Śaṭhakōpaṉ
are my refuge.

Taṉiyaṉ 4: Ēynta

Attributed to Anantāḻvāṉ

ca. 11th–12th century

I bow to Rāmanuja's feet,
that sage of steadfast fame
so I might hold in my mind
illustrious Śaṭhakōpaṉ's
perfect Tamiḻ Veda.

Taṉiyaṉ 5: Vāṉ Tikaḻum

Attributed to Parāśara Bhaṭṭar

ca. 12th century

Śaṭhakōpaṉ is the mother
who birthed the Tamiḻ Veda
in a thousand verses
praising the glory of Araṅkar,
in his city of gardens and firm walls,

and Rāmānuja is the mother
who nurtured them, made them flourish.

Taṉiyaṉ 6: Mikka Iṟai

Attributed to Parāśara Bhaṭṭar
ca. 12th century

The Veda sweet as a lute
composed by the king of Kurukūr
speaks of the nature of the supreme lord,
and the nature of the deathless self,
it speaks of the right path
the obstacles of past actions,
and the final goal.

Annotations on the Taṉiyaṉ

Taṉiyaṉ 1

In this verse, the *Tiruvāymoḻi* is compared to an ocean and is the distillation of the Upaniṣad.

Taṉiyaṉ 2

Here, the poet does not use the word Tamiḻ, and simply describes the text as rendering the precious and obscure Veda as an antāti (*arumaṟaikaḷ antāti ceytāṉ*). The poet praises not only Nammāḻvār but also his region (Vaḻuti) and his city (Kurukūr).

Taṉiyaṉ 3

This verse follows the lead of the *Tiruvāymoḻi*, which consistently praises devotion to fellow devotees. More specifically, it echoes

Nammāḻvār's decad on Tirukkurukur, which exhorts people to sing that city's fame (IV.10.2).

Taṉiyaṉ 4 and 5

Rāmānuja is evoked in both laudatory verses. In the first instance, he is venerated as the teacher, a mediator and guide, who will lead the devotee to and through the *Tiruvāymoḻi*. In the second instance, he is identified as the one to nurture the *Tiruvāymoḻi*. He is imagined here in his institutional role in ensuring the preservation, transmission and interpretation of the text. The fifth taṉiyaṉ also invokes the temple site of Srirangam, with which Rāmānuja was closely associated.

Taṉiyaṉ 6

This verse encapsulates the five major themes that the *Tiruvāymoḻi* explores—the nature of god, the nature of the self, the path to god, the obstacles to that path, and the final goal, which is mokṣa.

Appendix 4

Commentary on the Tiruvāymoḻi

There are five major traditional commentaries on the *Tiruvāymoḻi*, collectively called *Bhagavat Viṣayam* (Pertaining to God/Sacred Matters). They are composed during the intensely productive and formative period of the Śrīvaiṣṇava tradition between the eleventh and fourteenth centuries. The commentaries are named according to a unit of syllabic length called the paṭi, where each paṭi consists of thirty-two syllables (*grantha*). All of the commentaries are composed in prose in the hybrid Tamiḻ-Sanskrit admixture called Maṇipravāḷa.

The earliest extant commentary is the Āṟāyirappaṭi (the 6000) composed by Rāmānuja's student, Piḷḷāṉ (b.1161), and authorized by that great teacher. Śrīvaiṣṇavas equate Piḷḷāṉ's commentary to the Sanskrit *Viṣṇu Purāṇa*, for that text too consists of 6000 granthas. Piḷḷāṉ's Maṇipravāḷa consists of twice as many Sanskrit words as Tamiḻ words. He incorporates typical phrases from Rāmānuja's works directly into his commentary. Although this is the shortest commentary, he provides a prose explication for every verse of the *Tiruvāymoḻi*. Some verses receive extensive treatment, while for others the comments are cursory.* We find the first reference to the śaṭhāri (the crown inscribed with feet, placed on the head of devotees) as Nammāḻvār in Piḷḷāṉ's commentary. It thus equates for the first time Nammāḻvār to god's grace.†

A generation later, Nañjīyar (1182–1287) composed the *Oṉpatiṉāyirappaṭi* (the 9000). He is said to have learnt the text and its interpretation from his teacher, Parāśara Bhaṭṭar (1094–1174), a close associate and disciple of Rāmānuja. Bhaṭṭar did not produce a *Tiruvāymoḻi* commentary of his own, but two later commentaries—the 24,000 and the 36,000—record his comments. These observations taken together are known as *Bhaṭṭar Nirvāham*. According to the hagiographical tradition, Nañjīyar (original name Madhvācārya) was from present-day Karnataka, and initially a non-dualist (*advaitin*). He was a highly regarded scholar, and Bhaṭṭar wanted to convert him to the Viśiṣṭādvaita system. He was successful in this endeavour. Nañjīyar lived in Melkote for some time, until he gave up worldly life to join his teacher, Bhaṭṭar, in Śrīraṅgam. He is said to have written five major Maṇipravāḷa commentaries on the works of various āḻvārs, but only two survive.‡ Unlike Piḷḷāṉ, Nañjīyar's commentary glosses on words, offering multiple readings of the same. He is also the first to include an introduction (*avatārikai*) to the *Tiruvāymoḻi*, a practice that will be adopted in all subsequent medieval commentaries.

* K.K.A. Venkatachari. *The Maṇipravāḷa Literature of the Śrīvaiṣṇava Ācāryas*. pp. 61–64.

† Vasudha Narayanan. 'Oral and Written Commentaries on the *Tiruvāymoḻi*'. pp. 88–89.

‡ The surviving commentaries are those on the *Tiruvāymoḻi* and Madurakavi's *Kaṇṇinuṇ ciṟu tāmpu*. The missing commentaries are those on Āṇṭāḷ's *Tiruppāvai*, the three *Tiruvantātis* of the first three āḻvār, and Periyāḻvār's *Tiruppallāṇṭu*. Srilata Raman. *Self-surrender (Prapatti) to God in Śrivaiṣṇavism*. pp. 98–99.

Nañjīyar's introduction describes the reasons for the Āḻvār's birth, his nature and the reasons for the composition of the *Tiruvāymoḻi*. He also offers a rousing defence of elevating a Tamiḻ text composed by a poet from the fourth caste.* Nañjīyar entrusts the copying of his manuscript to his student, Nambūr Varadarājar. The student does so, but loses the manuscript while crossing the Kaveri. He rewrites the commentary from memory, but it is infused with new ideas and meanings, which Nañjīyar notices immediately. When Varadarājar confesses, Nañjīyar, rather than getting upset with his student, is pleased with the work. He bestows upon him the name Nampiḷḷai (my child), and appoints him his successor. Although famous as an interpreter of the *Tiruvāymoḻi*, Nampiḷḷai did not commit his own interpretations of the text to writing. This task fell to two of his disciples, Vaṭakku Tiruvīti Piḷḷai (1217–1312)† and Periyavāccāṉ Piḷḷai, who each composed a commentary.

Periyavāccāṉ Piḷḷai (b.1228) authored the *Iruppatinālāyirappaṭi* (the 24,000). Periyavāccāṉ Piḷḷai was also the first Śrīvaiṣṇava scholar to compose a commentary on all four thousand verses that comprise the *Nālāyira Divya Prabandham*, earning him the title *Vyākhyāna Cakravarti* (Emperor of Commentators).

The longest and most comprehensive commentary is Vaṭakku Tiruvīti Piḷḷai's *Muppatāyirappaṭi* (the 36,000). It is popularly referred to as the *Īṭu*. K.K.A. Venkatachari provides us three possible traditional interpretations of *Īṭu*. First, it is derived from the

---

* K.K.A. Venkatachari provides a summary of the proposed charges against elevating the *Tiruvāymoḻi* and Nañjīyar's response. *The Maṇipravāḷa Literature of the Śrīvaiṣṇava Ācāryas*. pp. 25–27.

† Piḷḷai is a very important link in the lineage of teachers, particularly in the Teṅkalai tradition. He was father to Piḷḷai Lokācārya, the foremost teacher of the Teṅkalai sub-sect, and to Aḻakiya Maṇavāḷa Perumāḷ Nāyaṉār, the author of the *Ācārya Hṛdayam*.

verb *īṭupaṭutal* (to be entangled), implying that the *Tiruvāymoḻi* ensnared the author of the commentary. The second meaning is 'equal to', for this commentary is seen as the equivalent of the commentary on Rāmānuja's Śrībhāṣya, which also has 36,000 granthas. The final meaning is that this is simply a record, and not an original work, as the Śrīvaiṣṇava tradition regards the commentary as a record of an oral discourse by the great teacher and scholar, Nampiḷḷai.

Each of these commentaries can be understood as representing a lineage of transmission, reaching back to Rāmānuja. The commentaries grow more long and detailed, providing analysis and interpretation for each verse of the text. Commentators generally identify a central theme in a given decad, and explicate individual verses accordingly.

Below, I follow the lead of the *Īṭu* to summarize the main themes inherent in each set of hundred verses. This summary is adapted from the second of the *Īṭu*'s three introductions (*śrīyaḥpati*), which provides a brief summary of each Hundred.

General Introduction

The god of gods (Sarveśvaraṉ), the beloved of Śrī, is the repository of all auspicious qualities (kalyāṇa guṇa). It's his very form. He gave his grace causelessly (*nirhetu*) to the Āḻvār (i.e. Nammāḻvār) who suffered many births, whose mind was restless and brought him clarity. All of this is expressed in the text's opening line, uyarvaṟa.

In the *Tiruvāymoḻi*, Nammāḻvār makes clear the meaning of the *dvayam* (*śrīman nārāyaṇāya caraṇau prapadye/śrīmate nārāyaṇāya namaḥ*).* In the first three centums (that is, *Tiruvāymoḻi*

* The dvayam is the second of three sacred mantras that comprise the rahasya traya (the secret three). These three mantras are understood as distilling the core

I, II and III), he explicates the meaning of the second line of the dvayam (śrīmate nārāyaṇāya namaḥ: obeisance to Nārāyaṇa). In the next three Hundreds (that is, *Tiruvāymoḻi* IV, V and VI), he explores the first part of the dvayam (śrīman nārāyaṇāya caraṇau prapadye: I take refuge at the feet of Śrī and Nārāyaṇa). In the next three sections (that is, *Tiruvāymoḻi* VII, VIII and IX), he explains the requirements for the upāya (way), the conditions of the self and the relationship with god that has developed that keeps him from the grief of attachment. The final Hundred (*Tiruvāymoḻi* X) describes the Āḻvār's achievement of his goal as he desired.

The First Hundred: Tiruvāymoḻi I (I.1–I.10)

The First Hundred opens with a quotation from the opening verse of the *Tiruvāymoḻi*

uyarvaṟa uyarnalam uṭaiyavaṉ evaṉ avaṉ
ayarvaṟum amarararkaḷ atipati evaṉ avaṉ
tuyararu cuṭaraṭi toḻutu eḻu eṉ maṉaṉē (I.1.1)

The Āḻvār begins by praising god as the one with all auspicious qualities (kalyāṇa guṇa), the one who has a form and attributes, who is dear to the gods, who is with Śrī, and is the cause of all things (*pramāṇam*). Thus, the Āḻvār decides to serve [at] his feet, for this is the only goal. Since he (god) is described as *uḷaṉ cuṭar miku curuti:* he's in the luminous śruti (I.1.7), he is the authority

principles of the Śrīvaiṣṇava philosophy and that path to surrender (prapatti). The dvayam is also called the *mantra-ratna* (the jewel among mantras) for it succinctly encapsulates both the way (upāya) and the goal (upeya) as the divine couple Śrī and Nārāyaṇa. The dvayam is as follows: śrīman nārāyaṇa caraṇau śaraṇam prapadye/śrīmate nārāyaṇaya namah: I take refuge at the feet of Śrī and Nārāyaṇa/Obeisance to Śrī and Nārāyaṇa.

spoken of in the flawless Veda. If you ask, 'who has these qualities, who has this nature', the Āḻvār describes him grandly as *vaṇpukaḻ nāraṇaṉ*: Nāraṇaṉ of limitless glory (I.2.10), *tiruvuṭai aṭikaḷ*: the feet of the one who is with Śrī (I.3.8) and *celva nāraṇaṉ*: auspicious Nāraṇaṉ (I.10.8).

He then asks his heart-mind (maṉam) to rise up—*toḻutu eḻu maṉaṉē* (I.1.1), and that he will sing of him, hold him, worship him, never forget him: *ayarppilaṉ alaṟṟuvaṉ taḻuvuvaṉ vaṇaṅkuvaṉ amarntē*: (I.3.10). As he begins by asking his mind to rise up (I.1.1) and concludes with *col paṇicey āyiram*: the thousand sung in service (I.10.11), the Āḻvār asserts that loving service (*kaiṅkaryam*) to god is the sole goal (puruṣārtha).

The Second Hundred: Tiruvāymoḻi II (II.1–II.10)

The thrust of the Second Hundred is on loving service, kaiṅkaryam, to god. The Āḻvār rids himself of the obstacles to kaiṅkaryam that emerge from living in the world (II.3.10). He wants this kaiṅkaryam to be shared with like-minded devotees. As he advised these devotees on entering the endless land of good, *nalam antam illatu ōr nāṭu pukuvīr* (II.8.4), god believes that he is fixed on Paramapadam (Vaikuṇṭha), and so he grants it to him. But as he is poised to enter, the Āḻvār says, *em mā vīṭṭu tiṟamum ceppam*: I don't ask for that great release. I have no compulsive desire for it. As he took me for himself: *taṉakkēyāka eṉṉaikkoḷum ītē* (II.9.4), and he asked me to serve only him, this is the only thing I want. In this way, he asserted that his goal (puruṣārtha) is not Vaikuṇṭha, but eternal service, kaiṅkarya.

The Third Hundred: Tiruvāymoḻi III (III.1–III.10)

When god (īśvaraṉ) witnessed the Āḻvār's pleasure in kaiṅkaryam (loving service) and the alacrity with which he took to it, he revealed to him undisturbed and peaceful Tirumalai (Tiruvēṅkaṭam), which is suited to such service. Being thus directed, the Āḻvar asserts the value of the devotees' service to other devotees, *vaḻu ilā aṭimai ceyya vēṇṭum nām*, (III.3.1), and sings of this service (III.7), which is itself the culmination of service to Viṣṇu.

The Fourth Hundred: Tiruvāymoḻi IV (IV.1–IV.10)

In the Fourth Hundred, he (the Āḻvār) shows the path to this goal (puruṣārtha), which is the feet of Nārayaṇa (*tirunāraṇaṉ tāḷ*, IV.1.1). He also takes on those with opposing points of view, saying that even if you reach heaven, you'll return to earth [if you don't think of him] (*kuṭimaṉṉum iṉ cuvarkkam*, IV.1.9); even those who have meditated [will return] (*ellām viṭṭa iṟukal iṟappu*, IV.1.10). He thus preaches that renunciation is inimical to the path. He too practises this, as one who fully experienced the five senses (*aiṅkuruvi kaṇṭa iṉpam*, IV.9.10), but it was only the sight of Viṣṇu and Śrī that enabled him to reach his feet.

The Fifth Hundred: Tiruvāymoḻi V (V.1–V.10)

In the Fifth Hundred, as the Āḻvār says that 'you showed me the way offering your feet as refuge' (*āṟu eṉakku niṉ pātamē caraṇākat-tantoḻintāy*, V.7.10), god offered his feet as the means (*upāyam*) to gain what one desires and to cease desire for what one does not want.

The Sixth Hundred: Tiruvāymoḻi VI (VI.1–VI.10)

In the Sixth Hundred, he seeks the aid of those who will guide the upāyam that he (Viṣṇu) has given, and thus accepts the great goddess (*periya piṟāṭṭiyār*) as the mediator (puruṣakāra) for he says, 'I sought refuge and settled at your feet, the one on whose chest resides the goddess Śrī' (*alarmēl maṅkai uṟai mārpā/uṉ aṭikkīḻ amarntu pukunentēṉ*, VI.10.10). Thus, the three successive Hundreds IV, V and VI, can be seen to express the meaning of the dvayam.

Additionally, in this Hundred, the two messenger decads, VI.1 and VI.8, may be interpreted as seeking the aid of the teacher, or ācāryas.

The Seventh Hundred: Tiruvāymoḻi (VII.1–VII.10)

In the Seventh Hundred, although he (the Āḻvār) had taken refuge and accepted Viṣṇu as the way to achieving his goal, as it did not bear fruit immediately, he was dejected. He calls out to him as the 'guardian of sea and earth, dark as storm clouds, with a disc bright as lightning' (*kaṭal ñālam kākkiṉṟa/ miṉṉu nēmiyiṉāy*, VII:1.2), and enumerates his virtues as the one who is the way (*upāyopayogi*). In the previous Hundred, he had called to him saying, 'come to me bearing your sharp disc and white conch' (*kūr ār āḻi veṇ caṅku ēnti vārāy*, VI.9.1), he gives him this vision, of him with a white conch and holding the disc (*veḷḷai curi caṅkōṭu āḻi ēnti*, VII.3.1), but as this is a mental experience and not a corporeal one, he speaks in the mode of separation (*viśleṣa*).

The Eighth Hundred: Tiruvāymoḻi (VIII.1–VIII.10)

In the Eighth Hundred, the Āḻvār, distressed that the internal vision that he had received earlier was not one he could experience bodily as he desired, said, 'You take the form your devotees love/ they rejoice in your feats, and your mysterious ways' (*umar ukantu ukantu uruvam niṉ uruvam āki uṉ taṉakku aṉparāṉār*, VIII.1.4). That he who takes the form devotees desire does not show himself must require that some value exists in the ātman. Thus, he composes with the intention of recognizing this value. (That is, god wants the Āḻvār to recognize the value of his own self [ātman], which is characterized by its exclusive dependence and servitude to god.)

The Ninth Hundred: Tiruvāymoḻi (IX.1–IX.10)

In the Ninth Hundred, in response to the doubts that besiege the Āḻvār, god reveals his nature as independent of all things, (*nirupādhika*, that is unlimited by *upādhi*s or attributes), and says that he is Nārāyaṇa, and possessed of all power and effort. He will bring all of your desires to fruition. In response, the Āḻvār says that god is the one of limitless perfection (*cīlam ellai ilāṉ*, IX.3.11) and becomes immersed in his nature.

The Tenth Hundred: Tiruvāymoḻi (X.1–X.10)

In the Tenth Hundred, witnessing his (the Āḻvār's) sorrow and his inability to bear this sorrow, he (Viṣṇu) came to Tirumōkūr as the object of his (the Āḻvār's) desire and revealed to him the path to Vaikuṇṭha (arccirāti gati), just as he (the Āḻvār) had wanted. He (Viṣṇu) makes him (the Āḻvār) sing of the treasure he (the Āḻvār) had received, saying, 'you cut even my great love for you, and engulfed me' (*eṉ avā āṟac cūḻntāyē*, X.10.10).

Appendix 5

Myths in the *Tiruvāymoḻi*

The myths are listed in the order in which they first appear in the text.

Myth	Verse Number
Eating/swallowing the worlds: Viṣṇu	I.1.7; I.1.8; I.1.10; I.8.7; I.10.5; II.2.1; II.3.4; II.6.2; II.6.7; II.7.12; II.8.8; III.6.1; III.7.10; IV.2.1; IV.4.9; IV.7.1; V.4.1; V.6.1; V.7.7; V.9.7; V.10.6; VI.1.2; VI.2.4; VI.2.7; VI.6.3; VI.9.11; VI.10.1; VII.3.9; VII.4.4; VIII.3.4; VIII.4.11; VIII.5.5; IX.1.1; X.7.6; X.8.2
Razing of the three cities: Viṣṇu	I.1.8; I.3.9 [as Śiva]; III.10.4 [Śiva-Tripurāntaka]; V.10.4*; VII.6.7
Kṛṣṇa steals/eats butter: Kṛṣṇa	I.3.1; I.5.1; I.5.8; I.8.5; II.3.8; II.10.6; III.8.3; IV.4.6; IV.8.11; V.10.3; VI.2.11; VII.7.2
Kṛṣṇa tied up [for stealing butter]: Kṛṣṇa	I.3.1; VI.4.4

Creating the world from his navel/ Brahmā rising from a lotus: Viṣṇu	I.3.9; I.9.9; II.5.2; II.8.3; V.10.8; VII.1.11; VII.6.1; VII.6.5; VIII.4.11; IX.3.10; X.10.3
Feet measured the world/took the world/crossing the world: Trivikrama	I.3.10; I.5.3; I.8.10; I.10.1; I.10.5; II.1.10; II.2.3; II.8.6; II.8.7; III.1.10; III.2.9; III.3.8; III.3.11; III.7.10; III.8.11; IV.3.7; IV.4.8; IV.5.10; IV.7.2; IV.7.3; IV.8.6; IV.10.3; V.3.5; V.4.4; V.4.10; V.6.1; V.9.8; V.10.5; V.10.9; VI.3.11; VI.4.6; VI.5.3; VI.6.1; VI.6.4; VI.9.6; VI.9.9; VI.10.6; VII.1.3; VII.2.2; VII.4.1; VII.6.1; VII.10.2; VIII.1.5; VIII.2.9; VIII.3.8; VIII.4.4; VIII.5.7; VIII.6.7; VIII.10.3; VIII.3.5; IX.2.2; IX.2.11; IX.3.2; IX.4.10; IX.5.5; IX.8.7; IX.9.2; IX.10.5; X.1.5; X.9.3
Churning of the ocean: Kūrma	I.3.11; III.4.9; III.8.1; IV.7.5; IV.9.1; V.6.5; V.10.10; VI.2.3; VII.1.7; VII.1.10; VII.2.5; VII.4.2; VIII.1.1; VIII.1.5; VIII.3.10; VIII.4.4; IX.2.11; IX.3.6; X.10.7
The youth who stole/took the world/asked for three steps/alms: Vāmana	I.4.3; I.8.6; I.10.1; III.2.2; III.3.3; III.8.2; III.8.5; III.8.9; IV.8.6; V.10.9; VI.1.11; VI.4.8; VI.9.2; VII.5.6
King/chief/leader of cowherds: Kṛṣṇa	I.5.1; I.5.6; IV.6.6; V.6.6; VI.2.10; VIII.6.9; IX.8.6; IX.9.1; IX.9.2; X.3.10; X.3.11
Taming/killing of the seven bulls: Kṛṣṇa	I.5.1; I.8.7; II.5.7; II.9.10; III.5.4; IV.2.5; IV.3.1; IV.8.4; V.6.6; V.7.9; V.10.2; VI.4.6; VII.2.9
Making/ordering Brahmā to make the world: Viṣṇu	I.5.3; II.2.4; III.1.7; VI.6.4; VII.5.4; VIII.10.7

The encounter with a hunchback: Kṛṣṇa or Rāma	I.5.5
Piercing the seven trees with a single arrow: Rāma	I.5.6; I.7.6; II.5.7; II.6.9; VI.10.5; IX.1.2
Eating and spitting out the worlds: Viṣṇu	I.5.8; II.8.7; III.1.10; III.4.9; III.6.8; IV.3.2; IV.3.6; IV.5.10; IV.6.4; IV.9.8*; IV.10.3; V.10.5; VI.4.11; VII.1.3; VII.2.2; VIII.1.5; VIII.9.4; VIII.10.4; IX.3.2; IX.9.2; IX.9.11; X.2.3; X.5.3
Suckling the poisoned breast/milk of the demoness (Pūtanā): Kṛṣṇa	I.5.9; I.9.5; II.10.9; IV.3.4; IV.4.6; IV.8.3; V.3.3; V.3.8; V.8.11; V.10.3; VI.4.4; VI.6.8; VII.3.5; X.5.6
Giving nectar to the immortals/ gods: Kūrma/Mohinī	I.6.6; I.7.9; III.7.5
Slashing the arms of Laṅkā's king/ killing him (Rāvaṇa): Rāma	I.6.7; IV.3.1; V.6.9; VIII.6.2
Child of cowherds: Kṛṣṇa	I.7.2; I.7.3; I.7.9
Kṛṣṇa beaten [for stealing butter]	I.7.3
Playing/flirting with the cowherd girls: Kṛṣṇa	I.7.5; IV.2.2
Lifting the earth/digging the earth/splitting the earth: Varāha	I.7.6; I.9.2; II.3.5; II.8.7; II.10.7; IV.5.10; IV.10.3; V.6.1; V.7.4; V.7.6; V.10.5; VI.6.5; VII.1.3; VII.2.9; VII.4.3; VII.5.5; VII.6.7; VIII.1.2; VIII.1.5; VIII.4.3; IX.3.2; IX.9.2; X.5.3; X.10.7
Embracing Piṉṉai/Piṉṉai's beloved	I.7.8; III.9.8; IV.8.4; VI.4.2; VIII.1.7; VIII.1.8; IX.8.2; IX.8.4; IX.10.4; X.4.3

Tearing the jaws of the horse (Keśin): Kṛṣṇa	I.8.2; II.1.10; IV.5.1; V.10.2; VI.5.9; VI.8.7
Lifting of the mountain (Govardhana): Kṛṣṇa	I.8.4; II.10.4; III.3.8; III.5.3; IV.5.7; V.6.5; V.6.6; V.10.5; VI.4.1; VII.2.8; VII.4.10; VII.4.11; VII.6.2; VII.6.3; VII.7.5; IX.4.3; X.4.8
Cowherd/caring for cows/grazing cows: Kṛṣṇa	I.8.8; II.2.2; III.2.9; III.3.9; III.8.3; III.10.4; IV.2.5; IV.3.4; IV.4.5; IV.8.4; VI.2.2; VI.2.4; VI.2.10; VI.4.2; VI.4.3; VI.5.3; VII.6.10; VIII.1.7; VIII.1.8; VIII.4.1; VIII.6.9; VIII.7.4; VIII.8.4; IX.9.5; X.3.1–X.3.7; X.3.9; X.4.8
Taking the form of the fish: Matsya	I.8.8; II.8.5; V.1.10
Taking the form of the pig/boar: Varāha	I.8.8; IV.2.6; IV.5.6; V.1.10; V.7.6; VII.5.5
Breaking the tusks of the elephant/killing the elephant (Kuvalayāpīḍa): Kṛṣṇa	I.9.2; II.7.2; IV.1.4; IV.3.1; IV.6.5; V.3.8; VI.4.3; VIII.4.1; VIII.10.6; IX.4.11; X.5.2; X.6.6
Resting on a banyan leaf: Kṛṣṇa	I.9.4; II.2.7; III.7.10; IV.2.1; VI.2.4; VII.1.4; VIII.3.4; IX.10.1; X.4.4
Burning/destroying of Laṅkā: Rāma	II.1.3; II.4.3; II.4.4; II.4.10; II.6.9; II.9.10; III.6.2; IV.2.8; IV.8.5; V.7.2; VI.1.10; VI.2.1; VII.3.7; VII.4.7
Kicking the cart (Śakaṭāsura): Kṛṣna	II.1.8; V.3.3; V.3.8; V.10.3; VI.4.4; VI.6.8; VI.9.4; VII.3.5
Crawling between the maruta trees: Kṛṣṇa	II.1.10; III.8.10; V.1.2; V.3.8; V.7.9; VI.10.5; VII.3.5
Giving alms to Śiva (Bhikṣāṭaṇa)	II.2.2
Cut the demon's nose (Śūrpanakhā): Rāma	II.3.6

Destroying the demon clan (Rāvaṇa): Rāma	II.3.11; II.7.10; VII.6.9
Cutting the arms of Bāṇa: Kṛṣṇa	II.4.2; III.8.9; IV.8.9; VI.4.8; VII.4.8; VII.10.7
Killing of Kaṁsa: Kṛṣṇa	II.4.8; III.5.5; III.8.9; VI.4.5; VII.6.10; VIII.4.1; IX.6.11
Pot-dancer: Kṛṣṇa	II.5.11; II.7.4; III.6.3; III.6.7; IV.2.5; IV.4.6*; IV.5.9; IV.10.10; VIII.5.6; VIII.6.5; IX.7.1; X.1.11
Killing of Hiraṇyaṉ: Narasiṁha	II.6.6*; IV.8.7; VII.2.5; VII.4.6; VII.5.8; VII.6.11; VIII.1.3; IX.3.7; IX.4.7; IX.10.6; X.6.4; X.6.10
Viṣṇu as Kāma's father: Kṛṣṇa	II.7.8; VIII.10.9; X.2.8
Rescuing the elephant (Gajendra): Viṣṇu	II.8.2; II.9.1; III.1.9; III.5.1; V.1.7; VII.10.8; VIII.7.2; IX.2.5
Viṣṇu as the horse: Hayagrīva	II.8.5
Viṣṇu as the turtle: Kūrma	II.8.5; V.1.10
Viṣṇu's avatāra as man: Paraśurāma, Rāma, Kṛṣṇa	II.8.5; VI.4.7
Pārthaṉ placing flowers at feet: Kṛṣṇa	II.8.6
Emerging from the pillar/ Hiraṇyaṉ: Narasiṁha	II.8.9
Roaming with cows: Kṛṣṇa	II.10.8
Bharata war: Kṛṣṇa	III.2.3; V.10.1; VI.4.8; VI.4.10; VII.4.5; VIII.1.4; VIII.5.10; X.6.4
Defeat of the hundred (Kaurava)/ blessing, protecting, advising the five (Pāṇḍava)	III.5.7; III.6.10; III.7.11; V.6.5; V.7.4; V.10.1; VII.3.10; VII.5.9; VII.6.10; VIII.5.8
Dancing of the kuravai: Kṛṣṇa	III.6.3; IV.2.2; V.10.2; VI.4.1
Anger towards Hiraṇyaṉ and grace towards Prahlāda: Narasiṁha	III.6.6

Son of Daśaratha: Rāma	III.6.8; X.1.8
Poison to/killer of Laṅkā's king: Rāma	III.8.2; V.6.9
Defeat of Bāṇa/protection of Bāṇa/defeat of Śiva: Kṛṣṇa	III.10.4; VII.4.8; VII.10.7
Retrieving from heaven the dead sons of the brahmin: Kṛṣṇa	III.10.5; VI.4.9
Hearing a flute/flute-player/ holding a flute: Kṛṣṇa	IV.4.6; IV.8.4; VI.2.2; VI.4.2; IX.9.5; IX.9.8; IX.9.10
Charioteer/fighting for the Five (Pāṇḍava): Kṛṣṇa	IV.6.1; VI.8.3; VII.5.9; VII.8.3; VIII.5.8; X.6.4
As the king of Dvārakā: Kṛṣṇa	IV.6.10; V.3.6
Spitting out the worlds: Viṣṇu	IV.9.8
Hiding the worlds: Viṣṇu	IV.10.3
Viṣṇu relieves Śiva-Bhikṣāṭaṇa of his curse: Viṣṇu	IV.10.4; X.2.6
Śiva saves Mārkaṇḍeya through Viṣṇu's grace/Mārkaṇḍeya: Viṣṇu	IV.10.8; V.2.7; VII.5.7
Viṣṇu as dwarf/cunning youth: Vāmana	IV.10.10; V.1.10; V.9.6; VI.1.11; VI.6.9; VI.9.2; VIII.2.8; VIII.2.9; VIII.4.4; VIII.10.3
Viṣṇu as man-lion: Narasiṁha	V.1.10; VII.5.8; IX.3.7
Viṣṇu as Kalki	V.1.10
Killing the bird (Bakāsura): Kṛṣṇa	V.3.8; V.7.8; V.7.9; VI.4.6
Viṣṇu in disguise to destroy demons: Buddha*	V.10.4
Eating food meant for the celestials: Kṛṣṇa	V.10.5
Marrying the earth: Varāha	V.10.5
Cutting down kings: Paraśurāma	VI.2.10

Vanquishing/dancing on the serpent Kāliya: Kṛṣṇa	VI.4.1
Killing the wrestlers: Kṛṣṇa	VI.4.3; VI.6.10; VII.4.5; VIII.4.1
Birth of Kṛṣṇa/born in Mathurā: Kṛṣṇa	VI.4.5; VII.10.4; VIII.5.9; IX.1.3–IX.1.10
Fells the kuruntu tree: Kṛṣṇa	VI.4.6; VI.6.8
Messenger to kings: Kṛṣṇa	VI.6.4
Throwing the calf-demon (Vatsāsura): Kṛṣṇa	VII.3.5
Viṣṇu as Rāma: Rāma	VII.5.1; VII.5.2
Enmity of Śiśupāla: Kṛṣṇa	VII.5.3
The killing of Māli: Viṣṇu	VII.6.8; IX.2.6
Gifting of Laṅkā: Rāma	VII.6.9
Defeat of enemies/marriage to Rukmiṇī: Kṛṣṇa	VII.10.6
Binding the ocean: Rāma	VIII.1.5
Kaṁsa's demons/henchmen: Kṛṣṇa	X.3.9; X.3.10
Kṛṣṇa and Balarāma: Kṛṣṇa	X.3.10

*reference to the myth is not explicit

Appendix 6

Viṣṇu's Names in the *Tiruvāymoḻi*

Viṣṇu's names are listed in the order in which they first occur in the text.

Name	Verse Number
Nāraṇaṉ (Nārāyaṇaṉ)	I.2.10; I.3.3; I.3.7; I.4.5; I.4.9; I.10.8, II.1.7; II.7.1; II.7.2; III.7.4; IV.3.3; IV.3.6; IV.4.2; IV.4.4; IV.4.7; IV.7.1; IV.9.11; IV.10.8; V.7.11; V.9.10; VII.5.2; VIII.2.7; VIII.6.10; IX.3.1; IX.8.3; IX.8.7; X.5.1; X.5.2; X.6.2; X.6.3; X.9.1; X.9.2
Bhagavan	I.3.5
Hari	I.3.6; III.10.4; VII.6.10; VII.8.11; VIII.2.7; VIII.6.10; IX.3.3; X.10.11
Tirumāl	I.4.7; I.5.7, II.1.1; III.1.1; III.5.2; III.9.6; IV.1.2; IV.4.8; V.6.11; V.8.7; VI.5.11; VI.7.3; VI.7.5; VI.7.6; VI.9.11; VII.9.9; VII.9.11; VIII.3.8; VIII.3.9; VIII.6.11; VIII.7.11; VIII.8.11; VIII.9.1; IX.4.1; IX.8.7; IX.8.10; X.6.9; X.7.6; X.7.8; X.8.1
Neṭumāl	I.4.8; I.5.10; I.6.6; II.7.13; IV.4.4; IV.4.7; V.8.1; VI.1.4; VI.1.9; VI.5.10; VI.7.7; VI.9.8; VII.10.7; VIII.9.11; VIII.10.1

Kaṇṇaṉ	I.4.11; I.5.7, I.8.2, I.9.1; I.9.4; I.9.10; I.9.11; II.2.1; II.2.9; II.3.7; II.3.9; II.4.7; II.5.5; II.7.1; II.7.13; II.8.8; II.8.9; II.8.10; II.9.3; II.9.4; III.2.7; III.2.8; III.2.10; III.4.1; III.4.2; III.4.6; III.4.8; III.4.9; III.5.1; III.6.5; III.6.10; III.7.2; III.7.6; III.9.2; III.9.11; III.10.2; III.10.6; III.10.8; III.10.10; IV.1.3; IV.1.11; IV.2.10; IV.2.11; IV.3.5, IV.3.11; IV.4.7; IV.4.8; IV.4.9; IV.4.10; IV.4.11; IV.6.9; IV.7.11; V.1.1; V.1.4; V.1.5; V.1.11; V.2.7; V.2.10; V.2.11; V.3.4; V.3.11; V.4.2; V.4.5; V.4.8; V.7.6; VI.1.4; VI.1.9; VI.3.4; VI.3.8; VI.5.4; VI.6.7; VI.7.1; VI.7.9; VI.8.1; VI.8.6; VI.8.9; VII.1.8; VII.1.9; VII.2.3; VII.2.7; VII.3.1; VII.3.2; VII.3.5; VII.3.9; VII.5.7; VII.5.11; VII.7.1; VII.7.4; VII.7.8; VII.7.11; VII.8.4; VII.8.7; VII.8.8; VII.8.9; VII.10.4; VII.10.7; VIII.1.2; VIII.2.3; VIII.2.11; VIII.5.1; VIII.5.6; VIII.9.6; VIII.9.7; VIII.9.9; IX.1.9; IX.1.10; IX.1.11; IX.3.4; IX.4.8; IX.5.1; IX.5.4; IX.5.6; IX.5.7; IX.5.8; IX.5.9; IX.6.5; IX.6.6; IX.6.7; IX.9.3; IX.9.7; IX.9.8; X.3.1; X.3.2; X.3.5; X.3.6; X.4.11; X.5.1; X.5.11
Mādhava(ṉ)	I.5.5; I.5.6; I.6.10; I.6.11; II.7.2; II.7.3; IV.3.4; V.2.2; VIII.2.7; X.2.10; X.4.10; X.5.6; X.5.7; X.9.4; X.9.5; X.9.8
Govinda(ṉ)	I.5.5; II.7.3; II.7.4; III.1.3; IV.4.3; IV.4.5; IV.4.6; VII.10.3; VIII.2.7; VIII.6.7; IX.5.2; X.2.6; X.2.7; X.3.4; X.6.7; X.9.8
Madhusūda(ṉ)	I.5.5; II.1.5; II.3.1; II.6.4; II.7.5; II.7.6; VI.7.11; VI.8.7; VI.8.11; VII.1.3; VII.8.1; VII.10.3; VIII.6.6; X.4.7
Keśava(ṉ)	I.5.6; I.9.2; II.6.11; II.7.1; III.10.11; IV.9.11; VI.4.11; VII.5.3; VII.5.6; VIII.2.7; X.2.1; X.6.2; X.9.7
Śrīdhara(ṉ)	I.5.6; III.5.4; IV.4.2

Māl	I.5.11; II.2.3; II.8.7; III.4.6; III.4.9; III.5.10; III.6.6; V.1.8; V.3.5; VI.6.1; VI.10.8; VIII.2.6; VIII.2.7; VIII.7.9; IX.9.11; IX.10.1; X.4.2; X.7.6
Narasiṅka/ Narasiṁha	II.4.1; IX.3.7; IX.4.7
Vāmaṉaṉ	II.4.11; II.7.7; II.7.8; III.2.2; III.8.5; IV.3.4; IV.3.7; IV.4.1; IV.7.2; VII.5.6; VII.8.1; VII.8.6; VIII.5.1; VIII.6.10; VIII.7.1; X.2.9
Lord of Vaikuṇṭha/Master of Vaikuṇṭha (Vaikuntaṉ/ Vaikuṇṭha Nāthaṉ)	I.5.4; II.6.1; V.2.5; VII.9.6; VII.9.7; VIII.2.7; X.9.9
Kunta(ṉ)	II.6.1; VII.9.7
Kōvalaṉ (Gopāla)	II.7.4; VII.6.4; VII.6.5; X.1.6; X.9.7
Viṣṇu	II.7.4; II.7.5
Trivikrama(ṉ)	II.7.6; II.7.7; V.7.11
Śrīdhara(ṉ)	II.7.8; II.7.9; IV.4.2
Hṛṣīkeśa(ṉ)	II.7.9; II.7.10
Padmanābhaṉ	II.7.10; II.7.11; VII.6.1
Dāmodara(ṉ)	II.7.11; II.7.12; IV.7.3; X.4.1
Aḻakar	II.10.2
Puruṣa	III.4.4; IV.8.3*
Acyutaṉ	III.4.4; III.4.5; III.4.9; III.5.11; III.6.8; III.10.4; IV.4.3; IV.5.3; V.2.9; VII.3.11; VII.8.2; VII.8.10
Aṉantaṉ	III.4.9
Tirunāraṇaṉ	IV.1.1
Ādippirāṉ	IV.10.1; IV.10.2; IV.10.8; IV.10.9
Polintu Niṉra Pirāṉ	IV.10.5

Vāsudevaṉ	V.3.6
Kākuttaṉ (Kākutstha)	V.4.3; VI.6.9; VII.2.3; VIII.1.2; IX.5.6
Tirukkuṟuṅkuṭi Nambi	V.5.1–V.5.10
Vāṉamāmalai	V.7.6
Deyvanāyakaṉ	V.7.10; V.7.11
Kōlappirāṉ	V.9.6
Oppārillappaṉ	VI.3.9
Devapiraṉ	VI.5.2; VI.5.11
Aravindalocaṉa	VI.5.8
Varāha	VI.6.5; X.10.7
Vaittamānidhi [Perumāḷ]	VI.7.11
Makara Neṭuṅkuḻaik Kātaṉ	VII.3.10
Rāma	VII.5.1
Tirukkuṟaḷappaṉ	VII.10.2
Māyakkūttaṉ	VIII.2.4
Imaiyavarappaṉ	VIII.4.2
Māyappirāṉ	VIII.9.10
Kāyciṉa Vēntaṉ	IX.2.6
Kātkarai Appā/ Appaṉ	IX.6.2; IX.6.3; IX.6.4; IX.6.5; IX.6.8; IX.6.10
Kālamegha [Perumāḷ]	X.1.1
Āttaṉ [Āptaṉ]	X.1.6

*As Paramapuruṭaṉ (Puruṣa)

Appendix 7

Sacred Sites in the *Tiruvāymoḻi*

The sacred sites (Divya Deśa) are listed in the order in which they first occur in the text. Wherever applicable the site's current name is also listed. The region in which the site is located is also provided.

Name	Contemporary Name	Region	Verse Number
Kurukūr/ Tirukkurukūr	Alvar Tirunagari *Nava Tirupati site*	Pāṇṭiya Nāḍu	All phala-śruti verses except I.6.11; II.8.11; VI.9.11; VII.1.11; VII.4.11; VIII.8.11; IX.2.11; X.5.11 IV.10.1–IV.10.11 (entire decad)

The cosmic sea/ ocean of milk (Pāṟkaṭal)	N/A	Non-terrestrial	I.4.10; I.5.4; I.6.6; I.9.2; II.2.6; II.4.7; II.5.7*; II.6.5*; III.5.6; III.6.2; III.6.3; III.7.1*; III.10.2; IV.1.6; IV.3.3; IV.4.2; V.1.3; V.2.4; V.3.7; VI.5.3; VI.6.5; VI.9.5; VII.1.11; VII.2.7; VII.8.4; VIII.1.5; VIII.1.8; VIII.2.8*; VIII.4.6; VIII.5.4; VIII.6.8; VIII.7.10*; VIII.7.11; VIII.10.8; X.5.4; X.7.8*; X.9.7

Vaikuṇṭha	N/A	Non-terrestrial	I.5.4; II.1.11; II.5.11; II.6.1**; IV.4.1; IV.4.11; IV.7.11; IV.8.11; IV.10.11; V.2.5**; V.3.11; V.4.11; V.10.11; VI.9.5***; VII.6.5***; VII.6.10; VII.9.6**; VII.9.7**; VIII.2.7**; VIII.2.8; VIII.6.5; VIII.6.8; VIII.6.11; IX.2.4; IX.3.7; IX.3.11; IX.7.5***; IX.8.5***; IX.10.5; X.6.5***; X.7.8; X.8.4***; X.9.3; X.9.8; X.9.9

Vēṅkaṭam	Tirumala *Svayam vyakta kṣetra*	Vaṭa Nāḍu	I.8.3; II.6.9; II.6.10; II.7.11; III.3.1–III.3.10 (entire decad); III.5.8; III.9.1; IV.5.11; VI.6.11; VI.9.5***; VI.10.1–VI.10.11 (entire decad); VIII.2.1; VIII.2.8; IX.3.8; X.4.4***; X.5.6; X.7.8
Kuṟuṅkuṭi/ Tirukkuṟuṅkuṭi	Tirukkuṟuṅkuṭi	Pāṇṭiya Nāḍu	I.10.9; III.9.2; V.5.1–V.5.11 (entire decad)
Māliruñcōlai/ Tirumāliruñcōlai	Aḻakar Kōyil	Pāṇṭiya Nāḍu	II.10.1–II.10.11 (entire decad); X.7.1–X.7.11 (entire decad); X.8.1; X.8.6

Dvārakā	Dvārakā	Vaṭa Nāḍu	IV.6.10; V.3.6
Śrīvaramaṅgalam Vāṉamāmalai	Nanguneri *Svayam vyakta kṣetra*	Pāṇṭiya Nāḍu	V.7.1–V.7.11 (entire decad)
Tirukkuṭantai	Kumbakonam	Cōḻa Nāḍu	V.8.1–V.8.11 (entire decad); VIII.2.6; X.9.7
Tiruvallavāḻ	Tiruvallavāḻ	Cēra Nāḍu/ Malai Nāḍu	V.9.1–V.9.11
Tiruvaṇvaṇḍūr	Tiruvaṇvaṇḍūr *Pāṇḍava temple—Nakula*	Cēra Nāḍu/ Malai Nāḍu	VI.1.1– VI.1.11
Tiruviṇṇakar	Oppillāppaṉ Kōyil	Cōḻa Nāḍu	VI.3.1– VI.3.11
Tolaivillimaṅgalam	Iraṭṭai Tirupati *Nava Tirupati site*	Pāṇṭiya Nāḍu	VI.5.1– VI.5.11
Tirukkōḷūr	Tirukkōḷūr *Nava Tirupati site*	Pāṇṭiya Nāḍu	VI.7.1– VI.7.11; VIII.3.5
Tiruvaraṅkam	Śrīraṅgam *Pañcaraṅga kṣetra* *Svayam vyakta kṣetra*	Cōḻa Nāḍu	VII.2.1– VII.2.11 (entire decad)
Tiruppērai	Tentiruppērai *Nava Tirupati site*	Pāṇṭiya Nāḍu	VII.3.1– VII.3.11
Ayodhyā	Ayodhyā	Vaṭa Nāḍu	VII.5.1
Tiruvāṛaṉviḷai	Tiruvāṛaṉviḷai *Pāṇḍava temple—Arjuna*	Cēra Nāḍu/ Malai Nāḍu	VII.10.1– VII.10.11

Mathurā	Mathurā	Vaṭa Nāḍu	VII.10.4; VIII.5.9; IX.1.3–IX.1.10
Kuḷantai	Peruṅkuḷam *Nava Tirupati site*	Pāṇṭiya Nāḍu	VIII.2.4
Puḷiṅkuṭi	Tiruppuḷiṅkuṭi	Pāṇṭiya Nāḍu	VIII.3.5; IX.2.1–IX.2.11 (entire decad)
Vaṇparicāram	Tiruvaṇparicāram/ Tiruppatticāram	Cēra Nāḍu/ Malai Nāḍu	VIII.3.7
Tiruccenkuṉṟūr	Tiruccenkuṉṟūr *Pāṇḍava temple—Yudhisṭhira*	Cēra Nāḍu/ Malai Nāḍu	VIII.4.1–VIII.4.11 (entire decad)
Tirukkaṭittāṉam	Tirukkaṭittāṉam *Pāṇḍava temple—Sahādeva*	Cēra Nāḍu/ Malai Nāḍu	VIII.6.1–VIII.6.11 (entire decad)
Tiruppuliyūr	Tiruppuliyūr *Pāṇḍava temple—Bhīma*	Cēra Nāḍu/ Malai Nāḍu	VIII.9.1–VIII.9.11 (entire decad)
Varaguṇamaṅgai	Tiruvaraguṇamaṅgai *Nava Tirupati site*	Pāṇṭiya Nāḍu	IX.2.4
(Tiru)Vaikuṇṭham	Śrīvaikuṇṭham *Nava Tirupati site*	Pāṇṭiya Nāḍu	IX.2.4; IX.2.8

Tirukkāṭkarai	Tirukkāṭkarai	Cēra Nāḍu/ Malai Nāḍu	IX.6.1–IX.6.11 (entire decad)
Tirumūḻikkaḷam	Tirumūḻikkaḷam	Cēra Nāḍu/ Malai Nāḍu	IX.7.1–IX.7.11 (entire decad)
Tirunāvāy	Tirunāvāy	Cēra Nāḍu/ Malai Nāḍu	IX.8.1–IX.8.11 (entire decad)
Tirukkaṇṇapuram	Tirukkaṇṇapuram	Cōḻa Nāḍu	IX.10.1–IX.10.10 (entire decad, except final verse)
Tirumōkūr	Tirumōkūr	Pāṇṭiya Nāḍu	X.1.1–X.1.11 (entire decad)
Aṉantapuram	Tiruvaṉantapuram/ anglicized as Trivandrum	Cēra Nāḍu/ Malai Nāḍu	X.2.1–X.2.11 (entire decad)
Vāṭṭāṟu	Tiruvāṭṭāṟu	Cēra Nāḍu/ Malai Nāḍu	X.6.1–X.6.11 (entire decad)
Tiruppēr	Tiruppēr/Kōyilaṭi *Pañcaraṅga kṣetra*	Cōḻa Nāḍu	X.8.1–X.8.11 (entire decad) Last decad on a single sacred site

* specific mention of pārkaṭal, the ocean of milk

** mentioned as an epithet for Viṣṇu—he is lord of Vaikuṇṭha

*** the reference is oblique

Glossary

An asterisk indicates another term in the glossary. It is intended for cross-reference.

A

Akanāṉūṟu: An anthology of four hundred love poems composed in Tamiḻ* between the first and third centuries, CE

Arcā: The iconic form of Viṣṇu*

Adhyayanotsavam: The twenty-one-day Festival of Recitation celebrated in Śrīvaiṣṇava* temples during the month of Mārkaḻi* (December–January)

Akil: The aromatic resin from the Eaglewood tree, also known as Agarwood or Aloeswood, *Aquilaria agallocha*

Alli: Red water lily

Aniruddha: Kṛṣṇa's* grandson and son of Pradyumna.* A vyūha* of Viṣṇu.*

Antaryāmin: The in-dwelling form of Viṣṇu.* One of the five forms of Viṣṇu.

Antāti: Interlinked verses; end to beginning. The form of the *Tiruvāymoḻi.**

Anubhava: Enjoyment, relish, experience, particularly as it pertains to āḻvārs'* enjoyment of god, and of the ācāryas'* enjoyment of the āḻvārs'* enjoyment

Ayodhyā: One of the 108 Divya Deśas.* The kingdom of Rāma.*

Aṉṟil: A type of lovebird used to evoke constancy

Araiyar: Hereditary Śrīvaiṣṇava* brahmin male performer of the *Nālāyira Divya Prabandham**

Araiyar Cēvai: Service of the Araiyar. A hereditary performance that combines recitation, gestural interpretation and commentary. It survives at three temples in Tamil Nadu—Srirangam, Srivilliputtur and Alvar Tirunagari—and in Melkote in Karnataka.

Arjuna: One of the five Pāṇḍava brothers, and a famed archer. Kṛṣṇa serves as his charioteer in the Bharata* war.

Aṟaṉ: Hara (Sanskrit); Śiva*

Ayaṉ: Brahmā*

Avatāra: Descent of god, commonly translated as incarnation

Ācārya: Teacher or preceptor

Ācārya Hṛdayam: Heart of the teacher. A collection of Maṇipravāḷa* aphorisms summarizing the meaning of the *Tiruvāymoḻi.**

Āḻvār: Those who are immersed [in god]. The twelve Tamiḻ* Vaiṣṇava* poets who lived between the sixth and ninth centuries. Their compositions comprise the *Nālāyira Divya Prabandham.**

Āṇṭāḷ: The sole female āḻvār* poet, and author of the *Tiruppāvai* and *Nācciyār Tirumoḻi*

B

Bakāsura: The crane-demon killed by Kṛṣṇa*

Balarāma: Kṛṣṇa's* older brother

Bāṇa: A demon vanquished by Kṛṣṇa.* Aniruddha* falls in love with Bāṇa's* daughter, Uṣā.

Bhakti: Devotion, particularly as expressed in passionate, ecstatic and affective ways

Bhagavad Gītā: The Song of God. Kṛṣṇa's* discourse to Arjuna* on the eve of the great Bharata* war.

Bharata war: The eighteen-day internecine war between the five Pāṇḍava* brothers and their hundred Kaurava* cousins, described in the epic *Mahābhārata**

Bhāgavata: A devotee of Viṣṇu*

Bhāgavata Purāṇa: A Sanskrit Vaiṣṇava* legend-text likely compiled between the ninth and thirteenth centuries, particularly significant for Kṛṣṇa* devotion

Bhikṣāṭaṇa: Śiva* as a wandering beggar

Bhū: The goddess earth, and Viṣṇu's* secondary consort

Brahmā: The god of creation. In Vaiṣṇava* mythology, he arises from Viṣṇu's* navel and creates the world.

C

Carama Śloka: Verse 18.66 of the Bhagavad Gita.* It is the third of the rahasya traya.*

Cōḻa: One of three legendary dynasties of southern India. The historical Cōḻas were at the height of their power between the mid-ninth through the late thirteenth century. Much of their power was consolidated in the Kaveri* region.

Cēra: One of three legendary dynasties of southern India. Their seat of power was in the western region, and overlaps with the present-day state of Kerala.

Cilappatikāram: One of the five great Tamiḻ epics that relates the story of a married couple, Kaṇṇaki and Kōvalaṉ, composed between the fifth and sixth centuries CE by Ilaṅkō Aṭikaḷ. The story traverses the three major royal regions—the Cōḻa*, Pāṇṭiya* and Cēra* regions. It is a Jain work.

D

Daśaratha: Rāma's* father and the king of Ayodhyā*

Dānava: The sons of Danu, often the antagonists of the devas* (gods)

Deva: The gods, with Indra* as their king

Devakī: Kṛṣṇa's* birth mother, and sister of Kaṁsa.* She had to give the child up because of a threat to his life.

Divya Deśa: The 108 sacred sites praised by the twelve āḻvār* poets

Divyasūricaritam: A Sanskrit hagiography of the āḻvār* and Śrīvāiṣṇava* ācārayas.* The dating is disputed. It may be dated either to the thirteenth century or to the fifteenth century.

Dramiḍopaniṣad Tātparya Ratnāvali: The gem-necklace of meaning of the Southern/Tamiḻ Veda,* a summary work of the *Tiruvāymoḻi,** composed by Vedānta Deśika*

Drāviḍa Veda: Tamiḻ* Veda or Southern Veda. It refers to the *Tiruvāymoḻi.**

Droṇa: A major character in the epic, *Mahābhārata.** He was the teacher to both the Pāṇḍavas* and the Kauravas.*

Dvārakā: One of the 108 Divya Deśas,* and Kṛṣṇa's* capital city

Dvayam: The second of three sacred and secret mantras for Śrīvaiṣṇavas*

F

Five (The): Refers to the five Pāṇdava* brothers, the heroes of the epic, the *Mahābhārata**

G

Garuḍa: The divine eagle; Viṣṇu's* vehicle (vāhana)

Gopī: Cowherd women, and Kṛṣṇa's* beloveds during his childhood

Guṇa: Quality or virtue. There are three, lucidity (sattva), darkness (tamas) and passion (rajas).

Guruparamparaprabhāvam: Maṇipravāḷa* hagiography of the āḻvār* and Śrīvaiṣṇava* ācāryas.* There are two major versions known as the 6000 and 3000.

H

Hayagrīva: The horse-headed avatāra* of Viṣṇu.* He is believed to have taken this form to slay the two demons, Madhu and Kaiṭhabha.

Hiraṇyaṉ/Hiraṇyakaśipu: The demon who was killed by Narasiṁha, the man-lion avatāra* of Viṣṇu*

Hiraṇyākṣa: Brother of Hiraṇyaṉ,* killed by Varāha,* Viṣṇu's* boar/pig avatāra*

Hundred (The): The hundred Kaurava brothers. The antagonists of the epic, the *Mahābhārata.**

I

Indra: The king of the celestials/king of the gods

Iyaṟpā: One of the sections of the *Nālāyira Divya Prabandham,** which contains many experimental and unsigned works

Īṭu: The largest commentary on the *Tiruvāymoḻi,** also called the 36,000 (*muppattāṟayirappaṭi*)

J

Jyeṣṭhā: The goddess of ill fortune and poverty. She is Śrī-Lakṣmī's* older sister, and is her opposite in every regard.

K

Kaiṅkarya: Loving service to Viṣṇu*

Kali: The last of the four ages (Yuga*), which sees a complete breakdown of society, with loss of virtue, wisdom, morality and wisdom

Kamuku: Areca palm, *Areca catechu*

Kaṁsa: Kṛṣṇa's* uncle and the king of Mathurā*

Karma: Action that produces a result, either positive or negative, which keeps you bound to the endless cycle of birth and death

Kaurava: The hundred brothers, who are the Pāṇḍavas'* antagonists in the *Mahābhārata**

Kākkutaṉ: Rāma. Refers to Rāma* as a descendent of Kakutstha, a king of the solar dynasty. He was the son of Bhagiratha, who brought the Gaṅgā down to earth. Kakutstha's son was Raghu.

Kalpaka tree/creeper: Wish-fulfilling tree or creeper

Kāma: The god of love. He is Viṣṇu's* son.

Kāveri: One of the largest rivers in south India. It begins in the south-western mountains (ghats) and empties into the Bay of Bengal.

Kāya: A dark-purple flower

Keśī: The horse-demon killed by Kṛṣṇa*

Kiṉṉara: A mythical divine creature that is half-human and half-horse

Kōvai: The ivy gourd (*Coccinia indica*), a common creeper that produces a crimson red fruit

Kōyil Oḻuku: The chronicle of the Srirangam* temple

Kōyil Tiruvāymoḻi: Temple Tiruvāymoḻi. A shortened *Tiruvāymoḻi,** consisting of 143 verses, used in domestic and temple liturgy, particularly when one is short on time.

Kṛṣṇa/Kaṇṇaṉ: One of the human avatāras of Viṣṇu.* He is born into a princely family, but is raised in secret among cowherds. He kills his uncle, Kaṁsa,* and becomes the king of Dvārakā.* He is an ally of the Pāṇḍavas.*

Kuravai: A circle dance performed by Kṛṣṇa* with Nappiṉṉai* and cowherd women, similar in formation to the rās*

Kurukūr: The city associated with the poet Śaṭhakōpaṉ-Nammāḻvār,* located in the Pāṇṭiya* country, on the banks of the Tamiraparani* river

Kuruntu: Wild lime tree

Kuṟiñci: A dark-blue flower found in the Nilgiri hills that blooms every twelve years. It is also the name of a melodic mode.

Kuṭṭanāṭu: Kerala

Kuyil: Indian cuckoo

Kuvalayāpīḍa: The elephant killed by Kṛṣṇa* before he entered the wrestling arena in Mathurā*

Kūrattāḻvāṉ: An eleventh-century Śrīvaiṣṇava* teacher and one of Rāmānuja's* closest disciples. He was the father of Parāśara Bhaṭṭar.*

L

Lakṣmaṇa: Rāma's* younger brother, who followed him into his twelve-year forest exile

Laṅkā: The kingdom of Rāvaṇa,* identified with present-day Sri Lanka

Līlā Vibhūti: The realm of play; the terrestrial world

M

Madaṉaṉ: Kāma,* the god of love

Madurakavi: One of the twelve āḻvār* poets, and Nammāḻvār's* disciple; the author of the *Kaṇṇinuṇ ciṟu tāmpu*

Mahat/Mahān: The first entity produced through the interaction of Puruṣa* and Prakṛti.* It is also identified with intellect.

Mahābali: The king who was tricked into granting Viṣṇu* three measures of land by Vāmana.* Viṣṇu as Trivikrama* measured the earth and heavens with two steps. When he had no place left for the third step, Bali offered his head. Trivikrama accepted his offer and pushed him into the underworld.

Mahābhārata: The Sanskrit epic, whose main narrative arc is the internecine battle between the hundred Kaurava* brothers and their five Pāṇḍava* brothers

Makara: A fish

Makiḻ: *Mimusops elengi.* An evergreen tree with edible fruit and fragrant flowers. The flowers are small and pale white. Also referred to as the Vakula/Bakula in Sanskrit. In English, it is sometimes called the Bullet Tree or Spanish Cherry.

Maṇavāḷa Māmuṉikaḷ (1370–1450): An important teacher of the Śrīvaiṣṇava* traditions, particularly associated with the Teṅkalai* school

Maṇipravāḷa: Gems and coral. A hybrid situational language combining Tamiḻ* and Sanskrit used by the Śrīvaiṣṇava* community, particularly for the purposes of commentary.

Mantarā: An adviser to Kaikeyī, one of Rāma's stepmothers. She is responsible for engineering his twelve-year exile to the forest.

Maruts: Divine entities, associated with rain

Maruta/Maruti: *Terminalia Arjuna*, commonly known as the Arjuna tree

Mathurā: One of the 108 Divya Deśas. The site of Kṛṣṇa's* birth.

Maṭal: It refers to the practice of riding a horse made of palmyra leaves in a public square to declare one's love. It is described in the classical Tamiḻ* poems, and the Tamiḻ grammars insist that it is meant to be undertaken only by men.

Māli: An ancestor of Rāvaṇa.* He was defeated and killed in battle by Viṣṇu.*

Mārkaḻi: The Tamiḻ* month that falls between mid-December and mid-January. Considered a particularly sacred time for Vaiṣṇavas.*

Mārkaṇḍeya: An important seer, who is claimed by both Śaiva* and Vaiṣṇava* sources. He was saved from death by Śiva,* and entered the body of Viṣṇu* during the final deluge.

Māṟaṉ: An epithet of Nammāḻvār. Also a title often used by Pāṇṭiya* kings and functionaries, thus suggesting the poet's connection to Pāṇṭiya kings.

Mātavi: *Hiptage benghalensis*. An evergreen liana native to India that produces fragrant pinkish-white flowers.

Meru: A sacred mountain that serves as the axis mundi in Hindu, Jain and Buddhist cosmology

Mokṣa: Final release from the cycle of rebirth and redeath, saṁsāra*

N

Namaṉ: Yama, the god of death. He rides a buffalo and carries a noose, which catches the soul.

Nammāḻvār: Our Āḻvar. The most important of the twelve āḻvār* poets. Also known by the name Śaṭhakōpaṉ.*

Nampiḷḷai: Twelfth century. An important teacher of the Śrīvaiṣṇava* traditions. He did not write a commentary on the *Tiruvāymoḻi,** but was an influential orator and interpreter of the text.

Nanda/Nandagopāla: Kṛṣṇa's* foster father, and the chief of cowherds

Nañjīyar: Twelfth century. Author of the 9000, the second commentary on the *Tiruvāymoḻi.** The teacher of Nampiḷḷai.*

Nappiṉṉai: A distinctly Tamiḻ* goddess, who is Kṛṣṇa's* cowherd wife. He defeats seven bulls to win her.

Nava Tirupati: A pilgrimage circuit of nine temples located on both banks of the Tamiraparani* river in southern Tamil Nadu

Nālāyira Divya Prabandham: The Divine Collection of Four Thousand verses; the anthology collecting the works of the twelve āḻvār* poets

Nāmakaḷ: The goddess of speech; Sarasvatī

Nāṉmukaṉ: Four-faced one; Brahmā

Nāthamuni: The first preceptor of the Śrīvaiṣṇavas, who is credited with rediscovering the *Nālāyira Divya Prabandham** and institutionalizing its recitation

Neṭumāl: Lofty/tall lord

Nityasūri: The eternal ones

Nityavibhūti: The eternal realm. Refers to Vaikuṇṭha.*

P

Pampā: A sacred river in south India, which has its origin in the Western Ghats

Pañcaraṅga Kṣetra: Five temples to reclining Viṣṇu* as Raṅganātha* that are located along the banks of the Kaveri*

Paraṅkuśa Nāyikā: Nammāḻvār's* female persona

Parāśara Bhaṭṭar: An influential twelfth-century teacher and commentator, and one of Rāmānuja's* foremost disciples

Pāñcajanya: Viṣṇu's right-turning conch, which he holds in his left hand. Also known as the Valampuri.*

Pāṇḍava: The five sons of Pāṇḍu, and the heroes of the *Mahābhārata**

Pāṇḍava Temples: A group of five temples in Kerala associated with the Pāṇḍava* brothers

Pāṇṭiya: One of three legendary dynasties to rule the southern regions. Their capital was Madurai.

Pārkaṭal: The ocean of milk, the cosmic sea on which Viṣṇu* reclines on a serpent, Ādiśeṣa

Pārthan: Arjuna,* famed archer and warrior of the *Mahābhārata** and one of the five Pāṇḍava* brothers

Periyavāccāṉ Piḷḷai: A thirteenth-century commentator who authored the first commentary on the entire *Nālāyira Divya Prabandham**

Piḷḷāṉ: Early twelfth century. The first commentator of the *Tiruvāymoḻi,** and a student of Rāmānuja.* His commentary is called the 6000.

Piḷḷai Lokācārya: A thirteenth-century Śrīvaiṣṇava* teacher, particularly important to the Teṅkalai* school

Piṉṉai: Nappiṉṉai*; Krsna's* cowherd wife

Porunal: Another name for the sacred Tamiraparani. The city of Kurukūr,* identified in the eleventh verse of most decads of the *Tiruvāymoḻi,* is located on the river's south bank, going downstream.

Pradyumna: The son of Kṛṣṇa and Rukmiṇī.* He is also considered to be Kāma* reborn. One of the vyūhas* of Viṣṇu.*

Prahlāda: A great devotee of Viṣṇu, and the son of Hiraṇyaṉ*

Prakṛtī: Nature, the material energy of things. The active principle that animates Puruṣa.*

Praṇaya Kalaka Utsavam: Quarrel Festival celebrated in several Śrīvaīṣṇava* temples that enacts a quarrel between Viṣṇu* and his consorts

Prapatti: Self-surrender, complete dependence on god, particularly in the Śrīvaiṣṇava* schools

Puṉṉai: Alexandrian Laurel Tree, *Clusiaciaea calophyllum*

Puṟanāṉūṟu: An anthology of four hundred Tamiḻ poems, concerned with public life. Composed between the first and third centuries, CE.

Puruṣa: Cosmic or primordial man, whose body pervades the universe. In the Ṛg Veda Saṁhitā,* the gods sacrifice Puruṣa to constitute the universe. In the contemplative traditions that follow, Puruṣa is the unchangeable principle that pervades the universe. In the Vaiṣṇava* traditions, Viṣṇu* is Puruṣa.

Puruṣārtha: In the context of the Śrīvaiṣṇava* tradition, it refers to the purpose and goal of life, which is eternal service (kaiṅkarya)* to Viṣṇu*

Pūtanā: A demon who tried to kill the infant Kṛṣṇa* by nursing him at her poisoned breast

R

Rajas: One of the three guṇas,* which can be translated as passion

Rāma: One of Viṣṇu's* human avatāras.* He's the hero of the *Rāmāyaṇa*,* and Rāvāṇa's* antagonist.

Rāmānuja: The most important teacher of the Śrīvaiṣṇava* tradition. His traditional dates are 1017–1137 CE.

Rāmāyāṇa: The epic story of Rāma,* the prince of Ayodhyā,* and husband of Sītā.* It recounts his adventures and eventual battle with Rāvaṇa.*

Rās: The circular dance of Kṛṣṇa* with the gopī* women, in which he duplicates for every woman

Rāvaṇa: Rāma's* chief antagonist in the *Rāmāyaṇa**

Rudra: Another name for Śiva*

Ṛg Veda: The oldest of the four Vedas*

S

Sampradāya: Tradition, lineage

Saṁsāra: The eternal cycle of birth and death

Sattva: One of the three guṇas,* which can be translated as purity or lucidity

Sāma Veda: One of the four Vedas.* The *Tiruvāymoḻi** is equated to it.

Sārṅga-bow: The name of Viṣṇu's* celestial bow

Sītā: The heroine of the *Rāmāyaṇa*.* Rāma's* wife.

Sugrīva: The monkey-king in the *Rāmāyaṇa*,* and an important ally of Rāma*

Svayamvyakta Kṣetra: Eight Vaiṣṇava pilgrimage sites, where the image is believed to have self-manifested

Śacī: The wife of Indra*

Śaiva: Associated or pertaining to Śiva; devotees of Śiva*

Śaraṇāgati: To take refuge, surrendering oneself

Śaṭhakōpaṉ: The name the poet uses in the *Tiruvāymoḻi*.* He comes to be known as Nammāḻvār.*

Śaṭhāri: The crown used in Śrīvaiṣṇava* ritual. It consists of a domed metal crown with a pair of feet atop it. It is placed on the bowed head of the devotee. It is also a name of Nammāḻvār,* and is also called the Śrī Śaṭhakōpam, or simply the Āḻvār.

Śiva: The auspicious one, who is responsible for destroying the world in the end times. He's a supreme deity for his devotees, but Vaiṣṇavas* subordinate him to Viṣṇu.*

Śrī-Lakṣmī: Also just Śrī. Viṣṇu's primary consort, and the goddess of wealth, auspiciousness, sovereignty and good fortune. She is inseparable from Viṣṇu, and rests on his chest. The Tamiḻ* equivalent is Tiru.

Śrīraṅgam: An island bound by the Kāveri.* The most important temple site for Śrīvaiṣṇavas.*

Śrīvaiṣṇava: A Vaiṣṇava* sect that reveres the twelve āḻvār* poets and was organized by Rāmānuja*

Śruti: That which is heard/revealed; i.e. the Veda*

T

Talaivi: The heroine of a poem

Tamas: One of the three guṇas,* which can be translated as dullness or darkness

Tamil̲: A language that developed in the south-eastern part of the Indian subcontinent. It has a long and continuous literary history, with the oldest written extant texts, datable to the first century CE.

Tamiraparani: See Porunal

Tan̲iyan̲: Laudatory verse appended to the main text

Teṅkalai: The southern sub-sect of the Śrīvaiṣṇava* tradition

Tirukkuṟaḷ: A text of 1330 couplets, dealing with various aspects of ethical life, dated to the fifth century, CE

Tirukkōnēri Dāsyai: A thirteenth-century(?) woman, who authored a commentary on the *Tiruvāymol̲i**

Tirumaṅkai: One of the most important āl̲vār* poets, whose contributions to the *Nālāyira Divya Prabandham** are second only to those of Nammāl̲vār*

Tiruvāymol̲i: Sacred Utterance/Sacred Truth. Nammāl̲vār's* poem of 1102 verses. Each decad of the text is also called a Tiruvāymol̲i.

Tiruvāymol̲i Nūṟṟantāti: The *Tiruvāymol̲i** in a Hundred Antāti.* A composition of Maṇavāḷa Māmun̲ikaḷ,* summarizing the *Tiruvāymol̲i* in a hundred verses.

Tuḷasi (Tiruttuḻāy): Sacred basil

Trivakrā: A great devotee of Viṣṇu,* whose curved back Kṛṣṇa* straightened

Trivikrama*: One of the avatāras* of Viṣṇu,* in which he measured the world

Toṇṭai: A creeper that produces a red fruit

V

Valampuri: Viṣṇu's right-turning conch, which he holds in his left hand. Also known as the Pāñcajanya.*

Val̲uti: Refers to Pāṇṭiya* country, which generally comprises the regions south of Madurai

Vasus: They are the eight attendants of Indra,* and the sons of Aditī, a celestial mother goddess

Vaikuṇṭha: Viṣṇu's* paradise

Vaiṣṇava: Associated or pertaining to Viṣṇu; devotees of Viṣṇu*

Vāmana*: Viṣṇu* in his diminutive form. He appears in this form before Mahābali* to extract the promise of three measures of land. After receiving the gift, he assumes gargantuan proportions and measures the world as Trivikrama.*

Varāha: Viṣṇu's third avatāra* as the boar, in which he rescued the submerged earth from the clutches of the demon, Hiraṇyākṣa*

Vaṭakalai: The northern school of the Śrīvaiṣṇava* tradition. One of their most important teachers is Vedānta Deśika.*

Veda: Compilation of hymns composed in Sanskrit between 1200–900 BCE. They are considered to be revealed.

Vedānta Deśika: A thirteenth-century teacher, philosopher, theologian and poet, who composed the *Dramiḍopinaṣad Tātparya Ratnāvali,** a summary of the *Tiruvāymoḻi.** One of the most important teachers of Vaṭakalai* Śrīvaiṣṇavas.*

Velala: An agricultural-caste group

Vibhīṣaṇa: Rāvāṇa's* younger brother, and one of Rāma's* allies in the battle against Rāvaṇa*

Viṣṇu: The pervader, the deity who protects the world. For Vaiṣṇavas, he is the supreme deity.

Viṣvaksena: Viṣṇu's* attendant

Vyūha: Manifestation, emanation. One of the five forms of Viṣṇu.*

Y

Yaśodā: Kṛṣṇa's* foster mother

Yuga: Age or aeon. There are four such ages of decreasing length, and of gradual decay. At the end of the Kali* age, the last age, the world will end. Vaiṣṇavas* believe that Kalki, Viṣṇu's* final avatāra, will appear to end the Kali age.

Bibliography

PRIMARY SOURCES

Aṉṉapukaḻ Muṭumpai Aḻakiya Maṇavāḷap Perumāḷ Nāyaṉār Aruḷicceyta Ācārya Hṛdayam. Madras: Madras Rattiṉam Press, 1950.

Bhagavat Viṣayam. 10 Vols. Ed. Vai Mu Gopālakiruṣṇamācāriyār and A. Vi Narasimmācāriyār. Ce. Tiruvallikkēṇi: Kiruṣṇamācāriyar Publishers, 1924–1930.

Divyasūricaritam. Garuḍavāhana Paṇḍita. Sanskrit text ed. T.A. Sampath Kumaracharya and K.K.A. Venkatachari. Bombay: Ananthacharya Research Institute, 1978.

Guruparamparaprābhavam 3000. Maṇipravāḷa text. Tiruvallikkēṇi: Sri Vanibhusanam Publishers, 1913.

Nālayira Divya Prabandham. Tamiḻ text ed. P.B. Aṇṇaṅkarācarya. Kanci: Aṇṇaṅkarācarya Institute, 1972.

Nālayira Divya Prabandham. Tamiḻ text ed. Krishnaswami Iyengar. Trichy: Srinivasa Press. Publication date unavailable.

Naidu, Purushottam, B.R. *Tiruvāymoḻi Īṭṭiṉ Tamiḻākkam.* 10 Vols. 2nd Edition. Madras: University of Madras Press, 1973.

Piṉpaḻakiyaperumāḷ Cīyar. *Guruparamparaprabhāvam 6000.* Maṇipravāḷa text. Tiruvallikkēṇi: Nōpil Accakkūṭam, 1927.

Varadarajan, M. *Tiruvāymoḻi Paṉṉīrāyirappaṭi Uraiyum Tamiḻākkamum.* 10 Vols. Chennai: Bhakatamrutam Sri Ananth Publications, 2009–2012.

SECONDARY SOURCES

Aiyangar, Krishnaswami S. *Early History of Vaishnavism in South India.* Oxford: Oxford University Press, 1920.

Ayyangar, Kurrattalvar N. *A Free Translation of Tiruvaymoli of Sathakopa: Tenth Hundred.* Trichinopoly: British India Press, 1926.

Ayyangar, Kurrattalvar N. *A Free Translation of Tiruvaymoli of Sathakopa: Sixth Hundred.* Trichinopoly: Jananukoola Branch Press, 1927.

Ayyangar, Kurrattalvar N. *A Free Translation of Tiruvaymoli of Sathakopa: Fourth Hundred.* Trichinopoly: Jananukoola Branch Press, 1927.

Ayyangar, Kurrattalvar N. *A Free Translation of Tiruvaymoli of Sathakopa: First Hundred.* Trichinopoly: Thayar Press, 1925.

Ayyangar, Satyamurthi S. *Tiruvāymoḻi English Glossary.* 2 Vols. Bombay: Ananthacharya Indological Research Institute, 1981.

Anandkichenin, Suganya. *My Sapphire-hued Lord, My Beloved: Kulacēkara Āḻvāṟ's Perumāḷ Tirumoḻi.* Pondicherry: École Française d'Extrême-Orient and French Institute of Pondicherry, 2018.

Bard, Amy. '"No Power of Speech Remains": Tears and Transformation in South Asian *Majlis* Poetry'. *Holy Tears: Weeping in the Religious Imagination.* Princeton, N.J.: Princeton University Press, 2005. pp. 145–164.

Benton, Catherine. *God of Desire: Tales of Kāmadeva in Sanskrit Story Literature.* Albany: State University of New York Press, 2006.

Bharati, Srirama. *The Sacred Book of Four Thousand: Nalayira Divya Prabandham Rendered in English with Tamiḻ Original.* Chennai: Sri Sadagopan Tirunarayanaswami Divya Prabandha Pathasala, 2000.

Bharati, Srirama and Sowbhagya Lakshmi. *The Tiruvaimoli of Nammalvar Rendered in English.* Melkote: Tyaga Bharati Music Education Mission, 1987.

Bronner, Yigal. *Extreme Poetry: The South Asian Movement of Simultaneous Narration.* New York: Oxford University Press, 2010.

Bryant, Edwin. *Krishna: The Beautiful Legend of God: Śrīmad Bhāgavata Purāṇa Book X.* New Delhi: Penguin Books, 2003.

Carman, John. 'Dissolving One Paradox and Discovering Another: Pillan's Interpretation of Nammalvar's Poem'. *Religion and*

Public Culture: Encounters and Identities in Modern South India. Richmond, Surrey: Curzon Press, 2000.

Carman, John and Vasudha Narayanan. *The Tamil Veda: Piḷḷāṉ's Interpretation of the Tiruvāymoḻi.* Chicago and London: University of Chicago Press, 1989.

Champakalakshmi, R. *Religion, Tradition, and Ideology: Pre-colonial South India: Collected Essays.* New Delhi: Oxford University Press, 2011.

Chari, S.M.S. *Philosophy and Theistic Mysticism of the Āḻvārs.* Delhi: Motilal Banarasidass, 1997.

Clooney, Francis X. 'The Use of Sanskrit as a Theological Resource in the Interpretation of *Tiruvāymoḻi*'. *International Journal of Hindu Studies.* Vol. 19, 1–2 (2015). pp. 7–38.

Clooney, Francis X. *His Hiding Place Is Darkness: A Hindu-Catholic Theopoetics of Divine Absence.* Palo Alto: Stanford University Press, 2014.

Clooney, Francis X. 'By the Power of Her Word: Absence, Memory and Speech in the *Song of Songs* and a Hindu Mystical Text'. *Exchange*, Vol. 41 (2012). pp. 213–244.

Clooney, Francis X. 'Divine Absence and the Purification of Desire: A Hindu Saint's Experience of a God Who Keeps His Distance'. *Knowing the Unknowable: Science and Religions on God and the Universe.* Ed. John Bowker. London: I.B. Tauris, 2009. pp. 227–255.

Clooney, Francis X. *Seeing through Texts: Doing Theology among the Śrīvaiṣṇavas of South India.* Albany: State University of New York, 1996.

Clooney, Francis X. *The Art and Theology of Śrīvaiṣṇava Thinkers: The De Nobili Endowment Lectures.* Madras: Satya Nilayam Research Institute, 1994.

Clooney, Francis X. 'Nammāḻvār's Glorious Tiruvallavāḻ: An Exploration in the Methods and Goals of Śrīvaiṣṇava Commentary'. *Journal of the American Oriental Society*, Vol. 111, No. 2 (April–June 1991). pp. 260–276.

Clooney, Francis X. '"I Created Land and Sea": A Tamil Case of God-Consciousness and Its Śrīvaiṣṇava Interpretation'. *Numen*, Vol. 35, Fasc. 2 (December 1988). pp. 238–259.

Cutler, Norman. 'Four Spatial Realms in *Tirukkōvaiyār*'. *Tamil Geographies: Cultural Constructions of Space and Place in South India.* Albany: State University of New York Press, 2008. pp. 43–57.

Cutler, Norman. *Songs of Experience: The Poetics of Tamil Devotion.* Bloomington and Indianapolis: Indiana University Press, 1987.

Cutler, Norman. *Consider Our Vow: Translation of Tiruppāvai and Tiruvempāvai into English.* Madurai: Muttu Patippakam, 1979.

Damodaran, G. *The Literary Value of Tiruvāymoḻi.* Tirupati: Sri Venkateswara University, 1978.

Damodaran, G. *Ācārya Hṛdayam: A Critical Study.* Tirupati: Tirumalai Tirupati Devasthanams, 1976.

Decès, Isabelle Clark. *The Encounter Never Ends: A Return to the Field of Tamil Rituals.* Albany: State University of New York Press, 2007.

Decès, Isabelle Clark. *No One Cries for the Dead: Tamil Dirges, Rowdy Songs and Graveyard Petitions.* Berkeley: University of California Press, 2005.

Dehejia, Vidya. *Slaves of the Lord: Path of the Tamil Saints.* 1st Edition. South Asia Books, 2002.

Doniger, Wendy. *Hinduism: The Norton Anthology of World Religions.* Ed. Jack Miles. New York: W.W. Norton and Company, 2015.

Doss, Vittal K.R. *Alwars and the Indian Vaishnavite Literatures.* New Delhi: Munshiram Manoharlal, 2017.

Dutta, Ranjeeta. *From Hagiographies to Biographies: Rāmānuja in Tradition and History.* New Delhi: Oxford University Press, 2014.

Egnor, Margaret T. 'Internal Iconicity in Paraiyars' "Crying Songs"'. *Another Harmony: New Essays on the Folklore of India.* Ed. Stuart H. Blackburn and A.K. Ramanujan. Berkeley: University of California Press, 1986. pp. 294–344.

Govindacharya, Alkondavilli. *The Holy Lives of the Azhvars or the Dravida Saints.* Bombay: Ananthacharya Indological Research Institute, 1982.

Govindâchârya, Aḷkoṇḍavilli. *The Divine Wisdom of the Drâvida Saints.* Madras: C.N. Press, 1902.

Handelman, Don and David Shulman. *Śiva in the Forest of Pines: An Essay on Sorcery and Self-Knowledge.* New Delhi: Oxford University Press, 2004.

Hardy, Friedhelm. 'South Indian Visnu Temples and the Performing Arts'. *South Asia Research.* Vol. 18, No. 1 (1998). pp. 99–114.

Hardy, Friedhelm. 'A Radical Reassessment of the Vedic Heritage—The Ācāryahṛdayam and Its Wider Implications'. *Representing Hinduism: The Construction of Religious Traditions and National Identity.* Ed. Vasudha Dalmia and Heinrich von Stietencron. New Delhi: Sage Publications, 1995. pp. 35–50.

Hardy, Friedhelm. 'The Formation of Srivaisnavism'. *Charisma and Canon: Essays on the Religious History of the Indian Subcontinent.* Ed. Vasudha Dalmia, Angelika Malinar and Martin Christof. New Delhi: Oxford University Press, 2001. pp. 41–61.

Hardy, Friedhelm. 'The ŚrīVaiṣṇava Hagiography of Parakāḷa'. *Indian Narrative: Perspectives and Patterns.* Ed. Christopher Shackle and Rupert Snell. Wiesbaden: Otto Harrassowitz, 1992. pp. 81–116.

Hardy, Friedhelm. *Viraha-Bhakti: The Early History of Kṛṣṇa Devotion in South India.* New Delhi: Oxford University Press, 1983.

Hardy, Friedhelm. 'The Tamil Veda of a Śūdra Saint: The Śrīvaiṣṇava Interpretation of Nammāḻvār'. *Contributions to South Asian Studies* I. Delhi: Oxford University Press, 1979. pp. 29–87.

Hart, George L. *The Four Hundred Songs of Love: An Anthology of Poems from Classical Tamil, the Akanāṉūṟu.* Pondicherry: French Institute of Pondicherry, 2015.

Hart, George L. *The Poems of Ancient Tamil: Their Milieu and Their Sanskrit Counterparts.* Berkeley: University of California Press, 1988.

Hart, George L. *Poets of the Tamil Anthologies: Ancient Poems of Love and War.* Princeton, N.J: Princeton University Press, 1979.

Hart, Kausalya. *Divya Prabandham: Nammazhvar's Tiruvaymozhi.* Self-published, 2015.

Hart, George L. and Hank Heifetz. *The Four Hundred Songs of War and Wisdom, the Puṟanāṉūṟu*. New York: Columbia University Press, 1999.

Hancock, Mary. 'The Dilemmas of Domesticity: Possession and Devotional Experience among Urban Smārta Women'. *From the Margins of Hindu Marriage*. Ed. Lindsey Harlan and Paul B. Courtright. New York: Oxford University Press, 1995. pp. 60–91.

Hawley, John Stratton. *A Storm of Songs: India and the Idea of the Bhakti Movement*. Cambridge, MA: Harvard University Press, 2015.

Hawley, John Stratton. *The Memory of Love: Sūrdās Sings to Krishna*. New York: Oxford University Press, 2009.

Hawley, John Stratton. 'The *Gopīs'* Tears'. *Holy Tears: Weeping in the Religious Imagination*. Princeton, N.J.: Princeton University Press, 2005. pp. 94–111.

Hawley, John Stratton. 'Author and Authority in the Bhakti Poetry of North India'. *The Journal of Asian Studies*, Vol. 47, No. 2 (May 1988). pp. 269–290.

Hooper, J.S.M. *Hymns of the Ālvārs*. Calcutta: Association Press, 1929; Oxford: Oxford University Press, 1929.

Hopkins, Steven P. '"I Walk Weeping in Pangs of a Mother's Torment for Her Children." Women's Laments in the Poetry and Prophecies of William Blake'. *Journal of Religious Ethics*, Vol. 37, No. 1 (2009). pp. 39–81.

Hopkins, Steven P. 'Extravagant Beholding: Love, Ideal Bodies and Particularity'. *History of Religions*, Vol. 47, No. 1 (August, 2007). pp. 1–50.

Hopkins, Steven P. *An Ornament for Jewels: Love Poems for the Lord of Gods by Vedāntadeśika*. New York: Oxford University Press, 2007.

Hopkins, Steven Paul. *Singing the Body of God: The Hymns of Vedāntadeśika in Their South Indian Tradition*. New Delhi: Oxford University Press, 2002.

Hudson, Dennis D. *Krishna's Mandala: Bhagavata Religion and Beyond*. Ed. John Stratton Hawley. New Delhi: Oxford University Press, 2010.

Hudson, Dennis. 'Piṉṉai: Krishna's Cowherd Wife'. *The Divine Consort: Rādhā and the Goddesses of India*. Ed. John Stratton Hawley and Donna Marie Wulff. Boston: Beacon Press. pp. 238–262.

Jagannathan, Bharati. *Approaching the Divine: The Integration of Āḻvār Bhakti in Śrīvaiṣṇavism*. New Delhi: Primus Books, 2015.

Jagadeesan, N. *Collected Papers on Tamil Vaishnavism*. Madurai: New Rathna Press, 1989.

Jagadeesan, N. *History of Sri Vaishnavism in the Tamil Country (Post-Ramanuja)*. Madurai: Koodal Publishers, 1977.

Jeyarajan, Kokkalai. *Nammāḻvār Aruḷiya Tiruviruttam: Oru Tiṟaṉāyvu*. Chennai: Maharani Publications, 1997.

Kaylor, R.D. and K.K.A. Venkatachari. *God Far, God Near: An Interpretation of the Thought of Nammāḻvār*. Bombay: Ananthacharya Indological Research Institute, 1981.

Kaylor, David R. 'The Concept of Grace in the Hymns of Nammāḻvār'. *Journal of the American Academy of Religion*, Vol. 44, No. 4 (1976). pp. 649–660.

Kingsbury, F. and G.E. Phillips. *Hymns of the Tamil Śaivite Saints*. London: Oxford University Press, 1921.

Krishnaswami, K.R. *Iyarpa: 4000 Divya Prabandham Series*. Vol. 8. Bangalore: A&K Prakashana, 2010.

Kumaran, Sampath Tamarapu. *Guide to 108 Divya Desams*. Chennai: Hindu Dharma Paripalana Trust, 2005.

Mumme, Patricia. 'Śrīvaiṣṇava Hagiography: Lessons from Biblical Scholarship'. *Journal of Vaiṣṇava Studies*. Vol. 5. No. 2 (Spring 1999).

Monius, Anne. 'Dance before Doom: Krishna in the Non-Hindu Literature of Early Medieval South India'. *Alternative Krishnas: Regional and Vernacular Variations on a Hindu Deity*. Ed. Guy L. Beck. Albany: State University of New York Press, 2005. pp. 139–149.

Nabokov, Isabelle. *Religion against the Self: An Ethnography of Tamil Rituals*. New York: Oxford University Press, 2000.

Nandakumar, Prema. *Nammalvar's 'Tiruviruttam': The Drama of the Love Divine*. Calcutta: Writers Workshop Publications, 1979.

Narayanan, Vasudha. '"With the Earth as a Lamp and the Sun as the Flame": Lighting Devotion in South India'. *International Journal of Hindu Studies*, Vol. 11, No. 3 (December 2007). pp. 227–253.

Narayanan, Vasudha. 'A Wedding Procession and a Procession to Vaikuntha: Selections from the Poetry of Andal and Nammalvar'. *Journal of Vaishnava Studies*. Vol. 12, No. 1 (Fall 2003). pp. 67–87.

Narayanan, Vasudha. 'Casting Light on the Sounds of the Tamil Veda: Tirukkōnēri Dasyai's "Garland of Words"'. *Jewels of Authority: Women and Textual Tradition in Hindu India*. Ed. Laurie L. Patton. New York: Oxford University Press, 2002. pp. 122–136.

Narayanan, Vasudha. 'Music and the *Divya Prabandham* in the Śrīvaiṣṇava Tradition'. *Journal of Vaishnava Studies*. Vol. 4. No. 2. (Spring 1996). pp. 37–56.

Narayanan, Vasudha. 'The Realm of Play and the Sacred Stage'. *Gods at Play: Līlā in South Asia*. Ed. William Sax. New York: Oxford University Press, 1995. pp. 177–204.

Narayanan, Vasudha. 'The Rāmāyaṇa in the Theology and Experience of the Śrīvaiṣṇava Community'. *Journal of Vaishnava Studies*. Vol. 2. No. 4. (Fall 1994). pp. 55–89.

Narayanan, Vasudha. *The Vernacular Veda: Revelation, Recitation and Ritual*. Columbia, S.C.: University of South Carolina Press, 1994.

Narayanan, Vasudha. 'Oral and Written Commentary on the *Tiruvāymoḻi*'. *Texts in Context: Traditional Hermeneutics in South Asia*. Ed. Jeffrey R. Timm. Albany: State University of New York Press, 1992. pp. 85–107.

Narayanan, Vasudha. *The Way and the Goal: Expressions of Devotion in the Early Śrī Vaiṣṇava Tradition*. Washington, D.C.: Institute for Vaishnava Studies and Center for the Study of World Religions, Harvard University, 1987.

Nayar, Nancy Ann. *Praise-poems to Viṣṇu and Śrī: The Stotras of Rāmānuja's Immediate Disciples, a Translation from Sanskrit with Introduction and Notes*. Bombay: Ananthacharya Indological Research Institute, 1994.

Nayar, Nancy Ann. *Poetry as Theology: The Śrīvaiṣṇava Stotra in the Age of Rāmānuja*. Wiesbaden: Otto Harrassowitz, 1992.

Orr, Leslie. 'Words for Worship: Tamil and Sanskrit in Medieval Temple Inscriptions'. *Bilingual Discourse and Cross-Cultural Fertilisation*. Ed. Whitney Cox and Vincenzo Vergiani. Pondicherry: French Institute of Pondicherry and École Française d'Extrême-Orient, 2013. pp. 325–357.

Pandian, Anand. *Crooked Stalks: Cultivating Virtue in South India*. Durham, N.C.: Duke University Press, 2009.

Parameswaran, M.R. and Uma Parameswaran. 'Singing to the Feet of the Lord: On A.K. Ramanujan's Translations from Nammalvar's Poetry'. *Journal of South Asian Literature*. Vol. 19, No. 2 (Summer/ Fall 1984). pp. 137-151.

Parthasarathy, R. Trans. *The Tale of an Anklet, an Epic of South India: The Cilappatikāram of Ilaṅkō Aṭikaḷ*. New York: Columbia University Press, 1992.

Parthasarathy, S. *Nammazhwar's Tiruvaaimozhi (Tamiḻ Vedam)*. Ahmedabad: Sri Desika Darsana Sabha, 1989.

Patton, Kimberly Christine and John Stratton Hawley. 'Introduction'. *Holy Tears: Weeping in the Religious Imagination*. Princeton, N.J.: Princeton University Press, 2005. pp. 1–23.

Pillai, Vaiyapuri. *History of Tamil Language and Literature: Beginning to 1000 A.D.* Madras: New Century Book House, 1956.

Peterson, Indira Viswanathan. *Poems to Śiva: The Hymns of the Tamil Saints*. Delhi: Motilal Banarasidass Publishers, 1991.

Raghavan, V. 'The Name Pāñcarātra: With an Analysis of the Sanatkumāra-Saṁhitā in Manuscript'. *Journal of the American Oriental Society*. Vol. 85, No. 1 (January–March 1965). pp. 73–79.

Raman, K.V. *Srī Varadarājaswāmi Temple—Kāñchi*. New Delhi: Abhinav Publications, 1975.

Raman, Srilata. *Self-surrender (Prapatti) to God in Śrīvaiṣṇavism: Tamil Cats and Sanskrit Monkeys*. London: Routledge, 2007.

Ramanujan, A.K. and Norman Cutler. 'From Classicism to *Bhakti*'. *The Collected Essays of A.K. Ramanujan*. Ed. Vinay Dharwadker. New Delhi: Oxford University Press, 1999. pp. 232–259.

Ramanujan, A.K. 'Towards an Anthology of City Images'. *The Collected Essays of A.K. Ramanujan*. Ed. Vinay Dharwadker. New Delhi: Oxford University Press, 1999. pp. 52–72.

Ramanujan, A.K. 'Is There an Indian Way of Thinking?' *The Collected Essays of A.K. Ramanujan*. Ed. Vinay Dharwadker. New Delhi: Oxford University Press, 1999. pp. 34–51.

Ramanujan, A.K. 'Where Mirrors Are Windows: Towards an Anthology of Reflections'. *History of Religions*, Vol. 28, No. 3 (1989). pp. 187–216.

Ramanujan, A.K. 'On Translating a Tamil Poem'. *The Collected Essays of A.K. Ramanujan*. Ed. Vinay Dharwadker. New Delhi: Oxford University Press, 1999. pp. 219–231.

Ramanujan, A.K. 'Men, Women, and Saints'. *The Collected Essays of A.K. Ramanujan*. Ed. Vinay Dharwadker. New Delhi: Oxford University Press, 1999. pp. 279–294.

Ramanujan, A.K. *Hymns for the Drowning: Poems for Viṣṇu by Nammāḻvār*. Princeton, N.J.: Princeton University Press, 1981.

Ramanujam, B.V. *History of Vaishnavism in South India Up to Ramanuja*. Chidambaram: Annamalai University Press, 1973.

Ramesh, M.S. *108 Vaishnavite Divya Desams*. 6 Vols. Tirupati: Tirumala Tirupati Devasthanams, 1995–2000.

Rangachari, R. Trans. Vedanta Desika's *Dramidopanishad Tatparya Ratnavali and Sara*. Madras: Vedanta Desika Research Society, 1974.

Rao, Gopinatha T.A. *Sir Subrahmanya Ayyar Lectures on the History of the Śrī Vaiṣṇavas*. Madras: Government Press, 1923.

Rao, Hari V.N. *Kōil Olugu: The Chronicle of the Srirangam Temple with Historical Notes*. Madras: Rochouse and Sons, 1961.

Reddiar, Subbu N. *Religion and Philosophy of Nālāyira Divya Prabandham with Special Reference to Nammāḷvār*. Tirupati: S.V. University Press, 1977.

Reddiyar, Venkatacami K. *Śrī Nammāḻvār aruḷicceyta Tiruviruttam*. Srirangam: Srirangam Srimat Andavan Asramam, 1984.

Renganathan, Vasu. 'The Element of Beauty and the Use of Similes in Tamiḻ Poetics'. Paper Delivered at the 8th Annual Tamil Conference, UC Berkeley, 21 April 2012.

Richards, F.J. Review of *The Heritage of India Series. Hymns of the Āḻvārs*. J.S.M. Hooper. *Journal of the Royal Asiatic Society of Great Britain and Ireland*, No. 3 (July 1934). pp. 590–592.

Sastri, Nilakantha K.A. *A History of South India: From Prehistoric Times to the Fall of Vijayanagar*. 3rd Edition. Madras: Oxford University Press, 1966.

Sastri, Nilakantha K.A. *Development of Religion in South India*. Madras: Orient Longman, 1963.

Seastrand, Anna. 'Tracing a Line: Guruparamparā in the Murals of Āḻvār Tirunakari'. *Journal of Vaishnava Studies*, Vol. 21, No. 2 (2013). pp. 43–63.

Selby, Martha Ann. *Tamil Love Poetry: The Five Hundred Short Poems of the Aiṅkuṟunūṟu*. New York: Columbia University Press, 2011.

Selby, Martha Ann. 'Dialogues of Space, Desires, and Gender in Tamil *Caṅkam* Poetry'. *Tamil Geographies: Cultural Constructions of Space and Place in South India*. Albany: State University of New York Press, 2008. pp. 17–42.

Selby, Martha Ann. *Grow Long Blessed Night: Love Poems from Classical India*. New York: Oxford University Press, 2000. pp. 17–21.

Sethuraman, N. *The Later Pandyas (A.D. 1371–1759)*. Paper Presented at the 19th Annual Congress of the Epigraphical Society of India, 12–14 February 1993. Tiruchirappalli: Bharatidasan University.

Sethuraman, N. *Medieval Pandyas (A.D. 1000–1200)*. Kumbakonam: Raman and Raman Private Limited, 1980.

Sethuraman, N. *The Imperial Pandyas: Mathematics Reconstructs the Chronology*. Kumbakonam: Raman and Raman Private Limited, 1978.

Shulman, David. *Tamil: A Biography*. Cambridge, MA: Harvard University Press, 2016.

Shulman, David. '*Tirukkōvaiyār*: Downstream into God'. *Self and Self-Transformation in the History of Religions*. Ed. David Shulman and Guy G. Stroumsa. New York: Oxford University Press, 2002. pp. 131–149.

Shulman, David. 'Embracing the Subject: Harṣa's Play within a Play'. *Journal of Indian Philosophy*. Vol. 25 (1997). pp. 69–89.

Shulman, David. 'On Being Human in the Sanskrit Epic: The Riddle of Nala'. *Journal of Indian Philosophy*. Vol. 22 (1994). pp. 1–29.

Shulman, David. 'The Yogi's Human Self: Tāyumāṉavar in the Tamil Mystical Tradition'. *Religion*. Vol. 21 (1991). pp. 51–72.

Smith, Frederick M. *The Self Possessed: Deity and Spirit Possession in South Asian Literature and Civilization*. New York: Columbia University Press, 2006.

Stein, Burton. *Peasant State and Society in Medieval South India*. Delhi: Oxford University Press, 1980.

Soifer, Deborah A. *The Myths of Narasiṁha and Vāmana: Two Avatars in Cosmological Perspective*. Albany: State University Press, 1991.

Stoker, Valerie. *Polemics and Patronage in the City of Victory: Vyāsatīrtha, Hindu Sectarianism and the Sixteenth Century Vijayanagara Court*. Berkeley: University of California Press, 2016.

Subramaniam, Arundhathi. *Eating God: A Book of Bhakti Poetry*. New Delhi: Penguin Books, 2014.

Takahashi, Takanobu. *Poetry and Poetics: Literary Conventions of Tamil Love Poetry*. PhD Dissertation, University of Utrecht, 1989.

Trawick, Margaret. *Notes on Love in a Tamil Family*. Berkeley: University of California Press, 1992.

Trawick, Margaret. 'Ambiguity in the Oral Exegesis of a Sacred Text: Tirukkōvaiyār (Or, the Guru in the Garden, Being an Account of a Tamil Informant's Responses to Homesteading in Central New York State).' *Cultural Anthropology*, Vol. 3, No. 3 (August 1988). pp. 316–351.

Trawick, Margaret. 'Spirits and Voices in Tamil Songs'. *American Ethnologist*, Vol. 15, No. 2 (May 1989). pp. 193–215.

Van Buitenen, J.A.B. 'Pañcarātra'. *History of Religions*. Vol. 1, No. 2 (Winter 1962). pp. 291–299.

Varadadesikan, R. 'Vaiṣṇava Literature in Tamil'. *Mapping the Chronology of Bhakti: Milestones, Stepping Stones, and Stumbling Stones*. Ed. Valerie Gillet. Pondicherry: French Institute of Pondicherry and École Française d'Extrême-Orient, 2014. pp. 287–301.

Varadarajan, M. *A Compendium of Nalayira Divya Prabandham and Its Commentaries*. Chennai: Bhaktamrutam Sri Ananth Publications, 2017.

Venkatachari, K.K.A. 'Abhayapradānasāra'. *Journal of the Oriental Institute*. Vol. XLVIII. No. 1–4 (1998–1999). pp. 201–212.

Venkatachari, K.K.A. *The Maṇipravāḷa Literature of the Śrīvaiṣṇava Ācārya-s*. Bombay: Ananthacharya Institute, 1978.

Venkatesan, Archana. *Nammāḻvār: A Hundred Measures of Time, Tiruviruttam*. New Delhi: Penguin Classics, 2014.

Venkatesan, Archana. 'A Different Kind of Āṇṭāḷ Story: The *Divyasūricaritam* of Garuḍavāhana Paṇḍita'. *Journal of Hindu Studies*, Vol. 6, No. 3 (November, 2013). pp. 243–296.

Venkatesan, Archana. *The Secret Garland: Āṇṭāḷ's Tiruppāvai and Nācciyār Tirumoḻi*. New York: Oxford University Press, 2010.

Venkatesan, Archana. 'Double the Pleasure: Reading Nammāḻvār's *Tiruviruttam*'. *Passages: Relationships between Tamiḻ and Sanskrit*. Ed. M. Kannan and Jennifer Clare. Pondicherry: French Institute of Pondicherry, 2009. pp. 267–279.

Venkatesan, Archana. 'A Woman's Kind of Love: Female Longing in Tamil Alvar Poetry'. *Journal of Hindu Christian Studies*. Vol. 20 (2007). pp. 16–24.

Venkatesan, Archana. *Āṇṭāḷ and Her Magic Mirror: Her Life as a Poet in the Guises of the Goddess*. PhD Dissertation, University of California, Berkeley, 2004.

Venugopal, I.P. *Nammāḻvār Tiruviruttamum Māṇikkavācakar Tirukkōvaiyārum*. Vellore: Sukuntalā Veḷiyiṭṭakam, 1992.

Verghese, Avey. *108 Vishnu Temples: Architectural Splendour, Spiritual Bliss*. New Delhi: Niyogi Books, 2017.

Wilden, Eva. 'Nammāḻvār as a Master of *tiṇaimayakkam*—Transposition Technique in the *akam* Songs of the *Tiruvāymoḻi*'. *Mapping the Chronology of Bhakti: Milestones, Stepping Stones, and Stumbling Stones*. Ed. Valerie Gillet. Pondicherry: French Institute of Pondicherry and École Française d'Extrême-Orient, 2014. pp. 317–333.

Wilden, Eva. *Kuṟuntokai: A Critical Edition and an Annotated Translation of the Kuṟuntokai* (Vol. 1). Pondicherry: École Française d'Extrême-Orient and Tamiḻmaṇ Patippakam, 2010.

Yocum, Glenn E. 'Shrines, Shamanism, and Love Poetry: Elements in the Emergence of Popular Tamil Bhakti'. *Journal of the American Academy of Religion*, Vol. 41, No. 1 (March 1973). pp. 3–17.

Young, Katherine. 'Śrīvaiṣṇava Topoi: Constructing a South Indian Sect through Place'. *Mapping the Chronology of Bhakti: Milestones, Stepping Stones, and Stumbling Stones*. Ed. Valerie Gillet. Pondicherry: French Institute of Pondicherry and École Française d'Extrême-Orient, 2014. pp. 335–364.

Young, Katherine. '*Om*, the Vedas, and the Status of Women with Special Reference to Śrīvaiṣṇavism'. *Jewels of Authority: Women and Textual Tradition in Hindu India*. Ed. Laurie L. Patton. New York: Oxford University Press, 2002. pp. 84–121.

Young, Katherine. *Beloved Places: The Correlation of Topography and Theology in the Śrīvaiṣṇava Tradition of South India*. PhD Dissertation, McGill University, 1978.

Younger, Paul. 'Singing the Tamiḻ Hymn Book in the Tradition of Rāmānuja: The Adyayanotsava Festival in Srirangam'. *History of Religions*. Vol. 21. No. 3 (1982). pp. 272–293.

Zvelebil, Kamil. *Companion Studies to the History of Tamil Literature*. Leiden: E.J.Brill, 1992.

Zvelebil, Kamil. *Tamil Literature*. Leiden: E.J. Brill, 1975.

Zvelebil, Kamil. *A History of Indian Literature: Tamil Literature*. Wiesbaden: Otto Harrassowitz, 1974.

Zvelebil, Kamil. *The Smile of Murugan: On Tamil Literature of South India*. Leiden: E.J.Brill, 1973.

Index